Santa Catalina Cookbook

VOLUME II

*A Collection of Recipes
Representing the Uniqueness of the
Santa Catalina School Community
Monterey, California*

First Printing: November 1983

ISBN Number 0-9612300-1-0

Santa Catalina Cookbook
Santa Catalina School
Mark Thomas Drive
Monterey, California 93940

Editors

TERRI CORRELL BRAZINSKY   KATHI BOWDEN

Acknowledgments

The Sisters of Santa Catalina School for support, encouragement and guidance.

Jay and Glenn Sullivan for their efforts and support, for the typing, and for the assembly of the indexes.

John Brazinsky for the cover photography and for his shopping, testing, and tasting expertise.

Kim and April for patience, support and assistance.

Sheila Lamson for historical information.

Katie Claire Mazzeo for her contribution to the Gourmet Cooking Seminar.

Harry Timmins for advice, friendship and expertise.

Josie Weiss for the typography.

Jim Hall, Filmcraft of Carmel, for use of the aerial photograph.

The contributors to our collection of recipes.

Illustrator

BUD EVENSON

All proceeds from the sale of this cookbook benefit the Santa Catalina Scholarship Fund.

Dear Friends,

In September 1980 the Santa Catalina Cookbook was published as part of the School's 30th anniversary on this campus. Its format and contents were so appealing that a sequel was inevitable.

Volume II has more pages than its predecessor because the response to the editors by the Santa Catalina family was most generous. Alumnae, board members, parents, grandparents, faculty members, students and other friends of the School sent in a bountiful selection of choice recipes. The result is a collection that will appeal not only to the willing but inexperienced beginner, but also to the gourmet chef.

Because of the dedication, thoroughness and skill of editors Terri Brazinsky and Kathi Bowden, this book came into being. Their close attention to quality, their unstinting gifts of time and personal talents to the myriad details that go into the making of a book before it reaches the printer are contributions from the heart and spirit, which we recognize with deep appreciation. Unique to this volume is a menu created and served by students of the senior class of 1983 as a project for their Independent Studies. One section alone is dedicated to pasta recipes, an area that enjoys universal favor. The artwork is by Architect Bud Evenson, a warm and enthusiastic friend, who has two daughters enrolled in the school. His sketches of the campus bring into focus the beauty of the buildings and grounds which has always been a distinction of the School.

Some contributors have said that they often read cookbooks, even when they are not intending at the moment to cook, but for enjoyment, as a source of information, or of local history. This prompted the editors to contribute again in this volume, as in the first one, outlines of School traditions, history, activities and campus customs. Santa Catalina School has been a part of California history since its founding in 1850 and the subsequent re-establishment of a campus in Monterey in 1950. We enjoy a singular continuity of tradition and spirit personified by our pioneer founders and emphasized through our 20th Century co-founders. Our tradition is the challenge of academic excellence and the encouragement of intellectual curiosity offered each student. The spirit motivating this educational approach is the vision of our founders' commitment to Judeo-Christian values and the uncommon effort of each successive member of the modern day Santa Catalina family to honor that commitment.

Over the decades of our history, our loyal supporters have recognized that formation of a student's character is as important as attaining academic excellence in mastering the problems of living life outside the classroom. Part of the motivation for contributing to this cookbook is the realization that proceeds from its sale go toward endowed scholarships. Beyond the fact that this project has a warm and universal appeal is the sensitivity of participants and purchasers to an educational approach that should have utmost support in a world grown complex in its knowledge and ambiguous in its choices.

We hope that you will refer often to this addition to your kitchen library. We believe that any recipe you may choose from among the many here will delight you and your guests and will quite possibly become part of your gourmet repertoire.

Bon appetit!

Sister Carlotta
Principal

Summer 1983

v

Contents

Hors d'Oeuvres and Beverages

BRIE EN CROUTE

2 (4½ ounce) packages spiced
cheese with garlic and herbs
(Rondele or Boursen)
2 tablespoons whipping cream
2 pounds Brie cheese (8" in
diameter)

1 (1 pound) package frozen puff
pastry, defrosted
1 egg, beaten
1 tablespoon water

In mixing bowl, beat spiced cheese and whipping cream until smooth.
Spread on Brie, covering the top completely. Remove one sheet of puff
pastry. Place on lightly floured board and roll into a square approximately 14 inches. Brush with egg wash, made by beating the egg with 1
tablespoon water.

Place Brie in center. Trim pastry into a circle 2 inches larger than the
cheese. Brush edges of pastry with egg wash again. Press a portion of
dough along the side of the cheese. Cut along cheese and place cut edge
of pastry against bottom edge of cheese. Repeat with remaining dough,
covering entire sides of cheese. Roll second pieces of pastry into a 14"
square. Brush with egg wash. Turn Brie over and place in center of pastry. Cut pastry into a circle 2" larger than the cheese. Brush edges of
pastry with egg wash. Repeat folding and cutting the dough, covering
the sides with a double thickness of pastry. Brush top and sides with
egg wash. Reroll pastry scraps and cut out decorations. If making a border, place it ½" from outer edge. Place decorations on top and brush
them with egg wash. NOTE: At this point the appetizers may be
covered and refrigerated overnight or may be frozen for 2 weeks.
Before baking, bring to room temperature. Preheat oven to 400°. Place
on ungreased baking sheet and bake 35-45 minutes or until pastry is
golden. Let rest for at least 2 hours before serving or else the cheese will
be too soft to cut. Serve with crackers. Serves 16-20.

Joanne Cohen (Mrs. Sheldon)
Mother of Poppy, '86
Fresno, California

"This may be served cold as an hors d'oeuvre, or served after a meal with crackers and fruit."

BRIE TART

1½ cups flour
¼ teaspoon salt
12 tablespoons cold, unsalted
butter (sweet butter)
4-6 tablespoons cold water

½ pound very ripe brie cheese
1-2 tablespoons light cream
2 eggs, beaten
1½ teaspoons sugar
1 teaspoon ground ginger
Dash of nutmeg

Make a pastry by combining flour, salt, butter and cold water in a food processor, turning machine on and off until dough forms a ball. Place dough on wax paper in the refrigerator to chill. Roll out chilled dough ¼ inch thick. Line a pie pan with the dough and bake in a 400° oven for 15 minutes. Remove rind from brie; melt over low heat, adding cream if necessary to insure a smooth consistency. Add beaten eggs, sugar, ginger and nutmeg, mixing well. Pour into the pre-baked pie shell. Bake at 375° for 30 minutes, or until lightly browned and puffy.

Rosemary Violante
Marin County, California

SMOKED OYSTER SPREAD

3 (3 ounce) packages cream
cheese
2 tablespoons cream
½ teaspoon Spice Island Beau
Monde
2 teaspoons A-1 sauce

1 (3-2/3 ounce) can smoked
oysters
1 tablespoon chives or green
onion, chopped
1 teaspoon Chervil

Soften cream cheese with cream and blend with Beau Monde and A-1 sauce until smooth. Add chopped oysters, chives or green onion and Chervil. Serve with crackers or toast squares. Yields 3½ cups.

Mrs. Lee B. Price
Monterey, California

CREAM CHEESE SALMON BALL

1 (8 ounce) package cream
cheese
1 (16 ounce) can salmon
1 tablespoon lemon juice

1 tablespoon horseradish
1 (2½ ounce) package
slivered almonds

Blend cream cheese, salmon, lemon juice and horseradish together until smooth. Place in freezer until firm enough to shape into a ball. Roll in chopped nuts and refrigerate. Serve with crackers.

Joan B. Miller
Mother of Jennifer '81
North Palm Beach, Florida

SHEPHERDS CRAB AND CHEESE PIE

1 round loaf sourdough bread
2 (8 ounce) packages cream
    cheese
1 (6½ ounce) can crab meat

1½ cups shredded cheddar cheese
2 tablespoons milk
1 teaspoon horseradish
½ cup green onions, chopped

Cut a thin slice off top of the round loaf; hollow out loaf, being careful not to cut into sides or bottom of crust. Combine remaining ingredients, reserving 1 tablespoon of the green onion. Fill loaf with the mixture and top with the reserved green onions. Bake at 350° for 30-45 minutes until thoroughly heated. Serve with sliced sourdough bread. EDITORS' NOTE: Bread removed from the round sourdough loaf may be cut into bite-sized pieces and served surrounding the loaf. Furnish a small knife to spread filling on each piece.

Maria Vessey
Class of '68
La Jolla, California

HOT CRAB COCKTAIL

1 (8 ounce) package cream
    cheese
1 tablespoon milk
2 teaspoons Worcestershire sauce

7½ ounces crab
2 tablespoons green onion
Slivered almonds

Cream together the cheese, milk and Worcestershire sauce. Fold in the crab and green onion; top with almonds. Bake in pie pan at 350° for 15 minutes. Place on warming tray and serve with crackers.

Patricia S. Johnson (Mrs. Richard A.)
Mother of Kaaren '83
San Francisco, California

There were six sisters on the faculty in 1950: Sister Pierre, who taught the 5th and 6th grades, Sister Marie de Lourdes, who had charge of the 7th and 8th grades, and Sister Kieran and Sister Matthew, who taught the first and second years of high school. They were assisted by two lay teachers, Antoinette Haberl in physical education, and Lee Crow, drama. Sister Imelda Marie taught all the music and Sister Carmelita helped with tutoring.

HOT CRAB DIP

2 (3 ounce) packages cream
  cheese
4 ounces Jack cheese, grated
6 ounces dungeness or snow crab
2 eggs

¼ onion, pureed
1 tablespoon horseradish
6-10 drops Tabasco sauce
Chopped parsley

Cream together cream cheese, Jack cheese and crab. Beat in eggs, one at a time. Add onion, seasonings and pour in buttered souffle dish or other oven proof dish. Heat at 375° for 20-25 minutes until bubbly and brown. Serve with crackers.

Theresa A. May
Class of '69
Tahoe Vista, California

CRAB DIP

2 (7½ cans crab, drained
  (or fresh crab)
½ cup mayonnaise
2 teaspoons horseradish

2 tablespoons lemon juice
2 tablespoons snipped
  scallions
½ teaspoon salt

Mix all ingredients well. Refrigerate 3-4 hours before serving to allow flavors to blend. Serve with crackers or avocados.

Joan B. Miller
Mother of Jennifer '81
North Palm Beach, Florida

SALMON MOUSSE

1 envelope gelatin
¼ cup hot water
½ cup mayonnaise
¼ teaspoon paprika
1 teaspoon dill

1 small onion, diced
1 (1 pound) can salmon
1 cup heavy cream
2 tablespoons lemon juice

Dissolve gelatin in hot water; add lemon juice. Combine in a large mixing bowl the gelatin mixture with the mayonnaise, paprika, dill and diced onion. Blend in drained salmon; slowly add heavy cream, 1/3 at a time. Place in oiled mold and chill. Serve with crackers.

Patricia Bondeson
Class of '54
Sausalito, California

TUNA ALMONDINE

2 envelopes unflavored gelatin
½ cup cold water
1 cup boiling water
2 (8 ounce) packages cream
   cheese
2 tablespoons lemon juice
1 tablespoon curry powder
½ to 1 teaspoon salt

¼ teaspoon garlic powder
1/3 cup finely chopped green
   onions
1 (2 ounce) jar pimientos
2 (7 ounce) cans tuna, drained
   flaked
1¼ cups sliced toasted almonds

In a large bowl, sprinkle gelatine over cold water and let stand 1 minute. Add boiling water and stir until gelatine is completely dissolved. With wire whip or rotary beater blend in cream cheese until smooth. Stir in lemon juice, curry powder, salt and garlic powder. Fold in green onions, pimiento, tuna and ½ cup of the almonds. Turn into oiled 5½ cup fish mold and chill until firm. To serve, unmold onto platter. Garnish with remaining almonds, overlapping to form scales, green olives and pimiento strips may be used for a face. Serve with crackers or party breads.

Kathy Anderson
San Jose, California

CRAB OR SHRIMP MOUSSE

1 (6½ ounce) can crab or
   ½ pound fresh
½ cup chopped celery
1 green onion, thinly sliced
1 cup mayonnaise

1 (8 ounce) package cream
   cheese
1 (10 ounce) can cream of
   mushroom soup
1 envelope unflavored gelatin
Dash of lemon juice

Heat soup. (Works perfectly heated in a 4 cup measuring cup in the microwave.) Soften gelatin with 3 teaspoons cold water and quickly add to hot soup. Add remaining ingredients and mix with hand mixer. Place in serving dish or oiled mold and chill for several hours. Serve with crackers. NOTE: Shrimp or a combination of crab and shrimp may be substituted for the crab. This may also be served as a salad.

Marianne Wolfsen Chaney (Mrs. James)
Class of '57
Lemoore, California

SHRIMP MOLD

1 envelope gelatin
Juice of 1 lemon
2 (8 ounce) packages cream
   cheese, softened
1 pound shrimp
4 tablespoons mayonnaise
2 tablespoons Worcestershire
   sauce
½ cup minced celery

2-3 minced green onions
3 tablespoons minced parsley
2 teaspoons curry
Dash Tabasco sauce
Salt
Pepper
Parsley for garnish

Soften the gelatin with lemon juice; set aside. In a large bowl, soften the cream cheese and blend in remaining ingredients. Fold in gelatin mixture. Carefully spoon into a lightly greased mold and refrigerate for three or more hours. Invert and garnish liberally with chopped parsley. Serve with Euphrates crackers.

Jennifer English (Mrs. John A.)
Mother of Lauren '85
Lafayette, California

"This curried shrimp and cheese canape is one of those tasty hors d'oeuvres neither you nor your guests can leave alone."

AMANDAS

¼ pound tiny shrimp
1 (3 ounce) package cream
   cheese
½ cup grated sharp cheddar
   cheese
½ cup freshly grated Parmesan
   cheese

½ cup mayonnaise
¼ cup diced green olives
2 tablespoons grated onion
2 tablespoons snipped chives
1 teaspoon curry powder
Cocktail loaf of French bread
Minced fresh parsley

Cook, shell, devein and chop shrimp. In a small bowl, mix shrimp, cheeses, mayonnaise, olives, onion, chives and curry powder. Cut the loaf of French bread into ½ inch slices and place on broiler pan. Toast one side under preheated broiler until golden. Turn slices over and spread untoasted sides with shrimp mixture; broil until heated through. Remove from broiler and sprinkle canapes with minced parsley. NOTE: The shrimp mixture can be made 1-2 days before using, but bring to room temperature before spreading.

Bia Osmont Wahl (Mrs. Dale)
Class of '62
Portland, Oregon

OUT-OF-THIS-WORLD SHRIMP

1½ pounds small cleaned shrimp 1/3 cup vinegar
½ cup minced onion 1 clove minced garlic
1 cup snipped parsley 1 teaspoon salt
2/3 cup salad oil Dash of pepper

Combine shrimp, onions and parsley. Set aside. Blend salad oil, vinegar, garlic, salt and pepper; beat well with rotary beater. Pour over shrimp; refrigerate overnight. Serve with tooth picks. Escort and sesame crackers go well with this. NOTE: Instead of using small shrimp, one may use baby shrimp and provide a spoon to serve the mixture on crackers.

Uta Zener (Mrs. Julian)
Mother of Juliette '83
Stockton, California

SHRIMP SALAD CANAPES

1 (6 ounce) can baby shrimp 1 tablespoon sweet pickle relish
1 large egg, hard cooked 1 tablespoon mayonnaise

Rinse and drain the shrimp well, patting dry if necessary to remove all moisture; place in a small serving bowl. Grate the hard-cooked egg over top of the shrimp; add remaining ingredients. Mix well until thoroughly blended, being careful not to break the shrimp. The amount of mayonnaise may be adjusted, using just enough to bind. Serve on your favorite cocktail breads, crackers or toasted rounds.

Roxanne Terrell (Mrs. Mark)
Monterey, California

ALLIES' SHRIMP SPREAD

3 (8 ounce) packages cream 2 bunches finely chopped
  cheese green onions
2½ cups finely chopped celery Juice of 1 lemon
1½ cups mayonnaise 2 cups small shrimp

Thoroughly blend cream cheese and mayonnaise. Add celery, onions and lemon juice. Mix well. Gently fold in shrimp. Chill several hours or overnight. Serve with Triscuits or small rye bread slices. NOTE: Any leftovers are delicious spread on toasted English muffins!

Tina Goodrich (Mrs. John, Sr.)
Mother of Mary Kris and John
Fort Ord, California

"This recipe comes from an English friend, Sir Arthur Harris, K.G., Marshall of the Air Force."

POTTED SHRIMP

1 pound fresh tiny shrimp
1 teaspoon black pepper,
medium grind

1 teaspoon ground nutmeg
¼ pound butter, melted

Cook, shell and clean the shrimp. Spread in a single layer on wax paper. Sprinkle evenly with the pepper, then the nutmeg. Place shrimp in a bowl, covering completely with melted butter. Refrigerate until butter is hardened. Turn out on a plate, if desired, or serve directly from bowl, with small squares of hot fresh toast. NOTE: This is an excellent appetizer with drinks and may be kept in the refrigerator for about a week as the spices and butter act as a preservative.

Mrs. Gordon T. Southam
Mother of Nancy '74
Vancouver, British Columbia
Canada

ROQUEFORT STUFFED PRAWNS

24 medium sized prawns,
cooked
3 ounces cream cheese

1 ounce Roquefort cheese
½ cup finely chopped fresh
parsley

Shell and devein the prawns. With a sharp knife split the prawns down the spine, about half way through. Blend the cheeses together and stuff the mixture into the split backs of the prawns. Roll the cheese side in the parsley.

Mrs. Lee B. Price
Monterey, California

The Science Building opened in the fall of 1971 and was dedicated to the memory of Countess Bernardine Murphy Donohue. Included in the building's design are four laboratories with a research room adjacent to each; two seminar rooms, six instructor-counselor offices, a three room unit dark room and film composing area, a separately ventilated animal room for mammals, an astronomy deck with Questar telescope, and a 100 seat lecture amphitheatre and projection room. It was patterned from the Lawrence Hall of Science on the Berkeley campus of the University of California.

"All one needs is a good can opener!"

ANTIPASTO

1 pound boiled shrimp, cut into
   bite-sized pieces
2 (4 ounce) cans skinless boneless
   sardines, washed, drained and
   cut in half
1 (2 ounce) can flat anchovies,
   washed, drained and cut in
   half
2 (6 ounce) jars artichoke hearts,
   cut in half

1 large dill pickle, cut in thirds
   and then in strips
1 (2 ounce) jar pimento, diced
1 (7 ounce) can white tuna,
   drained and broken into pieces
1 (3 ounce) jar stuffed olives,
   sliced
2 (3 ounce) cans sliced
   mushrooms, drained

MARINADE:
1 cup oil
Juice of 2 lemons

1 tablespoon tomato paste
¼ teaspoon pepper

In a large bowl combine the antipasto ingredients. Make a marinade by blending the oil, lemon juice, tomato paste and pepper. Pour over the antipasto and marinate for a minimum of two days. During the marinating period, mix gently two or three times each day. To serve, allow to stand at room temperature for about ½ hour.

Teisah Miller
Monterey, CA

CAVIAR PIE

2-3 avocados, mashed
Lemon juice
1 large purple onion, finely
   chopped
3 hardcooked eggs, chopped

Mayonnaise
Salt
Pepper
1 (3½ ounce) jar lumpfish
   caviar

In a 9½ inch ceramic quiche dish, spread a layer of mashed avocado, sprinkled with a little lemon juice so it won't discolor, followed by a layer of the finely chopped onion. Mix the eggs with the mayonnaise, salt and pepper; mixture should not be too creamy. Spread on top of the onion. Cover and chill several hours or overnight. Immediately before serving, add a layer of lumpfish caviar. Serve with Triscuits or Melba toast. NOTE: This is much lighter than the recipes containing cream cheese.

Wynn Woodward
Class of '67
Vancouver, B.C.
Canada

CHICKEN LIVER PATE

1 pound chicken livers
½ pound sweet butter or
  margarine
4 shallots, minced
3 large hard cooked eggs
1½ tablespoons brandy
1½ tablespoons Madeira

2 teaspoons salt (½ teaspoon if
  margarine is used)
1/8 teaspoon powdered cloves
¼ teaspoon (scant) pepper
¼ teaspoon thyme
¼ teaspoon marjoram
¼ teaspoon ginger
¼ teaspoon cinnamon

Cut chicken livers into coarse pieces and cook slowly in ¼ pound of the sweet butter or margarine with the minced shallots. Be careful not to brown the livers; remove from heat when they are firm but still tender, reserving pan juices. In a bowl, cream remaining butter or margarine and add the cooked livers with all the pan juices. Finely chop eggs, or force through a sieve; add to livers along with remaining ingredients, mixing well. Puree the mixture, one-third at a time, in an electric blender or food processor. Fill 4 half-pint jars with the pate; cover and chill thoroughly before serving. NOTE: If the pate is covered with a thin layer of melted butter it will keep well in the refrigerator for 2 weeks. This recipe also freezes well.

Dorothy Kirk (Mrs. Northrop)
Mother of Elizabeth '84 and Northrop
Pacific Grove, California

WYNN'S PATE

½ cup chopped onion
2 tablespoons green onions or
  shallots, chopped
1 tart apple, peeled and sliced
Butter for sauteeing
1 pound chicken livers (cleaned)

¼ cup brandy
2 large handfuls pistachio nuts
2-4 tablespoons heavy cream
10 tablespoons soft butter
1 teaspoon lemon juice
1 teaspoon salt
¼ teaspoon pepper

Saute in butter the onion, shallots and apple; remove from pan. Saute the chicken livers in butter over high heat. When nearly cooked, add brandy and flambe. Process in blender all sauteed ingredients with 1 large handful of the pistachio nuts. Place in a bowl and set aside to cool. When cooled, add remaining ingredients, including the second handful of pistachio nuts, and mix well. Pack in a tureen or ceramic dish and seal with a thin layer of melted butter. Serve with toast rounds or thinly sliced baguette.

Wynn Woodward
Class of '67
Vancouver, B.C.
Canada

CHICKEN LIVER PATE A L'ORIENTALE

½ pound (1 cup) chicken livers
1 tablespoon shoyu
½ cup soft butter
½ teaspoon salt
½ teaspoon dry mustard
Dash cayenne

1 (5 ounce) can water chestnuts,
  finely chopped
6 slices bacon, cooked and
  crumbled
4 tablespoons finely chopped
  green onion

Cook and chop the chicken livers. Add remaining ingredients in order listed, combining well after each addition. Refrigerate until needed. Serve on crackers or toasted bread rounds. EDITORS' NOTE: Shoyu is a Japanese soy sauce.

Connie Sage (Mrs. Gary)
Lower School Faculty
Mother of Renee St. Amour
Pacific Grove, California

CHICKEN LIVER PATE

4 tablespoons butter
1 pound chicken livers
½ pound sliced mushrooms
½ cup sliced scallions
1 teaspoon salt
½ cup dry white wine

1 clove garlic, minced
½ teaspoon dry mustard
¼ teaspoon dried rosemary
¼ teaspoon dried dill weed
¼ cup yogurt cheese
1 cup walnuts

Melt the butter in a large saucepan; add chicken livers, mushrooms, scallions and salt. Saute for five minutes, stirring occasionally (livers should be slightly pink). Add wine, garlic, mustard, rosemary, and dill; cover and simmer over low heat for approximately ten minutes. Uncover pan; raise heat to cook down liquid until almost gone. Let cool briefly. Place in food processor and puree. Add the yogurt cheese and blend thoroughly. Add walnuts and blend again. Pack in large crock and chill for at least 8 hours. Yields 2½ cups. NOTE: Pate keeps about two weeks in the refrigerator.

CriCri Solak-Eastin
Class of '71
Pasadena, California

The Mack estate was a haven for artists. One of the artists in residence was Salvadore Dali, whose small cottage studio near the main house has been turned into a music classroom.

LIVER PATE

1 pound chopped liver (from deli)
1 cup butter at room temperature
5 tablespoons minced onion
3 tablespoons cognac
2 teaspoons dry mustard

1 garlic clove, minced
½ teaspoon hot pepper sauce
½ teaspoon nutmeg
¼ to ½ teaspoon ground cloves
Salt
2 hard cooked eggs

Combine all the ingredients except the eggs in a blender or food processor and mix well, or put through a food mill to thoroughly combine. Strain, if necessary, to make a completely smooth paste. Pack into a three-cup terrine and refrigerate until thoroughly chilled. Just before serving, garnish with chopped eggs, the whites and yolks chopped separately.

Jennifer Michaels (Mrs. Paul)
Mother of Christina
Salinas, California

"This is a professional looking and tasting party hors d'oeuvre which I first saw and tasted at a Washington D.C. cocktail party. It has always been successful."

PATE NORRIS

1 (10½ ounce) can beef consomme
2 tablespoons sherry (or to taste)
1 envelope gelatin

2 (4½ ounce) cans pate de foie gras
1 (8 ounce) package cream cheese
1 tablespoon whiskey

Heat consomme with sherry over low fire until warm; remove from heat. Soften gelatin in consomme mixture until dissolved. Pour ½ inch consomme into a buttered ring mold and chill until set. Reserve the remaining liquid at room temperature. Blend well together the pate, cream cheese and whiskey. Gently place into mold on top of set gelatin mixture, being careful not to touch sides of mold. Pour remaining consomme into mold. Chill until set. Serve, unmolded, with crackers. NOTE: Raw or cooked vegetables may be added to consomme prior to chilling.

Winthrop Boswell (Mrs. James)
Mother of Rosalind '67
Hillsborough, California

PATE

4 slices crisp bacon
1 (2¼ ounce) can deviled ham
16 ounces Oscar Meyer
   Braunschweiger liver sausage
1 small onion
Pepper to taste

2 teaspoons butter
½ teaspoon dill weed
½ teaspoon basil
Brandy to taste
Dijon mustard
Parsley

Mince onion in food processor; add bacon, ham, liver sausage, butter and spices. Check frequently, adding brandy a little at a time. Place in serving container, cover with Dijon mustard; top with chopped parsley. Leave uncovered at room temperature for several hours to allow flavors to blend. Cover and refrigerate. This yields approximately 2 cups.

Bonnie McWhorter Bertelsen (Mrs. Jeffery)
Class of '63
Foster City, California

CHEESE OR PATE IN ASPIC

2 (10½ ounce) cans consomme
2 envelopes gelatin
6 tablespoons cold water

2 tablespoons sherry
Cheese or a liverwurst mixture

Heat consomme and add the gelatin which has been dissolved in the cold water. Add the sherry and set aside to cool. Pour the consomme mixture about one inch deep in a lightly greased mold, either round, oblong or melon. Place in the refrigerator to congeal. Mound cheese mixture or liverwurst mixture in appropriate shape to mold you are using. Place in mold on well-set consomme, centering carefully. Pour in remaining consomme, covering sides and top of cheese or liverwurst mixture. Chill. Unmold and serve with crackers or melba toast.

Linda Hall (Mrs. John)
Mother of Amy '86
San Francisco, California

On the campus is the former residence of Colonel Harold Mack, financier, art patron, and authority on Spanish architecture. It is a 26 room house that was finished in 1938 after seven years of architectural research and building. There are 17th century tiles set in the floors, stairways and window recesses. There are early hand-blown Spanish window glass and Flemish primitive paintings.

"This recipe is similar to Mediterranean taponade."

OLIVE PATE

1 cup pitted black olives
  (Greek or Italian)
3 tablespoons butter or olive oil
2 cloves garlic, minced
½ teaspoon crushed thyme
1 tablespoon capers

2 teaspoons minced onion
Anchovies or anchovy paste
  (optional)
Black or cayenne pepper and/or
  Tabasco

Put the olives, butter or olive oil, garlic, thyme, capers, onion and anchovies (to taste as desired) into the container of a blender or food processor and process until smooth. Taste, adjust seasonings and add more butter or olive oil to adjust texture if needed. Serve with crisp crackers or hard bread. NOTE: This can be varied by adding canned tuna, more anchovies, or strong brandy. It is wonderful when spread thickly on the crust of an onion tart.

Cheri Sullivan
Aunt of Kim Bowden '87
Urbana, Illinois

CURRIED SHERRY PATE

2 (3 ounce) packages cream
  cheese
1 cup grated cheddar cheese
½ teaspoon curry powder
½ teaspoon garlic powder

¼ teaspoon salt
4 teaspoons sherry
1 (9 ounce) jar chutney
½ bunch green onions

Bring the cream cheese and the grated cheese to room temperature; thoroughly blend with the curry and garlic powders, the salt and sherry. Shape into a ball and place on a round serving platter. Flatten ball until it is approximately ¾ to 1 inch thick. Process chutney in a blender or food processor until thick (drain off a small amount of the excess liquid, if desired, to produce a thicker topping) and spread over the flatened cheese ball covering only the top of the cheese. Sprinkle generously with the finely sliced green onions and serve with Sociable crackers. NOTE: This recipe is best made 2 to 3 days in advance to allow the flavors to blend. Refrigerate. Do not top with the chutney or onions until ready to serve.

Jody Stockwell (Mrs. Robert)
Garmish, Germany

CHEESE AND CHUTNEY BALL

1 (8 ounce) package cream
  cheese
1 (4 ounce) package blue cheese

1 (8 ounce) jar Major Grey's
  mango chutney
1 (2½ ounce) package chopped
  pecans or walnuts

Soften cream cheese with a fork, blend in the blue cheese and then stir in the chutney (if chutney pieces are large, cut into smaller pieces before adding). Stir until thoroughly mixed. Place in freezer until firm enough to shape into a ball. Roll the ball in the chopped nuts. Store in refrigerator. Serve with crackers. NOTE: If your taste doesn't run to blue cheese, eliminate the blue cheese, use only about 2/3 jar chutney and add a little curry powder to taste. Proceed as above.

Joan B. Miller
Mother of Jennifer Lynn '81
North Palm Beach, Florida

SWISS CHEESE BALLS

1 (8 ounce) package cream
  cheese
4 tablespoons grated Swiss
  cheese
2 tablespoons horseradish

1 tablespoon chopped pimiento
½ teaspoon onion powder
Salt to taste
Parsley, chives or ham

Mix well the cheeses, horseradish, pimiento, onion powder and salt. Form into small balls, adding a small amount of thick cream, if necessary, to bind. Roll balls in finely chopped parsley, chives or ham.

Mrs. Lee B. Price
Monterey, California

PAPRIKA CHEESE SPREAD

2 (8 ounce) packages cream
  cheese
2 cloves garlic, minced
2 teaspoons paprika

¼ cup chopped walnuts
1-2 ounces vodka
¼ cup finely minced onion

Blend all ingredients until smooth and creamy. Serve on small squares of pumpernickel bread.

Marilyn Ramos Ospina (Mrs. Eduardo)
Class of '60
Mother of Maria Christina '86
Bogota, Colombia

CHEESE SPREAD

1½ pounds cheddar cheese
¼ teaspoon salt
¾ teaspoon dry mustard
¼ cup chopped parsley
¼ cup chopped onion

2 tablespoons soft butter
Dash of Tabasco sauce
Dash of Worcestershire sauce
¼ cup tomato ketchup
1/3 cup sherry

Cut cheese in small pieces and put through a food processor, using metal blade. Add salt, mustard, parsley and onion and process until well blended. Add remaining ingredients and process until mixture is smooth and creamy. Place in small bowl and serve with crackers. NOTE: This spread is better when made at least 24 hours before using and stored in refrigerator. The cheese may be grated and the remaining ingredients gradually worked in with a wooden spoon if a food processor is not available.

Helen O'Hara (Mrs. Gerald P.)
Mother of Catherine '60, Mary '66,
Virginia '72
San Francisco, California

"COMPANY'S COMING AND I FORGOT"
OR UNEXPECTED COMPANY DROPPED IN

1 (8 ounce) package cream
  cheese

Pick a Peppa sauce or soy sauce
and browned sesame seeds

Place cream cheese on serving platter. Cover with Pick a Peppa sauce OR soy sauce and sesame seeds. To brown sesame seeds, place on cookie sheet, dot with butter, bake in a 350° oven until golden brown, stirring frequently. Cover cream cheese with the browned sesame seeds. Pour soy sauce over all. Serve with crackers. EDITORS' NOTE: Cream cheese makes a wonderful base for many quick and easy hors d'oeuvres. Other toppings to consider are: chutney, salsa, chopped sweet midget pickles, shrimp or crab cocktail, Jalepeno pepper jelly, a mixture of chopped olives and walnuts, drained crushed pineapple or pimento jelly.

Juana D. Mestres (Mrs. Lee)
Mother of Nicole '85
Tahoe City, California

"This is great on Valentines or Christmas. This recipe is actually stolen from my older sister, Lynn Tomlinson Elliott, Class of '65."

RED BELL PEPPER SPREAD

6 red bell peppers
1 cup vinegar

1½ cups sugar
1 (8 ounce) package cream
cheese

Dice bell peppers; combine with vinegar and sugar in a frying pan or iron skillet; simmer one hour. Drain off liquid. Bring the cream cheese to room temperature, spread on a plate and cover with bell pepper sauce. Serve with crackers.

Tina Tomlinson Del Piero (Mrs. Marc)
Class of '73
Salinas, California

ROQUEFORT CANAPES

1 (3 ounce) package cream
cheese, softened
8 ounces Roquefort cheese
1 tablespoon white wine
½ teaspoon onion powder

1 teaspoon dill weed
¼ teaspoon salt
½ pint whipping cream
¼ cup chopped, toasted
pecans

Blend cream cheese, Roquefort and wine until smooth; add onion powder, dill weed and salt. Whip cream until stiff. Fold whipped cream and pecans into cheese mixture until well blended. Refrigerate about an hour to allow flavors to blend. Serve with crackers. Yields about 3½ cups.

Mrs. Lee B. Price
Monterey, California

FROSTED HAM BALL

2 (4½ ounce) cans deviled ham
1 tablespoon Gulden's spicy
mustard
Few dashes of Tabasco
8 ounces cream cheese
2 teaspoons milk or cream

¼ cup sour cream
2½ teaspoons Gulden's spicy
mustard
½ teaspoon onion powder
(optional)

Blend the ham, mustard and Tabasco. Form into a ball and place in the refrigerator. Combine the remaining ingredients to make a frosting and frost ham ball when hard. Remove from refrigerator about 15 minutes before serving.

Mrs. Lee B. Price
Monterey, California

ARTICHOKE SPREAD

3 (6 ounce) jars of marinated
  artichoke hearts
1 teaspoon dill

¼ cup sour cream
Garlic salt to taste

Drain marinade from artichoke hearts; chop artichokes into small pieces. Add remaining ingredients and mix well. Serve with crackers of your choice or Armenian cracker bread. NOTE: This can be made two days in advance and refrigerated until needed.

Candy Hazard Ducato (Mrs. John)
Class of 1960
Mother of Caroline '85
Hillsborough, California

"This is so easy to do and it's delicious. People have a hard time guessing the ingredients. I have also used grated Cheddar cheese which is less expensive."

HOT ARTICHOKE DIP

1 cup Parmesan cheese, freshly
  grated
1 cup mayonnaise

1 (14 ounce) can artichoke
  hearts, packed in water

Chop artichokes; mix with mayonnaise and Parmesan cheese. Bake, uncovered, in a 350° oven for 15-20 minutes. Serve with tortilla chips.

Ann Craig Hanson (Mrs. John)
Class of '66
Hanover, New Hampshire

ARTICHOKE DIP

1 (14 ounce) can artichoke
  hearts, drained and chopped
½ cup mayonnaise

1 (4 ounce) can chopped green
  chiles
½ cup grated Parmesan cheese

Mix ingredients together. Place in greased casserole and bake at 350° for 30-45 minutes or until bubbly. Serve with crackers or tortilla chips. May be made ahead and frozen.

Joanne Cohen (Mrs. Sheldon)
Mother of Poppy, '86
Fresno, California

ARTICHOKE HEART DIP

¾ cup mayonnaise
¾ cup Parmesan cheese, grated
6 green onions, chopped

1 (8½ ounce) can artichoke hearts
Lemon juice to taste

Blend all the ingredients in a food processor, or chop artichoke hearts and process ingredients in a blender until thoroughly mixed. Bake in an oven-proof dish at 350° until brown and bubbly (approximately 45 minutes). Serve at room temperature with corn chips.

Katherine Hayes Carrington (Mrs. David)
Class of '65
Los Angeles, California

SPINACH DIP

1 cup mayonnaise
1 pint sour cream
1 (10 ounce) package frozen
    chopped spinach
    defrosted and well drained

1 small onion, chopped
1 package Knorr's leek soup
1 (8 ounce) can water chestnuts,
    chopped

Combine all ingredients and chill. Serve with fresh vegetables or chips.

Joanne Cohen (Mrs. Sheldon)
Mother of Poppy, '86
Fresno, California

JUST FOR THE WIDOW

1 cup powdered mustard
    (Coleman's)
1 cup white wine vinegar

1 cup granulated sugar
3 eggs, beaten

Soak mustard in vinegar for 8 hours. In top of double boiler, blend mustard mixture with sugar and beaten eggs; simmer for about 20 minutes, stirring constantly to prevent lumping. Cool; keeps indefinitely in refrigerator. Use as a dip with pretzels or fresh vegetables. Yields 2½ cups.

Catherine Flynn Doig (Mrs. Barry)
Class of '53
Sarasota, Florida

ECONOMICAL BLENDER SURPRISE

1 (10 ounce) can cream of
   chicken soup
1 diced cucumber

1 diced onion
¾ cup vermouth or white wine

Combine all ingredients in blender and blend well; place in serving dish and chill thoroughly. Serve with small pretzels.

Catherine Flynn Doig (Mrs. Barry)
Class of '53
Sarasota, Florida

DIXIE'S CHILI DIP

1 (15 ounce) can chili without
   beans
1 pound Velveeta cheese

3 green onions
2 jalapeno peppers

Cube the cheese and melt over low heat. Set aside. Rinse, seed and finely chop the peppers and slice the green onions, including stems. Add to melted cheese; stir in chili. Place in 1½ quart casserole dish and bake 1 hour at 225°. Serve with taco or corn chips.

Polly Reese (Mrs. Robert)
Mother of Heather
Monterey, California

CHILI CHEESE APPETIZER

1½ cups grated sharp cheddar
   cheese
1 (4 ounce) can diced chile
   peppers
1 (2¼ ounce) can chopped olives

4 ounces tomato sauce
2-4 ounces salad oil
1 small onion, grated
1 clove garlic, minced

Mix all ingredients together and pat into a greased mold. Chill. Unmold on serving dish. Serve with corn chips.

Lanie Waters (Mrs. N. Roger)
Aunt of Lauren and Adrianne Humiston
Sherman Oaks, California

AZTEC CALENDAR APPETIZER

1 (16 ounce) can refried beans
1 (1¼ ounce) package taco
  seasoning
3 avocados, mashed
3 tablespoons sour cream
2 tablespoons lemon juice
¼ teaspoon garlic salt
1 (4 ounce) can chopped green
  chiles

4 green onions, chopped
½ pound Cheddar cheese,
  shredded
½ pound Monterey Jack cheese,
  shredded
1 (2¼ ounce) can sliced olives
1 tomato, chopped

For first layer, mix refried beans and taco seasoning; spread into 12-inch pie plate. For second layer, mash avocados with sour cream, lemon juice and garlic salt; spread on top of bean mixture. For third layer, sprinkle chiles and onions over avocado mixture. For fourth layer, combine cheeses and sprinkle over chiles and onions. Arrange sliced olives and tomato on top; sprinkle lightly with chili powder and fresh parsley. Serve with cheese spreaders and large round tortilla chips. Serves 12.

Lilly Harman Huppert (Mrs. Lee)
Class of '58
Albuquerque, New Mexico

"This is a big hit with young and old alike."

KRIS' TACO DIP

1 large corn tortilla or
  3 small ones
1 (10½ ounce) can bean dip
2 avocados, sliced
6 tablespoons sour cream
½ of 1 (1¼ ounce) package taco
  seasoning mix

2 tomatoes, diced
½ pound cheddar cheese,
  grated
½ pound Monterey Jack cheese,
  grated
1 bunch green onions, diced
1 (2¼ ounce) can sliced olives

Place 1 large tortilla, or 3 small tortillas, overlapping on a plate. Layer with bean dip, avocado and sour cream mixed with the taco seasoning, being careful to spread each layer evenly over the tortillas. Cover with a mixture of the cheeses; then layer the tomatoes, the onions, and top with olives. Serve with corn chips. NOTE: Two cans of frozen avocado, thawed, may be used in place of the fresh avocado, if desired.

Mrs. Joseph Deming
Mother of Susan '63
Grandmother of Kathleen '84
Zephyr Cove, Nevada

"This is similar to quiche, but with the flavor of Baja, California."

BAJA BITES

5 eggs
1 cup cottage cheese
¼ cup flour
½ teaspoon baking powder
¼ cup butter, melted

2 tablespoons minced green
  onions
2 cups Monterey Jack cheese
1 (4 ounce) can chopped
  green chiles

Grease an 8-inch square baking pan; set aside. Preheat oven to 350°. In a large bowl, beat eggs; add cottage cheese and beat until almost smooth. Beat in flour, baking powder and melted butter until thoroughly blended. Stir in chiles, green onions, and cheese. Pour evenly into prepared pan. Bake 30-40 minutes until center is firm. Cool slightly. Cut into 5 rows horizontally and 5 rows vertically; serve warm. Makes 25 appetizer servings.

Sandra Robinson (Mrs. Edward)
Mother of Aundra '85
La Jolla, California

HAM AND CHEESE QUICHES

3 (9½ ounce) packages pie crust
  mix
1½ pounds Swiss cheese, grated
6 eggs, beaten
3½ cups light cream
½ cup chopped onion

2 teaspoons salt
2 teaspoons Worcestershire sauce
¼ teaspoon black pepper
4 (4½ ounce) cans deviled ham
Parmesan cheese

Prepare pie crust mix according to directions. Chill dough. Combine cheese, eggs, cream, onion, salt, Worcestershire sauce, pepper and deviled ham. Set aside. Roll out chilled dough; cut into 4-inch circles. Place circles of dough in small muffin tins (about 2" in diameter) and fill with ham-cheese mixture. Sprinkle with Parmesan cheese. Bake at 450° for 5-8 minutes. Reduce heat to 300° and continue baking for 15-20 minutes. Cool slightly. Remove from pans. Makes about 50. NOTE: These freeze well and keep for about six months. Reheat in a 350° oven for 10-15 minutes. Serve hot.

Marianne McFadden
Class of '62
Salinas, California

" . . . simple, casual, satisfying snack-type food — marvelous for a children's lunch or supper."

FRENCH BREAD PIZZA

1 loaf French bread
1 teaspoon vegetable or olive oil
1 (15 ounce) can tomato sauce
1 (6 ounce) can tomato paste
8 ounces Mozarella cheese,
 shredded

1 teaspoon Italian seasoning
1 teaspoon parsley
½ teaspoon oregano
½ teaspoon garlic salt
Optional pizza topping

Cut loaf of bread in half lengthwise. Drizzle oil over cut surface of bread; set aside on a cookie sheet. Combine tomato sauce, tomato paste and seasonings; spread evenly over bread. Sprinkle with cheese, being careful to cover completely, as this will prevent bread from becoming soggy. If desired, hamburger, sausage or pepperoni may be used as a topping. Place in a preheated 350° oven for 20 minutes or until pizza is crisp and cheese is melted. Serves 12-16 as an hors d'oeuvre; 4-6 as a lunch.

Ellen (Eleanor) Hills Klos
Duneland Beach, Indiana

PIZZA CON PATE FEUILLETEE

6½ ounces puff pastry
1 large ripe tomato, peeled
Salt
Pepper
Oregano

1½ ounces flat anchovies
Mozzarella cheese
1 teaspoon anchovy oil or
 olive oil

Roll the puff pastry out very thinly and cut into a circle about 8 inches in size. Place on lightly buttered baking tray, or pizza tray. Prick the pastry well and partially cook in 400° oven for 10 minutes. Cut the tomato into thin slices and remove seeds. Arrange the slices over the partly cooked pastry, keeping clear of the edges. NOTE: More than 1 tomato can make the pastry soggy. Season the tomato with salt, pepper and some oregano. Cut the anchovies into small pieces and arrange on the top. Cover with Mozzarella cheese, keeping clear of the edges as the cheese spreads as it melts. Sprinkle a teaspoon of anchovy oil or olive oil over the pizza and bake 10 minutes in a 400° oven. Cut into wedges. Serves 8-10 as an hors d'oeuvre, 6 as an entree.

Denise LeBlanc deForest (Mrs. Lockwood)
Class of '57
Melbourne, Australia

BOB'S FAVORITE HORS D'OEUVRES

1 small loaf sourdough French
  bread
4 tablespoons butter
Garlic powder

2 large dill pickles
12 slices sharp Cheddar cheese
12 (4 inch) strips of bacon

Slice bread into 12 pieces. Spread with butter and sprinkle with garlic powder. Cut pickles lengthwise into 12 slices. Place a slice of pickle on each piece of bread. Cover with cheese; top with bacon. Broil 10 inches from heat until bacon is cooked and cheese is melted.

Mr. Robert W. Covert
Father of Robin, '86
Salinas, California

CHEESE-MUFFIN DELIGHT

6 English muffins, split
1½ cups mild Cheddar cheese,
  grated
1 (2¼ ounce) can chopped ripe
  olives

½ cup chopped scallions
¼ cup mayonnaise
½ teaspoon curry powder
½ teaspoon chili sauce
½ teaspoon salt

Slightly toast muffin halves. Combine remaining ingredients and mix well; spread onto muffins and place on cookie sheet. Broil until bubbly (approximately 5 minutes). Remove from oven. Cut in halves or quarters before serving.

Pamela Becking (Mrs. Paul)
Mother of Frank and Paul
Salinas, California

CHEESE ROLLS

1 loaf thinly sliced sandwich
  bread
¼ cup butter, melted
¼ cup mayonnaise

1 (2 ounce) jar pimiento, finely
  diced
1 cup grated Cheddar cheese
¼ cup chopped parsley
1 teaspoon finely chopped
  green onion

Remove crust from bread. Brush lightly with melted butter. Combine remaining ingredients and spread mixture on bread slices. Roll bread in the fashion of a jelly roll, using a damp cloth. Place seam side down on wax paper and freeze. Before serving, place on cookie sheet and spread with the remaining melted butter. Place in an oven preheated to 350° for about 5 minutes or until cheese is melted. Broil until golden brown, watching carefully. Serve immediately.

Mary Jane Wesson (Mrs. W.P.)
Mother of Jameen '77
Modesto, California

CHEESE STRAWS

1 pound sharp Cheddar cheese
  grated
1½ cups butter, softened

4 cups flour
1 teaspoon salt
1 teaspoon cayenne pepper

Mix the softened butter and grated cheese until well blended. Sift flour with salt and cayenne; blend with butter and cheese mixture. When the mixture has been kneaded until creamy, fill cookie press fitted with the star disc. Press onto greased cookie sheet in long parallel strips. Bake at 350° until barely brown (about 18 minutes). Cut into desired lengths while slightly warm. Makes 10-12 dozen.

Ruth Barres
Shreveport, Louisiana

CHEESE WAFERS

½ pound very sharp Cheddar
  cheese
½ pound margarine (not butter)
2 cups flour

½ teaspoon salt
¼ teaspoon dry mustard
¼ teaspoon cayenne (or to taste)
1½ to 2 cups Rice Krispies

Grate cheese, mix with margarine; add remaining ingredients. Drop by teaspoonfuls and flatten on ungreased cookie sheet. Bake 350° for 15-20 minutes, or until lightly brown. Will keep for weeks in a tin container, or may be made ahead and frozen. Reheat to serve.

Lucille Bowman (Mrs. Merle F.)
Mother of Barbara '66 and Melinda '67
Monterey, California

"This recipe was given to me by a 98 year old friend, Zena Seabrook. She said, "It's nice to have a blotter when you have a drink!"

BLOTTER CRISPS

2 heaping teaspoons powdered
  cardamon

¾ cup butter
12 flour tortillas

Cream butter with cardamon and spread evenly over tortillas. Bake in a shallow pan at 250° until crisp (45 minutes to 1 hour). Cool. Break into irregular pieces before serving. NOTE: Some people may prefer cinnamon instead of cardamon for another occasion.

Marie Cressey Belden (Mrs. Lester M.)
Mother of Cressey Joy Belden '87
Santa Rosa, California

JACIMA SLICES

1½ pounds Jacima

Peel and rinse jacima. Slice thoroughly and chill until served. It is best kept in ice water if stored for longer than 20 minutes. Serve on a platter with hot Mexican food, use instead of crackers with a guacamole dip, or eat by itself as a snack. Jacimas are a nice substitute if one is allergic to apples. NOTE: Most supermarkets carry this Mexican vegetable in the produce department.

Penny Nichols
Portress' Office
Pacific Grove, California

BAKED POTATO PEEL

6 small baking potatoes   *Salt*
1 tablespoon melted butter   *Onion powder*

Peel the potatoes so that the skins are ¼ inch thick. (Refrigerate the unused portion of the potatoes in a container of cold water for other use.) Place the potato skins in a single layer on a greased baking sheet. Bake uncovered in a 450° oven until brown and crisp, about 40 minutes. Brush melted butter over the peels, coating well; sprinkle with salt and/ or onion powder as desired. Serve immediately.

Mrs. Lee B. Price
Monterey, California

"This is a summer treat if you grow your own zucchini or know someone who does. Pick only the "male" blossoms early in the morning when they are wide open. The "male" blossoms are the ones without the tiny zucchini developing on the stem end."

SQUASH BLOSSOMS

1 (8 ounce) package cream   *¼ teaspoon pepper*
  cheese   *20-24 zucchini squash*
1 (4 ounce) can chopped green   *blossoms*
  chiles   *Flour*
¾ cup Parmesan cheese   *1-2 eggs, beaten*
2½ tablespoons milk   *Oil*

Blend the cream cheese, chiles, Parmesan, milk and pepper. Stuff the blossoms with the cheese mixture, dip in flour, then in milk and egg. Fry in small amounts of oil until golden on both sides, turning once.

Mary Ann Taylor (Mrs. James)
Mother of James, Katie and Asher
Monterey, California

ZUCCHINI APPETIZERS

3 large or 4 medium zucchini
½ cup chopped green onion
1 clove garlic, minced
1 cup Bisquick
4 beaten eggs
½ cup oil
½ cup grated Parmesan cheese

1 cup grated Cheddar cheese
1 teaspoon garlic salt
1 teaspoon oregano
¼ teaspoon hot pepper sauce
1 cup cheese crackers, crumbled
½ cup hard salami, chopped

Thinly slice zucchini; mix well with onion, minced garlic, Bisquick, eggs, oil, Parmesan cheese, ½ cup of the Cheddar cheese, garlic salt, oregano, hot pepper sauce and salami. Place in greased 13x9x2 pan; top with crumbled crackers and remaining ½ cup Cheddar cheese. Bake at 350° for 35-45 minutes. Let stand 5 minutes after removing from oven; cut in squares. Serves 12. NOTE: This may also be used as a brunch or luncheon dish.

Marie Degnan (Mrs. Michael)
Mother of Michelle '83
Dhahran, Saudi Arabia

ZUCCHINI PUFFS

2 medium zucchini (about 12
ounces)
1/3 cup grated Parmesan cheese

1/3 cup mayonnaise
½ teaspoon basil

Slice zucchini into 36 ¼ inch rounds. In small bowl combine the remaining ingredients. Spread each zucchini slice with a thin layer of mayonnaise mixture and place on broiler pan. Broil 5 inches from heat in preheated broiler, about 30-60 seconds or until top is golden brown. Each round is about 20 calories. This recipe can be made ahead and placed, covered, in refrigerator for up to 24 hours.

Joan Courneen (Mrs. Peter)
Mother of Karrie '86
Santa Cruz, California

Since 1973 the University of California at Berkeley has used our facilities in the Science Building for their annual seminars in January on the California Grey Whales and the Sea Otter.

MONTEREY ARTICHOKE BAKE

2 (6 ounce) jars marinated
   artichoke hearts
1 small onion, finely chopped
1 clove garlic, crushed
4 eggs, beaten
¼ cup dry breadcrumbs
2 cups grated Monterey jack
   cheese

¼ teaspoon salt
¼ teaspoon crushed basil leaves
¼ teaspoon dried oregano leaves,
   crushed
2 tablespoons finely chopped
   green chiles
Pimiento strips, if desired

Drain artichoke hearts, reserving 1 tablespoon marinade in a small saucepan. Set artichoke hearts aside. Add onion and garlic to reserved marinade. Saute until onions are soft. Preheat oven to 375°. Grease an 8-inch square baking pan; set aside. Finely chop artichoke hearts and combine with beaten eggs, breadcrumbs, cheese, salt, basil, oregano, pepper, green chiles and sauteed onion mixture. Spoon into prepared baking pan. Bake 25-30 minutes until mixture is firm. Cut into 25 to 30 small bars or squares. Garnish each piece with a strip of pimiento, if desired. Serve warm or cold. Makes 25-30 appetizer servings.

Sandra Robinson (Mrs. Edward)
Mother of Aundra '85
La Jolla, California

MUSHROOM CRESCENT SNACKS

3 cups sliced mushrooms
2 tablespoons butter
½ teaspoon garlic salt
2 tablespoons finely chopped
   onion
1 teaspoon lemon juice

1 teaspoon Worcestershire sauce
1 (8 ounce) can crescent dinner
   rolls
1 (3 ounce) package cream
   cheese, softened
¼ cup grated Parmesan cheese

Preheat oven to 350°. Brown mushrooms in butter. Stir in salt, onion, lemon juice and Worcestershire sauce. Cook until liquid evaporates. Separate dough into 2 rectangles. Place in ungreased 13"x9" pan and press over bottom and ¼ inch up the sides. Spread cream cheese over dough. Top with mushrooms, then Parmesan cheese and bake 20-25 minutes or until brown. Cut into squares. NOTE: This is a very versatile hors d'oeuvres. You can use the cream cheese and chives, add black olives, use grated Monterey Jack cheese and chiles along with the cream cheese, omitting the mushrooms and Parmesan cheese.

Mary Munhall Holl (Mrs. Stephen)
Class of '70
San Bernardino, California

"This is most attractive during the Christmas season."

MUSHROOM CANAPE

½ pound mushrooms, chopped   Bread rounds
1 teaspoon grated onion   Paprika
4 tablespoons butter   Parsley
½ cup sour cream

Mix together mushrooms, onions, butter and sour cream. Place on small rounds of thinly sliced breads — rye, wheat, white or black. Dust half of the round with paprika; sprinkle the other half with chopped parsley. Broil quickly or brown at 350° for 15 minutes.

Marie Cressey Belden (Mrs. Lester M.)
Mother of Cressey Joy Belden, '87
Santa Rosa, California

"Quickee hors d'oeuvres in five minutes, tastes like you slaved for hours."

MAGIC MUSHROOMS
This Recipe in Honor of the Late Tink Dollar, Class of 1971

1 package of Rondele, or   18 medium to large mushrooms
   Boursin with herbs, without   2 tablespoons olive oil
   peppercorns   Paprika

Wash and dry mushrooms. Remove stems. Grease bottom of mushrooms with the olive oil, using a paper towel. Place in a 8x8 inch baking dish, and fill each mushroom with cheese, softened to room temperature. Broil until top is browned and bubbly. Sprinkle with paprika before serving.

Kathleen Sullivan
Class of '71
ABC News
Washington, D.C.

The Santa Catalina campus is involved in many community activities on the Monterey Peninsula. The Bach Festival holds concerts in our Performing Arts Center as does the Jazz Festival. The University of California has held extension programs on the campus, and the Knights of the Vine sometimes hold their installations here. Some of the other groups using our facilities are the Sierra Club, Save the Otters, the Audubon Society, and the local Stanford Alumni.

CRAB-STUFFED MUSHROOMS

20 medium sized mushrooms
½ cup melted butter
1 (8 ounce) package cream
  cheese, softened
1 (6½ ounce) can crab meat,
  drained

1 tablespoon minced onion
1/3 cup Parmesan cheese
2 tablespoons milk
¼ teaspoon onion powder
dash garlic salt
1/8 teaspoon paprika

Wash mushrooms and remove stems. Coat mushrooms with melted butter and place on cookie sheet. Mix well the remaining ingredients except the paprika. Stuff the mushrooms lightly with the mixture. Sprinkle with paprika and bake 15 minutes at 350°. Serve immediately.

Mary Munhall Holl (Mrs. Stephen)
Class of '70
San Bernardino, California

BANANA-BACON HORS D'OEUVRES

Bacon
Bananas

Lemon juice
Brown sugar

Cut bananas into one inch pieces. Wrap one slice of bacon (or stretch and use half slices) around each piece of banana. Dip in lemon juice and a touch of brown sugar. Place seam side down and saute until brown. Serve immediately.

Mrs. M.B. Cooper
Monterey, California

"Very easy and so good. These go quickly!"

BESS'S CHEESEBALLS

1 pound sharp Cheddar cheese
3 cups Bisquick

1 pound hot bulk sausage

Melt cheese in a double boiler and set aside. Work Bisquick and sausage together. Pour cooled melted cheese over all and blend well. Roll into walnut-sized balls. Bake at 350° for 15-25 minutes or until brown on top. NOTE: These may be made ahead and frozen before baking. Place cheeseballs on cookie sheet; when frozen, remove and store in plastic bag.

Nina Davis Gray (Mrs. Elisha)
Class of '62
Winnetka, Illinois

SWEET AND SOUR SAUSAGE BALLS

4 pounds bulk sausage or use 2
  pounds hamburger and 2
  pounds sausage
4 eggs
1½ cups soft bread crumbs

3 cups catsup
¾ cup brown sugar
½ cup white wine vinegar
½ cup soy sauce

Combine meat, eggs and breadcrumbs. Form into balls about the size of a walnut. Saute until brown on all sides. Drain and set aside. Combine remaining ingredients to make a sauce. Pour over sausage balls. Cook 30 minutes, stirring occasionally. Serve hot. NOTE: These freeze well and keep for 3-6 months. Reheat slowly in saucepan on top of stove or in 350° oven for 20 minutes.

Marianne McFadden
Class of '62
Salinas, California

LAMB MEATBALLS

2 pounds lean ground lamb
2 teaspoons ground cumin
2 teaspoons chopped fresh mint
  or ½ teaspoon dried mint
2 green onions, finely
  chopped

2 teaspoons salt
¼ teaspoon pepper
¼ cup dry bread crumbs
2 eggs
1 cup sour cream
1 teaspoon caraway seed

Mix together all ingredients except the sour cream and caraway seeds. Shape into one-inch meatballs and place on a flat pan. Bake at 425° for 15 minutes until thoroughly cooked. Arrange on a platter or chafing dish. In a small bowl, combine sour cream and caraway seeds. Serve as a dip for meatballs.

Mary Malcolm Ford (Mrs. Peter)
Class of '63
Atlanta, Georgia

TARRAGON MUSTARD CHICKEN PUFFS

1 cup minced cooked chicken
1 (8 ounce) package cream cheese

2 tablespoons Tarragon mustard
1½ diameter bread rounds

Blend together the chicken, softened cream cheese and mustard. Mound on bread rounds and bake in a 350° oven until golden brown.

Mrs. Lee B. Price
Monterey, California

DEVILED CHICKEN WINGS

30 chicken wings
1 cup butter
½ cup honey

4 or 5 tablespoons prepared
mustard
2 teaspoons curry powder or
to taste

Remove tip of chicken wing with kitchen shears. Place wings on a baking sheet with 1 inch sides. Combine remaining ingredients to make a sauce and pour over wings making sure that all are coated. Bake at 325° until done about 50-60 minutes.

Heather Peirce (Mrs. Robert)
Mother of Lisa Peirce '85
Calgary, Alberta, Canada

CHICKEN DRUMETTES

3 packages chicken drumettes
  (14 per package)
1 cup honey
½ cup soy sauce
2 tablespoons vegetable oil

2 tablespoons catsup
Salt
Pepper
½ clove garlic, chopped

Make a sauce by combining all ingredients except chicken. Place chicken drumettes in a large shallow baking pan (10 x 14) in a single layer. Pour sauce evenly over chicken and bake at 375° for 1 hour, turning drumettes once or twice.

Polly Reese (Mrs. Robert)
Mother of Heather
Monterey, California

DELICIOUS CHICKEN DRUMETTES

1 package chicken drumettes
½ cup olive oil
Juice of 1 lemon
½ cup mayonnaise
½ teaspoon curry powder

3 heaping tablespoons sour
  cream
2 tablespoons chutney, pureed
1 tablespoon lemon juice
Rice Krispies

Make a marinade by combining the juice of 1 lemon with the olive oil. Marinate chicken approximately 8-12 hours, turning several times. Remove from marinade and pat dry with a paper towel. Thoroughly mix the mayonnaise, curry powder, sour cream, chutney and remaining 1 tablespoon lemon juice to make a sauce. Coat each drumette liberally with the sauce, then roll in Rice Krispies until well covered. Place on a baking sheet and bake 45 minutes at 375° until brown.

Mrs. M. B. Cooper
Monterey, California

Beverages

"This punch is very refreshing and not too sweet."

TRUDY'S PUNCH

For Punch:
2 quarts grapefruit juice
2 quarts cranberry juice
1 quart apple juice or apple cider
2 (28 ounce) bottles ginger ale
½ gallon raspberry sherbet (optional)

For Mistletoe Ring:
Ginger ale
Mint sprigs
Water
Raspberry sherbet

Chill juices and ginger ale thoroughly. Prepare mistletoe ring several days in advance. Pour chilled juices and ginger ale into a large punch bowl at the last minute. Add mistletoe ring or ½ gallon of raspberry sherbet, a quart at a time. Yields 7 quarts. Mistletoe ring: Pour ¾ inches of ginger ale into a six cup ring mold and freeze. Arrange mint sprigs on ice in ring to simulate sprigs of mistletoe; add ¾ inches water; freeze. Fill mold with softened raspberry sherbet. Cover tightly and freeze until solid, at least 24 hours.

Dorothy Kirk (Mrs. Northrop)
Mother of Elizabeth '84 and Northrop
Pacific Grove, California

ORANGE JULIUS

1 (12 ounce) can frozen orange juice
3 cups milk
2 teaspoons vanilla

2 eggs
2 tablespoons sugar
10 ice cubes

Combine all ingredients except ice in the blender and blend well. Add ice cubes and blend until ice is crushed. Serve immediately.

Corinne Renshaw
Class of '77
Logan, Utah

STRAWBERRY-BANANA DAIQUIRI

Ice cubes
2-3 jiggers rum
1 (8 ounce) can lemonade
    concentrate

1 (10 ounce) can sweetened
    frozen strawberries
¼ cup liquid sweet n' sour mixer
1 banana

Fill blender container 1/3 full of ice cubes and add 2-3 jiggers of rum, or to taste; process until ice is crushed and mixture is smooth. Add the partially thawed can of lemonade and the partially thawed can of strawberries and process again. Pour in the sweet n' sour mixer; process. Add the banana and blend until smooth. Add additional ice, if necessary, to equal 5 cups; processing to insure a smooth consistency.

Jerry Bettencourt
Meadow Vista, California

DUDDY DELIGHT

1½ cups fresh strawberries
1 (6 ounce) can frozen limeade
    concentrate

6 ounces Vodka

Place ingredients in blender with enough crushed ice to fill blender approximately 2/3 full. Blend until smooth. Serves 4.

Mr. Lon Dudley
Husband of Bev Harman '62
Folsom, California

HOLIDAY PUNCH

1 quart cranberry juice
1 quart apple cider
¼ cup brown sugar

2 tablespoons whole cloves
4 cinnamon sticks, broken
1 pint Burgundy wine

Combine the cranberry juice, apple cider, and brown sugar in a large kettle; simmer until sugar is dissolved. Make a cheesecloth bag and put the spices in it; suspend in liquid for 15 minutes while the punch is simmering on low heat. Remove spices and add the wine. Serve hot. NOTE: A short cut for this recipe is to put the liquids in a percolator and the sugar and spices in the basket and perk.

Beezie Leyden Moore (Mrs. H. Walker)
Class of 1953
Clovis, California

JANIE'S HOT MULLED CIDER

½ cup brown sugar
2 quarts cider
1½ teaspoons whole cloves
1 teaspoon whole allspice

2 pieces stick cinnamon
Orange slices (if not available,
 use 1 teaspoon dried orange
 peel)

In a large pot, dissolve brown sugar in cider. Tie spices in cheesecloth or put into a tea strainer (include dried orange peel if used). Add to cider and simmer. Float orange slices on top. Yields 8 one-cup servings. EDITORS' NOTE: A large electric coffee urn may be used instead of a pot, placing spices in coffee basket before perking.

Yolanda Scaccia Manuel (Mrs. Chris)
Class of '67
San Mateo, California

CIDER WASSAIL

4 cups apple cider
¼ to 1/3 cup dark brown sugar
½ cup dark rum
2 tablespoons apple brandy
1 tablespoon orange liqueur
2 tablespoons brandy

¼ teaspoon cinnamon
¼ teaspoon ground cloves
1/8 teaspoon ground allspice
Pinch of salt
1 rounded tablespoon orange
 juice concentrate
Whipped cream

Bring cider to boil. Add sugar and stir until dissolved; remove from heat. Stir in rum, brandies, orange liqueur and spices. Stir in orange juice concentrate. Heat over moderate heat, stirring for 2 minutes. Pour into demitasse cups or wine glasses and top with a generous amount of slightly sweetened whipped cream. Garnish with fresh nutmeg, if desired. Serves 10-15. NOTE: The whipped cream makes a big difference. Don't omit.

Russell Anderson
San Jose, California

In 1949, Mother Margaret Thompson negotiated for the purchase of a 28 acre estate on the Monterey Peninsula and announced that the houses thereon could be converted to school dormitories, classrooms, and living quarters for the Sisters by September, 1950. Sister Mary Kieran Hannifan was appointed Superior and Santa Catalina was re-established.

"This is most enjoyable when it is 40° below zero and the snow is five feet deep as it sometimes is in Minnesota."

TOM AND JERRY

5 eggs for 6 servings (OR 8 eggs   Brandy
  for 10 servings)   Dark Rum
Powdered sugar   Nutmeg

TO MAKE BATTER: Separate the eggs and beat the egg whites until they hold their shape. In a separate bowl, beat the egg yolks until light, then beat the egg yolks into the egg whites. Fold in quantities of powdered sugar, a little at a time, beating constantly until the batter becomes very thick. Do not add cream or any other ingredients to the batter. FOR AN INDIVIDUAL SERVING: Pour hot water into a large china cup to heat it, empty out the water and place a heaping tablespoon of the batter in the cup. Add 1 jigger of brandy and ¾ jigger of dark rum while stirring with a teaspoon. Pour in boiling water, continuing to stir until cup is filled. Garnish with a sprinkling of nutmeg. Serve immediately. Guaranteed:a good night's sleep! NOTE: leftover batter may be refrigerated and used again the next evening. Stir before using.

Sister Carlotta
Principal
Santa Catalina School

BOHEMIAN SPICED WINE

1½ cups water   ½ cup blanced almonds
20 whole cloves   2 (24 ounce) bottles red
10 cardamon seeds (without   Bordeaux
  pods)   2 (24 ounce) bottles Port
5 tablespoons grated orange peel   3½ cups vodka
2 cups pitted prunes   Sugar (optional)
1¼ cups raisins

Bring water to a boil. Tie cloves, cardamon seeds and orange peel in cheesecloth and add to water. Reduce heat, cover and simmer 10 minutes. Add prunes, raisins, almonds, and additional water to cover. Simmer 10 minutes more. Pour in wine, port and vodka. Increase heat and bring just to boil. Remove from heat and allow to cool. Cover and refrigerate overnight. Before serving, remove spice bag and reheat wine to warm thoroughly. Do not boil. Add sugar to taste. Transfer to pitcher and pour into glasses, spooning a few raisins and almonds into each serving. Yields about 20 glasses or mugs.

Dr. Paul Michaels
Father of Crissey
Salinas, California

"This is a recipe from Katherine and Melissa's great-grandmother, Clara Louisa Schmidt Breuner, and has been a tradition at family gatherings during the holidays . . ."

HOLIDAY EGGNOG

12 ranch eggs, separated
2 cups sugar
1 pint whiskey
1 pint rum

1 pint brandy
2 quarts half and half
1 quart vanilla ice cream

Due to the large quantity, mix the eggnog in two separate batches, using half the ingredients each time.

In the large bowl of the electric mixer, beat 6 egg whites until foamy, gradually adding ½ cup sugar; beat until stiff and set aside. In a second bowl, beat 6 egg yolks with ½ cup sugar until light and fluffy; slowly add 1 cup each whiskey, rum and brandy. In another bowl, combine the two mixtures, adding 1 quart half and half; pour into punchbowl. Repeat process with remaining ingredients. Place the brick of ice cream in the punchbowl and allow it to stand until it melts. NOTE: For best results, bottle and store the eggnog in the refrigerator for five days. If you don't want to wait five days, it's also delicious served immediately!

Kitty Davis (Mrs. Gerard H.)
Mother of Katherine '84 and Melissa '86
Sacramento, California

FROSTY EGGNOG

6 eggs
¼ cup sugar
½ cup light corn syrup

½ pint half and half cream
¼ cup rum, optional
1 pint vanilla ice cream
Nutmeg

In large bowl, with mixer at high speed, beat 6 egg whites until foamy. Gradually beat in sugar until stiff peaks form. In small bowl, with mixer at medium speed, beat the egg yolks and the corn syrup about five minutes or until thick and lemon colored. Add half and half. Beat until well mixed. Fold into egg white mixture. If desired, stir in rum. Cover and refrigerate. Unmold vanilla ice cream from carton and place in punch bowl. Pour eggnog over ice cream. Sprinkle with nutmeg. Makes 24 (½ cup) servings.

Joan Courneen (Mrs. Peter)
Mother of Karrie, '86
Santa Cruz, California

KAHLUA

1 scant cup good quality
  instant coffee
4 cups boiling water
4 cups sugar

1 good quality vanilla bean
1/5 brandy or vodka
Large empty jug with cap

In a large saucepan, dissolve coffee and sugar in the boiling water. Add liquor after the coffee mixture cools. Break the vanilla bean into 4 parts and put in a jug. Pour coffee-liquor mixture over the vanilla bean. Cap jug for 30 days; turning upside down every 2-3 days to mix. Uncap for 1 day before serving. NOTE: It is important to use the best quality coffee, vanilla bean and liquor. This will insure the best flavor.

John H. Brazinsky, M.D.
Father of April
Carmel, California

APRICOT LIQUEUR

12 even unblemished apricots
1 fifth of vodka

1 pound hard rock sugar

Put apricots and vodka in a glass quart jar container and leave for four months. Remove fruit and strain liquid into a new clean jar and add the rock sugar broken in small pieces. Add the apricots and let stand for one additional month. Strain again into a pretty liqueur decanter. NOTE: The apricots make a good dessert.

Marlene Kellogg (Mrs. Clarence)
Mother of Kellene '79 and Christina '85
Pacific Grove, California

Soups and Sauces

Often the difference between a good soup and a great soup is the stock. There is no true substitute for the rich flavor of a good homemade stock, and so we begin our recipes with two stocks that will offer a wonderful beginning to many soups, sauces, gravies and stews.

BASIC WHITE OR CHICKEN STOCK
(Bouillon de poulet)

1 hen or stewing chicken, plus
   some wings
Veal bones
Cold water to cover
1 large onion, peeled and
   and quartered
1 carrot, sliced
10 sprigs parsley

2 whole cloves
2 cloves of garlic
8 peppercorns, slightly crushed
2 celery stalks with leaves, cut up
2 teaspoons salt

Cut the hen and place in a large kettle with the wings and veal bones. Cover with cold water, bring slowly to a boil and skim off the scum as it forms on the surface. When all the scum has been removed, add the remaining ingredients and seasoning and simmer, covered for 3 hours. Remove the meat pieces and strain through a sieve. Cool rapidly, uncovered, and refrigerate or freeze. NOTE: It will keep one week in the refrigerator or 6 months in the freezer. To freeze, cool first; remove layer of fat on top and freeze. If to be kept in the refrigerator, leave the layer of fat on top as it serves to exclude air and preserve the stock. TO CLARIFY: Remove fat from stock. Correct seasoning. For each quart of bouillon, add 1 egg white beaten with a little water, and the crushed shell of the egg after the white skin has been removed. Bring to a boil for 2 minutes, stirring constantly and then simmer gently for 20 minutes. Strain through a fine sieve lined with a double thickness of cheese cloth.

Pauline Cantin (Mrs. Giles)
Music Department
Mother of Marie '70
Monterey, California

BASIC BROWN STOCK
(Bouillon de boeuf)

1 or 2 pounds bone marrow	*3 whole cloves*
4-6 pounds soup meat (beef	*1 teaspoon whole black pepper*
shin, knuckles, neck)	*2 teaspoons salt*
2 large onions	*1 bay leaf*
1 carrot, sliced	*2 garlic cloves*
1 rib celery, cut in 1" lengths	*Water to cover*

Cut one of the onions in half crosswise, and "burn" it, cut side down in a heavy pan. While this is cooking; Remove marrow from bones and melt in a large kettle; remove some of the meat from the bones and brown in the melted marrow; add all the bones, remaining meat and cover with cold water. Bring slowly to a boil and skim off scum as it forms at the surface. When all the scum has been removed, add remaining ingredients, the burned onion, and simmer, covered for 4 to 5 hours. When cooked, strain stock through a fine sieve. Cool quickly and refrigerate. NOTE: It will keep 1 week in the refrigerator or 6 months in the freezer. To freeze, cool first; remove layer of fat on the top and freeze. If it is to be kept in the refrigerator, leave the layer of fat on top as it serves to exclude air and preserve the stock. TO CLARIFY: Remove fat from stock. Correct seasoning. For each quart of bouillon, add 1 egg white beaten with a little water, and the crushed shell of the egg after the white skin has been removed. Bring to a boil for 2 minutes, stirring constantly, and then simmer gently for 20 minutes. Strain through a fine sieve lined with a double thickness of cheese cloth.

Pauline Cantin (Mrs. Giles)
Music Department
Mother of Marie '70
Monterey, California

In 1976, students in the Advanced Placement Art History class were honored by the National Trust for Historic Preservation in Washington, D.C. for their work in preparing an architectural resource inventory of the Monterey Peninsula. The project involved cataloguing, documenting, and photographing more than 400 structures to show the history of architecture on the Peninsula from 1770 to the present, including examples of how features of the architecture of the past were incorporated in more modern structures. The inventory was published as a book, "Architecture of the Monterey Peninsula" which has been sold in book stores and in connection with a show of some of the photographs at the Monterey Peninsula Museum of Art.

FRENCH ONION SOUP GRATINEE

½ cup sweet butter
8 cups thinly sliced yellow
   onions
1 teaspoon salt (or to taste)
3 tablespoons flour
1 teaspoon dry mustard

8 cups basic beef stock (see
   previous recipe)
Freshly ground pepper
8 slices French bread
8 slices Swiss cheese

Melt butter in a large, heavy skillet and add the onions and salt. Cook over medium heat, stirring frequently, for about 25 minutes or until the onions are golden brown. Sprinkle flour and mustard over onions and stir until well blended. Remove from heat. In another skillet, heat 8 cups of brown stock over high heat. Pour hot stock over the onions and mix well. Reduce the heat, cover and simmer 40 minutes. Season with pepper and additional salt if needed. Butter the bread slices on both sides with melted butter. Place on a cookie sheet and bake 25 minutes (or butter on one side and place under the broiler). Remove from oven; place a slice of Swiss cheese on each slice of bread. Ladle the soup in individual ovenproof bowls, and top each one with a slice of bread with its cheese. Put the bowls on a pan and place under the broiler (6 inches below heat) and broil for 3 to 4 minutes or until cheese is melted and golden brown. Serve immediately.

Pauline Cantin (Mrs. Giles)
Music Department
Mother of Marie '70
Monterey, California

" 'Serendipitous' because most great inventions occur when one is not looking for these results. Thus we created the most delicious soup which has become a meal in itself. Just add a loaf of hot French bread and 'voila' a superb dinner for cold evenings."

"SERENDIPITOUS" SOUPE L'OIGNON

3 (12 ounce) bottles tarragon
   vinegar
2 quarts water
6 pounds mixed onions (Spanish,
   Bermuda, leeks, shallots)
3-4 tablespoons olive oil
½-1 pound butter
Salt
Pepper

Tarragon
1 tablespoon flour
2 quarts chicken broth (canned
   or bouillon cubes)
2 quarts beef broth (canned or
   bouillon cubes)
French bread slices
Swiss cheese
Parmesan cheese

Combine tarragon wine vinegar and 1 quart of water in a large bowl; set aside. Fill container or sink with tepid water and place onions in water. Slice onions under water (this prevents tears). Place cut up onions in vinegar and water container. The liquid needs to cover all the onions. Let soak for 1 hour. Heat olive oil and ½ pound of butter in a skillet; add onions to soften. Season onions with a pinch of salt, pepper and tarragon. Cook onions until tender and slightly brown. Sprinkle with 1 tablespoon flour and stir. Combine all the broths and 1 quart water in a soup kettle. Heat slowly. Add the browned onions to the broth and simmer slowly for 30-40 minutes. Scoop the soup into oven proof bowls. Float toasted French bread slices on top. Cover with slices of Swiss cheese and/or sprinkle with Parmesan cheese. Place bowls under broiler for a few seconds or until cheese has melted and is slightly brown. Leftovers may be frozen and used another day. Serves 6-8. NOTE: If you want to make your own croutons, take sliced French bread and generously brush the top with a combination of butter and freshly pressed garlic. Place in oven at 325° and bake until crisp and lightly browned.

Roberta Gladstone (Mrs. Marvin)
Mother of Karen '81
La Habra, California

"There are many versions of French onion soup, but this one I find has guests dancing in the streets. A tossed green salad on the side is all you need for a complete meal with Baguette and wine accompanying."

FRENCH ONION SOUP

4 medium onions, thinly sliced
4 tablespoons olive oil
1 clove garlic, finely chopped
1 teaspoon salt
1 teaspoon Worcestershire sauce
½ teaspoon sugar
½ teaspoon cracked pepper

6 cups beef bouillon
¾ cup Burgundy (or Fortissimo)
3 tablespoons brandy
6 rounds hard-toasted French
  bread
Grated Parmesan cheese
Grated Gruyere cheese

Cook onions slowly in olive oil until yellow, about 10 minutes. Stir in seasonings and continue cooking until onions are golden brown, 20 to 30 minutes, stirring frequently. Add broth and wine, simmer, covered, 30 minutes more, adjust seasonings. Stir in brandy, pour soup into individual bowls over toasted French rounds. Grated Parmesan and Gruyere may be sprinkled over all. Serves 6. NOTE: Butter or margarine may be substituted for olive oil.

Sheila Lamson (Mrs. Perry)
Upper School Faculty
Pebble Beach, California

GREEN ONION SOUP

1 quart milk
Salt
Pepper
2 bunches green onions, sliced

4 tablespoons butter
4 eggs
Parmesan cheese

Scald milk, season to taste; cool just until warm. Saute the onions in the butter. Beat the eggs and add the onion mixture. Combine with the milk. Pour soup in oven-proof bowls, top with a generous amount of Parmesan cheese and broil for 5-10 minutes, watching carefully.

Mrs. Lee B. Price
Monterey, California

"This recipe is from my restaurant, Penelope's, located in Montecito, and has appeared in L.A. Magazine, Gourmet and Bon Appetit."

MUSHROOM SOUP WITH GREEN ONION

1 large onion
1 carrot
2 stalks of celery
1 leek
Few sprigs parsley
¼ teaspoon thyme
4 bay leaves
¼ teaspoon fennel seed

Salt
Freshly ground pepper
1 pound fresh mushrooms
4 tablespoons butter
1 quart chicken broth
1 tablespoon cornstarch
½ pint whipping cream

Finely chop all of the vegetables, either by hand or in a food processor. Melt butter in a large pot and add the vegetables and seasonings. Cook over low heat until tender. Add chicken broth and simmer for 1 hour. Dissolve cornstarch in a little cold water. Stir into the boiling soup and reboil for 1 minute. Strain the soup and reheat. Add warmed whipping cream and check seasoning. Do not boil. Serve in warm bowls garnished with sliced green onions. Makes 6 (6 ounce) servings.

Penelope R. Williams
Class of '64
Santa Barbara, California

In the library foyer is a sculpture of St. Catherine of Siena, the patron saint of the school. It is an original by Sculptress Frances Rich of Palm Desert, and commissioned by a parent in 1967.

"We are all so fond of this soup that we grow our own sorrel. It is easy to raise and fun to gather and cook."

SORREL SOUP

8-10 green onions, including tops
2 tablespoons butter
1 large potato, diced
2 cups fresh sorrel leaves
   (at least ½ pound)

8 cups chicken broth
Salt
Pepper
Half and half or milk

Wash sorrel and cut into thin strips; chop onions. Saute sorrel and onions in melted butter until sorrel is wilted and changed in color and the onions are soft. Add potatoes and toss until coated. Add chicken broth and simmer until potatoes are cooked. Season. Place in blender and blend until smooth. Add cream or milk to taste; reheat. Serves 6. NOTE: If sorrel is not available, an equal amount of spinach may be substituted.

Margaret Zuckerman (Mrs. David)
Mother of Eleanor '80
Stockton, California

ZUCCHINI SOUP

6 small zucchini
Salt
2 tablespoons olive oil
2 tablespoons butter
2 medium onions, finely minced
1 clove garlic, finely minced

5 cups chicken stock
2 tablespoons fresh minced herbs
   (parsley and chives)
2 tablespoons dried herbs
   (basil and oregano)
Pepper

Cut unpeeled zucchini into 1-inch cubes, salt, and place in a colander to drain for 30 minutes. In a large pan, heat oil and butter; add onion and garlic and cook 5 minutes over low heat without browning. Dry zucchini well on paper towels and add to pan, cooking an additional 5 minutes. Add stock and simmer for 15 minutes. Cool; puree in blender. Add herbs, salt and pepper to taste. At this point, the soup may be frozen or stored for several days in the refrigerator. Before serving, garnish with sour cream and chives if soup is to be served cold, or reheat and garnish with heavy cream. In either case, top with grated zucchini. Serve as a first course or as a meal with French bread and salad. NOTE: This is a good dish to double and serve half now and freeze half to serve later. Serves 8.

Holly Guy (Mrs. Garth)
Mother of Holly Ayn
Pebble Beach, California

"This is a delicious, easy soup and was invented as a result of a surplus of zucchini in our summer garden."

CREME OF ZUCCHINI SOUP

2 tablespoons butter
1 medium onion, chopped
5 cups (2-2½ pounds) zucchini,
  thinly sliced
1 (14 ounce) can chicken broth
¼ teaspoon sugar
¼ heaping teaspoon marjoram
  leaves

½ teaspoon salt
¼ - ½ teaspoon pepper
½ cup half-and-half
½ cup water
1 heaping teaspoon seasoned
  chicken stock base
¾ cup Basic Cream Sauce with
  parsley

Saute onion in butter in a large pan; add zucchini and simmer a few minutes longer. Add chicken broth, sugar, salt, pepper, marjoram, water and chicken stock base. Simmer 20 minutes; cool slightly. Divide into 2 portions, pour 1 portion into a blender with half of cream sauce and blend. Repeat with second portion. When both portions have been blended, return to pan, add half-and-half and heat just to boil. Serves 4-6.

BASIC CREAM SAUCE

4 tablespoons butter
3 tablespoons flour
1½ cups milk or half-and-half

Salt
Pepper
Nutmeg

Heat butter, add the flour and cook for a few minutes, stirring constantly. Gradually add milk and continue stirring until nicely thickened. Cook 5 minutes more and season to taste with salt, pepper, and a dash of nutmeg, if desired. For parsley cream sauce, add 1/3 cup finely chopped parsley. NOTE: Heat milk to almost boiling before adding to flour and butter as blending goes much faster and easier with hot milk.

Sally von Drachenfels (Mrs. Alec)
Mother of Chris '67
Monterey, California

MARY'S LEEK SOUP

2 tablespoons butter
3 medium leeks
1½ pounds potatoes, peeled
  and quartered
6 cups water

1 tablespoon salt
1 egg yolk
1 cup milk
6 slices french bread

Melt butter in a large saucepan; shred leeks and add to pan, cooking until leeks are slightly browned. Add potatoes, water and salt. Bring to a boil. Cover and simmer 30 minutes; strain, reserving liquid. Mash vegetables. Stir cooking liquid into vegetables and return to pan. Bring to a boil. Stir in milk and egg yolk. Bring back to boiling point but do not allow to boil. Serve hot with french bread fried in butter. Serves 6-8. NOTE: A dry white wine goes well with this soup.

Anne Grupe (Mrs. Greenlaw)
Mother of Susan '66
Linden, California

KATY'S TOMATO ONION SOUP

2 large sweet or red onions
3 tablespoons butter
1 cup celery, chopped
¼ pound fresh mushrooms
1 (28 ounce) can tomatoes

2 (10½ ounce) cans condensed
* beef broth*
1 teaspoon salt
½ teaspoon pepper
½ teaspoon basil
½ cup chopped parsley

Peel and thinly slice the onions and celery (may be done in food processor). Saute in butter with the mushrooms and cook until tender. Add the tomatoes, broth, salt, pepper and basil. Cover and simmer for 1 hour. Serve with croutons and/or grated parmesan cheese and parsley. Serves 4-6. NOTE: This also makes a delicious chili! Add ground beef, kidney beans and chili powder.

Mrs. Francis E. Sammons, Jr.
Menlo Park, California

"Put it all together to serve ice cold or piping hot!"

ORANGE AND TOMATO SOUP

4 cups beef stock or consomme
1 tablespoon cornstarch
¾ cup orange juice
1 cup canned tomatoes, finely
* chopped*

1 tablespoon butter
1 tablespoon sugar
Salt
Pepper

Dissolve the cornstarch in the beef stock or consomme; add the orange juice, tomatoes, butter and sugar. Simmer until flavors are blended and season to taste with salt and pepper. Serve hot or chilled.

Catherine Flynn Doig
Class of '53
Sarasota, Florida

"Original recipe from The Garden Cafe, Honolulu Academy of Arts, Honolulu, Hawaii."

BROCCOLI SOUP

*1 pound fresh or 1 (10 ounce)
    package frozen chopped
    broccoli
2/3 cup chopped carrots
1½ cups chicken broth
¾ cup chopped celery
¾ cup chopped onion*

*1 tablespoon butter
½ teaspoon rosemary
½ teaspoon Hawaiian rock salt
1 cup half-and-half
½ teaspoon salt
¼ teaspoon fresh lemon juice
Sour cream*

Cook broccoli and carrots in 1 cup of the chicken broth for 15 minutes or until done. Saute onion and celery in butter until golden. Place both mixtures in a blender or processor; add rock salt and rosemary. Blend *very well.* Return to saucepan and add remaining ingredients except for sour cream. Heat over low heat. Serve with a dollop of sour cream. Makes 4 (1-cup) servings.

Kathy Shipley (Mrs. Richard)
Mother of Eric
Ft. Ord, California

POTAGE ST. GERMAIN

*2 tablespoons margarine
2 tablespoons flour
2 tablespoons minced green
    onion
1/8 teaspoon nutmeg
1/8 teaspoon white pepper*

*1 cup scalded milk
1 cup chicken broth
2 cups frozen peas
1 tablespoon fresh mint
½ cup whipping cream
Parsley for garnish*

Saute onions in margarine until soft. Add flour, nutmeg and pepper; cook, stirring constantly for 2 minutes. Remove from heat and gradually add scalded milk, while stirring with a whisk. Return to heat and cook until thickened. Add broth, peas and mint. Cook an additional 5 minutes over low heat; pour into a blender and puree. Return to saucepan, add whipping cream and heat gently. Serve in warmed soup bowls. Garnish with snipped parsley. Serves 4-6.

Kay Covert (Mrs. Robert W.)
Mother of Robin '86
Salinas, California

CORN-POTATO CHOWDER

6 strips bacon
½ cup chopped onion
4 tablespoons chopped green
    pepper
Butter
2 (10-ounce) cans cream of
    potato soup

2-3 soup cans of milk
1 (17 ounce) can creamed
    corn
Salt
Pepper

Cook and crumble the bacon; set aside. Saute the onion and green pepper in butter. Combine all ingredients and heat thoroughly. This is a meal in itself and is good with French bread and white wine. Serves 6.

Marjorie E. Talbot (Mrs. Fred C., Jr.)
Mother of Suzanne '64 and Pamela
Menlo Park, California

POTAGE CULTIVAUER
(French Vegetable Soup)

¼ cup minced leeks
¼ cup minced carrots
¼ cup minced turnips
¼ cup minced celery
½ cup coarsely chopped cabbage
4 tablespoons butter
6 cups chicken broth

1 medium baking potato, cut
    in ½" cubes
1 tomato, peeled, seeded and
    chopped
Salt
Pepper

Make slashes and clean leek well to remove all sand. Use only the white part or very tender green in the soup. Peel turnip before mincing. Melt butter in soup pot (do not brown) and add the minced vegetables; coat well. Soften about 10 minutes. Add the chicken broth and the potato. Simmer about 15 minutes, remove potatoes, crush and return to soup pot. This will thicken the soup. Add the tomato and cook 15 minutes more, being careful not to overcook the vegetables; check the seasoning. NOTE: The soup is more delicate and elegant if it is not overloaded with vegetables and if the ones you add are very finely minced. To save time, and if you don't need to be elegant, you can chop the vegetables casually or grind them in a food mill or very carefully in a blender. Serves 6.

Anne Tredway (Mrs. Frederick)
Belvedere, California

BEEF AND VEGETABLE SOUP

Beef short ribs from a rib roast
4 cups water
1 cup one-inch carrot strips
1 cup sliced celery
1 cup diced potatoes
1 cup green beans

2½ cups canned tomatoes
2 teaspoons salt
¼ cup chopped onion
1/8 teaspoon chopped parsley
1/8 teaspoon white pepper

Remove meat from bones and cut into cubes. Place meat, bones and water in an electric fry pan set at 250°. Cover and simmer for 2½ hours. Skim to remove fat from surface; add vegetables, seasonings and parsley. Cover and simmer 1 hour longer. Remove bones from soup before serving. Serves 6-8.

Anne L. Baggiolini (Mrs. Severo)
Mother of Chad Pattee
Salinas, California

STEAK SOUP

1 pound lean round steak
½ pound margarine
1 cup flour
2 quarts water
1 package frozen mixed vegetables
1 (20 ounce) can tomatoes

1 large or 2 small stalks celery
1 large or 2 small carrots
1 medium sized onion
4 tablespoons beef bouillon granules
2 tablespoons Kitchen Bouquet

Coarse grind or chop the steak; brown and cook until dry. Make a roux with the margarine and flour in a large kettle. Slowly add the water, stirring while heating until smooth. Chop carrot, onion, celery and cut tomatoes in small pieces; add to the roux in the kettle. Add the browned meat, bouillon granules and frozen mixed vegetables to the kettle. Add Kitchen Bouquet, salt and pepper to taste. Bring to a boil, reduce heat and simmer for 2 hours, covered.

Priscilla Hathorn
Monterey, California

HAM AND PEA SOUP

1 pound dried peas
4 cups water
1 medium onion
1 clove garlic
3 stalks celery with tops

3 cups water
¼ - ½ cup liquid smoke
¼ teaspoon soda
1½ cups cubed ham

Soak peas overnight in 4 cups of water. In a blender, puree the onions, garlic and celery with 3 cups water. Pour into a crock pot; add liquid smoke, soda, ham and peas which have been drained. Mix well. Cook on high 7-9 hours in crock pot. Serves 6-8.

Dianne Klech Saugier (Mrs. Joseph)
Class of '72
Shawnee, Kansas

THE COACH HOUSE BLACK BEAN SOUP

3 pounds beef bones
¾ beef shin
3 pounds smoked ham shank
with bones and rind
15 cups water
3 cloves
¾ teaspoons black peppercorns
¼ teaspoon celery seed
2½ cups dried black beans
10 cups water
1 cup chopped onions
½ cup chopped celery

2 cups water
9 cups stock
2 large cloves garlic, chopped
1 teaspoon salt
½ teaspoon freshly ground
pepper
¼ cup sherry or Madeira
Garnishes:
Thin slices lemon
Chopped parsley
Chopped hard cooked egg
Chopped watercress
Sour cream

First day: Make the stock 1 day before serving. Prepare stock by placing beef bones, beef shin, ham shank, 15 cups water, cloves, peppercorns and celery seed in a large soup pot or kettle. Bring to boiling, reduce heat and simmer half covered 8-10 hours. Strain stock into a large container, reserve meat for other uses; discard bones. Refrigerate stock. Soak beans in 10 cups water overnight in refrigerator. Second day: Remove fat from surface of cold stock. In soup pot, place onions, celery and 2 tablespoons fat from the stock; cook, stirring until soft. Add drained, soaked beans, garlic, 2 cups of water and 9 cups of stock, adding water to make the 9 cups. Bring to boiling, reduce heat and simmer uncovered 2½-3 hours, stirring occasionally. Keep beans covered with liquid; if necessary, adding more water. When beans are very soft, puree the soup. Use a food processor or blender, pureeing a little at a time until fairly smooth. Return pureed soup to the soup pot. Add salt, pepper and sherry; heat until soup boils and is piping hot. Ladle into warm soup bowls and garnish with lemon slices, chopped parsley and chopped hard-cooked egg, or you can garnish with chopped watercress and sour cream. Makes 12 servings. NOTE: Soup may be made several days in advance and reheated, or it may be frozen.

Terri Correll Brazinsky (Mrs. John)
Mother of April
Carmel, California

61

SOUP SCALLOPS BOB

3 cups Court bouillon
1 medium onion, sliced
½ cup celery, thinly sliced
½ cup carrots, thinly sliced

3 cups water
1 cup white wine
½ pound scallops

Boil all but the scallops until the vegetables are not quite tender. Add the scallops and poach for 5 minutes — no longer! Serve in soup bowls with dollops of hollandaise sauce as a garnish and hot French bread.

Mrs. Francis E. Sammons, Jr.
Menlo Park, California

CRAB SOUP

10 small crabs
3 tablespoons olive oil
2 leeks, diced
1 celery stalk
6 tomatoes
3 garlic cloves

Saffron
Salt
Vermicelli
Croutons
Parmesan cheese
Gruyere cheese

Heat olive oil in a kettle or soup pot. Add crabs, leeks, celery, tomatoes without their juice and seeds, and garlic cloves; cook for 2-3 minutes, then crush the crabs. Add a pinch of saffron and 2 quarts of water; bring to a boil. Add salt and simmer for 20 minutes. Strain. Add 2-3 tablespoons vermicelli and simmer for another 10 minutes. Serve with croutons, Parmesan cheese and grated gruyere cheese. NOTE: Can be made with small crabs (etrilles) or Norway lobster heads (Pangoustines).

Leticia Gascoin-Ruffie (Mrs. Jean Paul)
Class of '65
St. Agne, France

CLASSIC OYSTER BISQUE

1 sprig parsley, chopped
1 small carrot, diced
1 small onion, chopped
1 small celery stalk, chopped
2 tablespoons melted butter
1½ pints oysters (3 dozen)
½ cup The Monterey Vineyard
   Classic California White Wine

1 cup soft bread crumbs
2 cups chicken broth
1 cup milk
1½ cups heavy cream
Salt
Pepper
Butter

Saute carrot, onion, celery and parsley in butter until shiny, about 3 or 4 minutes. Drain and reserve liquid from 1 pint (2 dozen) oysters; finely chop the oysters and add to vegetables. Stir over low heat 3 minutes. Stir in wine and continue to simmer 3 minutes more. Soak bread crumbs in oyster liquid; spoon into vegetable-oyster mixture. Add chicken broth, milk and cream; heat but do not boil. While bisque is heating, saute remaining oysters in a small amount of butter until edges ruffle; combine with bisque. Pour into heated tureen or individual bowls. Serves 8-10. NOTE: French or Italian bread is preferable for making the soft crumbs.

Monterey Vineyard
Hayward, California

"Tastes delicious, but my favorite part is the directions! This soup is a supper in itself — and so quick!"

CRAB BISQUE

3 (10 ounce) cans tomato soup
3 (10 ounce) cans pea soup
(without ham)
2½ quarts half-and-half and or milk

2/3 cup dry sherry (or to taste)
2 pounds crab meat
White pepper

Combine all ingredients. Heat and serve. This is wonderful with French bread and salad and is good reheated. Serves 12. NOTE: Shrimp or lobster tails may be substituted for the crab.

Sister Mary Ellen
Santa Catalina School
Monterey, California

"This mixture provides a generous serving for one, the master of the home . . . can be stretched to pamper the lady's palate."

LEMON LEVES

¾ cup dry white wine
¾ cup purified water
2 egg yolks

Rind of 1 lemon
Pinch of sugar

Combine the wine with the bottled water and heat gently; beat in egg yolks. Add sugar and lemon rind and bring to a boil. Serves 1.

Dr. A. Bela Janko
Father of Julia '82, Isabelle '83, and Alexander
Carmel, California

"This was given to me by a friend who lived years in Ceylon. It is very delicate and delicious."

CASHEW NUT SOUP

½ pint raw cashew nuts
2 tablespoons butter
1 tablespoon flour
1 quart chicken broth, heated

1 pint heavy cream
Salt
Pepper
Dash of nutmeg

Carefully cull the nuts and grind to a powder. Melt butter in the top of a double boiler. Add flour and cook 8-10 minutes. Add to this the heated broth and heavy cream; season with salt, pepper and nutmeg. Stir in nuts and cook until thick and velvety.

Mrs. Walter H. Sullivan, Jr.
Mother of Paula '66, Erica '71, and
Dagmar '77
San Francisco, California

"We celebrated my thirtieth birthday at the King's Arms Tavern in Williamsburg, Virginia. This soup was our first course and is delicious."

KINGS ARMS TAVERN CREAM OF PEANUT SOUP

1 medium onion, chopped
2 ribs celery, chopped
¼ cup margarine
3 tablespoons flour

2 quarts chicken stock or
  canned chicken broth
2 cups smooth peanut butter
1¾ cups light cream
Chopped peanuts

Saute onion and celery in margarine until soft, blend in flour well. Add peanut butter and blend in quickly. Gradually add chicken stock, stirring constantly; bring to a boil. Remove from heat and add cream, blending well. Warm over low heat, do not boil. Garnish with peanuts, if desired. This can be served warm or chilled. Makes 10-12 first course servings or 5-6 main dish servings.

Mary Ann Taylor (Mrs. James)
Mother of James, Katie and Asher
Monterey, California

Gina Jansheski, class of 1977, was the first daughter of an alumnae to graduate from Santa Catalina. Her mother is Gloria Felice Jansheski, class of 1954.

"My cousin wrote this one in our family cook booklet. It's amusing to see if guests can guess all the ingredients!"

HOT WEATHER SOUP

2 quarts buttermilk
1 large or 2 small cucumbers,
   peeled and seeded
1 tablespoon sugar (or sugar
   substitute)
2 teaspoons creamed horseradish
2 teaspoons salt (or salt substitute)

1 tablespoon parsley, minced
1 teaspoon curry powder
Fresh ground white pepper
½ cup very dry Vermouth
   (optional)
Garnish

Place all ingredients in a food blender or Osterizer and blend thoroughly. Chill. Garnish with very thin slices of lemon or lime or a sprinkling of chopped chives.

Marie Cressey Belden (Mrs. Lester M.)
Mother of Cressey Joy '87
Santa Rosa, California

"The very Renaissance-type man who gave me this recipe said it was often served in Italy at times of stress . . . perhaps there is more truth than poetry in the contention that garlic lowers blood pressure and removes cholesterol from the blood . . . Whatever, this soup is marvelous in relaxed settings also . . . Good followed by steamed mussels or clams and light salad."

COLD GARLIC SOUP

PER SERVING:
1 slice dry Italian bread or
½ cup crumbs
1 large clove garlic
16 blanched almonds
1 teaspoon olive oil

6 peeled, seedless grapes
½ teaspoon vinegar
pinch salt
¾ cup ice water

Finely grind bread, almonds and garlic in blender; add remaining ingredients except grapes and process until well blended. Pour into small bowls or cups and top each serving with grapes. NOTE: About 4 servings can be prepared in a standard blender. Process crumbs in small batches; then almonds and garlic, return all to blender and add remaining ingredients.

Beth Gill (Mrs. David)
Mother of Coco
Pebble Beach, California

"This soup is not only a nice hot weather 'cooler' but is also a welcome addition for those watching their weight."

GAZPACHO SOUP

1 (32 ounce) can tomato juice
1 (2 ounce) can pimientos
1 (4 ounce) can chopped
  mushrooms
1 cucumber, chopped (use
  Armenian cucumber, if
  available
1 onion chopped

2 tablespoons vinegar
4 tomatoes, peeled and quartered
2 tablespoons Worchestershire
  sauce
Salt
4 drops Tabasco sauce

Combine all ingredients and chill several hours to allow flavors to blend. Provide sour cream or yogurt, croutons and green onions to garnish soup as desired.

Gail Wagner (Mrs. Charles)
Mother of Beth '86
Stockton, California

BEET BORSCHT

1 (16 ounce) can Julienne beets,
  drained
1 (10 ounce) can consomme
1 pint sour cream

1 teaspoon salt (or less)
1 tablespoon lemon juice
Chopped parsley

Combine the beets, consomme and sour cream. Chill. Add salt and lemon juice. Sprinkle with finely chopped parsley and serve in a small bowl.

Mrs. Lee B. Price
Monterey, California

"This soup is a specialty of the Coburg Inn, Coburg, Oregon."

BEER CHEESE SOUP

4 tablespoons grated carrots
4 tablespoons minced onions
4 tablespoons butter
4 cups chicken broth
½ teaspoon dry mustard
½ teaspoon paprika

1 teaspoon Worchestershire sauce
2 tablespoons cornstarch
¼ cup milk
1 cup grated sharp Cheddar
1 cup beer, room temperature
Chopped parsley

Cook carrots and onions in butter over medium heat for 10 minutes, stirring occasionally. Add the chicken broth, dry mustard, paprika and Worcestershire sauce; cover and cook over low heat for 15 minutes. Mix cornstarch with milk and stir into soup. Cool for 5 minutes, then add the cheese and beer. Stir over low heat until the cheese melts. Serve garnished with chopped parsley. Makes 6 servings.

Donna Wilson
Mother of Pamela '84
San Diego, California

"This sauce goes well on lamb, chicken or fish."

AUGOLOMONO SAUCE (LEMON SAUCE)

1 cup chicken stock
3 egg yolks
1 tablespoon fresh lemon juice
1 teaspoon arrowroot

1 teaspoon salt
Pinch of cayenne
1 tablespoon chopped parsley

Place in top of a double boiler over simmering hot water the egg yolks, lemon juice, arrowroot, salt and cayenne, mixing lightly with a whisk. Slowly stir in chicken stock; stir constantly with a whisk until thickened, being careful not to boil. Garnish with parsley. Keeps 1 hour. NOTE: Use less salt if stock is not homemade.

Laura Stahl (Mrs. William)
Mother of Kevin
Carmel Valley, California

DEVINE SAUCE

2 carrots
1 onion
2 stalks celery
3 tablespoons butter
1 pound brown sugar

Juice and zest of 2 oranges
1 cup red wine vinegar
1 quart rich brown sauce
1 cup Grand Marnier

Coarsely chop the carrots, onion and celery; saute in butter until the onion is transparent. Add sugar and cook over low heat until caramelized. Add orange juice, orange zest and vinegar; simmer until reduced by half. Stir in rich brown sauce and simmer for 10 more minutes. Pour in Grand Marnier and cook an additional 5 minutes. This sauce may be served with duck, chicken or roast. Entree may be garnished with grated orange rind or twists of thinly sliced oranges.

Beverlee R. Becker (Mrs. George)
Mother of Joan '83
Carmel, California

CURRANT GLAZE FOR ROAST PORK

2/3 cup red currant jelly
3 tablespoons port

2 tablespoons vinegar
1 teaspoon dry mustard

Combine all ingredients in a small saucepan; bring to a boil. Reduce heat and simmer for 10 minutes, stirring occasionally. Baste a pork roast frequently with the glaze during the final half hour of roasting.

Mrs. Lee B. Price
Monterey, California

SAUCE FOR KIELBASE
(Polish Sausage)

6 tablespoons butter
2 tablespoons dry mustard
2/3 cup brown sugar

2/3 cup catsup
6 tablespoons vinegar
6 tablespoons water

Melt butter in saucepan. Add remaining ingredients and cook, stirring until well blended. Pour heated sauce over sausages which have been cut in ½-inch slices and sauteed in butter. NOTE: This sauce is also *great* for glazing boiled corned beef for about 20 minutes in a 350° oven.

Mrs. Lee B. Price
Monterey, California

SPARERIB SAUCE

3 cups catsup
2½ cups sugar
¼ cup salt

3 cloves garlic, minced
1 cup hoisin sauce
½ cup salad oil

Combine all ingredients and marinate spareribs for 2-3 hours. NOTE: This makes enough sauce for 3 slabs of spareribs. Ribs may be grilled, broiled or baked in a 350° oven for 1-1½ hours.

Marian Kageyama
Monterey, California

At the time of the original founding of Santa Catalina, Monterey was largely a Spanish settlement, and so the school was named Santa Catalina in honor of the great Dominican Saint Catherine of Siena.

"This recipe has taken the place of bottled barbecue sauce in our family, and it's so simple to prepare."

BAR-B-QUE SAUCE FOR CHICKEN

1 cup catsup
½ cup water
½ cup chopped onion
1 clove garlic, minced
1 teaspoon salt

¼ teaspoon pepper
1 teaspoon paprika
1 tablespoon Worchestershire
  sauce
¼ cup lemon juice
2 tablespoons butter

Mix together and simmer all ingredients except lemon juice and butter for 20 minutes. Remove from heat and add lemon juice and butter. Cool and refrigerate. Yields 2 cups.

Barbara Jo Burton Szemborski (Mrs. Stanley)
Class of '66
Sandbank, Scotland

SAUCE FOR ASPARAGUS

1 cup mayonnaise
1 cup sour cream
2 teaspoons lemon juice
2 teaspoons grated onion

1 teaspoon salt
1 teaspoon dry mustard
1 teaspoon dill weed

Combine all ingredients, mixing well. Serve over cold asparagus. Sliced tomatoes or other cold vegetables.

Jameen Ann Wesson
Class of '77
Modesto, California

SAUCE FOR STEAMED ARTICHOKES

½ cup mayonnaise
¼ cup plain yogurt

1 tablespoon mustard
1 tablespoon artichoke liquid

In a small bowl, combine yogurt and mayonnaise until well mixed. Add mustard and 1 tablespoon of the water in which artichokes have been steamed. Serve in small cups for dipping.

Terri Solberg (Mrs. Morton E.)
Mother of Brandy and Monet
Carmel, California

PESTO SAUCE

2 garlic cloves
1 cup FRESH basil leaves
1 cup parsley sprigs

½ to ¾ cup olive oil
½ cup grated Parmesan cheese
¼ cup pine nuts

Peel garlic and remove stems from basil and parsley; puree in blender. Add olive oil a little at a time; add cheese and nuts and puree. Continue adding olive oil until finished sauce is like creamed butter, adding more if necessary. Preparation time: 5 minutes or less! Yields 1-1½ cups. NOTE: This sauce freezes well and is best if fresh ingredients are used.

Louise Harris (Mrs. Joseph)
Mother of Gingy '83
San Francisco, California

CHRISTMAS QUINCE SAUCE

4 quinces
2 cups water
3 cups brown sugar

Cinnamon to taste
1 teaspoon rum extract

Wash, peel, core and thinly slice quinces. Boil the water in a saucepan and add quinces, cooking until tender. Add sugar, cinnamon and rum flavoring. Cook ½ to 1 hour longer, stirring occasionally with a wooden spoon. Serve as a sauce for meat; or on hot biscuits or toast; or with whipped cream as a dessert.

Serena Underwood (Mrs. Donald)
Mother of Belinda and Melissa
Carmel Valley, California

CHOCOLATE SAUCE FOR ICE CREAM

¼ cup butter
4 tablespoons Nestles Quick
  (chocolate)

2 tablespoons powdered sugar

Melt butter in a saucepan; add Nestles Quick to pan and mix well. Add the powdered sugar, blending until smooth. Pour over ice cream.

Alyson Coniglio
Lower School Student
Monterey, California

Salads and Dressings

SALAD TROPICANA

4 cups fresh or frozen lobster
  tails, cooked and cubed
1 cup chopped celery
2 cups cantaloupe balls
2 cups honeydew melon balls
2 cups seeded red grapes
2 small ripe avocados

1 tablespoon lemon juice
½ to 1 cup cashews, optional
Mayonnaise
Taylor California Cellars
  Johannesberg Riesling
Salt
Pepper

Cook lobster; chill thoroughly. Chop celery into desired size cubes. Cut lobster into cubes about 1¾ inches in diameter. Prepare melon ball; refrigerate separately. About 1 hour before serving, combine lobster, celery and mayonnaise-wine dressing (1/3 Johannesberg Riesling wine to 2/3 mayonnaise). Toss together thoroughly. Season with salt and pepper. About ½ hour before serving, cube avocados; sprinkle with lemon juice. Just before serving, toss all ingredients together. Add additional dressing and season to taste. Serve on a bed of Bibb lettuce or other desired greens. Garnish as desired. Approximately 12 to 15 servings.

Monterey Vineyards
Hayward, California

ALPINE COMBINATION SALAD

2/3 cup crab meat
2/3 cup shrimp
3 hard cooked eggs, chopped
3 marinated artichoke hearts,
  chopped
2 green onions, chopped,
  including stems
½ cup celery hearts, chopped
1 (16 ounce) can spring peas

1 (16 ounce) can kitchen-cut
  string beans
2 tablespoons pimientos,
  chopped
2 tablespoons sweet relish
Salt
Pepper
Oil and vinegar salad dressing

GARNISHES:
Sliced hard cooked egg
Green olives
Thousand Island Dressing

Asparagus spears
Lettuce leaves

72

Combine all ingredients except garnishes, adding the salt, pepper and oil and vinegar dressing according to taste. Refrigerate at least 4 hours. Serve on a bed of crisp lettuce leaves, top with a slice of hard cooked egg and a green olive, placing 2 asparagus spears alongside the salad. Garnish the egg and asparagus spears with a small amount of Thousand Island dressing. Serve with bread sticks or crunchy French rolls. Serves 8-10. NOTE: Crab or shrimp amounts may be adjusted according to taste.

Mr. August Armansco
Upper School Faculty
Father of Perla Lee '72
Carmel, California

ELEGANT SALAD

2½ pounds chicken breasts
1½ pounds shrimp, cooked and cleaned
4 heads iceberg lettuce, chopped
1 quart ranch dressing
1 pound bibb lettuce

½ cup French dressing
12 devilled eggs
1 (2 ounce) jar caviar
1 pound bacon, cooked and crumbled
1 quart cherry tomatoes, marinated in Italian dressing

Cook and cube the chicken in ¾ inch pieces. Combine the chicken, shrimp and chopped iceberg lettuce with the ranch dressing. (A large roasting pan is useful for this.) Mound in the center of a large platter or tray. Toss the bibb lettuce leaves in the French dressing and arrange around the chicken mixture. Garnish the devilled eggs with the caviar and arrange on the bibb lettuce. Evenly distribute the bacon and cherry tomatoes over the chicken mixture. Serves 20.

Martha Johnsen (Mrs. Bruce)
Lower School Faculty
Pacific Grove, California

The Sister Mary Kieran Memorial Library built in 1967, houses over 35,000 volumes with expansion capacity, has four listening rooms for tapes and recordings, a lecture and projection room, art rooms, and a seminar room.

RICE-TUNA SALAD

1 (7 ounce) can tuna, drained
  and flaked
3 cups cold cooked rice
6 pimiento stuffed olives, sliced
1/3 cup chopped sweet pickle
2 tablespoons minced green
  pepper
1½ cups finely chopped celery
2 tablespoons minced parsley
½ cup mayonnaise
½ cup sour cream

2 tablespoons lemon juice
½ teaspoon salt
¼ teaspoon pepper
Dash of cayenne
1 (2 ounce) jar pimientos, diced
¼ cup sour cream
¼ cup mayonnaise
1 hard cooked egg yolk
Salad greens
Parsley for garnish

Combine the tuna, rice, olives, pickle, green pepper, celery and parsley; set aside. Blend together the mayonnaise, sour cream, lemon juice, salt, pepper and cayenne; add to the tuna mixture and mix well. Stir in the pimiento and pack into an oiled 1 quart mold; chill. Make a mask by combining the sour cream and mayonnaise; refrigerate. Before serving, unmold salad on a serving plate, spread with the mask and sprinkle with sieved hard cooked egg yolk. Garnish with chicory or other salad greens and sprigs of parsley. Serves 6-8. NOTE: This recipe doubles well, using a 10-inch bundt pan.

Yolanda Scaccia Manuel (Mrs. Chris)
Class of '67
San Mateo, California

CURRIED SHRIMP AND PEA SALAD

2 (16 ounce) packages "fancy"
  frozen green peas
1 (8 ounce) can sliced water
  chestnuts
1 (3¾ ounce) package diced
  walnuts
1 bunch green onions, finely chopped

6 ounces fresh-cooked baby
  shrimp
1 (2 ounce) jar pimientos
1 cup mayonnaise
2 teaspoons curry powder

Defrost the peas in a bowl at room temperature for 2 hours (the peas will still be slightly frozen). In a salad bowl mix the peas, water chestnuts, walnuts, onions, shrimp and pimientos. Combine the mayonnaise and curry powder for a dressing and toss with the salad mixture. Serves 10.

Jacquie Johnson Lindemann (Mrs. George)
Mother of Kaysie '86
Los Banos, California

CAROLINE'S SHRIMP SALAD

1 cup cooked shrimp
1 cup chopped celery
½ cup chopped green onion
1 cup chopped green pepper

½ cup chopped coriander
Spinach leaves
Peanuts

DRESSING:
¾ tablespoon grated lime peel
3 tablespoons fresh lime juice
¾ cup olive oil

¾ teaspoon ground red pepper
¾ teaspoon cumin powder

Combine all dressing ingredients and mix well; set aside. In a salad bowl, mix the shrimp, celery, onion, bell pepper and coriander. Chill. Just before serving, arrange spinach leaves on individual serving plates; divide the salad evenly on the plates; pour dressing over the salad and garnish with peanuts.

Caroline Lord MacKenzie (Mrs. Gordon)
Class of '65
Singapore

SHRIMP MOLD

1 envelope unflavored gelatin
½ cup Chablis or other white wine
1 (10 ounce) can consomme
1 tablespoon wine vinegar
2 tablespoons chili sauce
1 teaspoon chopped mint, optional
2 teaspoons chopped green onion or chives

Dash Tabasco
¾ cup cucumber, seeded and chopped or celery
12 ounces bay shrimp
Dill weed
½ cup sour cream
½ cup mayonnaise

Soften the gelatin in ¼ cup of the wine. Heat the consomme and add to the gelatin mixture; stir well. Blend in the remaining wine, vinegar, chili sauce, Tabasco, onion and mint, if used. Cool until slightly thickened. Add shrimp and cucumber and spoon into molds. Refrigerate. Serve on salad greens with a dressing made by combining the sour cream and mayonnaise. Top with dill.

Helen L. Howard
Mother of Elinor '54, Jane '56, and
Katherine '58
Grandmother of Michele McGrath '79,
Joan Goodfellow '80 and Kathleen McGrath '81
Walnut Creek, California

SOUR CREAM CHICKEN MOLD

2 envelopes unflavored gelatin
2 cups boiling water
4 chicken bouillon cubes
3 tablespoons lemon juice
2½ teaspoons curry powder
1 teaspoon dry mustard

1 teaspoon onion salt
2 cups sour cream
3 cups cooked, diced chicken
¼ cup diced green pepper
¼ cup slivered almonds

Soften the gelatin in ½ cup cold water. Dissolve the bouillon cubes in the boiling water; add the lemon juice, curry powder, mustard and onion salt. Pour this mixture over the softened gelatin; cool 5 minutes. Stir in the sour cream and refrigerate for 45 minutes. Fold in the chicken, green pepper and almonds. Pour into an oiled 1½ quart mold and chill several hours or until firm. Serve on a bed of lettuce. It is best when prepared a day before serving. Serves 6-8.

Diane Ditz Stauffer (Mrs. Wilbur)
Class of '63
Stockton, California

BEAN SPROUT SALAD

4 cups fresh bean sprouts
3 green onions, chopped
1 clove garlic, crushed

DRESSING:
4 tablespoons soy sauce
2 tablespoons rice vinegar

1 tablespoon toasted sesame seed
1 fresh pimiento or red pepper,
chopped (optional)

2 tablespoons sesame seed oil

Make a dressing by combining the soy sauce, rice vinegar and sesame seed oil. Lightly steam the bean sprouts and rise with cold water. Mix with remaining ingredients in a salad bowl. Pour dressing over the salad and toss; allow to stand at room temperature for at least an hour before chilling. Serve on beds of lettuce. It is best when prepared a day ahead. Serves 6-8. NOTE: Toasted sesame seeds can be found in the oriental section of the grocery.

Diane Kajikuri (Mrs. Hisashi)
Mother of Amy '80 and Miya
Carmel, California

TITA McCALL'S ORIENTAL SALAD

1 head cabbage, shredded
5 green onions, chopped
½ cup toasted sesame seeds

½ cup toasted slivered almonds
1 steamed chicken, shredded
2 (3 ounce) packages Top Ramen
    soup noodles, chicken flavor

DRESSING:
1/3 cup rice vinegar
2/3 cup sesame oil
¼ cup salad oil

2 flavor packets from chicken
    flavored Top Ramen soup
¼ teaspoon pepper

Combine dressing ingredients and chill. Make the salad by combining the cabbage, onions, sesame seeds, almonds and chicken. Just before serving, toss salad with dressing; crumble the noodles, add to salad and toss again. NOTE: Sunflower seeds may be substituted for the toasted slivered almonds.

Sherry Blair
Tennis Pro, Santa Catalina School
Carmel Valley, California

ORIENTAL ONION SALAD WITH SESAME SEED DRESSING

1 medium onion, thinly sliced
4-6 pineapple rings
1 cup bean sprouts
1 cup small shrimp

½ cup water chestnuts, sliced
½ green pepper, cut in strips
Salad greens

SESAME SEED DRESSING
1/3 cup syrup, drained from
    pineapple
1/3 cup salad oil

3 tablespoons vinegar
1 tablespoons soy sauce
2 tablespoons sesame seeds

Thoroughly mix all dressing ingredients and set aside. Combine the onion, pineapple rings, bean sprouts, shrimp, water chestnuts, green pepper and greens of your choice to make a salad. Serve with the sesame seed dressing.

Mrs. Lee B. Price
Monterey, California

In 1951, the second year of the school, the first four grades and the Junior class of the high school were added.

ALL SEASONS BUFFET SALAD

1 (16 ounce) can green beans
1 (17 ounce) can peas
1 (16 ounce) can pitted black
olives
1 (19 ounce) jar salad olives
with pimiento

2 (6 ounce) jars marinated
artichoke hearts
½ cup minced green onion
½ cup chopped celery
½ cup sliced mushrooms
¼ cup wine vinegar
½ teaspoon garlic powder

Drain canned vegetables, except artichoke hearts. Combine gently with all ingredients, adding the artichokes and their marinade last. Marinate in the refrigerator for 6 hours in a 1 gallon jar. Turn jar 3-4 times to distribute marinade. Serves 10-12.

Kay Covert (Mrs. Robert)
Mother of Robin '86
Salinas, California

BEET AND KIDNEY BEAN SALAD

3 cups canned kidney beans
1 cup sweet pickle relish
3 green onions, chopped
5 hard cooked eggs, sliced
¾ cup celery, diced
2 (16 ounce) cans beets,
shredded

¾ cup creamy cucumber
dressing or mayonnaise
1 tablespoon lemon juice or
vinegar
Salt
Pepper
Egg for garnish

Drain beans and beets and combine in a large bowl with the pickle relish. Add eggs, onions and celery. Toss together lightly with the lemon juice and cucumber dressing or mayonnaise; season to taste. Chill thoroughly. Before serving, garnish with wedges of hard cooked egg. Serves 8.

Dr. Gail Frick Barmby
Class of '69
Walnut Creek, California

JICAMA TOMATO SALAD

1½ cups cherry tomatoes, halved
1 cup jicama, cut in ½" cubes
2 tablespoons sliced green
onions
¼ cup salad oil

3 tablespoons wine vinegar
½ teaspoon salt
¼ teaspoon dried tarragon
1/8 teaspoon garlic powder
Dash pepper

Combine the tomatoes, jicama and green onions in a salad bowl; set aside. Make a dressing by combining the remaining ingredients. Pour dressing over the salad mixture and toss well. Cover and refrigerate for several hours, stirring and spooning the dressing over on occasion. Serve in lettuce cups.

Roxanne Terrell (Mrs. Mark)
Monterey, CA

MARINATED VEGETABLE SALAD

2 cups Jarlsberg cheese	*1 cup halved cherry tomatoes*
1 cup sliced carrots	*1 cup sliced zucchini*
1 cup cauliflowerettes	*1/3 cup sliced green onions*
1 cup sliced celery	*3 tablespoons chopped parsley*
1 cup baby mushrooms	*1/3 cup Italian dressing*
1 cup cubed green peppers	*½ teaspoon dry mustard*

In a large bowl, combine all ingredients. Toss well. Chill several hours; tossing occasionally. Serve on crisp salad greens. Serves 6-8.

Teresa Annotti Rogers
Class of '59
Modesto, California

"This is a favorite dish with our springtime asparagus."

ASPARAGUS VINAIGRETTE

Fresh asparagus, cooked al dente
1 hard cooked egg, chopped

DRESSING:

6 tablespoons chopped green onions	*1 tablespoon chopped Kosher baby dill pickle*
2 tablespoons chopped parsley	*½ cup red wine vinegar*
1 tablespoon chopped fresh thyme	*1½ cups olive oil*
1 tablespoon chopped capers	*Salt*
1 tablespoon caper juice	*Pepper*

Combine dressing ingredients in a blender and blend for 15 seconds. Add salt and pepper to taste; blend again. Spoon over asparagus; top with chopped hard cooked egg. NOTE: For full flavor, serve asparagus at room temperature. Dressing improves if kept in refrigerator for a few days.

Margaret Zuckerman (Mrs. David)
Mother of Eleanor '80
Stockton, California

"This salad has a magical quality of pleasing all the people who thought they didn't like cauliflower or broccoli."

CAULIFLOWER AND BROCCOLI SALAD

2 heads of cauliflower	*1 (4 ounce) package Buttermilk*
1 large bunch of broccoli	*dressing mix*
1 bunch green onions	*2 tablespoons sugar*
1 cup mayonnaise	*2 tablespoons vinegar*

Wash the cauliflower and broccoli and separate into small flowerets; finely chop the green onions. Combine the mayonnaise and the envelope of buttermilk dressing mix; add the sugar and vinegar and blend well. Toss the vegetables with the dressing and marinate overnight. Serves 10-12.

Mildred Ramos (Mrs. Emile)
Mother of Marilyn '60
Grandmother of Maria Christina Ospina '86
Salinas, California

CAULIFLOWER SALAD

1 head lettuce, torn in	*½ pound bacon, cooked and*
bite-sized pieces	*crumbled*
1 cauliflower, broken into	*1 small onion, chopped*
flowerettes	*1½ cups Miracle Whip*
	½ cup Parmesan cheese

In a salad bowl, layer in order the lettuce, cauliflower, bacon, onion, Miracle Whip and Parmesan cheese. Chill overnight. Toss just before serving.

Eileen C. Sullivan (Mrs. Richard)
Mother of Erin '85
Monterey, California

"I have used this salad year 'round for a throw-together meal when people unexpectedly drop by. Served with light buttered French bread, it is wonderful."

SALAD THAT'S A MEAL

1 head romaine lettuce	*1 green pepper*
1 head iceberg lettuce	*1 large crisp red apple*
3 large tomatoes	*3 hard cooked eggs*
2 cucumbers	*½ pound cooked bacon*
1 red onion	*Dill weed*
4 green onions	*Cracked java pepper*
1 (8 ounce) jar artichoke hearts	*Seasoned salt*

DRESSING:
½ cup red wine vinegar   *½ teaspoon seasoned salt*
¼ cup olive oil   *½ teaspoon pepper*
1 tablespoon sugar or honey   *½ cup mayonnaise*
2 tablespoons catsup

To make the salad dressing, mix until blended well in a medium sized mixing jar, the vinegar, sugar, salt and pepper. Add the catsup and shake vigorously; add olive oil and shake again. Set aside. Wash, dry and shred the lettuce. Slice the tomatoes, the peeled cucumbers and the green pepper. Chop the green onion, the apple and the red onion. Drain the artichoke hearts and cut into bite-sized pieces. Assemble in layers in a large salad bowl, beginning with the lettuce. Top with grated hard cooked egg and crumbled bacon; sprinkle heavily with dill weed and pepper, adding seasoned salt to taste. Shake the dressing to mix well and pour over salad; add the mayonnaise and toss until salad is coated. Serves 10-12.

Laura Ann Knoop
Class of '72
New York City, New York

CALIFORNIA SALAD BOWL

4 tablespoons olive oil   *1 soft-ripe avocado*
4 tablespoons salad oil   *1 tablespoon lemon juice*
1 clove garlic, crushed   *1 teaspoon tarragon vinegar*
2 quarts bite-size pieces romaine *3 tablespoons grated Parmesan*
  (about 2 heads)   *cheese*
1 (2 ounce) tin flat anchovy   *Salt*
  fillets   *Freshly ground pepper*

Combine oils and garlic; let stand. Wash romaine, dry completely in towel and chill. Drain and finely chop the anchovies. Place lettuce in a large bowl. Add anchovies and mixture of oils and garlic; toss until coated. Peel and dice an avocado into the salad; sprinkle with lemon juice, vinegar and Parmesan. Toss lightly but well. Season with pepper and salt, if desired, remembering that anchovies are salty. Makes 4 luncheon servings or 5-6 dinner salads.

Alice Cloran
Upper School Staff
Carmel Valley, California

ZUCCHINI AND SWISS SALAD

1 raw zucchini
¼ pound Swiss cheese
4 mushrooms
½ cup sliced celery
¼ cup sour cream

½ teaspoon Dijon mustard
½ teaspoon horseradish
Salt
Pepper
2 radishes, grated for garnish

Grate the zucchini and set aside to drain. Meanwhile, cut the Swiss cheese into Julienne strips and thinly slice the mushrooms and celery. Mix the vegetables and cheese in a salad bowl. Combine the sour cream, mustard, horseradish, salt and pepper. Pour over the salad and toss well. Garnish with grated radishes.

Mrs. Lee B. Price
Monterey, California

"The Elizabethan merchant seaman brought back many new vegetables: the Virginia potato, the Jerusalem artichoke (known as the Canadian potato), globe artichokes, asparagus, cauliflower, chard and beet. In the seventeenth century raw vegetables were included in 'boiled' salads, from which many modern ideas about salads derive — the inclusion of cooked beef, most of all."

SEVENTEENTH CENTURY SALAD

6 hard cooked eggs
4 leeks, white part only, cooked
12 asparagus spears, cooked
½ head cauliflower, in flowerets,
   lightly cooked

DRESSING:
½ cup oil
2 tablespoons vinegar

3 French or Belgian endives,
   halved
¼ cup currants
6 fresh sorrel leaves, chopped
1 bunch watercress, shredded

Cinnamon
Ginger

Combine the oil and vinegar with a pinch of cinnamon and ginger and mix well. Arrange the salad ingredients on a plate with the sorrel, currants and watercress sprinkled evenly over all. Just before serving, pour the dressing over the salad. Serves 6. NOTE: The amount of dressing may be adjusted, using 3 parts oil to 1 part vinegar, adding cinnamon and ginger to taste.

Nancy Rembert (Mrs. Paul)
Mother of Grey '81
Concord, Massachusetts

SPINACH SALAD

1 pound fresh spinach   ¾ pound bacon

DRESSING:
1 tablespoon sugar   1 teaspoon paprika
1 teaspoon salt   ¼ cup plus 2 tablespoons lemon
1 teaspoon dry mustard   juice
¼ teaspoon pepper   2 tablespoons powdered sugar
     ¾ cup olive or salad oil

Combine the dressing ingredients and chill 1 hour before serving. Wash and drain well the fresh spinach; tear leaves into bite-sized pieces. Fry ¾ pound bacon until crisp; crumble. Toss with spinach and dressing just before serving. NOTE: Sliced and cooked eggs may be added to the salad if desired.

Jeanne Adams (Mrs. Michael)
Mother of Sarah '83
Fresno, California

TACO SALAD

3 cups shredded lettuce   ½ cup sliced ripe olives
1 (16 ounce) can kidney beans,   1 tablespoon chopped green
     drained and rinsed   chiles
2 medium tomatoes, chopped   Salt
     Pepper

DRESSING:
1 large avocado, mashed or 1 can   1 teaspoon instant minced onion
     frozen guacamole   ¾ teaspoon chili powder
½ cup sour cream   ¼ teaspoon salt
2 tablespoons Italian salad   Dash of pepper
     dressing

TOPPING:
½ cup shredded sharp cheddar   Whole pitted olives for garnish
     cheese
½ cup coarsely crushed corn chips

Combine dressing ingredients in a bowl or blender and chill. In a large bowl mix the lettuce, beans, tomatoes, chiles and sliced olives. Season with salt and pepper. Just before serving, toss with chilled dressing and top with the cheese and corn chips. Garnish with the whole pitted olives. Makes 6-8 servings.

Mr. Robert S. Beaumont
San Carlos, California

TEN-LAYER SALAD

1 large head iceberg lettuce,
  shredded
½ cup finely chopped green
  onions
½ cup chopped celery
1 (6 ounce) can water chestnuts,
  sliced
2 (10 ounce) packages frozen
  peas
2 cups mayonnaise

1 tablespoon sugar
1 pound bacon, fried, drained,
  crumbled
4 hard-cooked eggs, chopped
4 tomatoes, peeled, seeded and
  diced
Grated Parmesan and Romano
cheese
Chopped parsley for garnish

A day ahead, place the lettuce in a large shallow serving bowl. Sprinkle the onions, celery and water chestnuts in layers. Break apart the frozen peas and sprinkle on the top without defrosting. Sprinkle with sugar. Spread mayonnaise on the top like frosting. Cover and refrigerate overnight. Before serving, add layers of crumbled bacon, eggs and tomatoes. Sprinkle with grated cheeses. DO NOT TOSS. To serve, spoon from the bottom of the bowl to taste all layers. Serves 8-10.

Linda Hall (Mrs. John H.)
Mother of Amy Hall '86 and Annie
San Francisco, California

POPPY SEED DRESSING AND SALAD

SALAD:
1 or 2 heads lettuce
1 papaya
1 or 2 oranges

1 or 2 avocados
1 red onion

DRESSING:
½ cup sugar
1 teaspoon salt
1 teaspoon dry mustard
½ teaspoon onion powder or
  onion salt

1/3 cup wine vinegar
1 tablespoon lemon juice
1 cup salad oil
1½ tablespoons poppy seeds

Combine all dressing ingredients and mix well; set aside. Wash, pat dry and tear the lettuce. Cut papaya, oranges and avocados into bite-sized pieces. Thinly slice the onion. Mix all salad ingredients in a large bowl and toss with the dressing.

Marlene Kellogg (Mrs. Clarence)
Mother of Kellene '79 and Christina '85
Pacific Grove, California

"This recipe, my own creation, is proving to be very popular. It's convenient to prepare ahead of time and is easily tossed together at the last minute."

MARINATED MUSHROOMS, GREENS AND SEEDS

½ pound mushrooms, thinly
   sliced
3 tablespoons tarragon vinegar
¼ cup olive oil
¼ cup safflower oil
1 teaspoon salt

½ teaspoon pepper
½ teaspoon dry mustard
¼ clove garlic, minced
1 head lettuce
½ bunch spinach
½ cup sunflower seeds, toasted

Mix vinegar, oils, salt, pepper, mustard and garlic in a quart jar. Add sliced mushrooms and place in refrigerator 2 hours or more to marinate. Tear lettuce and spinach into bite-sized pieces in a large salad bowl. At serving time, pour jar of mushrooms and marinade over green; toss. Sprinkle with sunflower seeds which have been toasted for 6 minutes in a 400° oven. Serves 8-12.

Martha Rice (Mrs. Chester T.)
Mother of Peggy '78
Kentfield, California

"Friends have called from distant states to get this recipe."

POPPY SEED DRESSING

1½ cups sugar
2 teaspoons dry mustard
2 teaspoons salt
2/3 cup vinegar

3 tablespoons McCormick onion
   juice or 1 medium white onion
2 cups salad oil (never olive oil)
3 tablespoons poppy seeds

In a blender mix the sugar, mustard, salt, vinegar and onion juice. Slowly add the oil and poppy seeds and blend until thickened. Store in refrigerator. Should it separate, pour off the clear oil and reblend it with the other part. This is excellent with fresh fruit. Yields about 3½ cups.

Jeanne Adams (Mrs. Michael)
Mother of Sarah '83
Fresno, California

In September, 1971, the Santa Catalina Pre-school opened with 25 boys and girls attending. Within a year, both morning and afternoon classes were required to meet the demand.

"This salad dressing seems to appeal especially to men."

A MAN'S DRESSING

½ cup sugar
¾ cup catsup
½ cup vinegar
1 teaspoon salt

1 cup oil
1 teaspoon paprika
1 teaspoon lemon juice
1 clove garlic, crushed

Blend sugar, catsup, vinegar and salt until dissolved. Add remaining ingredients and mix well. Store in the refrigerator.

Jeanne Adams (Mrs. Michael)
Mother of Sarah '83
Fresno, California

OLD DEMONICO'S CRESS SALAD DRESSING

1½ teaspoons dry mustard
1 teaspoon paprika
1½ teaspoons sugar
1½ teaspoons salt (or less)
¼ teaspoon pepper
1/3 cup vinegar
1 cup olive oil

1 clove garlic
Dash Worcestershire sauce
1 teaspoon chili sauce
Dash Tabasco sauce
4 tablespoons chopped
   watercress leaves

Combine all ingredients except watercress and beat until well blended and slightly thick, about 3 minutes. Stir in watercress and mix thoroughly. Makes 1¾ cups.

Mrs. Lee B. Price
Monterey, California

FOOD PROCESSOR MAYONNAISE

1¼ cups cooking oil
1 egg
1 teaspoon sugar
1 teaspoon salt

1 teaspoon dry mustard
Dash of cayenne
3 tablespoons lemon juice

In a food processor bowl with chopping blade, put ¼ of the oil, the egg, sugar, salt, mustard and cayenne. Begin processing, slowly adding ½ cup more of the oil. Stop and add the lemon juice. Process again, slowly adding the remaining oil, only until mixture is thick and smooth. Do not overprocess. Yields 1½ cups. This recipe may be tripled and keeps well in the refrigerator.

Dr. Tom McGuire
Oakland, California

VEGETABLE SALAD MEDLEY

2 (6 ounce) packages lime
  gelatin
4 cups boiling water
3½ cups cold water
¼ cup wine vinegar

½ cup mayonnaise
Shredded carrot
Chopped celery
Chopped red onion
Cucumber, peeled and sliced

Dissolve the gelatin in the boiling water; add the cold water, vinegar and mayonnaise and chill until slightly thickened. Add the vegetables in the desired amounts and pour into an oiled bundt pan. Chill until set. Unmold to serve and garnish with parsley. Serves 8-10.

June Boyle
Aunt of Sister Mary Ellen and
Kathleen Ryan
San Mateo, California

GREEN GODDESS CUCUMBER MOLD

1 envelope plain gelatin
¼ cup cold water
½ medium cucumber, pared and
  sliced
½ cup plain yogurt
½ pint dairy sour cream
½ tablespoon white vinegar
¼ teaspoon garlic powder

¼ teaspoon salt
1/8 teaspoon pepper
1 tablespoon anchovy paste
¼ cup chopped onion and
  parsley combined
1/8 teaspoon chives
1 tablespoon Dijon mustard
1 tablespoon horseradish

Sprinkle gelatin over the water to soften, and stir over low heat until dissolved. Combing all the remaining ingredients in an electric blender and blend until smooth. Add gelatin mixture and mix thoroughly. Pour into a greased mold and chill until firm. This makes 2 medium or 1 large mold.

Vera Nichols
Monterey, California

In 1979 Mr. Ferdinand Ruth of our Science faculty wrote two Nature Trails self-guiding tours for the general public and school groups visiting Point Lobos. These relieve the Rangers there of a heavy teaching load, in that numbered stakes are now placed at strategic locations and the visitor may read of the flora and fauna surrounding him by referring to the corresponding number in his guide book.

SWEET TOMATO MOLD

2 (6 ounce) packages cherry
  gelatin
3 (29 ounce) cans tomatoes,
  seasoned with onion and
  bell pepper

1 cup dehydrated onion
1 tablespoon dehydrated
  sweet bell pepper
½ cup water

Drain the juice from the cans of tomatoes into a saucepan. Add ½ cup water and bring to a boil, taking care not to scorch liquid. Dissolve gelatin in the hot liquid; add tomatoes, onion, bell pepper and mix thoroughly. Pour into an oiled 3-quart mold. Refrigerate 6 hours before serving. Serves 20-30.

Jane Foster Carter (Mrs. Robert B.)
Mother of Ann '71
Colusa, California

PEACH CHUTNEY ASPIC

1 envelope unflavored gelatin
½ cup boiling water
1 (16 ounce) can sliced peaches,
  drained
¼ cup white vinegar

¼ cup hot chili sauce
¼ cup chutney
3 tablespoons lemon juice
½ teaspoon salt
½ thinly sliced onion

Combine boiling water and gelatin in a blender and blend on low speed until dissolved. Add remaining ingredients; cover and blend on high speed until completely smooth. Chill until firm in a ring mold or a loaf pan. Unmold to serve.

Vera Nichols
Monterey, California

SHERRY GELATIN

2¼ tablespoons gelatin
½ cup of cold water
1 cup boiling water
1 cup sugar

1-1/3 cups sherry
2/3 cups strained orange juice
2 tablespoons lemon juice

Soak gelatin in the cold water; add boiling water. Mix the sugar, sherry, orange juice and lemon juice. Add to the gelatin and chill.

Mrs. Lee B. Price
Monterey, California

PINEAPPLE, NUT AND PICKLE SALAD

1 (20 ounce) can pineapple, cut
  in small pieces
½ cup chopped pecans
1 (12 ounce) jar sweet pickles,
  'sliced

1 cup sugar
2 packages lime gelatin
½ envelope unflavored gelatin
Salt

Drain the juice from the pineapple and add the sugar and enough water to the juice to make 2 cups liquid. Dissolve lime gelatin in 2 cups boiling water and add to the pineapple juice. Dissolve unflavored gelatin in ½ cup cold water; add to the lime gelatin mixture. Chill until slightly thickened; add fruit, pickles and nuts. Pour into a 9x13 glass dish and chill until firm. Serves 15.

Lucie G. de Guajardo
Mother of Gabriela '84
Monterrey, Mexico

APRICOT MOLD

1 (3 ounce) package lemon
  gelatin
1 (3 ounce) package orange
  gelatin
3 tablespoons lemon juice
½ cup water

1 (12 ounce) can apricot nectar
1 cup sour cream
1 (20 ounce) can apricot halves
1 (20 ounce) can grapes
1 (20 ounce) can pineapple
  chunks

Heat the water, lemon juice and apricot nectar; remove from heat, add the gelatins and stir until dissolved. Chill until slightly thickened, beat in the sour cream, fold in drained fruits and chill until firm. Serves 8.

Jean Quinlan (Mrs. W. Edward)
Mother of Mary Jean '65, Ann '66, and
Nancy '68
Salinas, California

Shortly after the opening of school every year, the Mothers' Service League hosts a Welcoming Tea. This is an opportunity for new mothers to become acquainted with other mothers, faculty, and administration. It is an event which includes the Upper School, Lower School, and Pre-school.

"We always serve this with our Easter, Christmas and Thanksgiving dinner."

SUNSHINE SALAD

1/3 cup sugar
1 (3 ounce) package orange
  gelatin
1 cup hot water

1 (8¾ ounce) can crushed
  pineapple
1 (11 ounce) can mandarin
  oranges
1 cup sour cream

In a mixing bowl, combine the sugar and gelatin; add hot water and stir until gelatin is dissolved. Chill until slightly thickened. Add pineapple, mandarin oranges and sour cream.

Marlene Kellogg (Mrs. Clarence)
Mother of Kellene '79 and
Christina '85
Pacific Grove, California

CHRISTMAS RIBBON SALAD

2 (3 ounce) packages lime
  gelatin
1 (3 ounce) package lemon
  gelatin
1 cup hot water
½ cup small marshmallows
1 (20 ounce) can crushed
  pineapple

1 (8 ounce) package cream
  cheese
½ cup mayonnaise
½ cup heavy cream, whipped
1 cup pineapple juice
2 (3 ounce) packages cherry
  gelatin

For first layer: Prepare the 2 packages of lime gelatin according to package directions and chill until firm in a 13x9 inch glass pan. For second layer: In a mixing bowl, dissolve the lemon gelatin in the cup of hot water; add the marshmallows and stir until melted; set aside. Drain the pineapple, reserving the juice. Cream the cheese with the pineapple juice, add to the lemon gelatin mixture and beat until well blended; stir in 1 cup of the pineapple. Chill until slightly thickened; fold in the mayonnaise and whipped cream. Spread over the set lime gelatin; chill until firm. For third layer: Prepare the 2 packages of cherry gelatin according to package directions. Chill until partially set and pour over the second layer; chill until firm. Makes 12 servings.

Nancy Quinlan Kincade (Mrs. Michael B.)
Class of '68
San Jose, California

"A holiday season would be incomplete without this salad."

CRANBERRY SALAD

1 (16 unce) package fresh
  cranberries
1 cup sugar
2 (3 ounce) packages raspberry
  gelatin
1 (17 ounce) can crushed pineapple

½ cup chopped apple
2/3 cup chopped celery
2/3 cup chopped nuts
1-2 oranges, peeled and
  chopped

Chop cranberries and mix with sugar; let stand a few hours or over-night. Add 2 cups hot water to the raspberry gelatin; cool and add to cranberries. Add the remaining ingredients, including juices of pine-apple and oranges. Chill until set. Serves 8 or more. NOTE: This can be varied to suit your taste by adding more apple, etc. If it is too thick, add ½-1 cup water.

Margaret Lotz (Mrs. John)
Lower School Faculty
Monterey, California

"A family tradition for Thanksgiving and Christmas!"

RUSSIAN CREAM MOLD

1 envelope unflavored gelatin
3 tablespoons cold water
½ cup sugar
1 cup heavy cream
2 cups water
1 cup dairy sour cream
1 teaspoon vanilla

1 (8 ounce) can crushed
  pineapple
1 (6 ounce) package strawberry
  gelatin
1 (16 ounce) can whole
  cranberries
1 cup chopped walnuts

Sprinkle gelatin over cold water; set aside. Bring sugar, cream and 1 cup of water to a boil, stirring constantly. Remove immediately from heat and add unflavored gelatin; mix thoroughly until gelatin is dissolved. Blend in sour cream, add vanilla and beat with rotary beater until smooth. Pour into greased 2-quart mold and chill until firm. Meanwhile, drain crushed pineapple. Measure juice and add enough water to make 1 cup liquid. Bring to a boil and pour over strawberry gelatin, stirring well. Add the cranberries and nuts and mix well; cool. Prick the sour cream layer in several places to prevent the second layer from slipping. Pour the pineapple mixture over the sour cream layer. Chill until set. Serves 12-16.

Brenda Guy (Mrs. Michael)
Mother of Jennifer
Pebble Beach, California

Breads

REFRIGERATOR ROLLS

1¾ cups warm water
2 packages active dry yeast
½ cup granulated sugar
1 tablespoon salt

1 egg
¼ cup soft butter
6 cups sifted flour
1 tablespoon melted butter

Sprinkle yeast, sugar and salt over warm (not hot) water; stir to dissolve. Add egg, soft butter and 3 cups of the flour. Beat with a mixer or wooden spoon until smooth. Gradually add remaining flour, using hands; continue to work the dough until smooth and elastic. Place dough in a large bowl that has been oiled with the melted butter. Cover with a double layer of plastic wrap. Let rise in refrigerator for at least 2 hours, and up to 3 days. Punch down as necessary. Shape dough into rolls and let rise until double, about 1 hour. Brush with butter, if desired; bake at 400° for 12-15 minutes.

Carole Steen (Mrs. Robert)
Salinas, California

SIXTY MINUTE YEAST ROLLS

1¾ - 2 cups unsifted flour
1½ tablespoons sugar
½ teaspoon salt
1 package dry yeast

½ cup milk
¼ cup water
2 tablespoons margarine

In a mixing bowl, combine ¾ cup of the flour, the yeast, sugar and salt. In a saucepan, heat the milk, water and margarine to 120° - 130° F. Add the heated liquid to the flour mixture and beat for 2 minutes. Gradually add the remaining flour and knead for 5 minutes. Place in a greased bowl; place the bowl in a warm place in a pan of warm water and let rise for 15 minutes. Divide the dough into 8-12 balls and place in a greased 8-inch round cake pan. Let rise for an additional 15 minutes. Bake in a preheated 425° oven for 15 minutes.

Dianne Klech Saugier (Mrs. Joseph)
Class of '72
Shawnee, Kansas

HERB BUBBLE LOAF

3 to 3½ cups flour
2 tablespoons sugar
1½ teaspoons salt
2 packages dry yeast
1¼ cup milk
2 tablespoons oil
1 egg

1/3 cup butter, melted
2 tablespoons grated Parmesan
cheese
1 tablespoon sesame seed
½ teaspoon garlic salt
½ teaspoon paprika
1 teaspoon oregano

Combine 1 cup of the flour, sugar, salt and yeast in a mixing bowl. Heat the milk and oil until warm and add the warm liquid and the egg to the flour mixture. Beat ½ minute at low speed, then 3 minutes at medium speed. Stir in the remaining flour gradually to form a soft dough. Knead on a floured board until smooth and elastic, about 1 minute. Cover and let rise in a warm place until light and doubled in bulk. Punch down. Pinch off walnut-sized balls of dough and dip in melted butter. Place half of the dough in an ungreased 2-quart casserole, forming 1 layer. Mix cheese and spices. Sprinkle half of the mixture over the layer of bubbles. Repeat a second layer of dough balls. Pour any remaining butter over the dough and top with remaining seasoning mixture. Cover and let rise in a warm place until light. Bake at 400° for 25-35 minutes until the top sounds hollow when lightly tapped. Cool in pan for 10 minutes. Remove and serve warm.

Carolyn Estrada (Mrs. Marshall)
Aunt of Kimberly Bowden '87
Whittier, California

CHERVIL-DILL BISCUITS

¼ cup butter
1/8 teaspoon dill or garlic
(optional)

1 tablespoon chervil
2 packages refrigerated biscuits
1 tablespoon Parmesan cheese

Melt butter in a 7 x 11 inch pan. Stir in dill or garlic powder with chervil. Arrange biscuits in butter and chervil mixture. Let stand in a warm place about 20 or 30 minutes. Turn biscuits over carefully with a spatula. Spoon some of the melted butter and chervil in the bottom of the pan on top of the biscuits. Sprinkle with Parmesan cheese. Bake in a 425° oven for 15 or 20 minutes or until biscuits are browned. Makes 20 biscuits.

Mrs. Lee B. Price
Monterey, California

DILLY BREAD

1 package dry yeast
¼ cup warm water
1 cup cottage cheese
1 tablespoon butter
2 tablespoons sugar

¼ teaspoon soda
1 tablespoon instant onion
2 teaspoons dill weed
1 beaten egg
2¼ - 2½ cups unsifted flour

Dissolve the yeast in the ¼ cup water for 10 minutes. Warm cottage cheese to lukewarm in a pan. Add the butter, sugar, soda, onion, dill weed, egg and yeast and beat well. Add flour and mix well. Cover and let rise for 1 hour. Stir down dough and divide into 2 round loaves. Cover and let rise again for 30-40 minutes. Bake at 350° for 30-40 minutes, checking after 30 minutes. Cover with foil for the final 5-10 minutes to prevent excess browning. Brush with melted butter and sprinkle with salt.

Suzanne Townsend Finney (Mrs. J. P.)
Class of '60
Hillsborough, California

MANNA BREAD

2 packages active dry yeast
8 slices bacon
1 tablespoon sugar
4 cups flour
1 (12 ounce) can beer

3 tablespoons dry onion soup
  mix
¼ cup milk
Cornmeal

In a bowl, combine the yeast, 2 cups of the flour and the soup mix. Cook bacon until crisp; drain, reserving 2 tablespoons of the drippings. Crumble bacon and set aside. Heat the beer, milk, sugar and reserved drippings just until warm (the mixture will look curdled); add to the dry ingredients. Beat in the mixer at low speed for 30 seconds; beat 3 minutes at high speed. Stir in crumbled bacon and enough of the remaining flour to make a moderately stiff dough. Knead until smooth and elastic. Place in a greased bowl, turning once to grease surface; cover. Let rise until almost double, 40-45 minutes; punch down. Shape into 16 rolls. Place in 2 (9x1½ inch) round baking pans. Brush tops of rolls with melted butter. Sprinkle with cornmeal and cover tightly. Let rise until almost double, about 25 minutes. Bake in a 375° oven for 20 minutes or until golden brown. Yields 16 rolls.

Kathleen Harman Greiten (Mrs. John E.)
Class of '60
Red Bluff, California

ENGLISH MUFFINS IN A LOAF

2 cups milk	1 tablespoon sugar
½ cup water	2 teaspoons salt
2 packages dry yeast	¼ teaspoon baking soda
5 cups flour	Cornmeal

FOR MICROWAVE: Heat together the milk and water to 120-130°; add the yeast, 3 cups of the flour, the sugar, salt and baking soda, beating well. Blend in the remaining flour. Grease and line with parchment paper 2 glass loaf pans. Sprinkle the parchment lightly with cornmeal and spoon batter equally into the 2 pans. Sprinkle tops lightly with cornmeal; cover and let rise 45 minutes. Cook each loaf on high for 6 minutes 30 seconds. Allow to rest in pan for 5 minutes. Slice in approximately 16 slices and toast. FOR CONVENTIONAL OVEN: Add an additional cup of flour to the batter and bake at 400° for 25 minutes. Remove from pans immediately; cool and slice. NOTE: This batter is more glutenous and slick than a traditional bread batter.

Frances Holodiloff (Mrs. Alexander)
Mother of Anastasia
Pacific Grove, California

GREEK CHEESE BUNS

1 package dry yeast	3 cups plus 2 tablespoons
¼ cup warm water	unsifted flour
½ cup milk	½ cup soft margarine
1 tablespoon sugar	3 eggs
¼ teaspoon salt	6 ounces feta cheese, crumbled
	3 teaspoons margarine, melted

In a large bowl, add yeast to the water and 1 cup of the flour. Mix in butter and eggs, add remaining flour and beat 10 minutes with a heavy-duty mixer or knead by hand 10 minutes. Cover and let rise until doubled. Divide dough into 16 equal pieces and roll into a rough 6-inch circle. Sprinkle with 2 teaspoons crumbled cheese, fold over edges and ends to make an egg-shaped bun. Place seam side down on a greased baking sheet; repeat. Let rise 30 minutes. Prick each roll 6 times with a toothpick. Brush with melted margarine. Bake at 375° for 15 minutes or until golden. These are delicious for breakfast and are wonderful with a green salad or soup for lunch. To reheat, place in a 325° oven for 15-20 minutes.

Mary Ann Taylor (Mrs. James)
Mother of James, Katie and Asher
Monterey, California

HONEY WHOLE WHEAT BREAD

3½ cups all-purpose flour
2½ cups whole wheat flour
2 packages dry yeast
1 tablespoon salt
1 cup milk

1 cup water
½ cup honey
3 tablespoons shortening
1 egg

In a large bowl combine 1 cup of the all-purpose flour, the whole wheat flour, the yeast, and salt. Set aside. In a saucepan, heat the milk, water, honey and shortening until warm (not hot — the shortening should not melt). Add the liquid mixture to the flour mixture. Add the egg and blend at low speed until moist. Beat for 3 minutes at medium speed. By hand, gradually stir in the remaining flour to make a firm dough; knead 5 minutes. Place in a greased bowl, cover and let rise in a warm place until light and double, about 1 hour. Punch down dough and divide into two 9x5 inch greased loaf pans. Cover and let rise about 30 minutes. Bake in a 375° oven for 35-40 minutes until golden brown. Remove from pans; cool on a rack.

Beezie Leyden Moore (Mrs. H. Walker)
Class of 1953
Clovis, California

BEER BREAD

3 cups self-rising flour
1 (12 ounce) can of beer

2 tablespoons sugar

Combine all ingredients and stir well. Pour batter in a greased 9 x 5 inch loaf pan. Let rise 20 minutes before baking. Bake in a 350° oven for 1 hour.

Dr. Tom McGuire
Oakland, California

IRISH SODA BREAD FROM UNCLE RAY AND TOM MCGUIRE

4 cups sifted flour
½ cup sugar
4 teaspoons baking powder
½ teaspoon soda

3 large eggs
1 cup currants
1 pint buttermilk

Combine the ingredients in a large bowl; mix well. In a large (10 inch or wider) cast iron fry pan, bake the mixture at 350° for 1 hour. Cool on a rack. NOTE: You must use a cast iron fry pan and you must use currants. This is best toasted and may be frozen.

Dr. Tom McGuire
Oakland, California

OATMEAL BREAD

1 cup rolled oats
1¼ cups buttermilk or sour milk
¼ cup brown sugar, packed
1 egg, beaten
¼ cup oil

1½ cups sifted flour
2 teaspoons baking powder
1 teaspoon baking soda
½ teaspoon salt
¼ cup grated cheddar cheese

Combine oats and milk in a medium bowl and let stand for 30 minutes. Beat in sugar, egg and oil. Sift together the dry ingredients and stir into oat mixture to blend. Pour into a greased 1½ quart casserole and sprinkle cheese over the top. Bake in a preheated 350° oven until a toothpick inserted in the center comes out clean, about 35 minutes. Cool 5 minutes; remove from casserole.

Patty Buchholz Madden (Mrs. Daniel)
Class of '75
Santa Rosa, California

OATMEAL-MOLASSES MUFFINS

1½ cups flour
1 teaspoon baking soda
1 teaspoon salt
2 cups quick-cooking oatmeal
1 egg, well beaten

¾ cup milk
½ cup molasses
1 mashed ripe banana
½ cup raisins

Mix the dry ingredients together, adding the oatmeal last. Combine the remaining ingredients, except for the raisins, and add to the dry ingredients. Stir only until moistened. Fold in the raisins. Bake at 375° for 30-40 minutes. Makes 12 muffins. NOTE: The banana makes the muffins extraordinarily tasty and moist, but the muffins may be made without a banana by increasing the milk to 1 cup.

Erica Swanson
Lower School Secretary
Monterey, California

CLOCKWATCHER MUFFINS

5 cups flour
5 teaspoons soda
5 teaspoons cinnamon
2 teaspoons salt
1 (20 ounce) box raisin bran

3 cups sugar
4 eggs, beaten
1 quart buttermilk
1 cup oil or melted shortening

Sift and measure the flour. Sift the flour again with the soda, cinnamon and salt; stir in the raisin bran and sugar. Add the eggs, buttermilk and oil to the dry ingredients, mixing until well blended. Line muffin tins with liners or grease well. Fill 2/3 full and bake at 400° for 20 minutes. Makes 5 dozen. NOTE: Keeps well in refrigerator and freezes well either raw or baked.

Dorothy Anderson (Mrs. A. R.)
Strathmore, California

"AMY'S BRAN MUFFINS"

2 cups All-Bran cereal
1 cup milk
1 teaspoon baking soda
2 cups whole wheat flour

½ teaspoon baking powder
½ cup sugar
1/3 cup oil
1 egg

Mix the cereal and milk together; set aside. In a separate bowl, mix the flour, soda, baking powder and sugar; set aside. Add the oil and egg to the cereal mixture; gradually add the dry mixture and mix well. Line muffin tins with cupcake papers or grease well. Fill 2/3 full and bake at 350° for 20-30 minutes. Yields 12 muffins.

Amy Berndt
Summer Camper
Reno, Nevada

WHEAT GERM MUFFINS

4½ cups flour
1 (20 ounce) jar wheat germ
1¼ cup sugar
1 cup packed brown sugar
5 teaspoons soda

2 teaspoons salt
4 eggs, slightly beaten
1 quart buttermilk
1 cup cooking oil
1½ - 2 cups raisins, optional

Combine dry ingredients in a large bowl; add remaining ingredients and stir until well blended. Fill greased or paper-lined muffin tins 2/3 full. Bake in a preheated 400° oven for 12-20 minutes. Yields 6 dozen muffins. NOTE: Batter may be stored in the refrigerator for up to 4 weeks. Increase baking time if batter has been chilled.

Hilary Wickersham Clark (Mrs. Richard H.)
Class of '71
Pasadena, California

BRAN-BERRY MUFFINS

¾ cup whole wheat flour
½ cup wheat germ
1 teaspoon baking soda
1 teaspoon grated orange rind
½ cup raisins
2/3 cup buttermilk or yogurt

¾ cup bran
¾ cup brown sugar
½ teaspoon salt
1 cup blueberries or cranberries
  (or half and half)
1 egg
¼ cup oil

Mix all ingredients well. Line muffin tins with cupcake liners or grease well; fill 2/3 full and bake at 400° for 20 minutes.

Marian Guiry Impey (Mrs. Guy)
Class of '72
Richmond, British Columbia
Canada

PERSIMMON MUFFINS

½ cup persimmon pulp
3 teaspoons lemon juice
½ teaspoon soda
1½ cups flour
½ cup sugar
2 teaspoons baking powder
½ teaspoon salt

½ teaspoon cinnamon
½ teaspoon nutmeg
¼ teaspoon cloves
1 egg, beaten
½ cup milk
½ cup melted butter
½ cup raisins

Add the lemon juice and soda to the persimmon pulp; set aside. Sift together the dry ingredients. Blend the beaten egg, milk, butter and persimmon pulp; and the dry ingredients and raisins and stir until mixed. Batter will be slightly lumpy. Spoon into greased or paper lined muffin tins and bake at 400° for 15 minutes. Yields 12 muffins. Freezes well.

Nancy Crane (Mrs. Bert)
Mother of Karen '83
Merced, California

"HOT DOG BUN" STICKS

Hot dogs buns
Melted butter
Parmesan cheese

Poppy seeds
Sesame seeds

Cut each hot dog bun lengthwise and then across to make rectangular "sticks". Dip each piece into melted butter, then into Parmesan cheese, then into the poppy seeds and sesame seeds. Bake on a cookie sheet in a 375° oven for 15-18 minutes.

Carolyn Humiston (Mrs. George)
Mother of Lauren and Adrianne
Carmel Valley, California

REAL SOUTHERN CORN BREAD

1 cup yellow cornmeal
¼ cup flour
1 egg, beaten
1 cup buttermilk

1 tablespoon melted butter
Pinch of salt
1 teaspoon baking powder

Sift together the dry ingredients. Combine the milk with the egg and add to the dry ingredients; add the melted butter and stir well. Pour into a well greased 8-inch pan and bake at 425° for 25 minutes. Serves 4.

Mr. Dudley Nix
Father of Joanne '60 and Sherrie '62
Carmel, California

"Best corn bread we've ever eaten!"

CONNECTICUT CORN BREAD

1 cup flour
1 cup sugar
1 cup milk
1 cup cornmeal

2 eggs
¼ cup vegetable oil
2 teaspoons baking powder

Combine all ingredients and beat at medium speed for 2 minutes. Pour into a greased and floured 8-inch square pan and bake at 350° for 35-45 minutes. NOTE: If recipe is doubled, use a 13 x 9 x 2 inch oblong pan.

B. J. Burton Szemborski (Mrs. Stanley)
Class of '66
Sandbank, Scotland

Three additions to the campus were opened in September 1971: a new Science Building equipped with aquariums and terrariums, a coeducational Pre-school and Kindergarten, and a newly furnished Day Student Lounge, which had formerly served as a physics lab.

FIESTA CORN BREAD

1 cup flour
1 cup cornmeal
4 teaspoons baking powder
¾ cup butter
¾ cup sugar
4 eggs
1 (4 ounce) can diced green
chiles

1 (2 ounce) jar pimientos,
chopped
1 (17 ounce) can cream style
corn
½ cup grated Monterey Jack
cheese
½ cup grated cheddar cheese
¼ teaspoon salt

Preheat oven to 350° and grease and flour a 9 x 13 inch baking dish. Sift together the flour, cornmeal and baking powder; set aside. In a large bowl, cream the butter and sugar until light. Add the eggs, one at a time, blending well after each addition. Stir in the chiles, pimiento and corn; add the cheeses, salt and dry ingredients. Mix well and pour into the prepared dish. Reduce oven to 300° and bake for 1 hour. Serve warm. Makes 10-12 servings.

Jay Sullivan (Mrs. Glenn R.)
Grandmother of Kim Bowden '87
Salinas, California

CORN SPOON BREAD

2 eggs, slightly beaten
1 (8½ ounce) box corn muffin
mix
1 (8 ounce) can corn, drained

1 (8 ounce) can creamed corn
½ cup melted butter
1 cup shredded Swiss cheese

Combine all ingredients except cheese. Spread in a greased 9 x 9 inch baking dish and bake at 350° for 35 minutes. Sprinkle cheese evenly over the top and bake an additional 10 to 15 minutes or until a knife inserted in the center comes out clean. Serves 8.

Judith Kennedy (Mrs. E. John)
Mother of Katie and J.J.
Pebble Beach, California

The Santa Catalina School Foundation was founded in 1953. Its first project was raising funds for the construction of a swimming pool.

APRICOT-SOUR CREAM BREAD

1/3 cup shortening
1 cup white flour
1 cup whole wheat flour
¾ cup sugar
3 teaspoons baking powder
Dash salt
1 cup chopped dried apricots

2 bananas, optional
½ cup nuts, optional
1 egg
1 cup buttermilk
½ cup molasses, optional
1½ teaspoons vanilla
½ cup sour cream

Melt and set aside the shortening. In a large bowl, sift together the flours, sugar, baking powder and salt. In a separate bowl, mix the fruit(s) and nuts; set aside. In a third bowl, mix until blended the egg, buttermilk, molasses, vanilla and sour cream; blend in the melted shortening. Make a well in the center of the dry ingredients and add the liquid mixture and the fruit(s) mixture all at one time. Stir only until moistened. Pour into a greased loaf pan and bake in a 350° oven for 1 hour. Freezes well.

Deadra Ophelia Nokes (Mrs. Ed)
Mother of Christine '86
Salinas, California

APRICOT NUT BREAD

½ cup dried apricots
1 egg
1 cup sugar
2 teaspoons melted butter
2 cups flour
3 teaspoons baking powder

¼ teaspoon soda
¾ teaspoon salt
½ cup strained orange juice
¼ cup water
1 cup broken walnut pieces

Chop apricots and soak in hot water. Set aside. Beat the egg, stir in the sugar and butter and mix well. Sift the flour with the baking powder, soda and salt. Add alternately with the orange juice and water to the sugar mixture. Drain the apricots and add with the nuts; mix well. Pour into a greased loaf pan and let rest for 15 minutes. Bake at 350° for 1 hour or until a toothpick inserted in the center comes out clean.

Mrs. Marjorie Bisgrove
Mother of Beth '78
Pebble Beach, California

Family Day in the Lower School is a time for students, parents, and faculty to get together for a day of games, socializing, and enjoying a barbeque.

PUMPKIN BREAD

1 (16 ounce) can pumpkin
4 eggs
1 cup oil
2/3 cup water
3½ cups flour
3 cups sugar

2 teaspoons baking soda
1 teaspoon nutmeg
1 teaspoon cinnamon
1½ teaspoon salt
1 cup chopped nuts (optional)

Preheat oven to 350°. Generously grease and flour 2 (9x5) loaf pans. In a large bowl, combine the pumpkin, eggs, oil and water. Sift together the dry ingredients and mix well with the pumpkin mixture. Add chopped nuts, if desired. Pour into loaf pans and bake for 1 hour or until a toothpick inserted in the center comes out clean. Yields 2 loaves.

Marian Evans (Mrs. William E.)
Mother of Billy and Sarah
Monterey, California

ORANGE QUICK BREAD

6 ounces orange juice
   concentrate, thawed
2 large very ripe bananas
2 eggs

2 cups self-rising flour
2½ teaspoons pumpkin pie spice
1 teaspoon soda
4 tablespoons white raisins

Combine orange juice, bananas and eggs in a mixing bowl and beat until fluffy. Add the flour, spice and baking soda and beat for 1 minute; stir in the raisins. Bake in a greased loaf pan at 350° for 35 minutes or until a knife inserted in the center comes out clean. This is delicious toasted and makes 20 slices, 85 calories each.

Polly Reese (Mrs. Robert)
Mother of Heather
Monterey, California

"This was my grandmother's recipe. She loved to make this bread and serve it with a little cream cheese. When I was little, it made a special tea time treat."

ORANGE BREAD

Rind of 2 oranges, chopped
1 cup sugar
1/3 cup boiling water
1 egg

1 cup milk
3 cups sifted flour
4 rounded teaspoons baking
   powder
(No shortening is used)

Cook rind of 2 medium oranges in salted water until tender; drain. In a saucepan, place the orange rind, sugar and 1/3 cup water; boil together until thickened. Cool. Add the well beaten egg, milk, flour and baking powder. Pour into a greased 5 x 9 loaf pan and bake 45 minutes in a 325° oven.

Jane Day (Mrs. Donald)
Mother of Kelly
Pebble Beach, California

"My mother told a story about this recipe: Her mother begged 'the best baker in Vallejo' for this recipe before he retired from his profession. He agreed to give her the recipe on the day he closed his shop."

NUT BREAD

3 cups flour
1 cup sugar
3 teaspoons baking powder
1 teaspoon salt
1 heaping teaspoon cinnamon

1 egg
1½ cups milk
½ teaspoon vanilla
1 cup raisins
1 cup chopped walnuts

Mix all ingredients in the order given. Let stand for 30 minutes in a well greased loaf pan. Bake in a 350° oven for 1 to 1¼ hours. Crust will be hard.

Kathleen Ryan
Director of Pre-School
Monterey, California

BANANA BREAD

2 eggs
1/3 cup soft margarine
2 medium ripe bananas
2/3 cup sugar

1¾ cup sifted flour
¾ teaspoon baking soda
1¼ teaspoon cream of tartar
½ teaspoon salt

Put eggs, margarine, banana and sugar in a blender; cover and blend until smooth. Pour blended mixture over sifted dry ingredients and mix gently until barely combined. Pour into a greased 8 x 4 inch loaf pan and bake in a 350° oven until lightly browned, about 45 minutes.

Kate Craft (Mrs. Jack)
Mother of Lisa '69
Carmel, California

"By far, the teenage favorite is walnut chocolate chip banana bread; but plain, nut and apricot are equally delightful!"

FIELD HOCKEY'S FAVORITE BANANA BREAD

2½ cups flour
1 cup sugar
3 tablespoons oil
1 egg
3½ teaspoons baking powder
1 teaspoon salt

¾ cup milk
1 cup mashed bananas (or 3 bananas)
1 cup "extras":
chopped walnuts, diced chocolate chips, diced dried apricots

Combine all ingredients in a large bowl and beat at medium speed for about 30 seconds. Pour into greased and floured loaf pans and bake at 350° until a knife inserted comes out clean. Baking times approximate: 9-inch loaf, 55 minutes; 5-inch loaf, 30 minutes, 4-inch loaf, 20 minutes. Makes 3 to 5 loaves depending on pan size.

Dave and Barb Stock
Upper School Faculty
Parents of Stephanie
Monterey, California

PEGGY'S BANANA LOAF

½ cup butter
1¼ cups sugar
2 eggs, beaten
4 tablespoons sour cream
1 teaspoon baking soda

2 ripe bananas, mashed
1½ cups flour
¼ teaspoon salt
1 teaspoon vanilla
½ cup pecans, optional

Cream together the butter, sugar and eggs; blend in the sour cream, soda and mashed bananas. Add the remaining ingredients and mix well. Pour into a greased loaf pan and bake in a 350° oven for 1 hour. This is excellent served warm with vanilla ice cream or cold with bananas and whipped cream. Serves 8.

Mrs. Julia Puleo
Mother of Theresa '83 and Julia '87
Pebble Beach, California

BLUEBERRY BREAKFAST CAKE

6 tablespoons butter
¾ cup sugar
2 eggs
1½ cups blueberries
2 cups flour

3 teaspoons baking powder
¾ teaspoon salt
1 (6 ounce) can evaporated milk
Confectioners sugar

Preheat oven to 350° and grease a 9 x 13-inch baking dish. Cream the butter, sugar and eggs until light and fluffy. Toss the blueberries with ¼ cup of the flour; set aside. Combine the remaining flour, baking powder and salt and add to the creamed mixture alternately with the evaporated milk. Gently fold in the blueberries. Bake for 30 minutes or until golden. Dust with confectioners' sugar before serving. Serves 12.

Mary Ann Taylor (Mrs. James)
Mother of James, Katie and Asher
Monterey, California

MOMMER'S COFFEE CAKE

2½ cups flour	*1 teaspoon baking powder*
1 cup brown sugar	*1 egg, beaten*
¾ cup sugar	*1 teaspoon soda*
¾ cup oil	*1 cup sour milk*
1 teaspoon nutmeg	*1 cup nuts*
¼ teaspoon salt	*1 tablespoon cinnamon*

Combine flour, sugars, oil, nutmeg and salt; mix well. Set aside ½ cup of the mixture. To the remaining portion of the mixture, add the baking powder, beaten egg, soda and sour milk, blending well. Pour into a greased 9 x 13 inch pan. To the reserved mixture, add the nuts and cinnamon and sprinkle over batter and bake at 350° for 30-45 minutes, or until done.

Marie Jones (Mrs. Charles)
Seattle, Washington

Brunches and Lunches

"This recipe came from my French grandmother."

"EGGS ODETTE"
POACHED EGGS IN CHEESE SOUFFLE

8 poached eggs
½ pint cream, warmed
¼ pound grated Gruyere (or ½
   Gruyere and ½ Parmesan)
3-4 tablespoons butter

1 heaping tablespoon flour
6 eggs, separated
2 tablespoons grated Parmesan
   cheese

Poach 8 eggs and set aside on a towel to drain well. Melt the butter in a double boiler, blend in the flour, salt and pepper and cook for about 10 minutes. Thoroughly stir in the warmed cream; remove from heat and add the yolks of the 6 separated eggs and the grated cheese. Blend well. When cool, fold in stiffly beaten egg whites. Generously butter a lower, flatter and wider dish than is generally used for a souffle. Pour in half of the souffle mixture and place the poached eggs, evenly spaced, over the top; cover with the remaining souffle mixture and then the Parmesan cheese. Bake approximately 30 minutes in a moderate (350°) oven.

Mrs. Walter H. Sullivan, Jr.
Mother of Paula '66, Erica '71 and Dagmar '77
San Francisco, California

EGGS BEARNAISE

4 slices sour dough bread, cut
   ½" thick
Softened butter or margarine
1 large tomato, cut in 4 slices

½ pound sliced cooked ham
   or smoked sausage
4 poached eggs
Bearnaise sauce

Toast bread on 1 side in a preheated broiler; brush with butter. Heat tomato slices on a lightly greased skillet. Place 2 or 3 slices of sausage or ham, 1 tomato slice and 1 poached egg on each toast slice. Top with Bearnaise sauce. Serves 4.

Mrs. Lee B. Price
Monterey, California

BREAKFAST CASSEROLE

6-8 slices of bread, cubed
1 pound bacon, ham or sausage
½ cup Swiss cheese, grated
½ cup cheddar cheese, grated
¾ cup light cream
Mushrooms, optional
Hot peppers, optional

1¼ cups milk
1 teaspoon Worcestershire sauce
1 teaspoon prepared mustard
5 eggs, slightly beaten
1 teaspoon salt
¼ teaspoon pepper

Butter a casserole or an 8 x 12-inch pan and line the bottom of the pan with the cubed bread. Cook and drain meat. Combine eggs, seasonings, cream and milk and beat with a rotary beater. Sprinkle meat, cheeses, mushrooms and hot peppers over the surface of the bread; pour liquid over casserole and let set overnight. Preheat oven to 400° and bake 45 minutes (less if using an oblong pan) or until a knife comes out clean when inserted in the center. Serves 8-10. NOTE: This recipe can be made ahead and frozen. Thaw before baking.

Brenda Guy (Mrs. Michael)
Mother of Jennifer
Pebble Beach, California

BRUNCH EGGS

10 slices white bread, quartered
2 cups chopped ham, optional
6 ounces cheddar cheese
1½ cups chopped pepper
1 cup chopped green onion

8 large eggs
3 cups milk
1½ teaspoons dry mustard
1½ teaspoons pepper
1½ teaspoons paprika

Arrange bread in overlapping rows in a buttered shallow casserole dish. Sprinkle with ham, cheese, pepper and onion. Beat together the eggs, milk, mustard, pepper and paprika and pour over the bread pieces in the baking dish. Refrigerate for 1 hour or overnight. Bake at 350° for 45-50 minutes. Let stand an additional 5-10 minutes before serving. Serves 6-8.

Jennifer Brazinsky
Sister of April
Iowa City, Iowa

EGG CHEESE CASSEROLE

8 slices bacon
4 chopped green onions
8 eggs
1 cup milk

2½ cups grated jack cheese
½ pound mushrooms
½ teaspoon salt

Fry the bacon; crumble and set aside. In 1 teaspoon of the bacon drippings, saute the green onions and the mushrooms. Beat eggs, milk and salt together. Stir the crumbled bacon, onions, mushrooms and 2 cups of the cheese into the egg mixture. Pour into a greased 13 x 9 inch pan. Bake, uncovered, at 350° for 35-45 minutes until set; cover with the remaining ½ cup of cheese and cook until cheese is melted and is a golden brown.

Margie Jennings
Upper School Faculty
Monterey, California

"A few years ago I read a description by a food writer of her favorite quiche. Alas, she did not provide the recipe, but her description was the basis of this creation."

ITALIAN SAUSAGE AND PEPPER QUICHE

1 (9 inch) pastry crust, partially baked
½ pound hot Italian sausage
3 thinly sliced medium onions
1 red bell pepper, julienned
1 green bell pepper, julienned
3 tablespoons butter
4 tablespoons flour

2 cups warm milk
Salt
Pepper
2 egg yolks
½ cup shredded Fontina cheese
½ cup shredded Saanen cheese
Freshly grated Parmesan cheese

Crumble the Italian sausage into a frying pan and saute until thoroughly cooked. Remove from pan and drain well, saving the drippings. Saute the onions and peppers in about 2 tablespoons of the drippings (or substitute butter) over low heat until soft, about 20 minutes. Stir often. To prepare the sauce, make a roux with the flour and butter. Add the warm milk and stir with a whisk over medium heat until the mixture thickens and comes to a boil. Season with salt and pepper. Remove from heat and whisk in egg yolks, then cheese. Put filling into the crust and top with sauce. Grated Parmesan cheese may be sprinkled over the top, if desired. Bake at 350° for about 30 minutes, or until the top browns.

Cheri Sullivan
Aunt of Kim Bowden '87
Urbana, Illinois

"This is Elizabeth's favorite!"

FOOL PROOF SAUSAGE QUICHE

1 egg
4 teaspoons flour
½ cup mayonnaise
½ cup milk
8 ounces (or more) Swiss cheese,
    grated

1 pound pork sausage
1 tablespoon (or more) finely
    chopped green onion
1 9-inch baked pie shell

Cook, drain and crumble sausage. In a blender or food processor mix the egg, flour, mayonnaise, milk and green onion. Combine grated cheese and crumbled sausage with the liquid mixture and pour into the prebaked pie shell. Bake in a preheated 350° oven for 45 minutes or until a knife blade inserted in the center comes out clean. Serves 4-6. NOTE: You can use less sausage, but 1 pound usually reduces considerably after cooking. This recipe can be varied with ham and diced green chile peppers, bacon or crab. I have even forgotten to put the egg in and the quiche still can be served!

Heidi Kennedy (Mrs. David)
Mother of Liz '84
Menlo Park, California

"This is simple and quick and always a hit. As a luncheon dish, I serve it with warm sour dough French bread and a green salad. It is excellent as a vegetarian entree for a buffet."

QUICK QUICHE

1 (10 ounce) package frozen
    spinach, thawed
1 (4 ounce) can diced green chiles
1 pound jack cheese, grated
½ teaspoon seasoned salt

3 green onions, chopped
1 cup Bisquick
3 eggs, beaten
3 cups milk
Nutmeg

Drain the thawed spinach; combine with the chiles, cheese, salt and onions and place in a baking dish (the more shallow the pan the less time it takes to bake). Mix together the Bisquick, eggs and milk and pour over the spinach mixture. Sprinkle a dash of nutmeg on top. Bake at 325° for 1 hour or until set.

Jeanne Adams (Mrs. Michael)
Mother of Sarah '83
Fresno, California

"This recipe won second place in the Main Dish category of the 1982 Monterey Peninsula Herald cooking contest. It evolved when I combined two recipes and then experimented with types and amounts of cheese, cream and meat."

KRISTIN'S QUICHE

½ cup mayonnaise
2 tablespoons flour
2 eggs, beaten
½ cup half and half cream
4 ounces Monterey jack cheese,

4 ounces Swiss cheese, grated
4 ounces cream cheese, cubed
½ cup chopped green onions
6-8 ounces crumbled bacon or
   cubed ham or crabmeat
1 (9 inch) deep dish pie shell

Combine the mayonnaise and flour; add, in order, the beaten eggs, the half and half, cheeses, green onions and the bacon (or ham or crabmeat), mixing well after each addition. Bake the pie crust for about 5 minutes in a 350° oven. Remove and add the filling; return to oven and bake 50-55 minutes. Serves 6. NOTE: The mixture can be made the day before baking. If using a frozen deep dish pie shell, let thaw before baking.

Kristin Searle (Mrs. Dan)
Mother of Danny
Salinas, California

"Another quick supper — easy and good for after work, or a treat for a 'fiesta' brunch."

CALIFORNIA QUICHE

1 (9 inch) deep dish pastry shell
1½ cups shredded jack cheese
2 ounces diced green chiles
1 cup shredded taco cheese

3 eggs
¾ cup half and half
¼ teaspoon salt
¼ cup shredded cheddar cheese

Prebake pastry shell for 5 minutes at 375°. Sprinkle jack cheese and taco cheese on cooled pie shell. Place chiles on top of cheese. Beat eggs with half and half and salt and pour over cheese and chiles. Sprinkle with cheddar cheese. Bake at 400° for 10 minutes and reduce heat to 350° for 30 minutes or until center is set. Serves 6. NOTE: If taco cheese is not available, try one of the seasoned cheeses in your market or use more jack cheese with ½ teaspoon chili powder.

Sister Mary Ellen
Santa Catalina School
Monterey, California

BAJA QUICHE

6 corn tortillas
1 pound ground beef
1 large onion, chopped
1 green pepper, chopped
1 clove garlic, minced
1 (7 ounce) can green chile salsa
1 teaspoon oregano

1 teaspoon cumin
1 tablespoon chili powder
2 cups cheddar cheese
1 (4 ounce) can diced green
  chiles
6 eggs
1 cup milk

Cut the tortillas in wedges and fry until crisp; salt. Brown the ground beef with the onion, green pepper and garlic; drain. Add the salsa, oregano, cumin and chili powder and mix well. Place the tortilla chips in a lightly oiled 2½ to 3 quart casserole, saving some for garnish. Layer the meat, shredded cheddar cheese and diced green chiles. Beat the eggs with the milk and pour over the casserole. Bake for 20-30 minutes in a 375° oven until eggs are set. Serves 6-8. NOTE: This casserole can be assembled ahead, with the egg mixture added immediately before baking.

Carol Steen (Mrs. Robert)
Salinas, California

SPANISH CHEESE PIE

1½ cups grated cheddar cheese
1 cup grated Monterey jack
  cheese
¼ cup chopped green chili
  peppers
½ cup milk

1/8 teaspoon salt
3 eggs, beaten
1 (3 ounce) can French-fried
  onion rings

Combine all ingredients and pour into a well oiled 8 inch pie pan. Bake in a 350° oven for 30 minutes.

Kathi Bowden
Mother of Kim '87
Monterey, California

PEPPER-CORN CASSEROLE

1 (7 ounce) can diced green
  chiles
4-6 thick slices Monterey jack
  cheese
1 (17 ounces) can creamed corn

½ cup brown or raw sugar
½ cup corn meal
1 (6 ounce) can Bloody Mary mix
Butter

Preheat oven to 350°. Butter an 8 x 8 inch casserole and line the bottom with the diced green chiles. Layer in order the cheese, corn, sugar and cornmeal. Dot generously with butter and pour Bloody Mary mix over all. Bake for 35-45 minutes. Serves 6. NOTE: Tomato juice or V-8 juice may be substituted for the Bloody Mary Mix.

Serena Underwood (Mrs. Donald)
Mother of Belinda and Melinda
Carmel Valley, California

CHILE RELLENO CASSEROLE

1 (7 ounce) can diced green chiles	3 cups milk
	1/3 cup flour
¾ pound grated cheese (cheddar and/or Monterey jack)	¾ teaspoon salt
	1 (7 ounce) can salsa
2-3 chopped green onions	Mozzarella cheese, grated
3 eggs	

Evenly distribute the chopped chiles on the bottom of a buttered casserole; add the cheddar and/or Monterey jack cheeses and onion. Combine the eggs, milk, flour and salt and pour over cheese and chiles. Bake in a 325° oven for 45 minutes or until center is firm. Remove from oven, spread with salsa and sprinkle with grated Mozzarella cheese. Return to oven and bake an additional 5-10 minutes or until cheese is melted.

Kate Craft (Mrs. Jack)
Mother of Lisa '69
Carmel, California

MOCK CHILE RELLENO SANDWICH

8 slices bread	1 (4 ounce) can diced chiles
2 tablespoons mustard	4 eggs
2 tablespoons butter	1 cup milk
4-6 slices ham	Paprika
4 slices cheese	

Remove crusts from the bread. Mix mustard and butter and spread over 4 slices of bread; place in a square baking dish. Place ham slices on bread and top with cheese and chiles. Spread mustard and butter mixture over the remaining slices and place on top. Beat together the egg and the milk and pour over the sandwiches. Sprinkle with paprika, if desired. Bake for 45 minutes to an hour at 350°. Makes 4 sandwiches.

Linda Frick
Class of '66
Washington, D.C.

HAM AND EGG ROULADE WITH CHEESE SAUCE

1 pound ground cooked ham
  (2 cups)
1 cup chopped celery
1 cup mayonnaise
¼ cup butter
½ cup unsifted flour

¾ teaspoon salt
1/8 teaspoon pepper
1/8 teaspoon dried thyme leaves
2 cups milk
4 eggs

Make ham filling by combining ham, celery and mayonnaise in a casserole. Mix well, cover and set aside until ready to bake. Make a roulade: Preheat oven to 325°. Grease at 15½ x 10½ x 1 inch jelly roll pan and line with wax paper which has been greased and floured. Separate the eggs, putting whites in a large bowl and the yolks in a medium sized bowl. Melt the butter in a medium saucepan and remove from heat. Stir in the flour, salt, pepper and thyme until smooth. Return to heat and gradually stir in the milk; bring to boiling, stirring constantly. Reduce heat and simmer, stirring until mixture becomes very thick, about 1 minute; remove from heat. With a wire whisk or wooden spoon, beat the yolks. Gradually beat in the cooked sauce. With the mixer at high speed, beat the egg whites just until stiff peaks form; fold egg yolk mixture into egg whites just until blended. Turn into prepared jelly roll pan, spread evenly. Bake the roulade 45-50 minutes or until it is golden brown and the top springs back when lightly pressed with fingertip. Bake ham filling in the oven at the same time as the roulade. Meanwhile, make cheddar cheese sauce and keep warm. Loosen edge of roulade with a spatula; cover with an oiled sheet of wax paper; top with a cookie sheet. Quickly invert; lift off jelly roll pan and peel off wax paper lining. Stir filling and spoon evenly over the roulade. Starting from the short side, roll up, using wax paper as a guide. Turn onto a serving platter and serve with the cheddar cheese sauce.

CHEDDAR CHEESE SAUCE

3 tablespoons butter
3 tablespoons flour
¼ teaspoon dry mustard
1 teaspoon Worcestershire sauce

½ teaspoon salt
2 cups milk
8 ounces sharp cheddar cheese,
  grated
1 tablespoon chopped parsley

Melt butter, stir in flour, mustard, Worcestershire and salt. Gradually stir in milk. Bring to a boil, stirring constantly. Boil 1 minute and remove from heat. Add cheese and parsley, stirring until cheese is melted. Serve over the ham and cheese roulade.

Mrs. Lee B. Price
Monterey, California

FRITTATA

1 medium onion, coarsely
  chopped
½ pound mushrooms, sliced
1 small zucchini, sliced
1 medium green pepper, diced
2 cups diced cooked ham
½ cup cooked, squeezed and
  chopped spinach
1 pound dry ricotta cheese

1 cup grated jack cheese
4 large eggs, lightly beaten
2 tablespoons olive oil
2 teaspoons dill weed
Salt
Pepper
Parmesan cheese
Paprika
Melted butter

Saute the mushrooms, zucchini, pepper and onion until soft. Add the ham and saute the mixture for 2 minutes. Cool. In a bowl, combine the ricotta and jack cheeses, 4 eggs, the cooled ham mixture, spinach, olive oil, dill, salt and pepper. Pour into a 9 x 12 inch pan and sprinkle with melted butter, Parmesan cheese and paprika. Bake at 350° for 45 minutes or until a knife inserted in the center comes out clean. Serves 8 to 10.

Donna Rico (Mrs. Ronald)
Registrar
Carmel, California

DILLY CHEESE CUSTARDS

2 (3 ounce) packages pimiento
  cream cheese
¼ cup white dinner wine
½ cup cream
1 teaspoon seasoned salt
½ teaspoon dry mustard

½ teaspoon dried dill weed
  (or to taste)
1 tablespoon finely chopped
  green onion
4 eggs

Blend the softened cream cheese with the wine and cream until smooth; stir in salt, mustard, dill and onion. Beat the eggs and blend with the cheese mixture until smooth. Lightly butter bottoms of ramekins or custard cups; pour in cheesy custard. Set cups in a shallow pan with about ½ inch hot water in the bottom. Bake in a 375° oven for 25 minutes or until custards are barely set in the center. Remove from water and let stand 5 minutes before turning out, or serve in baking dishes with a sprig of parsley on the top. Served with broiled tomatoes and asparagus, this makes an attractive and delicious luncheon dish.

Mrs. Lee B. Price
Monterey, California

RACHEL SANDWICH (REUBEN'S COUNTERPART)

For each sandwich:
2 slices French, Italian or rye
  bread
German-style sweet brown
  mustard
½ cup sauerkraut, well drained

2 ounces sliced or grated
  Swiss cheese
Butter
Sliced tomatoes
Sliced onions, optional

Lightly toast bread, butter 1 slice and set aside. Spread mustard on the other slice, spread sauerkraut to cover the mustard and then top with cheese. Place on a cookie sheet in a 425° oven until cheese is melted. Remove from oven. Place sliced tomatoes and onion slices on the cheese, top with the buttered slice of toast and serve. NOTE: Use mustard freely, for those who like it. This can be made from an entire loaf of bread sliced horizontally into 2 long halves. If made from the whole loaf, serve by slicing through the assembled sandwich in 1-inch slices.

Carole Erickson (Mrs. John)
Mother of Molly '79
Carmel, California

"This is easy to prepare, economical and delicious."

BURGUNDY-GLAZED HAMBURGERS

4 English muffin halves
1¼ pound ground beef
4 tablespoons chopped shallots
  or green onions
2 cloves garlic, minced

1 teaspoon beef stock base
1 teaspoon Dijon mustard
¾ cup red wine
3 tablespoons butter

Spread muffin halves with butter and toast until brown. Shape meat into 4 patties which are slightly wider than the muffins, and cook to the desired degree of doneness in a skillet. Place on the toasted muffins; keep warm. To the drippings in the skillet, add the shallots and garlic and saute lightly. Combine wine, stock base and mustard; pour into the skillet and bring to a boil. Reduce by half. Cover the warm hamburgers with the glaze and serve immediately.

Janice White (Mrs. Geoffrey)
Mother of Stephen and Patrick
Pebble Beach, California

Santa Catalina graduated its first Upper School class of nine students in 1953. Since then, it has graduated over 1600 students.

CHICKEN STUFFED MUSHROOMS

4 small hard whole wheat rolls
½ pound large mushrooms
    (about 12)
4 tablespoons unsalted butter
¼ cup chopped onion
1 tablespoon parsley
4 tablespoons grated Parmesan
    cheese
1/8 teaspoon pepper

1½ cups finely chopped cooked
    chicken
½ small head lettuce, finely
    shredded
2 tomatoes, finely diced
2 scallions, finely chopped
1 tart apple, finely diced
Lemon juice
¼ cup Parmesan cheese
¼ teaspoon garlic powder

Make bread crumbs from the whole wheat rolls; set aside. Remove and finely chop the stems from the mushrooms; set the mushroom caps aside. In a small saucepan, melt the butter; add the chopped stems and onion and lightly saute for 2-3 minutes. Remove from heat. Add the bread crumbs, parsley, 4 tablespoons cheese, pepper and chicken, blending well. Stuff each mushroom with the chicken mixture and place in a buttered 9 x 11 inch baking dish. Toss together the lettuce, tomatoes, scallions, apple, lemon juice, Parmesan cheese and garlic powder; evenly distribute over filled mushroom caps. Bake in a preheated oven at 375° for 15-20 minutes or until thoroughly heated. Serve immediately. Leftovers (if any) can be refrigerated and enjoyed cold as a snack.

Helen Foster (Mrs. Jacob)
Mother of Linsey '71 and Freddie '72
Salinas, California

BAKED AVOCADO STUFFED WITH CRABMEAT

1½ cups flaked crabmeat
2 tablespoons fine diced green
    pepper
¼ cup finely diced celery
¾ teaspoon grated onion

¾ teaspoon salt
1 teaspoon Worcestershire
1/3 cup chili sauce
3 avocados
Buttered bread crumbs

Combine crabmeat, green pepper, celery, onion, salt, Worcestershire sauce and chili sauce. Do not peel avocados. Cut in halves lengthwise, remove seeds and fill centers with crabmeat mixture. Top with buttered bread crumbs. Bake in a moderate oven (400°) in a pan for 15 minutes or until browned. Serve immediately. Makes 6 servings.

Mary Gazlay (Mrs. A. William)
Mother of Susan '63
Corona del Mar, California

CRABMEAT MONZA

1 pound mushrooms
4-6 green onions
2 ounces butter
Meat of 1 large crab
1 teaspoon Worcestershire sauce
Salt

Pepper
2 ounces of sherry
3 tablespoons flour
1 cup half-and-half
Parmesan cheese

Slice mushrooms and onions and saute in butter until tender. Add the crabmeat, seasonings, sherry, flour and half-and-half; cook until sauce is smooth. Fill individual shells or ramekins. Sprinkle with Parmesan cheese and bake 5 to 10 minutes in a 375° oven until just bubbly and lightly browned. Serves 4-6.

Beezie Leyden Moore (Mrs. H. Walker)
Class of '53
Clovis, California

POTTED SHRIMP

¼ pound unsalted butter
¼ pound shrimp

½ teaspoon nutmeg
½ teaspoon mace

Melt butter over low heat and add the remaining ingredients. Pour into a small ramekin, pressing shrimp down so that the butter covers. Refrigerate to set. Serve for breakfast with dry toast as the English do or serve for luncheon on lettuce with toast points.

Shirleelyn Arnaudo Grow (Mrs. John)
Class of '64
Anniston, Alabama

"This is a wonderful first course or a delightful luncheon dish."

DEVILED CRAB DELUXE

1 large onion, sliced
3 tablespoons butter
1 rounded tablespoon flour
2 cups milk
1/8 teaspoon paprika
Dash of Worcestershire sauce
1 teaspoon lemon juice
Salt

Pepper
1 cup sliced mushrooms
1 pound crab meat
2 hard-cooked eggs, sliced
Crushed Ritz cracker crumbs
Butter chips
Lemon slices

Fry onion in a lump of butter about the size of a small egg, approximately 3 tablespoons. When fried to a golden brown, add the flour and slowly stir in the milk; whisk until thickened into a cream sauce. Blend in the paprika, Worcestershire, lemon juice, salt and pepper. Stir in the mushrooms; add the crab and hard-cooked eggs. Stir over a low flame until warmed through. Place in large shells or ramekins. Sprinkle lightly with the cracker crumbs and top with butter chips and a think slice of lemon. Bake in a preheated 375° oven until gently browned. Serves 6-8. NOTE: This can be made ahead and refrigerated. Bring to room temperature for approximately 30 minutes before baking.

Diane Ortner (Mrs. Paul)
Mother of Kristin '85 and Stephanie '85
Hillsborough, California

TUNA-SPINACH AU GRATIN

1 (7 ounce) can tuna
1/3 cup fine dry bread crumbs
1 (10 ounce) package frozen
* chopped spinach*
1 tablespoon lemon juice

¼ teaspoon salt
Dash pepper
2 tablespoons grated Parmesan
* cheese*
½ cup mayonnaise

Combine the tuna, bread crumbs, thawed spinach, lemon juice, cheese, salt and pepper; fold in mayonnaise. Place in a small oiled casserole dish and sprinkle with additional Parmesan cheese. Bake in a 350° oven for 20 minutes. Serves 2.

Cleo Devoto (Mrs. Ralph)
Grandmother of Ulrike Devoto '86
Lakeport, California

SAM'S HOMEMADE SAUSAGES

2 pounds pork, ground once
1 teaspoon salt
1 teaspoon pepper
1 teaspoon oregano
1 teaspoon sage

1 teaspoon paprika
¼-½ teaspoon sweet anise
2 cloves minced garlic
* (¼ teaspoon garlic powder)*
¼ cup dry white wine

Mix all the ingredients together. If the mixture is too dry, add a little more wine. Stuff in casings or make patties. Cook until done. Serves 6-8.

Sam Scaccia
Father of Yolanda '67
Cloverdale, California

This is delicious with toasted sour dough bread for breakfast, lunch or dinner!"

LOW FAT COTTAGE CHEESE AND VEGETABLE SPREAD

32 ounces cottage cheese
1 tablespoon Guilden's spicy
  mustard
Few dashes of tabasco sauce
1 tablespoon Worcestershire
  sauce
1 tablespoon (or to taste)
  seasoned salt
1 tablespoon olive oil
1 tablespoon red wine vinegar

1 tablespoon dill weed (optional)
1 green pepper, finely chopped
3 green onions, finely chopped
2 carrots, finely chopped
½ red pepper or 1 (2 ounce) jar
  pimento, finely chopped
2 ribs of celery, finely chopped
½ cup finely chopped parsley

Season the cottage cheese with the spices and then add the vegetables, mixing well.

Mrs. Lee B. Price
Monterey, California

"This recipe was given to me by a Swiss friend. It makes a delicious luncheon entree served with a green salad."

ONION TART

PASTRY:
1 cup flour
½ cup butter, softened

1 egg yolk
3 tablespoons water

FILLING:
3 onions
2-3 tablespoons butter
1 tablespoon flour
Salt
Pepper
Chopped parsley

Basil
Marjoram
1 cup light cream
¾ cup Gruyere cheese
3 beaten eggs

For pastry: Blend together the flour, butter, egg yolk and water and refrigerate at least 1 hour. Roll out pastry and line an 8 or 9-inch tart pan; set aside. For filling: Coarsely chop the onions and saute in butter, in a covered skillet, until lightly browned. Stir in the flour and season to taste with salt, pepper, parsley, basil and marjoram. Add the cream, grated cheese and eggs and pour into the unbaked tart shell. Bake at 350° for 25 minutes or until lightly browned and set.

Anne Berolzheimer (Mrs. Philip)
Mother of Caroline '85
Stockton, California

"This pancake is like a giant popover, very spectacular when it first comes from the oven. Have everyone gathered at the table when you take it from the oven. Fruit may be placed inside or served along side. Plain yogurt is served as a topping. The menu may be completed with browned sausages or baked Canadian bacon."

DUTCH BABY

PAN SIZE	BUTTER	EGGS	MILK AND FLOUR
2-3 quarts	¼ cup	3	¾ cup each
3-4 quarts	1/3 cup	4	1 cup each
4-4½ quarts	½ cup	5	1¼ cup each
4½-5 quarts	½ cup	6	1½ cups each

Place butter in a shallow pan, not more than 3 inches deep and melt butter in a 425° oven. While butter melts, mix the batter quickly by putting the eggs in a blender or food processor and blending on high speed for 1 minute; with the motor running, gradually add the milk and then the flour; continue blending for 30 seconds. Remove pan from oven and pour in the batter. Bake 20-25 minutes until the pancake is puffy and well browned. Dust with powdered sugar or nutmeg, if desired. Cut in wedges, serve with fruit and plain yogurt. NOTE: Suggested fruits are sliced strawberries and/or peaches, any fruit in season cut and sweetened, or mixed frozen fruit plus fresh fruit (bananas, oranges, berries, etc.).

Karen Yedlicka (Mrs. Joseph)
Mother of Jennifer Richardson
Salinas, California

"This is very good for a quick breakfast. The kids have learned to make it, and we have to make 2 pans!"

PUFF PANCAKE

¼ cup butter
½ cup milk
½ cup flour

Nutmeg
2 eggs, beaten

Preheat oven to 425°. Melt the butter in a 13 x 9 inch pan in the oven. In a bowl, mix the flour and milk with a generous sprinkling of nutmeg; add the eggs (batter will be lumpy). Pour into the pan of melted butter and bake 10-15 minutes. Serve with syrup or dusted with powdered sugar and lemon.

Pamela DuPratt Gallaway
Class of '63
Sacramento, California

CREPES FOURREES GRANINEES

BASIC CREPE BATTER
1¼ cups flour
Pinch of salt
3 beaten eggs

1½ cups milk
2 tablespoons melted butter

Place all ingredients in a blender, mix well. Let stand at least 1 hour before using. Heat small skillet or crepe pan. Brush with melted butter, and pour in about 2 tablespoons batter. Cook about 1 minute or until just beginning to brown lightly around the edges. Turn and cook briefly on the opposite side. Remove and stack between wax paper. These may be cooked ahead and refrigerated or frozen. Warm or thaw to room temperature before handling.

DUXELLES
4 tablespoons butter
4 tablespoons finely chopped
* scallions*
¾ pound finely chopped
* mushrooms*

4 teaspoons finely chopped
* fresh parsley*
4 teaspoons finely chopped
* chives*
Salt
Pepper

Heat butter, stir in scallions and cook, stirring constantly for 1 to 2 minutes. Add mushrooms and cook until all the liquid has evaporated and all that remains is the butter. This takes about 15-20 minutes. Remove from heat and add parsley and chives and season to taste with salt and pepper.

VELOUTE SAUCE
6 tablespoons butter
½ cup flour
2½ cups hot chicken stock
2 egg yolks

¾ cup cream or half and half
1 teaspoon salt
¼ teaspoon white pepper
1 teaspoon lemon juice

FILLING AND TOPPING
1½ cups cooked diced ham
* (prepared in food processor)*
½ cup finely chopped artichoke
* hearts sauteed in butter*
1 package frozen chopped
* spinach, drained*

4 tablespoons finely chopped
* parsley*
Lemon juice
Salt
Pepper
1½ cups grated Swiss cheese

In a large bowl, combine the ham, artichokes and spinach with 4 tablespoons parsley. Stir in the deluxelles and ½ cup of the veloute sauce. The mixture should be thick enough to hold its shape in a spoon. Add up to ½ cup more sauce, if necessary. Taste and season with salt and pepper and lemon juice.

TO ASSEMBLE:
Spoon about 2 tablespoons filling on each crepe and roll it up. Thin the remaining sauce with cream until it flows heavily off a spoon. Butter a baking dish and spread a little of the sauce on the bottom. Arrange the filled crepes, side by side, in the dish and mask them with the sauce and sprinkle with the grated cheese, then dot them with the remaining butter. Bake in a preheated 375° oven for 15-20 minutes, or until the sauce bubbles. The top should be lightly browned; if it isn't, slide under the broiler for a few seconds until it is brown. Serve immediately. Makes about 16.

Mary Jane Wesson (Mrs. W. P.)
Mother of Jameen '77
Modesto, California

"This is excellent and beautiful and is good for a brunch or as a dessert."

APPLE AND CHEESE TART

1 cup flour	*3 tart apples, peeled and thinly*
6 tablespoons butter	*sliced*
1 cup shredded Jack cheese	*Juice of 1 lemon*
	Melted butter

STREUSEL TOPPING:
½ cup packed brown sugar	*1 teaspoon cinnamon*
1/3 cup flour	*¼ cup soft butter*

In a medium-sized bowl, cut butter into flour until crumbly. Add cheese and mix to form a dough. Pat mixture into a thin layer on the removable base of a 12-inch tart pan (do not use sides of pan). Pinch edges of dough to form a small rim. Make the streusel topping by combining all of the streusel ingredients until moist and crumbly. Sprinkle the dough with ½ of the streusel topping. Coat sliced apples with lemon juice and arrange in an attractive pattern on dough. Brush with melted butter; sprinkle with remaining topping. Bake at 450° for 20 minutes. Serve warm.

Pat Jekel
Jekel Vineyard
Greenfield, California

Pasta

GNOCCHI

2 pounds rough-skinned potatoes   1 teaspoon salt
  (not new potatoes)   1 tablespoon oil
4½ cups flour   Melted butter
2 eggs

Boil the scrubbed, unpeeled potatoes, drain and peel. Puree them in a food mill or a potato ricer while still warm. Place pureed potatoes in a large bowl and add the flour, eggs, salt and oil. Blend with a fork. Turn potato dough out onto a well-floured area to prevent sticking. Lightly cover with a dish towel. Pull off pieces of dough (about ½ cup at a time) and roll into a ½" thick cord on a very lightly floured board. Cut each cord into ¾" lengths and shape by rolling off the inside curved tines of a dinner fork, keeping your thumb on center of dumpling (Gnocchi). Gnocchi will have an indented center and shell ridge effect on back, giving it the traditional shape, which insures the lightness and traps the sauce necessary for tasty gnocchi. (Gnocchi may be frozen before cooking by placing on floured cookie sheets, freezing, and transfering to plastic bags for storage). When all the dough has been shaped, cook by dropping about 20 at a time into a large kettles of boiling salted water (5 quarts or more). When gnocchi return to surface of water, continue cooking 5 minutes, keeping water at a gentle boil. Remove cooked gnocchi from water with a slotted spoon, draining well. Place in a shallow, rimmed pan and mix gently with melted butter. Cover tightly with foil and place in a warm (150°) oven. Gnocchi will keep for as long as 1 hour if well covered to retain moisture. Flavor is best if gnocchi is not allowed to become cool after cooking. Drop more gnocchi in the boiling water and repeat the process until all have been cooked. When ready to serve, toss with the desired sauce and sprinkle generously with grated Parmesan cheese. Makes 4-6 main dish servings or 8 first course servings. NOTE: If using SWEET BASIL PESTO or WALNUT PESTO (recipes follow), mix a few tablespoons of the water used for boiling the gnocchi to thin enough of the pesto sauce to generously coat gnocchi. For a creamier texture, toss the cooked gnocchi with 1/3 cup cream just before mixing with the thinned pesto. Serve with additional Parmesan cheese and pesto sauce to be passed at the table.

Linda Cristofaro (Mrs. Joseph)
Mother of Nancy '78
Oakland, California

PESTO, BASILICO ALLA GENOVESE
(Sweet Basil Pesto)

2 cups fresh basil leaves,
  tightly packed
½ cup fresh parsley leaves,
  tightly packed
1 cup grated Parmesan cheese
1 cup olive oil

2 teaspoons salt
¼ teaspoon pepper
2/3 cup pine nuts, optional
12 blanched walnuts, optional
12 blanced almonds, optional
4-5 cloves garlic

Place all ingredients in a food processor or blender and puree to make a thick, smooth paste. A thin layer of oil may be added to keep pesto from darkening. Use at once or cover and refrigerate up to a week or freeze in small portions. NOTE: For fettucini, add 2-3 tablespoons of the Sweet Basil Pesto to your favorite fettucini cream sauce.

Linda Cristofaro (Mrs. Joseph)
Mother of Nancy '78
Oakland, California

WALNUT PESTO

1 cup walnuts
2-3 cloves garlic
2 tablespoons butter

1 tablespoon oil
½ cup grated Parmesan cheese

Puree all ingredients in a food processor or blender to make a smooth paste. Use at once or cover and refrigerate up to a week or freeze in small portions. Cover with a thin layer of oil to prevent turning brown. NOTE: For fettucini, add 2-3 tablespoons of the Walnut Pesto to your favorite fettucini cream sauce.

Linda Cristofaro (Mrs. Joseph)
Mother of Nancy '78
Oakland, California

"This is a delicious way to serve left over turkey."

TURKEY PARMESAN WITH TAGLIARINI

¼ cup flour
½ cup Parmesan cheese
½ cup fine corn flake crumbs
1 beaten egg

1 pound cooked turkey breast,
  sliced
2-3 tablespoons lemon juice
1 pound tagliarini
4 ounces pesto

Combine the flour, Parmesan cheese, and crumbs to make a coating mixture. Sprinkle the turkey with lemon juice; dip first in the beaten egg and then in the coating mixture, thoroughly coating each side. Fry quickly in a small amount of oil until golden; remove from skillet and keep warm. Cook tagliarini in boiling salted water until just tender; drain and toss with the pesto. Serve on a warm platter with the turkey steaks arranged on the top. Serve with additional grated Parmesan cheese. Makes 5-6 servings.

Mary Ann Taylor (Mrs. James)
Mother of James, Katie, and Asher
Monterey, CA

AUDREY'S CHICKEN SPAGHETTI PROVINCIAL

4 cups canned tomatoes
2 cups chicken stock
1 tablespoon chopped parsley
1 large onion, diced
1 clove garlic, crushed
1 tablespoon Worcestershire sauce
2 teaspoons salt
Pinch basil
Pinch thyme

Pinch pepper
5 cups cooked and cubed
* chicken*
Sliced mushrooms
2 tablespoons melted butter
2 tablespoons flour
1 cup light cream
½ pound Cheddar cheese, grated
½ pound spaghetti

Simmer tomatoes and chicken stock until liquid is reduced by one-half. Season with parsley, onion, garlic, Worcestershire sauce, salt, basil, thyme, and pepper; add chicken and mushrooms. In a saucepan, melt the butter and stir in flour. Add cream and half of the grated cheese; heat, stirring constantly until thickened. Combine with the tomato-chicken sauce. In boiling, salted water, cook the spaghetti until tender; drain. Add the spaghetti to the sauce and mix well. Place in a 10 cup casserole, sprinkle with the remaining cheese and heat in a 350° oven for about 45 minutes. Serves 8. NOTE: The sauce will freeze well.

Melissa King Matthews
Class of '67
Los Altos, California

On December 16, 1982, Bishop Thaddeus Shubsda, the new Bishop of the Monterey Diocese, assisted by Father Jakubiec, School Chaplain for seventeen years, celebrated Mass in the Rosary Chapel for the Upper School student body and faculty.

SPAGHETTI ALLA CARBONARA
(Coal Miner's Spaghetti)

¼ pound bacon	Freshly ground black pepper
½ pound spaghetti	2 well beaten eggs
½ cup Parmesan cheese	

Chop the thinly sliced bacon into bite sized pieces and cook slowly until done; set aside in pan with drippings. Cook the spaghetti in boiling, salted water until just tender, drain, and place in a warmed wide platter or bowl. Add the bacon and drippings, Parmesan cheese and a generous amount of pepper and mix well. Quickly pour in eggs, stirring vigorously to evenly coat all the strands. Top with additional pepper and Parmesan cheese. Makes 4 first course servings.

Giulia Gaglioti Fly
Mother of Gregory
Monterey, California

WOODMAN'S SPAGHETTINI

4 tablespoons olive oil	1 tablespoon salt
1 clove garlic, minced	Freshly ground black pepper
1 ounce dry mushrooms, soaked	½ cup cream
and chopped	1 pound spaghettini
3 Italian sausages	3-4 tablespoons finely chopped
1 (16 ounce) can Italian tomatoes	parsley

In a saucepan, heat the oil and garlic, add the mushrooms and cook for 5 minutes. Remove casings from the sausages, crumble or chop the meat, and add to the saucepan, cooking another 5 minutes. Coarsely chop the tomatoes and add to the saucepan; season with salt and pepper. Increase the heat for about 15 minutes to slightly reduce the sauce. Blend in the cream; turn off heat and cover to keep warm. In 5 quarts boiling, salted water, cook the spaghettini until tender; drain. Place in a large bowl, cover with the sauce, and garnish with the fresh parsley. Buon Appetito!

Marlo Musto Mugnani (Mrs. Renzo)
Class of '64
Florence, Italy

SPAGHETTI SAUCE

5 large cloves of garlic
¼ cup olive oil
4 onions, chopped
4 (29 ounce) cans pear shaped
    tomatoes
2 (29 ounce) cans six-in-one
    tomatoes, crushed
2 (29 ounce) cans Progresso
    tomato sauce with basil

2 carrots, sliced
1½ teaspoons salt
Pepper
4 teaspoons Italian seasoning
4 tablespoons butter
½ pound dried mushrooms,
    oiled and chopped
1½ tablespoons sugar
Pasta

In a large pot, brown the garlic in the olive oil; remove and discard the garlic. Saute the onions in the garlic-oil until soft and light brown, adding more oil if necessary. Add the tomatoes, tomato sauce, and carrots; season with the salt, pepper, and Italian Seasoning, and simmer for 1½ hours. Cool and put through a sieve. Return sauce to the pot, add the butter, mushrooms, and sugar and cook an additional hour. Serve over spaghetti or your favorite pasta.

Ada Barone (Mrs. Samuel)
Mother of Sister Claire
San Francisco, California

SPAGHETTI-A-LA-FRANCESCONI

1 pound ground beef (OR
    chopped chicken hearts, liver,
    giblets, or a combination)
Salt
Pepper
½ cup white wine
1 medium onion, minced
2 cloves garlic, minced
2 ribs celery, minced

2 sprigs parsley, minced
2 (10 ounce) cans tomato sauce
    (OR a 6 ounce can tomato
    paste and a 10 ounce can
    tomato sauce)
1 (4 ounce) can mushrooms
2 tablespoons butter
1 pound spaghetti
Grated Parmesan cheese or
grated hard Monterey cheese

In a saucepan or skillet, brown the meat in a small amount of oil; season with salt and pepper. Add wine, simmer for a few minutes and add the onion, garlic, celery and parsley; saute. Stir in the tomato sauce, adding ½ cup water if sauce is too thick. Simmer for 1-1½ hours, stirring frequently. Add mushrooms and cook an additional 15 minutes. Blend in the butter. Cook spaghetti in boiling, salted water; drain. On a platter or in a bowl, layer the spaghetti, then the sauce, then a small amount of grated cheese; repeat layers, ending with a generous amount of sauce and cheese.

Mrs. Mabel Francesconi
Grandmother of Stephanie Eppler '86
Bakersfield, California

SPAGHETTI SAUCE AND MEATBALLS

For Sauce:
1 onion, finely chopped
1 clove garlic, finely chopped
½ teaspoon parsley
½ teaspoon oregano
½ teaspoon rosemary
½ teaspoon sweet basil
2 tablespoons olive oil
1 pound lean ground beef
½ cup red wine
1 (16 ounce) can tomato puree
1 (10 ounce) can tomato sauce
1 (6 ounce) can tomato paste
Salt
Pepper

Sugar to taste
¼ teaspoon nutmeg
For Meatballs:
1 pound lean ground beef
½ onion, finely chopped
¼ clove garlic, finely chopped
¼ teaspoon parsley
¼ teaspoon oregano
¼ teaspoon rosemary
¼ teaspoon sweet basil
3 slices white bread, soaked in
water and squeezed
2 eggs, beaten
¼ cup red wine
½ tablespoon grated Parmesan
cheese

For Sauce: brown the onion and herbs in olive oil; add hamburger and brown until crumbly. Add wine, tomato puree, sauce and paste, mixing well; season with salt, pepper, sugar, and nutmeg. For Meatballs: combine all ingredients and form into 10 meatballs. Broil on both sides until brown. Add to sauce and simmer 1 to 1½ hours. Serve over or tossed with 2 pounds spaghetti or pasta of your choice.

Pat Coniglio (Mrs. Peter)
Mother of Alyson
Monterey, CA

ITALIANA SPAGHETTI SAUCE

2-3 tablespoons vegetable or
olive oil
1 pound ground beef
2-3 Italian sausages, sliced
3 cloves garlic, minced
1-2 tablespoons chopped parsley
1-2 tablespoons chopped celery
1 medium onion, chopped
½ teaspoon rosemary
½ teaspoon nutmeg

½ teaspoon marjoram
Salt
Pepper
2 (8 ounce) cans tomato sauce
1 (6 ounce) can tomato paste
1 cup white or red wine
2 cubes beef or chicken bouillon
1 cup chopped mushrooms
Pasta

In a large saucepan heat the oil, add the ground beef and sausage; saute until brown. Add the garlic, parsley, celery, and onion; season with rosemary, nutmeg, marjoram, salt and pepper. Simmer about ½ hour. Add the tomato sauce and paste, bouillon, wine, 2 cups water, and mushrooms; simmer two additional hours. After simmering for an hour, correct seasonings. If sauce becomes too thick, thin with small amounts of broth. This makes enough sauce for one or more pounds of pasta.

Mrs. Emma Bonora
Grandmother of Sandra Chiappe Swenson '75
Modesto, CA

"This is an adaptation of the Mushroom Clam soup recipe in Volume I of the Santa Catalina Cookbook."

CLAM SAUCE FOR SPAGHETTI

½ cup butter
1 onion, chopped
1 pound mushrooms, sliced
3 cloves garlic, minced
4 (6½ ounce) cans chopped clams
1 (8 ounce) bottle clam juice

1 cup heavy cream
½ teaspoon black pepper
Pinch of salt
¾ cup Parmesan cheese, grated
4 tablespoons flour for
*   thickening*

Saute the onion, mushrooms and garlic in the butter until soft; add the clams and cook until tender. Stir in the clam juice, cream and spices and bring just to a boil; reduce heat and thicken with the flour. Stir in the Parmesan cheese and serve over spaghetti. Serves 6.

Julie Anderson (Mrs. Doug Poffenbarger)
Boulder Creek, California

SHRIMP FETTUCINI (PASTA SALAD)

1 pound vermicelli
1 quart mayonnaise
12 green onions, chopped
½ bell pepper, chopped

5 ribs celery, chopped
1 (2 ounce) jar pimiento
1½ pounds shrimp

Cook vermicelli; drain and combine with remaining ingredients except shrimp while the vermicelli is still hot (this allows the flavors to blend). Refrigerate overnight. Add shrimp shortly before serving. Serves 15-20. NOTE: Use part or all of the green onion stems, depending on taste.

Leila Jensen (Mrs. James)
Mother of Susan '86
Hillsborough, California

VERMICELLI AND SHRIMP SALAD

½ green pepper
5 stalks celery
12 green onions
3 hard cooked eggs
1 (2 ounce) jar pimientos
Salt

Pepper
Tomatoes
1 quart mayonnaise
1 pound vermicelli
2½ pounds shrimp

Chop green pepper, celery, onions, eggs and pimiento. Combine with the mayonnaise. Break vermicelli into fourths and boil according to package directions; drain well. Mix well all ingredients except the tomatoes, seasoning to taste with salt and pepper. Garnish with sliced tomatoes. Serve cold. Makes 10-12 servings. NOTE: Diced ham or chicken may be substituted for the shrimp.

Suzanne Townsend Finney (Mrs. J.P.)
Class of '60
Hillsborough, California

PASTA SALAD

1 medium clove garlic, finely
  chopped
4 firm ripe tomatoes, coarsely
  chopped
½ cup coarsely chopped fresh
  basil
Optional:
  Chopped walnuts
  Oregano
  Black nicoise olives

¾ cup olive oil
1 pound rigatoni, shell, or
  fusilli pasta
1 tablespoon balsamic vinegar
¾ pound feta cheese

Marinate the garlic, tomatoes, basil, and optional ingredients if desired, in olive oil for one hour. Cook pasta until al dente and drain (can be rinsed to cool or left hot for a warmer dish). Add vinegar to the tomato mixture and toss with the pasta. Crumble feta cheese over pasta and toss to mix. Serves 4.

John and Nancy McCormack
The Cheese Shop
Carmel, CA

FETTUCINI WITH SHRIMP

Olive oil
4-6 cloves garlic, crushed
12 medium mushrooms, sliced
1 (4½ ounce) can shrimp
1 (4 ounce) can sliced olives
2 tablespoons parsley

1 pound fettucini
½ cup Parmesan cheese
½ cup melted butter
1 egg yolk
½ cup whipping cream

In a skillet over low heat, saute the garlic and mushrooms in olive oil. Add shrimp and olives until warmed; remove from heat and add parsley. Cover and set aside. Cook the fettucini in 4 quarts boiling salted water; drain and place in a heated serving dish. Melt the butter, add Parmesan cheese, and beat in the egg yolk and cream with a wire wisk; pour over the pasta and top with the shrimp and olive mixture. Serve immediately. Makes 4 servings.

Karen Nencini (Mrs. Cesare)
Mother of Nella '83 and Elisa '87
Carmel Valley, California

FETTUCINE ALFREDO

2 tablespoons butter
1 cup Creme Fraiche
¼ cup salt

1 pound fettucine, linguine, or
  thin spaghetti
1 cup grated Parmesan cheese
Freshly ground pepper

One hour before serving, set out butter and Creme Fraiche to come to room temperature. Cook the pasta until al dente in six quarts of boiling water to which ¼ cup salt has been added. Drain, and toss with butter, Creme Fraiche and ¾ cup of the grated Parmesan cheese. Pass remaining Parmesan at the table. Grind fresh pepper over fettucine to taste. Serves 4.

John and Nancy McCormack
The Cheese Shop
Carmel, CA

135

SPINACH NOODLES

1 (12 ounce) package twisted or wide noodles
2 (10 ounce) packages frozen chopped spinach, drained
1 (9 ounce) package frozen creamed spinach, cooked
½ cup butter
1 tablespoon chopped green onion
1 tablespoon chopped fresh parsley
4 eggs, beaten
1 pint sour cream
Slivered almonds

Cook noodles according to package directions and combine with all the spinach, the butter, onion and parsley; add the eggs and fold in the sour cream. Place in a buttered casserole dish, top with the slivered almonds and bake in a 350° oven for 45 minutes. Serves 8. NOTE: With the addition of one package of finely cubed cooked Canadian bacon or ham, this recipe makes a complete entree. It may be divided into small portions and frozen.

Mrs. Frank H. Pierce
Carmel, California

"This is great for a large group."

COMPANY LASAGNA

3 pounds ground beef
1 pound ground fresh pork
2 cups chopped onions
2 cloves garlic, minced
2 (28 ounce) cans tomatoes
1 (15 ounce) cans tomato sauce
4 teaspoons salt
3 tablespoons sugar
6 tablespoons parsley flakes
3 teaspoons crushed basil
2 cups grated Parmesan cheese
2 (32 ounce) cartons small curd cottage cheese
2 teaspoons crushed oregano
1 pound lasagne noodles, cooked drained
2 pounds shredded mozzarella cheese

Cook the beef, pork, onion and garlic until the meat is brown; drain off fat. Add tomatoes, breaking with a fork. Stir in tomato sauce, 2 teaspoons of the salt, sugar, 4 tablespoons of the parsley and the basil. Simmer, uncovered, for at least 1 hour, preferably 3 hours. Preheat oven to 350°. Mix together 1 cup of the Parmesan cheese, the cottage cheese, the remaining 2 tablespoons parsley, the remaining 2 teaspoons salt and oregano. In 2 oiled 13 x 9½ inch baking dishes, layer half of the lasagne noodles, half of the mozzarella cheese and half of the cottage cheese mixture. Repeat, saving enough sauce to cover. Sprinkle with the remaining 1 cup Parmesan cheese. Bake, uncovered, for 45 minutes. Let stand 15 minutes before serving. Serves 24.

Arlene Dryden (Mrs. William)
Mother of Lesley '83, Lyndy '84 and Deborah
Monterey, California

For almost 20 years, Saga Foods has met the nutritional needs of the Santa Catalina community. This recipe makes enough for a family reunion, an alumnae get-together, or a large social gathering, and is especially popular during Lent.

VEGETARIAN CHEESE LASAGNA

	24 Servings (1 pan)	96 Servings (4 pans)
Cream cheese, softened	1 pound 2 ounces	4½ pounds
Cottage cheese, fine curd	2 pounds	8 pounds
Sour cream	¾ cups	3 cups
Green onion, chopped	4 ounces	1 pound
Green pepper, diced	2 ounces	8 ounces
Salt	2¼ teaspoons	3 tablespoons
White pepper	1-1/8 teaspoons	1-1/3 tablespoons
Marinara sauce	3 quarts	3 gallons
Water	1 quart	1 gallon
Lasagna noodles, raw	2 pounds	8 pounds
(1¾" wide)	(20 each)	(80 each)
(or 3" wide)	(12 each)	(48 each)
Mozzarella cheese, shredded	8 ounces	2 pounds

Combine the cream cheese, cottage cheese, sour cream, onion, green pepper, salt and pepper; mix well. In a separate container, stir the water into the marinara sauce. Oil the 21 x 13 x 2½" pan(s) well. For each pan, layer in order the following amounts:

> *2 cups marinara sauce*
> *8 ounces raw noodles (5 each) (or 3 each)*
> *1 quart cheese mixture*
> *8 ounces raw noodles (5 each) (or 3 each)*
> *2 quarts cheese mixture*
> *8 ounces raw noodles (5 each) (or 3 each)*
> *1 quart cheese mixture*
> *8 ounces raw noodles (5 each) (or 3 each)*
> *1½ quarts marinara sauce*

Cover the pan with foil and bake in a 325° oven for 1¾ hours. Uncover and bake an additional 10 minutes. Remove from oven and sprinkle evenly with the mozzarella cheese. Let rest for 15 to 20 minutes before cutting into serving portions.

Jerry Munckton
Saga Foods
Monterey, California

JIMMY GLASER'S LASAGNA

1 pound ground beef
1 (1½ ounce) package Lawry's
   lasagne sauce mix
1 (16 ounce) can whole
   tomatoes, cut up
1 (8 ounce) can tomato sauce
   with cheese
1 cup red wine

Lasagna noodles, cooked in
   water and oil
1 (9 ounce) package frozen
   creamed spinach
1 (16 ounce) carton large curd
   cottage cheese
8 ounces Mozzarella cheese,
   grated
Parmesan cheese

Cook meat until brown; add the sauce mix, tomatoes, tomato sauce and wine. Bring to a boil, reduce heat and simmer about 10 minutes. Prepare pasta and spinach according to package directions. In a buttered lasagna pan, layer in order half of the meat sauce, half of the pasta, half of the cottage cheese, half of the mozzarella and all of the spinach. Repeat layers, using the remaining ingredients. Top with Parmesan cheese and bake, uncovered, in a 375° oven for 30 minutes. NOTE: This lasagne can be made ahead and frozen. Bake at 350° until thoroughly heated.

Kate Craft (Mrs. Jack)
Mother of Lisa '69
Carmel, California

CANNELLONI

8 tablespoons butter
¼ pound mushrooms, finely
   chopped
1 pound lamb, cooked and
   minced
4 tablespoons Parmesan cheese

Salt
Pepper
2½ cups Bechamel Sauce
   (recipe follows)
12 rectangular cannelloni
   noodles

In a skillet, melt all but one tablespoon of the butter and saute the mushrooms for 2-3 minutes. Add the lamb and cheese, season, and stir in enough of the Bechamel Sauce to make a soft mixture. Cook the canneloni noodles in boiling salted water for 5 minutes, drain, and rinse with cold water. Spread filling on each of the 12 cannelloni noodles, roll up, and place seam side down in a shallow buttered baking dish. Dot with remaining butter and sprinkle with additional Parmesan cheese. Pour remaining Bechamel Sauce in baking dish with the filled cannelloni noodles and bake in a 425° oven until golden. Serves 6.

BECHAMEL SAUCE

4 tablespoons butter
4 tablespoons flour
2½ cups chicken stock or
  bouillon

Pepper
Nutmeg
Salt

In a saucepan, melt the butter, add the flour, and cook until bubbly. Stir in the chicken stock and cook, stirring constantly, until thickened. Season with pepper, nutmeg and salt if needed.

Mary Ann Taylor (Mrs. James)
Mother of James, Katie and Asher
Monterey, California

Entrees

"This recipe was given to me by a lovely lady who really knows how to cook! Please honor her — Yvonne Conover from Palo Alto, California."

CREPES FLORENTINE

CREPES
4 unbeaten eggs
1-1/3 cups flour
2 cups half and half

1 tablespoon oil
4 tablespoons sherry

FILLING
2 pounds lean ground veal
1 pound mushrooms
2 shallots

3 pounds fresh spinach, cooked
  and drained
1 cup grated Swiss cheese

SAUCE
10 tablespoons butter
10 tablespoons flour
3 cups milk
2 cups half and half

Nutmeg
Salt
Pepper
1 cup grated Swiss cheese

For crepes: Mix the eggs with the flour and gradually add the milk. Strain and refrigerate overnight. In the morning, add the oil and sherry. Heat a 5 or 7 inch skillet or crepe pan until moderately hot. Brush lightly with oil and cook, using several tablespoons batter for each crepe. For filling: In a food processor, chop the shallots and mushrooms. Cook veal well and add the shallots, mushrooms and spinach; cook again. Remove from heat and add the Swiss cheese. This can be made the day before and refrigerated. For sauce: Melt the butter, add the flour and stir in the liquids. Add the nutmeg, salt and white pepper to taste. When thickened, add the Swiss cheese and stir until smooth. To assemble: Place 2 or 3 tablespoons of the filling in the center of each crepe and roll the crepes. Place seam side down in 2 (8 x 10 inch) buttered glass or earthenware pans. Cover with sauce and sprinkle with an additional cup of Swiss cheese. Warm through in a 350° oven about 20-30 minutes. NOTE: Crepes Florentine can be made ahead and kept covered in the refrigerator. Remove cover prior to baking. This is good accompanied by broiled tomatoes and a green salad.

Jennifer English (Mrs. John)
Mother of Lauren '85 and
Allison, Summer Camp
Lafayette, California

VEAL WITH HEARTS OF PALM

4 veal loin chops	2 tablespoons dark rum
Flour	½ cup port
7 tablespoons butter	½ cup heavy cream
Salt	3 tablespoons puree of foie gras
Pepper	or liver pate
4 hearts of palm	Truffles, optional

Allow 1 medium thick loin chop per serving. Dust the chops lightly with flour. Melt 3 tablespoons of butter in a large skillet and brown the chops on both sides. Salt and pepper to taste. Reduce the heat and continue cooking until the meat is tender. Cover the skillet for part of the cooking time. Heat the hearts of palm in 3 tablespoons of the butter over a low flame, turning them carefully. When the chops are cooked, remove them to a hot platter and keep them warm. Rinse the pan with the rum and add the port. Gradually add the heavy cream and reduce the sauce a little over a low flame. Turn off the heat and add the remaining 1 tablespoon of butter, the puree of foie gras or liver pate and salt and pepper to taste. Serve the chops covered with the sauce and garnished with the hearts of palm. Each chop may be decorated with a slice of truffle for a more elegant presentation. Serves 4. NOTE: There are 2 sizes of hearts of palm — very thick and much thinner. Thinner ones are best for this dish.

Pauline Cantin (Mrs. Giles)
Music Department
Mother of Marie '70
Monterey, California

VEAL STEW

3 pounds veal, cut in cubes	2 tablespoons butter
¼ cup flour	½ cup chopped onions
¼ teaspoon black pepper	½ cup sweet sherry
2 teaspoons salt	2 teaspoons tomato paste
½ teaspoon thyme	1 cup sliced mushrooms
2 tablespoons olive oil	2 cups green peas

Toss the veal in a mixture of the flour, salt, pepper and thyme. Heat the oil and butter in a Dutch oven and brown the veal and onions. Add the wine and tomato paste; cover and cook over low heat 45 minutes or until the veal is tender. Add the mushrooms and peas and cook 5 minutes longer. Serves 6.

Sandra Smith (Mrs. Stanley)
Mother of Laura
Pebble Beach, California

VEAL CASQUEIRO

1½ pounds boneless veal
4 tablespoons butter
½ pound mushrooms
1½ tablespoons lemon juice
1 teaspoon salt
¼ teaspoon pepper

¼ cup flour
¾ cup Weibel Amber Cream
   Sherry
1 beef bouillon cube
¼ cup hot water
Fresh parsley

Trim the fat from the veal and slice the veal into julienne strips (1 inch long by 1 inch wide by 1 inch thick). Melt two tablespoons of the butter in a large saute pan, add the mushrooms and the lemon juice and cook over a medium heat until the mushrooms are soft. Pour the mushrooms into a dish and set them aside. Season the veal with salt and pepper and dust with flour. Shake off the excess flour. Melt the remaining two tablespoons butter in the pan and saute the veal slices quickly on both sides. (Don't leave the veal in the pan for longer than a minute on each side or the veal will be tough.) Add the Amber Cream Sherry and the bouillon cube dissolved in ¼ cup of hot water. Pour over the veal, return the mushrooms to the pan, mix and heat for another minute. Garnish with parsley. This is delicious served over rice and accompanied by a 1975 or 1976 Weibel Mendocino Pinot Noir. Serves 4.

Weibel Champagne Vineyards
Mission San Jose, California

LAMB CARDINAL

¼ cup tarragon vinegar
¼ cup currant jelly
½ cup tomato catsup
1 tablespoon butter
1 teaspoon Worcestershire sauce

Salt
Pepper
Lamb
1 tablespoon Marsala, optional

Combine in a saucepan the vinegar, jelly, catsup, butter and Worcestershire sauce; cook until jelly is melted and all the ingredients are well blended; season with salt and pepper. Add thin slices of cold, cooked lamb and cook about 20 minutes over low heat. A tablespoon of Marsala added just before serving makes this dish delicious. NOTE: This is an excellent way to use left-over lamb.

Helen M. Tillotson (Mrs. E. S.)
Grandmother of Erin Sullivan '85
Chattanooga, Tennessee

"Don't let the length of this recipe keep you from trying it. Believe me, as my Mom raises sheep and I've cooked lamb every possible way, this is divine."

LAMB WITH LEMON SAUCE

3 tablespoons vegetable oil
3 pounds lean boneless lamb
  shoulder, cut into 1½ inch cubes
1½ teaspoons salt
¼ teaspoon pepper
¼ teaspoon garlic powder
2 tablespoons butter
1 large onion, finely chopped
2 tablespoons flour

½ cup water
½ cup dry white wine
2 tablespoons chopped fresh dill
2 tablespoons fresh parsley
3 ribs celery, with leaves
3 small zucchini, sliced
4 egg yolks
6 tablespoons lemon juice

Heat the oil in a Dutch oven. Add the lamb cubes; sprinkle with 1 teaspoon of the salt, pepper and garlic, and brown on all sides. Remove meat with a slotted spoon as it browns. Add butter to the pan and reduce heat. Add the onion and cook until tender. Stir in flour and blend well. Pour in the water and wine, stirring constantly until thickened and smooth. Return the meat to the pan. Add dill, parsley, the remaining ½ teaspoon salt; cover and simmer about 1 hour. Cut the celery diagonally into 2 inch slices; chop the celery leaves. Add the zucchini, celery and leaves to the Dutch oven. Cover and simmer 10 additional minutes. Beat the egg yolks in a small bowl until thick; beat in the lemon juice 1 tablespoon at a time. Gradually stir in 1 cup of the hot liquid from the lamb mixture into the egg yolk mixture, while beating with vigor! Slowly pour the egg yolk mixture back into the Dutch oven, stirring constantly until the mixture is smooth and thickened. Do not boil. Serves 6-8.

Susan Grupe Smith (Mrs. Wilbur H.)
Class of '66
Stockton, California

ROAST GOOSE-WINE FRUIT STUFFING

1 cup dried prunes
1½ cups Taylor California Cellars
  Cabernet Sauvignon
4 cups peeled, cored, sliced apples
½ cup minced onion
½ cup diced celery
1 teaspoon salt

1 teaspoon sugar
1 teaspoon poultry seasoning
6 cups fresh white bread cubes
1 goose, 8-10 pounds
Salt
Pepper

Wash and pit the prunes, cover with 1 cup of the wine and soak overnight. Next morning, combine the prunes and wine with the apples, onion, celery and seasonings in a large saucepan. Cook over low heat about 30 minutes, stirring often, until prunes and apples are soft and most of the wine is absorbed. Cool, stirring occasionally. Fold in the bread cubes. Remove neck and giblets from the goose; wash goose inside and out under running water and drain well. Rub well all over inside and out with the remaining ½ cup wine; rub salt and pepper inside goose. Stuff the neck with the wine fruit stuffing and secure the skin with a skewer. Stuff body cavity and tie the legs together, if necessary. Place goose, breast side up, in an open roasting pan. Heat oven to 350° and roast goose for 1 hour. Prick skin all over with a fork. Roast another hour and remove fat from roasting pan. An 8 to 10 pound stuffed goose should be roasted 4 to 4½ hours (if necessary, remove fat a second time). To test for doneness: Meat thermometer inserted in the thickest portion of the thigh should read 190°. Using double or triple thickness of paper towel, pinch leg at thickest portion. Meat should feel very soft. Let goose stand 10 minutes before carving. Garnish with orange cups or peach halves filled with jelly or cranberry sauce. Serves 8-10.

GRAVY FOR ROAST GOOSE

Goose neck and giblets	*1½ cups broth*
2 cups salted water	*½ cup Taylor California Cellars*
1 small onion	*Cabernet Sauvignon*
1 rib celery	*Salt*
2 tablespoons drippings	*Pepper*
2 tablespoons flour	

For broth, simmer the neck and giblets, a small onion, and a stalk of celery in two cups water for about 2 hours; strain. Remove all but 2 tablespoons fat from the roasting pan; add the flour, 1½ cups of the broth, the Taylor California Cellars Cabernet Sauvignon. Cook and stir until the mixture is thickened. Add chopped giblets; season with salt and pepper as needed. Makes 2 cups. NOTE: If drippings in the bottom of the roaster become black, do not make gravy in it. Prepare gravy in a saucepan.

Monterey Vineyard
Hayward, California

PHEASANT

1 pheasant
Flour
Vegetable oil
Olive oil
6 cloves garlic, chopped
4 onions, chopped
1 green pepper, chopped
Chopped parsley

1½ cups canned skinless
  tomatoes
1 cup consomme
¾ cup marsalla wine or vermouth
Salt
Pepper
Oregano
1 cup fresh mushrooms, sliced
½ cup sour cream

Flour and brown pheasant parts in vegetable oil, and place in a buttered casserole. Saute in olive oil the garlic, onions and green pepper; add the parsley, chopped or broken tomatoes, consomme and wine or vermouth. Season with salt, pepper and oregano. Pour over pheasant and bake, covered, in a 325° oven for 1 hour. Add the mushrooms and bake for an additional 45 minutes. Stir in the sour cream and bake 15 minutes more.

Mary Jane Wesson (Mrs. W. P.)
Mother of Jameen '77
Modesto, California

BARBECUED DUCK A LA BARBER

2 large wild ducks (Sprig or
  Mallard)
Celery stalks and tops
Salt

Soy sauce (4 generous shakes)
3 pinches Thyme
Fresh rosemary sprigs

One hour prior to cooking, dry inside cavity of ducks with a paper towel and salt lightly. Place celery stalks and leaves inside the bird. Sprinkle breasts with soy sauce, then thyme, rubbing in gently. Start coals on outdoor grill (preferably a Weber-covered cooker), ½ hour before cooking. Use Mexican charcoal; add fresh rosemary sprigs to coals. Keeping ducks slightly separated, place breast side up on the grill for 20 minutes or until juice is pinkish. Carve breast from carcass and serve with wild rice, a fresh green vegetable and currant jelly. Cabernet Sauvignon wine is excellent with this meal. Serves 4. The remaining carcass may be picked and enjoyed at the conclusion of the meal.

Susan and Kent Barber
Parents of Elizabeth '86
San Francisco, California

DUCKLING WITH ORANGE SAUCE

1 (4-5 pounds) ready to cook
  duck
2 teaspoons grated orange peel
½ cup orange juice
¼ cup currant jelly
1 tablespoon lemon juice
1/8 teaspoon dry mustard

1/8 teaspoon salt
1 tablespoon cold water
1½ teaspoons cornstarch
1 orange, peeled and sectioned
1 tablespoon orange flavored
  liqueur

Fasten the neck skin of duck to the back with skewers. Lift wing tips up and over back for natural brace. Place the duckling breast side up on a rack in a shallow roasting pan. Prick skin with fork. Roast, uncovered, in a 325° oven until done, about 2½ hours, removing excess fat occasionally (if duckling becomes too brown, place a piece of aluminum foil lightly over breast). The duckling is done when drumstick meat feels very soft. Let stand 10 minutes for easier carving. Heat orange peel, orange juice, jelly, lemon juice, mustard and salt to boiling. Mix the water and cornstarch; stir into sauce. Cook over medium heat, stirring constantly, until the mixture thickens and boils. Boil and stir 1 minute. Stir in orange sections and liqueur. Brush duckling with some of the orange sauce; serve with remaining sauce.

Dianne Johnson (Mrs. D. M.)
Pre-school faculty
Monterey, California

"This is an easy, never fail recipe."

WILD DUCK

4 ducks
Juice of 1 lemon
½ - 1 teaspoon red pepper
1 - 1½ teaspoons each of the
  following:
Seasoned salt
Lemon pepper
Hot curry powder

Oregano
Thyme
Rosemary
Basil
1 cup red wine vinegar
2 cups water

Thoroughly clean ducks in cold water and sprinkle with the lemon juice. Combine all seasonings and cover both the breasts and back sides of ducks. Place, breast side down, in a 4 quart casserole to which the vinegar and water have been added. Bake, covered, in a 400° oven approximately 1½ hours. Serve with juices in baking pan. Serves 4.

Eleanor Hutcheson Gardner (Mrs. Stephen)
Class of '63
Austin, Texas

PLUM DUCK

¼ cup butter
1 medium onion, chopped
1 (16 ounce) can purple plums
1 (6 ounce) can frozen lemonade
2 teaspoons Dijon mustard
1/3 cup chili sauce
¼ cup soy sauce

1 teaspoon dry ginger
2 drops Tabasco
6 ounces Weibel White Cabernet
Sauvignon
2 oranges, halved
1 duck, quartered
Garlic powder
Onion powder

Heat butter in a skillet, add onions and cook until tender. Remove pits from the plums; puree plums with their juice in a food processor or blender; add the onions and blend in lemonade, mustard, chili sauce, soy sauce, ginger, Tabasco and wine. Simmer in a saucepan for 15 minutes. Place orange halves on a rack, cut side up, in a roasting pan. Season duck with garlic and onion powder and place on each orange half. Bake in a 350° oven, uncovered, for 1 hour. Remove from oven and drain fat. Place duck and oranges, side by side, in the roasting pan, brush with plum sauce and continue baking at 350° for 1 additional hour, basting every 10 minutes with the plum sauce. Serve the duck with the remaining plum sauce and garnish with fresh orange halves. Wild rice pilaf, spinach salad, stuffed zucchini and Weibel Blanc de Pinot Noir champagne are perfect accompaniments for this special holiday meal. Serves 4.

Weibel Champagne Vineyards
Mission San Jose, California

DUCKLING A LA GOURMET WITH SAUCE ORIENTALE

1 (4-5 pound) duckling
1 egg, slightly beaten
½ cup grated coconut
¼ cup flour

1½ teaspoons salt
½ teaspoon ginger
1/8 teaspoon pepper

SAUCE
1½ tablespoons cornstarch
1 (11 ounce) can mandarin
oranges
½ cup maple syrup
2 tablespoons lemon juice

2 tablespoons dark seedless
raisins
1 tablespoon butter
1 tablespoon soy sauce

Quarter duck and prick with a fork every half inch to allow fat to drain as it cooks. Place skin side up on a rack in a baking pan. Bake in a 350° oven for 1 hour 15 minutes, basting once or twice with pan drippings. Remove from oven and brush duck with egg and coat with a mixture of the coconut, flour, salt, pepper and ginger. Return to oven and roast for 15-30 minutes until brown. For sauce orientale, combine the cornstarch, syrup from the can of mandarin oranges, maple syrup and lemon juice in a saucepan; stir until smooth. Add raisins. Bring to a boil over medium heat and boil for 3 minutes. Stir in the butter, soy sauce and oranges; simmer 2 minutes. Serve hot with the duck. Makes 1-2/3 cups sauce and enough duck for 4 people.

Cleo Devoto (Mrs. Ralph)
Grandmother of Ulrike Devoto '86
Lakeport, California

CHICKEN MAGNIFIQUE

12 ounces dried mushrooms
3-5 tablespoons butter
6 pounds chicken breasts
(16 deboned halves)
4 tablespoons brandy
3 tablespoons finely chopped
onion
4 cloves finely minced garlic
2 teaspoons Bovril

1 (6 ounce) can tomato paste
5 tablespoons flour
1 cup strong chicken bouillon
1 cup dry white wine
Salt
Pepper
1 cup sour cream
1/3 cup finely chopped parsley

Cover the dried mushrooms with boiling water and let steep for 2-3 hours. Melt the butter in a large skillet and brown chicken breasts, a few at a time, adding more butter if necessary. Transfer the chicken to an ovenproof casserole with a cover. Add the brandy to the skillet and scape to loosen all the browned bits. Drain mushrooms, reserving the liquid, and chop finely. Add mushrooms, onion and garlic to the pan juices and cook a minute or two. Stir in the Bovril, tomato paste and flour and blend thoroughly. Combine the mushroom liquid, chicken bouillon and white wine (4 cups total liquid) and gradually add to the mixture in the skillet. Cook slowly until thickened, stirring constantly. Season heavily with salt and pepper as the sour cream, which is added later, will cut the flavor. Pour over chicken and bake in a preheated 350° oven for 35 minutes. (Can be frozen at this point, if desired). Defrost, if frozen, and bake until thoroughly heated. Remove chicken pieces and stir in the sour cream. Place the chicken back in the sauce; sprinkle with parsley and serve with rice. Serves 8-12. NOTE: This recipe will hold in a 200° oven for 30 minutes.

Joanne Cohen (Mrs. Sheldon)
Mother of Poppy '86
Fresno, California

"This entree holds up so beautifully it's the perfect dish for a do-ahead occasion."

CHICKEN ALMONDINE

*8 whole chicken breasts
(8 pounds) halved, skinned
and boned
3 eggs
1 cup unsifted flour
1 cup milk
1 teaspoon grated lemon peel
2 teaspoons salt
¼ teaspoon pepper*

*3 cups dried breadcrumbs
2 cups sliced almonds
½ teaspoon tarragon, crushed
¾ cup butter
4 tablespoons salad oil
2 cups chicken broth
3 tablespoons minced parsley
Lemon wedges for garnish
Parsley for garnish*

Using the bottom of a small saucepan, slightly flatten chicken breast halves between 2 sheets of wax paper; set aside. For batter: In a blender container, combine eggs, flour, milk, lemon peel, 1 teaspoon of the salt and the pepper. Cover and blend until smooth. Place chicken in a large shallow dish. Pour batter over and stir until chicken is well coated. Cover and refrigerate at least 30 minutes or overnight. Combine bread crumbs, almonds, remaining 1 teaspoon salt and the tarragon on a large tray or pan. Remove chicken from batter, draining well. Coat chicken evenly in bread mixture. Set aside on waxed paper in a single layer. In a large skillet, heat 2 tablespoons of the butter and 1 tablespoon of the oil until foamy. Add 4 chicken breasts and saute 5 minutes on each side, turning once. Place chicken on paper towels in a large baking pan; keep warm. Wipe out skillet with paper towels. Repeat, sauteeing 3 more times with the remaining chicken. To skillet, add the chicken broth and lemon juice; heat to simmer. Stir in the remaining 4 tablespoons butter. (May be prepared in advance to this point. Place chicken, as it is cooked, in a 200° oven; keeps up to 3 hours. Leave sauce in skillet and cover; remove from heat. Set aside. At serving time, heat to boiling). Season to taste. Stir in parsley. To serve, arrange chicken on a serving platter. Spoon sauce over and garnish with lemon wedges and parsley.

*Kim Bowden
Class of '87
Monterey, California*

Ceremonies establishing the Santa Catalina Chapter of the Cum Laude Society were held on May 26, 1982. The Society, founded in 1906, is modeled on Phi Beta Kappa and has the purpose of encouraging and recognizing true scholarship. Santa Catalina joined 295 chapters established over the years in school across the nation noted for strong academic programs.

POULETTE EN FOILLETTE

6 chicken breasts
Salt
Pepper
Garlic
Onion powder
Oregano
¼ cup lemon juice
½ cup water

Paprika
2 tablespoons Italian seasoning
½ cup dry vermouth
½ pound phyllo dough
1½ cups melted butter
Fine bread crumbs
6 slices proscuitto
1½ pounds Mozzarella cheese,
    shredded

Season chicken breasts with salt, pepper, garlic, onion powder and ore-gano. Place in a roasting pan and pour in lemon juice and water. Sprinkle with paprika and Italian seasoning. Cover and bake at 375° for ½ hour. Add wine and continue baking for another ½ hour. Cool and remove from bone. To assemble, coat 1 sheet of phyllo dough with the melted butter and sprinkle lightly with bread crumbs. Place proscuitto and chicken pieces on 1 end of the phyllo dough; top with cheese. Fold the phyllo dough over, brush with butter and sprinkle with more cheese. Continue folding, tucking in the ends and coating with butter and cheese at each turn. Place the chicken rolls in a shallow pan, seam side down. Brush the tops with more melted butter. Sprinkle with paprika. Bake at 375° for 10-15 minutes or until golden brown. Use the drippings for gravy, if desired. Serves 6.

Carolyn Estrada (Mrs. Marshall)
Aunt of Kim Bowden '87
Whittier, California

POLLO DALLA COGNATA

1 (6 ounce) package long grain
    and wild rice
1 (10 ounce) can cream of
    celery soup
1 (10 ounce) can cream of
    mushroom soup

2 cups white wine
½ pound sliced mushrooms
8-10 pieces chicken breasts,
    boned and skinned

Combine the rice, soups, mushrooms and wine and place in a casserole dish. Lay chicken over the mixture and marinate all day. Bake, covered, in a 325° oven for 1 hour; remove cover and bake an additional half hour. Serves 8.

Melanie Dugan
Director of Lower School
Monterey, California

CHICKEN TARRAGON

2 chicken breasts, halved   2 cups white wine
2 tablespoons dried tarragon   Seasoned flour

Soak the tarragon in the wine for several hours to allow flavors to blend. Dredge the chicken in seasoned flour and brown in half butter and half vegetable oil. Place in an uncovered casserole and bake in a 350° oven for 30 minutes. Pour the mixture over the chicken and bake for an additional hour, basting frequently to keep moist. Serves 4.

Mrs. Price Berrien
Santa Barbara, California

CHICKEN OREGANO

1 chicken, cut up   2 teaspoons oregano
¼ cup lemon juice   1/3 cup olive oil
2 tablespoons chopped parsley ½ teaspoon salt
1 clove garlic, chopped   Dash of pepper

Make a marinade by combining the lemon juice, parsley, garlic, oregano, oil, salt and pepper. Marinate the chicken several hours, if possible. Broil first with the skin side down, brushing occasionally with the marinade. Turn chicken, brush again with the marinade and broil until done. Spoon the pan juice over the chicken and serve. Makes 4-6 servings.

Anne Anka (Mrs. Paul)
Mother of Alexandra, Alicia, Amanda, Anthea, Amelia
Carmel, California

CHICKEN SCALLOPPINE

2 whole chicken breasts, boned,   1/3 cup medium-dry sherry
  skinned and halved   Slivered ham, sauteed in butter
¼ cup butter   Sliced mushrooms, sauteed in
1 cup heavy cream   butter

Flatten the halved chicken breasts between 2 sheets of wax paper and sprinkle with salt and pepper; saute in the butter over moderately high heat for 1-2 minutes on each side. Transfer to a heated platter, cover and keep warm. To the butter and pan drippings, add the cream and sherry, cooking until thickened. To the sauce, add the ham, mushrooms and any accumulated juices from the chicken being kept warm. Pour sauce over the chicken breasts. Serves 4.

Anne Berolzheimer (Mrs. Philip)
Mother of Caroline '85
Stockton, California

CHICKEN PICCATA

4 whole chicken breasts,
  skinned, boned and halved
½ cup flour
1½ teaspoon salt
¼ teaspoon pepper
Paprika
¼ cup butter

1 tablespoon olive oil
2-4 tablespoons dry white wine
3 tablespoons fresh lemon juice
Lemon slices
3-4 tablespoons capers
Fresh parsley

Place chicken breasts between 2 sheets of wax paper and pound until thin. Combine the flour, salt, pepper and paprika in a bag. Add the chicken and coat well. Heat the butter and olive oil in a large skillet and saute the chicken breasts 2-3 minutes on each side. Do not overcook! Drain on paper towels and keep warm. Drain off all but 2 tablespoons of the butter and oil. Stir in wine and lemon juice, scraping browned bits off the sides of the pan. Return chicken to skillet and top with lemon slices and capers. Heat until sauce thickens. Garnish with parsley. Serves 4.

Mary Munhall Holl (Mrs. Stephen)
Class of '70
San Bernardino, California

LAST MINUTE CHICKEN

½ cup butter
1 cup apple butter
1 cup teriyaki sauce

1 tablespoon apricot jam
2 tablespoons chutney
Chicken pieces

Melt the butter and add to the apple butter, teriyaki sauce, jam, and chutney to make a marinade. Allow chicken to marinate in this mixture while preparing charcoal in the barbeque. When the coals are glowing, and white ash is showing (about 30-45 minutes), place the chicken on the grill, and baste frequently with the marinade while cooking. NOTE: Any flavor marmalade or jam may be substituted for the apricot jam. Chicken may be marinated several hours or even overnight if desired.

Sister Claire
Vice-Principal
Santa Catalina School

CHICKEN KIEV

8 whole chicken breasts, boned
1 cup butter
1 clove garlic, finely chopped
1 tablespoon chives, chopped
1 tablespoon parsley, chopped
1 teaspoon salt

½ teaspoon rosemary, crumbled
¼ teaspoon pepper
1 (2-3/8 ounce) package
    seasoned coating mix for
    chicken
¼ cup milk

Pound the chicken breasts to ¼ inch thickness between sheets of wax paper; set aside. Combine the butter, herbs and seasonings, blending well, and pat into a ¾ inch thick and 8 inch long roll on a sheet of wax paper. Freeze until hard; divide into 8 equal pieces. Place 1 piece of the herb-butter in the center of each flattened chicken breast and roll up, tucking the ends and securing with a toothpick. Preheat the oven to 400°. Moisten the chicken with the milk and coat heavily with the seasoned coating mix. Arrange in a single layer in a shallow baking dish, and bake for 45 minutes or until tender. This is good served with a parsley rice pilaf. Serves 8.

Mary Ann Taylor (Mrs. James)
Mother of James, Katie and Asher
Monterey, California

CHICKEN AUX DEUX MOUTARDES

¼ cup butter
8 chicken thighs
4 shallots, minced
1/3 cup Calvados, applejack or
    chicken broth
2 teaspoons Dijon mustard

2 teaspoons dry mustard
2 cups heavy cream
1/8 teaspoon mace
Salt
Pepper
Chopped parsley

Melt the butter in a skillet, add the chicken and saute gently, turning once, until golden brown (about 8 minutes). Add the shallots and Calvados; reduce heat, cover and simmer for 15 minutes. Remove chicken to a wam 9 x 13 inch casserole dish. Stir the mustards into the cream, pour into the skillet and boil vigorously for 5 minutes. Season with mace, salt and pepper; pour over the chicken. Garnish with parsley before serving. Serves 4. NOTE: Chicken breasts or other parts may be substituted for thighs.

Carolyn Humiston (Mrs. George)
Mother of Adrianne and Lauren
Carmel, California

DRUNKEN CHICKEN

4 whole chicken breasts, split
   deboned
2 tablespoons salad oil
2 tablespoons butter
1 onion, finely chopped
2 tablespoons chopped parsley
1 (16 ounce) can tomatoes, chopped

½ teaspoon ground cinnamon
¼ teaspoon ground cloves
1 cup dry sherry
½ cup raisins
¼ cup packed brown sugar
½ cup blanched slivered almonds

Remove skin from chicken; season with salt and pepper, dredge in flour. In a wide frying pan, heat the oil and butter over medium heat; add chicken pieces a few at a time and cook until lightly browned on both sides; transfer to a shallow casserole. Add onion, and more oil and butter if needed, to the pan; cook until onion is translucent. Add parsley, tomatoes and their liquid, cinnamon, cloves, sherry, raisins and sugar; simmer uncovered 15-20 minutes, stirring occasionally. Pour over chicken and sprinkle with almonds; bake uncovered at 375° for about 30 minutes or until done. Makes about 8 servings.

Bonnie McWhorter Bertelsen (Mrs. Jeffery)
Class of '63
Foster City, California

CHICKEN AND BEEF

5 ounces chipped beef, rinsed
8-10 skinned and boned chicken
   breasts halves
1 (16 ounce) container sour cream

2 (10 ounce) cans mushroom
   soup
8-10 strips bacon

Layer chipped beef on the bottom of a 12 x 16 inch casserole. Wrap a strip of bacon around each chicken breast and place on top of the chipped beef. Mix together the sour cream and mushroom soup and completely cover the chicken. Bake uncovered in a 275° oven for 3 hours. This can be made a day ahead. EDITORS' NOTE: Another method of preparation is to flatten the chicken breasts, top each with chipped beef which has been chopped, roll in the style of an enchilada and secure with a strip of bacon. Proceed as above.

Terry Byrne (Mrs. Gerald)
Mother of Tricia Nance
Carmel, California

CHICKEN SAUTE CHASSEUR

1 chicken, cut in pieces
Flour
Salt
Pepper
½ cup butter

2-3 green onions, finely chopped
½ pound sliced mushrooms
1 large tomato
½ cup sauterne

Coat the chicken with flour, season with salt and pepper and brown in the butter; remove to a Dutch oven. Saute the onion and mushrooms; peel, seed and chop the tomato. Combine the vegetables with the sauterne and pour over the chicken in the Dutch oven. Cover and simmer for 40 minutes. Serve over rice. NOTE: If a thicker sauce is desired, thicken with 1 teaspoon cornstarch and about 2 tablespoons water.

Nancy Rembert (Mrs. Paul)
Mother of Grey '81
Concord, Massachusetts

DELICIOUS BAKED CHICKEN

1 fryer, cut in serving pieces
Freshly ground pepper
Seasoned salt
Buttermilk

Sea Harvest rice flour
Minced parsley
Freshly grated Parmesan cheese

Season chicken with freshly ground black pepper and a little seasoned salt. Arrange in a flat baking dish. Cover with buttermilk and marinate overnight in the refrigerator. Shake off excess milk and dip each piece carefully into a mixture of rice flour, minced parsley and Parmesan cheese, covering well. Refrigerate for 2 hours or more. Heat vegetable oil in a heavy skillet and quickly saute the chicken until golden. Arrange chicken so that the pieces do not touch in a roasting pan or pyrex dish and bake in a preheated 375° oven for 45 minutes to an hour, or until chicken is crisp and very tender. Serve plain or with a light creamy gravy.

Norma Eversole (Mrs. Henry)
Mother of Alexandra '65, Gillian '69, Helena '70, Melinda '79
La Canada, California

OVEN FRIED CHICKEN PARMESAN

1 cup crushed packaged herb
  stuffing
2/3 cup grated Parmesan cheese
  parsley

1 clove garlic
½ cup butter, melted
1 (2½-3 pound) frying chicken,
  cut up

Combine stuffing crumbs, cheese, parsley and garlic. Dip chicken pieces in butter and roll in crumbs. Place the pieces, skin side up and not touching, in a shallow pan. Sprinkle with the remaining butter and crumbs. Bake in a 350° oven for 45 minutes or until the chicken is tender. Do not turn. Serves 4.

Linda Hall (Mrs. John)
Mother of Amy '86
San Francisco, California

"These are super for a picnic or bag lunch. They stay warm for quite some time."

CHICKEN BREAST IN FOIL BASKET

1 tablespoon butter, whipped
1 tablespoon shallots or green
onions, chopped
4 chicken breasts (about 3 ounces
each)
4 sheets of heavy duty foil

12 fresh mushrooms
½ cup dry white wine
Pinch of thyme or tarragon
Chopped parsley to taste
Vegetable salt to taste

Melt butter in skillet. Add the shallots and chicken and saute lightly. Grease 4 sheets of foil, 12 x 12 inches, with vegetable oil; place a chicken breast and 3 mushrooms in the center of each. Fold edges of foil upward to form a basket. Add wine to skillet and deglaze. Add the seasonings. Pour liquid into each foil basket and fold the edges together tightly to seal. Bake in a 350° oven for 1 hour. Open when ready to eat. Serves 4.

Marie Cressey Belden (Mrs. Lester M.)
Mother of Cressey Joy '87
Santa Rosa, California

HERBED CHICKEN

3 chicken breasts with skin
Poultry seasoning

Season all salt

Place chicken breasts in a greased 9 x 11 inch pan, skin side up. Sprinkle poultry seasoning and season-all lightly over each piece of chicken. Place in a 350° oven for 1 hour. Serves 3.

Elizabeth Pollock Dalton
Class of '74
Pebble Beach, California

GIGI'S SAUCY CHICKEN BAKE

1 teaspoon salt
½ teaspoon pepper
1 teaspoon paprika
½ teaspoon chili powder
2 tablespoons brown sugar
½ clove garlic
½ medium onion, finely chopped

1 cup catsup
1 teaspoon Dijon mustard
½ cup water
¼ cup butter
1/3 cup lemon juice
1 tablespoon Worcestershire
  sauce
1 whole chicken, cut up

Blend together the spices and sugar; add the garlic, onion, catsup, mustard and water. Heat to boiling, remove from the heat and add butter, lemon juice and Worcestershire sauce. Pour over the chicken. Bake in a 350° oven for 45 minutes to 1 hour.

Anne McFarlane (Mrs. W. F.)
Grandmother of Alison Gamble
Clovis, California

ZESTY CHICKEN

½ cup butter
1 medium onion, chopped
½ cup chopped celery
2 (15 ounce) cans tomato sauce

1 tablespoon brown sugar
1 tablespoon sugar
¼ cup red wine vinegar
4 chicken legs with thighs

Saute the onions and celery in the butter until soft. Add the tomato sauce, sugars and vinegar and cook over low heat for 20 minutes. Remove skin from chicken and place in a baking dish. Cover with sauce and bake for 1½ hours in a 350° oven. Serves 4. NOTE: This can be made ahead and reheated and is excellent with rice.

Grace Knoop (Mrs. Frederick)
Mother of Laura '72
Atherton, California

CHICKEN SAFFRON

1 medium onion, sliced
2 tablespoons butter
1 frying chicken, cut up
1 bay leaf
2 tablespoons chopped parsley
Salt

Pepper
1 teaspoon paprika
Large pinch of saffron
1 (10 ounce) can mushroom
  soup
3 tablespoons sour cream

In a large skillet, melt the butter and lightly brown the onion. Add the chicken, bay leaf, parsley, salt, pepper, paprika and saffron. Pour in ½ cup hot water; cover and simmer until tender, about 30 minutes. Remove chicken from skillet and blend in the soup and sour cream; return chicken to pan and reheat. This is excellent served with or over rice. Serves 4.

Mary Ellen Parsons (Mrs. William)
Mother of Rachael
Pacific Grove, California

CHICKEN FRICASEE CASSEROLE

4 pounds chicken pieces
½ - ¾ cup flour
1 teaspoon salt
2 teaspoons paprika
¼ teaspoons pepper
¼ teaspoon thyme
¼ teaspoon garlic salt

1 tablespoon instant minced onion
3 (10 ounce) cans cream of chicken soup
¼ cup dry sherry
1 tablespoon parsley flakes
1 (16 ounce) can whole carrots
1 (16 ounce) can whole onions

Coat chicken with flour, salt, pepper, paprika, thyme and garlic salt. Arrange in a single layer in a shallow baking dish; sprinkle with minced onion. Combine soups and sherry; pour over chicken and onion and sprinkle with parsley flakes. Bake in a 400° oven for 20 minutes uncovered. Cover with foil or a lid and bake at 350° for 30 minutes. Uncover and add onions and carrots. Cook 15-20 minutes longer until the chicken is tender. Serves 6-8.

Jane Howard Goodfellow (Mrs. John)
Class of '56
Mother of Joan '80
Claremont, California

CHICKEN IN ASPARAGUS CREAM

1 small onion, chopped
1 bell pepper, chopped
2 tablespoons butter
1 (10 ounce) can cream of asparagus soup

¼ cup chicken broth
1 cup whipping cream
1 cooked chicken

Cut or shred the chicken into bite-sized pieces; set aside. Saute the onion and pepper in the butter. Dissolve the soup in the chicken broth and add the whipping cream. Add the chicken and the sauteed onion and pepper. Mix well and bake in an oven-proof dish, covered, at 350° for 20 minutes.

Lucie G. deGuajardo (Mrs. Carlos)
Mother of Gabriela '84
Monterey, Mexico

CHICKEN BAKED IN ZINFANDEL

2 broilers or young fryers,
quartered
½ teaspoon salt
1/8 teaspoon freshly ground
black pepper

1 cup flour
¼ cup vegetable oil
1-1½ cups Taylor California
Zinfandel
1 small onion, sliced

Season chicken with salt and pepper and coat generously with flour. Lightly brown chicken in oil a few pieces at a time in a heavy fry pan, removing pieces as they brown; add more oil only as needed. Arrange chicken, skin side up, in a shallow preheated baking pan. Pour Zinfandel over all. Bake in a 425° oven for 30-45 minutes or until done, baste occasionally. Add more wine as necessary. Arrange sliced onion rings on top of the chicken during the last 15 minutes of baking. Serve sizzling hot. 4-8 servings.

Monterey Vineyard
Hayward, California

"My sisters and I served this dish for our mother's seventieth birthday party, and it was a big hit!"

CHICKEN STRATA

24 slices day-old white bread
8 cups diced cooked chicken
2 cups chopped onion
2 large green peppers, chopped
2 cups finely chopped celery
2 cups mayonnaise

1 tablespoon salt
¼ teaspoon pepper
6 eggs, slightly beaten
6 cups milk
4 (10 ounce) cans cream of
mushroom soup
2 cups cheddar cheese

Trim crusts from bread and cut bread into 1-inch cubes. Place half the cubes in the bottom of 2 ungreased 9 x 13 inch casseroles. Combine the chicken, onion, peppers, celery, mayonnaise, salt and pepper and spread evenly over the bread cubes. Place remaining bread cubes over the chicken mixture. Combine eggs and milk and pour over all. Cover and refrigerate overnight or up to 48 hours in advance. Before baking, bring casserole to room temperature. Spoon soup over the top. Bake in a 325° oven for 60 minutes or until set. Top with grated cheese and return to oven until cheese is melted. Serves 24. NOTE: Casserole will drip during baking. To save oven, place foil underneath the casserole dishes. This recipe can be cut in half very successfully.

Jane Howard Goodfellow (Mrs. John)
Class of '56
Mother of Joan '80
Claremont, California

"A great party dish and very popular with the men. It tastes even better if made the day before!"

CHICKEN AND SHRIMP CASSEROLE

*1 pound raw shrimp, shelled
and deveined
2½ teaspoons salt
¾ cup uncooked long grain rice
4 chicken breasts, split
3 tablespoons salad oil
½ cup chopped onion
½ cup chopped green pepper*

*1 (10 ounce) can tomato soup
1 cup heavy cream
½ cup dry sherry
½ teaspoon Worcestershire sauce
¼ teaspoon pepper
¼ teaspoon thyme
2 tablespoons chopped parsley*

Bring to a boil 1 quart of water, add the shrimp and 1 teaspoon of the salt; bring to boiling again, reduce heat and simmer for 10 minutes, covered. Drain. Cook rice according to package directions. Wash chicken, pat dry. Heat oil in a Dutch oven and brown chicken well. Remove chicken and discard all but 2 tablespoons of the drippings. Saute onion and pepper for 5 minutes; remove from heat. Stir in soup, cream, sherry, the remaining 1½ teaspoons salt, Worcestershire sauce, pepper and thyme until well blended. Add the cooked rice, chicken and shrimp. Bake, uncovered, for 60 minutes at 350° or until the chicken is tender. Sprinkle with parsley. Serves 6-8.

*Marsha Deming (Mrs. David)
Mother of Kathleen '84
Reno, Nevada*

PARTY CHICKEN

*2 tablespoons butter
4 strips bacon, minced
1 small yellow onion, chopped
1 carrot, diced
Garlic salt
1 cut-up fryer
2 tablespoons flour*

*2 tablespoons minced parsley
Freshly ground pepper
1 teaspoon marjoram
½ bay leaf
1 teaspoon salt
1½ cups dry white wine
1 (2½ ounce) can mushrooms*

Melt the butter in a large frying pan and cook the bacon, onion, carrot and garlic salt until the bacon is done; remove from pan using a slotted spoon. Brown the chicken in the butter and bacon drippings remaining in the skillet; remove. Blend the flour and seasonings with the remaining drippings; stir in the wine and drained mushrooms. Return the chicken, bacon and sauteed vegetables to the pan and simmer for 1 hour. If needed, the thickness of the gravy may be corrected.

*Jeanette Nordstrom (Mrs. Gerald)
Mother of Adrienne '85
Fresno, California*

"This recipe is for a large party of 15 or more. For normal family use, reduce quantities to one-third of amounts shown."

CHINESE CHICKEN

8 pounds chicken breasts,
  skinned and boned
1 cup salad oil
1½ cups sliced green onions
¾ cup soy sauce

1½ cups dry or medium sherry
1½ cups chicken stock
3 (9 ounce) cans crushed
  pineapple

Dredge chicken breasts with flour. Heat oil in a large heavy skillet; brown chicken slowly on all sides. Sprinkle onions over chicken. Add soy sauce, wine and stock; cover and simmer gently for 30 to 45 minutes, or until chicken is tender, turning and basting chicken occasionally. (Simmering may be done in a baking dish in the oven at 275° if preferred). Remove chicken to a heated platter and keep warm. Add undrained pineapple to drippings in skillet; heat thoroughly. Pour sauce over chicken or pass separately. Serve with rice, peas or green beans with mushrooms and a fruit salad. NOTE: For onion haters, equal parts of diced pepper and celery may be substituted for the green onion. Hint: To easily bone the chicken, parboil for 5 minutes.

Mr. Robert S. Beaumont
San Carlos, California

CHICKEN CHOW MEIN
(American version!)

1 (3-4 pound) chicken
1 (5 ounce) can chow mein
  noodles
1 (8 ounce) can sliced water
  chestnuts
2 (10 ounce) cans mushroom soup
2 cups coarsely chopped celery
4 slices green pepper

½ cup diced onions
1 carrot, grated
½ cup sherry
1 (3 ounce) can chow mein
  noodles
¼ cup sliced almonds
1 (11 ounce) can mandarin
  oranges

Cook the chicken and cut into bite-sized pieces; combine with the 5 ounce can chow mein noodles, the drained water chestnuts, the undiluted soup, celery, green pepper, onions, carrots, and sherry. Place in a shallow casserole dish. (Casserole may be frozen or refrigerated at this point.) Evenly distribute the 3 ounce can of chow mein noodles and the almonds over the chicken mixture and arrange the orange slices attractively on the top. Bake in a 350° oven about 35-45 minutes, adjusting time if casserole has been refrigerated or frozen. Serves 6-8.

Teisah Miller
Monterey, California

HAWAIIAN CHICKEN WAIKIKI

1 cup flour
2 chickens, cut up
Salt
Pepper
1 (20 ounce) can sliced pineapple
1 cup sugar
2 tablespoons cornstarch

¾ cup cider vinegar
1 tablespoon soy sauce
¼ teaspoon ginger
1 chicken bouillon cube
1 large green pepper, cut
 crosswise

Coat the chicken with flour, salt and pepper, and fry in hot oil. Drain the pineapple, pouring juice into a 2-cup measure. Add enough water to make 1½ cups. In a saucepan, combine the sugar, cornstarch, pineapple syrup, vinegar, soy sauce, ginger and bouillon cube; bring to a boil and pour over the chicken. Bake, uncovered, about 30 minutes in a 350° oven. Top with rings of green pepper and pineapple and bake an additional 10 minutes. Serve with rice, green beans with almonds and a fruit salad. Serves 6.

Marlene Kellogg (Mrs. Clarence)
Mother of Kellene '79 and Christina '85
Pacific Grove, California

SOY BAKED CHICKEN THIGHS

2½ pounds skinned chicken
½ cup soy sauce
½ cup soy sauce

1 (16 ounce) can sliced pineapple
Sesame seeds

Marinate thighs in soy sauce for 1 hour. Place pineapple slices in a 2 quart dish. Arrange chicken over pineapple and sprinkle with sesame seeds. Cover with a paper towel and bake in a microwave oven on high for 16-18 minutes, or 7 minutes per pound. Serves 4.

Brenda Guy (Mrs. Michael)
Mother of Jennifer
Pebble Beach, California

Independent Study and Independent Seminar for Santa Catalina Seniors was inaugurated in the Spring Semester of 1969. Although the approach and goals have been redefined and sharpened over the years, its value to the students is the opportunity for each to concentrate in a particular field that could possibly lead to a future career. Choices range from the professions, such as law, medicine, and education to government, drama, dance, social service, communication and the fine arts. Each participant is expected to submit a written and/or oral report which evaluates her project, as experienced.

CHICKEN CASSEROLE

1 (10 ounce) can cream of
mushroom soup
1 (10 ounce) can cream of
chicken soup
10 ounces milk
1 (4 ounce) can chopped green
chiles

1 (8 ounce) can chopped water
chestnuts
6 corn tortillas
6 chicken breasts, cooked and
shredded
1 cup grated cheddar cheese

In a saucepan over low heat, blend the soups, milk, chiles and water
chestnuts. Layer in an oiled 6 x 10 inch casserole half the tortillas, half
the chicken and half of the soup mixture; repeat. Cover with the grated
cheese and bake in a 350° oven for 20 minutes. Serves 6.

Charlene Harvey (Mrs. James)
Mother of Fiona Dorst '84
San Francisco, California

CHICKEN TORTILLA CASSEROLE

1 dozen corn tortillas
1 (7 ounce) can diced green
chiles
1 large onion, finely chopped
1 pound Monterey jack cheese,
grated
1 cup longhorn cheese, grated

1 (10 ounce) can cream of
chicken soup
1 (10 ounce) can cream of
mushroom soup
1 cup ripe olives, sliced
1 chicken, cooked, boned and
shredded

Fry tortillas lightly, one at a time, in oil. Blot with a paper towel and
line the bottom of a 9 x 15 inch casserole dish, overlapping slightly to
cover completely. Sprinkle a portion of the onions, chile, jack cheese
and chicken evenly over the tortillas. Combine the soups with 1 can of
water, heat and generously cover the chicken. Continue the process,
beginning with the tortillas, until there are several layers and the dish is
full, finishing with the remaining soup mixture. Garnish with the longhorn cheese and olives. Bake in a 350° oven for about 30 minutes until
the cheese is melted and the flavors are blended. Serves 6-8.

Manijeh Aghazadeh (Mrs. Kioumars)
Mother of Komran
Carmel, California

CHICKEN VIVA

4 whole chicken breasts
1 dozen corn tortillas
1 (10 ounce) can cream of
    chicken soup
1 (10 ounce) can cream of
    mushroom soup

1 cup milk
1 onion, grated
1 (7 ounce) can green chili salsa
1 (4 ounce) can whole green
    chiles
1 pound cheddar cheese,
    shredded

Wrap the chicken in foil and bake in a 350° oven for 1 hour; bone and cut into large strips. Tear tortillas into 1-inch pieces. Combine all the ingredients in a large bowl, mixing well. Place in a buttered casserole and bake for 1¼ hours. Serves 8. NOTE: a 4-ounce can of green chile may be used instead of a 7-ounce can if a milder flavor is desired. This recipe may be made and refrigerated up to 24 hours in advance. Increase the baking time slightly.

Rita Bixley Smith (Mrs. Llewellyn)
Mother of Sarah '85
Corona del Mar, California

FIESTA LASAGNA

6 chicken breast halves
2 (10 ounce) cans tomatoes
    with jalapeno peppers
1 (2¼ ounce) can sliced olives
8 (8") flour tortillas

2 large avocados, peeled and
    sliced
2 cups sour cream
1½ pounds Jack cheese, shredded

Cook, skin and debone the chicken; shred into bite-sized pieces. Combine tomatoes and olives, lightly crushing tomatoes with the back of a spoon. Spread a thin layer of the tomato mixture in the bottom of a 13 x 9 inch baking dish. Arrange four of the tortillas over the tomatoes, overlapping as needed to cover dish. Layer in order: one-half of the tomato mixture, one-half of the chicken, one-half the avocado slices, one-half of the sour cream, and one-half of the cheese, evenly distributing each layer over the previous one. Repeat layers, beginning with the remaining four tortillas. Bake uncovered in a 325° oven for 35-45 minutes. Cut into squares to serve. Makes 8-10 servings.

Ann Quinlan Knokey (Mrs. David)
Class of '66
Northridge, California

SWISS ENCHILADAS

1 onion, chopped
Cooking oil
1 clove garlic, minced
2 cups tomato puree
2 (4 ounce) cans chopped green
chiles
2 cups chopped cooked chicken

Salt
12 flour tortillas
6 chicken bouillon cubes
3 cups half-and-half cream
½ pound Monterey jack cheese,
grated

Saute onion in 2 tablespoons oil until soft. Add garlic, tomato puree, green chiles and chicken. Season with salt to taste and simmer 10 minutes. Fry tortillas in 1 inch hot oil. Do not let them become crisp, as they are to be rolled. Dissolve bouillon cubes in hot cream. Dip each tortilla in cream, cover generously with chicken filling and roll up. Arrange rolls in baking dish and pour remaining cream mixture over them. Top with cheese. Bake at 350° for 30 minutes. Freezes well. Serves 6.

Terri Correll Brazinsky (Mrs. John)
Mother of April
Carmel, California

"This recipe is called 'Early California' because any late-comers will find them all gone!"

EARLY CALIFORNIA EGG ENCHILADAS

12 hard cooked eggs
¾ cup sour cream
1 (10 ounce) can hot enchilada
sauce
1 (16 ounce) can regular
enchilada sauce

1 dozen sturdy flour tortillas
¾ cup finely chopped onion
¾ cup chopped green chiles
¾ cup sliced green olives
2 cups grated cheddar cheese

Coarsely chop the hard cooked eggs and blend with the sour cream. Combine and heat the enchilada sauces. For each enchilada, do the following: Dip each tortilla in the heated enchilada sauce to soften, shaking off the excess sauce. Place 2 tablespoons of the egg mixture, 1 tablespoon of the chopped onion, 1 teaspoon of the chiles and 1 tablespoon of the olives down the center of the tortilla. Roll the enchilada and tuck the ends; place in an oiled 7 x 11 inch baking dish and cover with the remaining enchilada sauce and 2 tablespoons of cheese on each enchilada. Bake in a 325° oven for 20 minutes or until heated through. Serves 6. NOTE: Traditionally, enchiladas have open ends, however cooking is easier and neater with the ends tucked in as with burritos.

Mr. Wally S. Bryant
Pebble Beach, California

MARLENE'S AUNTIE PAULINE'S TAMALE PIE

1 clove garlic
½ cup chopped onion
4 tablespoons drippings
1 (20 ounce) can cream style corn
1 pound hamburger
1 (29 ounce) can tomatoes

2 cups yellow cornmeal
2 cups tomato juice
Dash of cayenne
1 (4 ounce) can black olives
1 tablespoon chili powder
Salt

Cook garlic and onion in drippings until soft; add meat and brown slightly. Add corn, tomatoes and seasonings and simmer for 20 minutes. Add cornmeal gradually, stirring constantly. Mix in the tomato juice and olives. Pour into a 7 x 11 inch buttered baking dish and bake at 350° for 30 minutes. Serves 6-8.

Marlene Kellogg (Mrs. Clarence)
Mother of Kellene '79 and Christina '85
Pacific Grove, California

TACO PIE

1 (8 ounce) can refrigerated
    crescent rolls
2 cups crushed corn chips
1 cup sour cream
1 (8 ounce) can refried beans
1-1½ pounds ground beef

1½ packages taco seasoning mix
½ cup water
2 cups grated cheese
1 (4 ounce) can sliced olives
1 tomato, sliced
Lettuce

To make a crust, press crescent roll dough in a greased 9-inch deep dish pie pan. Sprinkle 1 cup of the crushed corn chips onto the dough. Mix together the sour cream and refried beans and pour into the pie pan until the pan is half full (all of the mixture will not be used). Brown the ground beef, add the taco seasoning mix and water, and simmer until the water has evaporated; pour over the bean mixture in the pie shell. Add the grated cheese, then the sliced olives; sprinkle with the remaining corn chips. Bake in a 350° oven for 30 minutes or until the cheese is melted. Before serving, top with sliced tomato and lettuce. Serves 5-6. NOTE: This can be made ahead and refrigerated for up to 24 hours before baking. This recipe is very adaptable; substitutions or additions may be made as desired.

Julie Lambert
Class of '80
Corvallis, Oregon

ENCHILADAS RANCHERAS

¼ pound cheddar cheese,   12 corn tortillas
  shredded   Ranchera sauce
1 pound jack cheese, shredded Additional jack cheese
4-6 green onions, finely chopped Sour cream
½ cup butter, softened   Guacamole

Mix the cheeses, onion and butter until well blended. Roll mixture into 12 sticks the length of a tortilla. Soften tortillas in hot oil; drain. Place a cheese stick on each tortilla and roll up. Place side by side in an oiled baking dish and cover with Ranchera sauce. Top with additional cheese. Bake in a 450° oven for 15 minutes. Serve with sour cream and guacamole. Serves 6.

RANCHERA SAUCE

¼ cup oil   1 teaspoon garlic powder
½ onion, chopped   ¼ teaspoon oregano
1½ stalks celery, chopped   ½ teaspoon MSG
1 green pepper, chopped   2 cups water
¼ cup flour   1½ teaspoon chicken stock base
¼ teaspoon marjoram   ½ cup chicken broth
½ teaspoon salt   2 cups crushed tomatoes
¾ teaspoon pepper

Heat oil and add the onion, celery and green pepper. Cook until vegetables are soft and onion is transparent. Mix together the flour and spices. Slowly add water and stir until smooth. Combine the vegetables, flour mixture and remaining ingredients. Cook over medium heat, stirring occasionally until the mixture boils and thickens, about 1 hour.

Carolyn Estrada (Mrs. Marshall)
Aunt of Kim Bowden '87
Whittier, California

BAKED CHILE RELLENOS

1 (7 ounce) can whole green 1 cup flour
  chiles   2 teaspoons salt
1 pound sharp cheddar cheese 4 cups milk
4 eggs

In the bottom of a 3-quart buttered casserole, arrange the chiles which have been rinsed, seeded and cut into 2-inch pieces. Cut the cheese into long fingers and arrange in an even layer over the chili peppers. Beat the eggs slightly, then beat in the milk, flour and salt and pour over the cheese. Bake in a 350° oven for 45-50 minutes or until custard is set. Serves 6.

Polly Reese (Mrs. Bob)
Mother of Heather
Monterey, California

CHILE RELLENO CASSEROLE

1 cup tomato sauce	*2 tablespoons flour*
2 (7 ounce) cans green chiles	*1 cup canned milk*
1 pound grated cheddar cheese	*4 eggs, slightly beaten*
1 pound grated Monterey jack cheese	*1 cup mild Ortega green chile salsa*

Preheat oven to 350°. Wash chiles and remove seeds. Layer the cheeses and chiles in a lightly buttered 9 x 12 inch casserole. Mix the eggs, milk and flour and pour over the cheese and chiles. Bake for 30 minutes; remove from oven and pour a mixture of tomato sauce and salsa evenly over the casserole. Bake 20 minutes more. Allow to rest 10 minutes before serving.

Diane Ortner (Mrs. Paul)
Mother of Kristin '85 and Stephanie '85
Hillsborough, California

EASY CHILE RELLENO

2 pounds bulk pork sausage	*¼ cup flour*
1 small onion, chopped	*2 cups Monterey jack cheese, grated*
2/3 cup bottled Taco sauce or relish	*2 (7 ounce) cans whole green chiles, seeded*
¾ cup milk	
4 eggs	

Cook pork until crumbly and well browned; add onion and saute until transparent. Drain fat, add the taco sauce and cook over medium heat until mixture thickens. Beat together the milk, egg and flour; add cheese. Layer chiles, pork mixture, cheese and egg mixture in a greased 9 x 11 inch baking pan. Bake in a 350° oven for 45 minutes to 1 hour. Let stand 5 to 10 minutes before serving. Makes 6-8 servings. This can be frozen prior to baking. Put in oven frozen and double the baking time.

Mrs. Frank G. Pitts
Aunt of Holly Ayn Guy
Pauma Valley, California

CHILI

3 pounds ground beef
3 medium sized onions, chopped
3 cloves garlic, chopped
3 green peppers, chopped
3 (16 ounce) cans tomato sauce
½ teaspoon celery seed
2 teaspoons crushed red pepper
2 tablespoons chili powder
1 bay leaf

2 teaspoons salt
1 teaspoon oregano
1 teaspoon ground cumin
1/8 teaspoon basil
1 small can mushrooms
1 teaspoon sugar
2 cups beef stock
½ teaspoon black pepper
6 tablespoons cornmeal

Saute the onions and garlic in oil until the onions are transparent; add the ground beef and brown. Add the remaining ingredients except the cornmeal; reduce heat and cook for 1 hour, stirring occasionally; skim off fat. Blend cornmeal with water until it becomes a thin, pouring consistency add to the chili approximately 10 minutes before serving, stirring constantly. NOTE: I like to add a touch of cayenne pepper to make it even spicier.

Joanne May
Class of '71
Oakland, California

CROCK POT CHILI

2½-3 pound chuck steak
1 cup chopped onions
2-3 cloves garlic, chopped
3-4 tablespoons chili powder
1½ teaspoon cumin
1 teaspoon oregano
½ teaspoon salt
1½ teaspoons pepper

42 ounces canned kidney beans
   drained
1 (16 ounce) can whole
   tomatoes, drained
1 (8 ounce) can tomato paste
1 (8 ounce) can beef broth
1 tablespoon flour
2 tablespoons cornmeal

Brown the chuck steak which has been cut into 1 inch cubes, with half the onions and garlic; drain. Combine all the ingredients, including the browned meat, in the crock pot and cook for 2 hours on low and 1 hour on high, or for 4-5 hours on low. Serves 6. NOTE: Flavor improves with age, even better the next night!

Mr. Stephen Holl
Husband of Mary Munhall Holl '70
San Bernardino, California

"This is a recipe that makes a large amount of chili, perfect for taking along to the mountains for a ski weekend, or for those times when you don't feel like cooking everyday. Freezes well, too."

CHILI

3-4 pounds hamburger
2 red onions, chopped
2 packages Lawry's Chili mix
4 (15 ounce) cans chili beans

2 (15 ounce) cans dark red kidney beans
3 (15 ounce) cans stewed tomatoes
1 can chili peppers, optional

Brown the hamburger and onions; drain and return to heat and season with the chili mix; add the undrained chili beans and the kidney beans and mix well. Salt and pepper to taste. Stir in broken or chopped stewed tomatoes with their juice, and bring to a boil. Add 1 cup water or more for desired consistency. Boil, reduce heat and simmer for 5 hours. Serves 8 generously.

Molly Mahaney Wardell (Mrs. Keith)
Class of '75
San Francisco, California

CHILI

3 pounds lean ground beef
2 pounds lean ground pork
4 tablespoons oil
2 cups chopped onions
4 cups canned, crushed tomatoes
8 tablespoons chili powder
2 teaspoons white pepper
1 teaspoon ground coriander
1 teaspoon ground cumin

1 tablespoon oregano
2 bay leaves
8 cloves garlic, crushed
1½ tablespoons salt
3 tablespoons vinegar
3 tablespoons sugar
2 tablespoons prepared mustard
2 tablespoons Worcestershire sauce
4 cups beef broth or consomme

Fry the ground meats in the oil until browned. Saute the chopped onions and add to the meat. Stir in all remaining ingredients and bake in a 325° oven for 3-4 hours in a large casserole. Serve with kidney beans and corn bread. NOTE: Bake in a 5 quart steel or enameled pan. Do not use aluminum.

Carolyn Wuerflein
Mother of Marlene Wakefield '84
Los Gatos, California

COWBOY STEW

6 slices bacon
1 cup sliced onion
½ cup chopped green pepper
1 clove garlic, chopped
1½ pounds ground chuck
2 (29 ounce) cans tomatoes
2 cups cubed pared potatoes

1 teaspoon salt
¼ teaspoon pepper
1 tablespoon chili powder
1 (12 ounce) can whole kernel
   corn
1 (16 ounce) can red kidney
   beans

Cook and crumble the bacon, reserving drippings. Saute the onion, green pepper and garlic in the bacon drippings until tender. Add the ground chuck and brown; stir in the tomatoes, potatoes, salt, pepper and chili powder. Cover and simmer 30 minutes, add the drained corn and kidney beans and simmer an additional 15 minutes. Garnish with the crumbled bacon.

Cynthia Mock
San Mateo, California

SOURDOUGH PIZZA

1 pound ground beef
½ teaspoon salt
1 large loaf sourdough bread
1 pound cheddar cheese, shredded
1 cup green onions, sliced

5 large mushrooms, sliced
½ teaspoon oregano
1 (8 ounce) can tomato sauce
2 tablespoons olive oil

Brown the ground beef, season with salt, and drain. Cut the loaf of bread in half lengthwise. Cover each half evenly in order, with the cheese, the ground beef, the green onions, the sliced mushrooms, the oregano and the olive oil. Bake for 5-8 minutes in a preheated 450° oven.

Mrs. Robert Spencer
Sonoma, California

SWEDISH MEATBALLS

2 slices fresh bread
1 egg, beaten
1 small onion, minced
1 teaspoon sugar
1 cup milk

1½ pounds ground chuck
Salt
Pepper
½ teaspoon allspice
2 (10 ounce) cans beef or
   mushroom gravy

Tear bread into small pieces and combine with the egg, onion, sugar, milk, ground chuck and spices. Chill in refrigerator at least 1 hour. Form into small balls and brown in butter. To serve, add the meatballs to the warmed gravy. NOTE: For richer flavor, used canned milk in place of the regular milk. These meatballs freeze well.

Grace Beacham (Mrs. Richard)
Mother of August and Amy
Carmel, California

"This was a favorite of my mother when I was growing up. We all loved it because of the name and because it was great tasting too! This dish is especially good for buffet dinner parties as you can prepare everything ahead of time and just let it stew. It is extra good on the second or third day when all of the flavors have become acquainted."

MEAL BALL GLOP

2 cups stale bread
(½ white, ½ rye)
Milk
2 eggs, beaten
2 teaspoons salt
½ teaspoon pepper
1 teaspoon MSG
2 pounds ground beef

Flour
4 medium zucchini sliced
1 medium eggplant, peeled and
cubed
2 large onions, sliced
3 cloves garlic, crushed
2 bell peppers, cut in strips
6 ripe tomatoes

Soak bread in milk until soft; combine well with eggs, salt, pepper and MSG, and add the ground beef. Shape into large meat balls and brown; remove. Lightly flour the zucchini and eggplant, set aside. Saute the onion and garlic in oil until the onion is soft. Add the eggplant and bell pepper; cover and cook slowly for 30 minutes, stirring occasionally. Add the tomatoes and zucchini and salt and pepper to taste. Cook, covered, for 15-20 minutes, stirring occasionally; add meat balls and cook an additional 15 minutes. Serve over rice (especially good if 1 teaspoon cumin seed is added with 1 tablespoon oil and mixed with the raw rice before cooking). Serves 6-8. NOTE: Canned tomatoes may be substituted for the fresh.

Cameron Miller Menghetti (Mrs. Charles)
Class of '76
Long Beach, California

SAUERBRATEN LOAF

2 pounds ground beef
1 cup bread crumbs
1 cup crushed ginger snaps
½ cup milk
½ cup finely chopped onions

2 eggs
Salt
Pepper
1/3 cup red wine vinegar
Dash ground cloves

Combine all ingredients and bake for 1 hour at 350° in a loaf pan. Serve with sour cream. Serves 8.

Mrs. Francis E. Sammons, Jr.
Menlo Park, California

"This is my mother's recipe and my husband's favorite meat entree. My mother serves this with garden fresh vegetables, salad, and her special soda biscuits for an early Sunday dinner."

DICKIE'S MEAT LOAF

4 slices dry bread or toast,
    broken in pieces
1 cup warm milk
2 beaten eggs
¼ cup minced onion
1 pound ground beef
½ pound ground pork

½ pound ground veal
2 teaspoons pepper
1 tablespoon salad oil
1 cup chili sauce
1 bouillon cube
½ cup hot water

Soften bread in milk; add eggs, onion, meats and pepper; mix thoroughly. Form into an 8 inch square loaf in a 9 inch square pan. Spread with salad oil, then with chili sauce. Dissolve the bouillon cube in the hot water and pour around loaf. Bake in a moderate oven (350°) 1½-2 hours, basting every 15 minutes. NOTE: Be sure to use ground pork, not sausage.

Sally Smith Rhodes (Mrs. Richard)
Class of '57
Salinas, California

Since its inception in 1953, the Santa Catalina Summer Camp for girls ages 8 through 14 has been very popular. Campers come together from many parts of the country and abroad and form a close knit camp community. A riding program, tennis clinic, dance and drama workshop, and academics are among the many offerings.

"For as long as I can remember, Halloween has been celebrated in our house by a special dinner to which we children each invited a friend and her whole family. Pride of place at this feast has always been a handsome stuffed pumpkin, delicious and impressive. The size of the pumpkin is limited only by the size of your parboiling kettle. We always have a large pumpkin and increase the recipe accordingly."

STUFFED PUMPKIN

1 beautifully shaped 10"
  pumpkin
Salt
3 pounds ground round
2½ cups chopped onion
1 green pepper, chopped
1 red pepper, chopped
2 teaspoons olive oil
1 teaspoon vinegar
2 teaspoons oregano

1 teaspoon black pepper
Dash of tabasco
2 large cloves garlic, minced
¾ cup raisins
½ cup pimento-stuffed olives,
  sliced
2 teaspoons capers
1 (8 ounce) can tomato sauce
3 eggs, beaten

Cut a 5" lid off the pumpkin and save. Scoop out the seeds and scrape clean. Place in a large pan of hot salted water to cover pumpkin. Bring to a boil and cook until somewhat tender when pierced with a fork, about 25 minutes. It must be firm and keep its shape well. Drain thoroughly and sprinkle insides with a little salt. Saute together the ground round, onions, and peppers and cook, stirring, until the meat is brown and crumbly. Mix together the olive oil, vinegar, oregano, pepper, tabasco and garlic and add to meat along with the raisins, green olives, capers, and tomato sauce. Mix well, cover and cook gently for 20 minutes. Remove from heat, cool slightly and add the beaten eggs. Fill the cooked pumpkin with the meat stuffing, pressing down firmly. Cover loosely with the pumpkin lid. Place in a shallow greased baking pan and bake in a 350° oven for 1 hour. Support the bottom with a wide spatula and carefully lift the hot pumpkin onto a serving platter garnished with autumn leaves. Cut wedges from pumpkin and serve with tossed green salad and crisp french bread. Serves 8. NOTE: For best flavor, prepare the meat filling a day in advance, or it can be made ahead and frozen.

Eleanor Zuckerman
Class of '80
Stockton, California

"A rice pie with an unexpected sizzling brown beef crust. The filling — ah-h-h! Tender, light, rosy and spicy, hearty with sunny melted cheese. My mother cooked this as a traditional Hallowe'en dinner. For Hallowe'en, garnish with sliced black olives on top of the pie for a Hallowe'en face — a Jack-o-lantern."

COUNTRY PIE

CRUST:
½ cup tomato sauce
½ cup bread crumbs
1 pound ground beef
¼ cup chopped onion
¼ cup chopped green pepper

1½ teaspoons salt
1/8 teaspoon pepper
1/8 teaspoon oregano
Dash of chili powder

FILLING:
1-1/3 cups minute rice
1½ cups tomato sauce
½ teaspoon salt

1 cup water
1 cup grated cheddar cheese
Dash of chili powder, optional

For crust: Combine all of the crust ingredients in a bowl and mix well with a fork. Pat the meat mixture gently into the bottom and sides of a well greased 9-inch pie plate. For filling: Combine the minute rice, tomato sauce, salt, water and ½ cup of the cheese. Spoon the rice mixture into the meat shell. Cover with aluminum foil. Bake at 350° for 25 minutes. Uncover and top with the remaining cheese. Bake, uncovered, 10-15 minutes more. Serves 5-6.

Kellene Kellogg Simon (Mrs. Michael)
Class of '79
Davis, California

CASSEROLE PEPPER STEAK

1 large flank steak
2 teaspoons cornstarch
1 teaspoon ground ginger
1 teaspoon sugar

3 tablespoons soy sauce
1 tablespoon sherry
¼ cup peanut oil
4 large green peppers

Place flank steak in the freezer until partially frozen, about 45 minutes. Trim off and discard any excess surface fat on the meat and slice steak on an angle into very thin crosswise pieces. Stir together the cornstarch, ginger, sugar, soy sauce and sherry until smooth. Mix in the meat and marinate for at least 20 minutes. Seed peppers and cut into ½ inch strips. In a wok or a large skillet, heat the oil over high heat; add the green pepper and stir-fry 1 minute. Add the meat, cook and stir until meat loses its red color, about 4 minutes. Serves 4. Serve with rice.

Marian Kageyama
Monterey, California

"This is a nice entree if you don't want to fuss in the kitchen while your guests are having fun in the living room."

MARINATED FLANK STEAK

1½ pounds flank steak
3 tablespoons honey
2 scallions, finely chopped

2 tablespoons oil
4 tablespoons lemon and lime juice
¼ cup soy sauce

Combine all ingredients except steak to make a marinade. Score steak lightly on each side with a sharp knife. Marinate overnight, turning several times. Broil 6-7 minutes on each side. Serves 4.

Tina Tomlinson Del Piero (Mrs. Marc)
Class of '73
Salinas, California

"Some of life's greatest joys come from sharing favorite wines, sumptuous food and good conversation with friends."

BEEF AND MUSHROOMS NOIR

2 large onions, sliced
1 tablespoon butter
2 tablespoons olive oil
3 pounds stewing beef, cut into 1" cubes
3 tablespoons flour
¼ teaspoon thyme

¼ teaspoon marjoram
Salt
Pepper
½ cup beef stock or broth
1 cup Weibel Pinot Noir
½ pound mushrooms, sliced

Saute the onions in butter and oil until limp; remove from pan and brown meat in the same oil. Once the meat is browned on all sides, sprinkle with flour, thyme, marjoram and salt and pepper to taste. Add the broth and wine and mix well. Simmer, covered (vent lid to allow some steam to escape) for 3 hours, until meat becomes tender. Return the onions to the pan and add mushrooms. Continue to simmer 45 minutes to 1 hour longer. While simmering meat, additional wine or stock may be added just to cover. Serves 6. This is good served on a bed of noodles with an avocado and tomato salad, artichoke hearts with pureed peas and Weibel 1976 Pinot Noir.

Weibel Champagne Vineyards
Mission San Jose, California

BOEUF BOURGUIGNONNE

¼ pound diced bacon
2 pounds lean beef, cubed
1½ teaspoons salt
Freshly ground pepper
2 tablespoons flour
1½ cups burgundy
1½ cups water

Herb bouquet: 1 carrot, sprig of
  parsley, 1 bay leaf, ½ teaspoon
  thyme
1 clove garlic, crushed
1 onion, diced
½ pound fresh mushrooms
Minced parsley

Fry bacon until crisp; drain. In 2 tablespoons of the drippings, brown the beef slowly on all sides. Sprinkle with salt, a few grindings of pepper and the flour. Toss to coat evenly and place in a heavy 2-quart casserole; add bacon. In the frying pan, add wine, water and herb bouquet and garlic. Bring to a boil and pour over meat. Cover tightly. Cook in a 350° oven until tender, about 2 hours. Skim off fat, saute the onion and mushrooms in a little of the fat for a few minutes. Add the onions to the beef and cook 30 minutes. Add fresh mushrooms and cook 10 minutes longer. Garnish with parsley. Serves 4-6. Serve with French bread, noodles or potatoes.

Christy Pollaci (Mrs. Mark)
Lower School Faculty
Monterey, California

CALIFORNIA STEAK BURGUNDY

1 pound boneless beef steak
2 tablespoons butter or oil
½ teaspoon salt
Freshly ground pepper to taste
1 large onion, sliced
1½ cups Taylor California
  Cellars Burgundy

1 (2½ ounce) jar sliced
  mushrooms and liquid
1 bouillon cube
2 cups bean sprouts, fresh or
  canned
1 tablespoon soy sauce
1 tablespoon cornstarch

Put steak in freezer for about half an hour and cut into thin slices while still partially frozen. Heat butter or oil in a large skillet until quite hot; add meat, salt, pepper and sliced onion, and stir-fry quickly until meat is lightly browned and onion slightly limp. Add burgundy, mushrooms with liquid and the bouillon cube. Cover and simmer about 15 minutes. Stir in bean sprouts and soy sauce which has been mixed with the cornstarch. Bring to a boil, cooking just enough to heat the bean sprouts. Serve over rice. Makes 3 to 4 servings.

Monterey Vineyard
Hayward, California

BEEF BROIL

3½-4 pounds (2" thick) top   2 tablespoons catsup
   round of beef   1 tablespoon red wine vinegar
½ cup Monterey Vineyard Classic   1 teaspoon sugar
   California red wine   1 teaspoon marjoram
1/3 cup salad oil   ½ teaspoon crushed rosemary
1 large clove garlic, crushed   leaves
1 tablespoon Worcestershire sauce 1 medium onion, sliced

Marinate the top round of beef several hours or overnight in the refrigerator in a marinade made by combining all the ingredients. Grill 6 inches from moderate coals for 10 to 12 minutes; turn. Grill an additional 10 minutes or to the desired degree of doneness. Baste occasionally while cooking with strained marinade.

Monterey Vineyard
Hayward, California

"Graciously accept the praise of your guests!"

BARBECUE BRISKET OF BEEF, TEXAS STYLE

3 to 4 pound beef brisket (1½ - 2" thick)

Barbecue Sauce:
¾ cup regular barbecue sauce   ½ teaspoon coarsely ground
½ cup hickory flavored barbecue   pepper
   sauce   2 tablespoons lemon juice
1/3 cup catsup   1 tablespoon soy sauce
1/3 cup water   ½ teaspoon dry mustard
        ½ teaspoon garlic salt

Combine all ingredients except meat to make a barbeque sauce. Marinate the brisket in sauce for 1 hour while preparing charcoal, let coals burn for ½ to ¾ hours; grill brisket for 1¼ to 1½ hours with lid down (roast in aluminum foil if grill does not have a lid); turn and baste with the sauce every 15 minutes. Slice very thinly across the grain for serving; heat extra sauce for use at the table. Can be baked in oven at 325° for 2 hours, uncovered in a 9" x 13" dish. Goes great with foil-baked, buttered potatoes and a green vegetable. Serves 6-8.

Mr. Leslie Zambo
Father of Jane '83, Jill '84, Leslie '85
Monterey, California

POT ROAST IN BURGUNDY

8 pounds beef brisket
Salt
Pepper
1 onion, sliced
3 carrots, sliced
3 ribs of celery
1½ cups burgundy
1 bay leaf

Garlic salt
1 tablespoon celery salt
1 (20 ounce) can tomatoes
1 (20 ounce) can tomato puree
1 tablespoon paprika
2 cups consomme
½ cup flour

Brown the meat very well; season with salt and pepper. Saute the onion, carrots and celery in a large pot; add the burgundy, bay leaf, garlic salt, celery salt, tomatoes, tomato puree, paprika and consomme; stir well and simmer for about 10 minutes. In a bowl, mix a small portion of the sauce with the flour, blending until smooth. Slowly combine with the remaining sauce and vegetables and pour over the browned brisket. Cover tightly and roast at 375° for about 3 hours or until tender. When done, remove meat from the roasting pan, let rest about 15 minutes, and slice. Return meat to vegetables and gravy in the pan and keep warm until ready to serve.

Teisah Miller
Monterey, California

CORNED BEEF WITH SAUCE

1 (3 to 4 pounds) corned beef
  brisket

2 garlic cloves
3 bay leaves

SAUCE:
1 cup 7-Up
1 teaspoon Worcestershire sauce
1 teaspoon mustard

1 tablespoon soya sauce
1 tablespoon burgundy wine

A day before serving, boil the corned beef at a low simmer with the garlic cloves and bay leaves until tender, about 2½ to 3 hours. After the brisket has cooled, trim off all fat. An hour before serving, make the sauce by blending well the ingredients in the order given. Pour over trimmed corned beef in a shallow pan and cover with foil. Bake in a 375° oven for about 1 hour. To complete the dish, quarter a small cabbage and steam for 8 minutes, and add boiled new potatoes in their jackets. Serves 4. NOTE: "Old fashioned, covered with spices" brisket may also be purchased, thus eliminating the need for garlic cloves and bay leaves.

Sheila Lamson (Mrs. Perry)
Upper School Faculty and Administration
Pebble Beach, California

"What you learn to do when your husband comes home with 200 pounds of caribou meat!"

CARIBOU STROGONOFF

1½ pounds caribou meat
Butter
1 small onion, chopped
2 tablespoons lemon juice
2 tablespoons flour
½ teaspoon basil

1/8 teaspoon nutmeg
Salt
Pepper
1 pint sour cream
1 tablespoon brandy
3 tablespoons chopped chives

MARINADE:
2 cups red wine
¼ cup chopped onions
¼ cup chopped carrots

Pepper
Bay leaf
Parsley
Thyme

Combine marinade ingredients and marinate caribou for at least 12 hours to tenderize the meat. Slice the caribou into small, thin pieces because game meat should be cooked thoroughly. Brown the meat in butter and a little of the marinade; set aside. Saute the onion in butter, add the meat, lemon juice, flour and seasonings. Cook, stirring for several minutes; blend in the sour cream and brandy, season to taste. Stir in the chives. Serve over hot rice. Makes 4 servings.

Meredith Nino Egbert (Mrs. John)
Former Faculty
Juneau, Alaska

HAM SMOKED PORK SHOULDER

1 smoked pork shoulder (about
  4 pounds)
2 cups pineapple juice

½ cup brown sugar
1 tablespoon vinegar

Wash smoked pork shoulder in cold water to remove excess smokey taste. Place in a roasting pan and prick the meat with a fork or sharp pointed knife to allow the marinade to penetrate. Blend together the pineapple juice, brown sugar and vinegar and pour over the ham. Marinate overnight, turning the meat occasionally. Simmer, covered, with the marinade for 1 hour, turning the meat once and basting with the sauce. Drain the ham, peel off skin and sprinkle with additional brown sugar. Bake, uncovered, in a 350° oven for 1 hour or until golden brown. May be served hot or cold. Serves 8. NOTE: Fruit syrup saved from drained canned fruits may be used to marinate and simmer ham.

Dr. Lila Ferrer-Ibabao (Mrs. Florentino)
Mother of Cheryl '82 and Emily '84
Orinda, California

"This has always been a great hit at dinner parties. It is even good served cold."

PORK TENDERLOIN ROAST CHINESE STYLE

1½-2 pounds whole pork
   tenderloin
1 clove garlic
1 walnut sized piece of peeled
   ginger
½ cup beef broth

2 tablespoons brown sugar
2 tablespoons soy sauce
2 tablespoons catsup
Thick soy sauce for glaze
Catsup for glaze

In a blender, blend the garlic, ginger, beef broth, brown sugar, soy sauce and 2 tablespoons catsup to make a marinade. Marinate the pork tenderloin for 1 to 3 hours. Remove from marinade and place the roast in a roasting pan. Bake in a 350° oven for 1 hour, basting often with the reserved marinade and turning once. When thoroughly cooked, remove from oven and glaze with a mixture of thick soy sauce and catsup, using slightly more catsup than soy sauce. Serves 4-6. NOTE: Thick soy sauce can be found in specialty or oriental markets. Regular soy sauce can be substituted, using somewhat less.

Paula Sullivan Escher (Mrs. Thomas)
Class of '66
San Francisco, California

"A joy to use for a party because you can visit with your guests instead of being in the kitchen, and the timing doesn't have to be exact."

ROAST PORK WITH WHOLE ONIONS

3-4 pounds loin of pork
Ground thyme
Salt
Pepper

1 clove garlic
½ cup dry white or red wine
½ cup hot water
1 (16 ounce) can whole onions

Rub the loin of pork with thyme, salt and pepper. Sliver the garlic into fourths and make 4 slits between the chops; insert a sliver of garlic in each split. Place in a greased roasting pan and roast, uncovered, in a preheated 425° oven for 20 minutes. Reduce heat to 325°; pour the water and wine over the meat and continue roasting until done, about 1½ hours more. About 10-15 minutes before the end of the cooking time, add the rinsed and drained onions, turning them once or twice to coat. Serves 4-6.

Joan Weaver Hauserman (Mrs. Dan)
Mother of Heidi '84
Tahoe City, California

PORK CHOPS-WILD RICE CASSEROLE

4 loin pork chops
2-3 tablespoons oil
4 slices of onion
4 thick slices fresh tomatoes
½ cup wild rice

1 cup dry white wine
1 cup water
Butter
Salt
Pepper

Brown the pork chops in oil; place in a greased casserole. Top each chop with a slice of onion and a slice of tomato; salt and pepper to taste. Pour rice around the chops and cover with wine. Add the water to the pan used for browning chops and simmer to loosen browned bits remaining in the pan. Pour over rice; dot with butter. Cover and bake in a 325° oven for 2 hours until the liquid is absorbed. NOTE: This recipe holds well if dinner is delayed. Serves 4.

Jane Auckenthaler (Mrs. Joseph)
Mother of Bonnie McWhorter '63 and Laurie McWhoter '72
San Mateo, California

MARIAN'S PORK CHOPS

8 thinly sliced pork chops
2 eggs
1 tablespoon Worcestershire sauce
2 tablespoons cooking sherry

¾ cup grated Parmesan cheese
½ to ¾ cup cracker crumbs
½ teaspoon onion salt

Mix the eggs, Worcestershire sauce and sherry together and marinate the pork chops in this mixture for 2 hours. Mix together the Parmesan cheese, cracker crumbs and onion salt and thoroughly coat the marinated pork chops. In an electric skillet set at 350°, fry the pork chops in a combination of oil and butter until brown and done (about 10 minutes), turning once. Serves 4.

Marian Anderson (Mrs. Ken)
San Jose, California

Because of its location, Santa Catalina is able to offer a Marine Biology course during the summer. The school is situated in an area where warm and cold water currents come together so there is a great diversity of marine life. There is also a great abundance because of the rich nutrient water. The area offers many different habitats for marine life: a rocky inner coast, a rocky outer coast, sand flat habitats, and mud flat habitats. After four weeks and 120 hours of study equivalent to a full year of high school biology, many of the students, and others who come from across the nation and abroad, travel to Hawaii for further study of marine biology accompanied by their instructor and his assistants.

CORN PUDDING WITH DEVILED HAM

1 (16 ounce) can whole kernel
  corn
1 cup evaporated milk (or
  whipping cream)
4 eggs, beaten

2 tablespoons melted butter
1 (4½ ounce) can deviled ham
1 tablespoon sugar
½ teaspoon salt
1/8 teaspoon pepper

Drain the corn, reserving liquid. Add the reserved liquid to the milk or whipping cream and enough water to equal 2 cups. Combine the eggs, butter, ham, sugar, salt and pepper and blend thoroughly; stir in the corn and milk mixture. Pour into a buttered 1½ quart casserole. Set casserole in a pan of hot water and bake in a 350° oven for about an hour, or until a knife inserted in the center comes out clean.

Mrs. Lee B. Price
Monterey, California

VOL AU VENT WITH HAM IN WINE SAUCE

1 (10 ounce) package frozen
  patty shells
4 tablespoons butter
½ onion, finely chopped
½ cup celery, thinly sliced
4 tablespoons flour
2 (10¾ oz) cans cream of
  mushroom soup

2 cups Taylor California
  Cellars chablis
3 cups diced cooked ham
½ pound fresh sliced
  mushrooms, sauteed
Pepper

Bake patty shells as directed on the package. Melt butter in saucepan, add the onion and cook over low heat until tender, but not browned; add celery and continue cooking 5 minutes. Stir in the flour; add soup and mix well. Gradually blend in the wine, cook and stir until the mixture boils and is thickened. Add the ham and mushrooms, season with pepper and heat thoroughly. Serve in patty shells. Makes 6 servings. NOTE: A variety of dishes can be planned around this basic wine sauce. Instead of ham, add 3 cups diced cooked chicken, or 2 cups cooked chicken and 3 hard cooked diced eggs; or combine the ham with the eggs. Other choices: 3 cups cooked peeled shrimp, or a mixture of shrimp and hard cooked diced eggs. A few sliced water chestnuts may replace all or part of the mushrooms. The sauce may be prepared ahead, refrigerated and reheated.

Monterey Vineyard
Hayward, California

FIREBAUGH FROG LEGS

3 pounds fresh frog legs
1 cup cream
1 cup flour

Salt
Pepper
1/3 cup butter

SAUCE:
½ cup butter
2 cloves garlic, minced
1 cup sliced mushrooms
2 tomatoes, peeled and chopped
1/8 teaspoon white pepper

1 teaspoon salt
1/3 cup dry vermouth
1 teaspoon flour
1 teaspoon butter

Soak the frog legs in salt water overnight; rinse and pat dry. Dip frog legs in the cream, then the flour which has been seasoned with salt and pepper. Brown in 1/3 cup butter, turning often. Place in a shallow baking pan and bake in a preheated 350° oven for 20 minutes. For the sauce, melt ½ cup butter in a skillet. Add the garlic, mushrooms, tomatoes, salt and pepper; simmer for 5 minutes. Thicken the sauce with the flour and butter which have been mixed together and thinned with the vermouth. Pour the sauce over the frog legs and return to the oven for 5 minutes. Garnish with parsley. Serves 4.

Bev Harman Dudley (Mrs. Lon)
Class of '62
Folsom, California

SQUID RATATOUILLE

Olive oil
2 medium onions, chopped
1 medium eggplant, diced
4-5 cloves garlic, minced
2 medium zucchini, sliced
½ pound mushrooms, sliced
4 large stalks celery, sliced

2 (28 ounce) cans tomatoes
1 (12 ounce) can tomato paste
1 tablespoon Italian seasoning
½ teaspoon crushed red pepper
2-3 dashes hot sauce
Salt
3 pounds squid

Saute the vegetables in a large pot. Dot with enough olive oil to thinly cover the bottom of the pot. Add tomatoes, coarsely chopped, tomato paste and spices. Simmer about 45 minutes, stirring occasionally. While the sauce is cooking, clean the squid and cut into rings. Immediately before you are ready to eat, turn off the heat under the pot and stir in the squid. Keep stirring until squid turns milky white and is cooked through, about 1 minute. Do not overcook as squid will become rubbery and tough. Serve with grated Parmesan cheese over spaghetti or in bowls with crusty sourdough French bread. Serves 6 generously.

Stella Sinner Lauerman (Mrs. David)
Class of '75
Registrar
Monterey, California

MOCK FISH SOUFFLE

1 pound cod or snapper
1 small onion
1 teaspoon salt
Pinch cayenne pepper
1 tablespoon lemon juice

4 eggs, separated
1 cup milk
½ cup cream
1½ cups finely crushed saltines

Using the knife blade in a food processor, process the fish; add the onion and process again. Beat the egg yolks and combine them with the milk, cream and saltines; stir in the processed fish and onion. Beat the egg whites until stiff and fold into the fish mixture. Bake in an oiled souffle dish for 35 minutes in a 350° oven. Serve with a sauce. NOTE: Sauce is important, as fish is bland. Use a favorite cream sauce with shrimp and/or crab or use the following:

SAUCE

½ cup butter
¼ cup chopped scallions
¼ cup chopped parsley
¼ cup finely chopped celery OR
¼ cup finely chopped water
   chestnuts
1-2 tablespoons capers

Juice of lemon
Pepper
Basil
Dill Weed
½ pound tiny shrimp
1 hard cooked egg, chopped

Melt the butter in a saucepan; saute the scallions; parsley and celery or water chestnuts. Add the capers, lemon juice and seasonings. Just before serving, stir in the shrimp and the finely chopped hard cooked egg. Serve sizzling hot. NOTE: If desired, the sauce may be thickened with 1 tablespoon cornstarch.

Katie Clare Mazzeo (Mrs. Rosario)
Upper School Faculty
Carmel, California

HALIBUT DIVAN

1 pound halibut fillets
1 (10 ounce) package frozen
   broccoli spears

½ teaspoon tarragon
1 (10 ounce) can condensed
   cream of shrimp soup

In a microwave oven, cook broccoli on high for 3 minutes. Place fish in a 2-quart baking dish and top with broccoli, arranged with the stems to the outside and the flowers to the center; sprinkle with tarragon. Bake on high, covered with wax paper, for 11 minutes or until fish flakes easily. Pour soup in a 2-cup measure and heat on high for 2-3 minutes. Stir and pour over fish and broccoli. (Fish and sauce are not cooked together). Standing time about 2 minutes. NOTE: Any white fish may be substituted for the halibut and any cream soup may be substituted for the cream of shrimp soup.

Brenda Guy (Mrs. Michael)
Mother of Jennifer
Pebble Beach, California

SOLE SAUTE WITH HONEY-WALNUT SAUCE

4 medium sole fillets (or any   Tamari sauce (naturally aged
*   mild white fish)   soy sauce)*
¼ cup butter   Lemon
¾ cup coarsely chopped walnuts   2 tablespoons honey
*   Dried spearmint leaves*

Melt the butter in a cast iron pan over low heat. Add the chopped walnuts and saute lightly for a minute or two. Push walnuts to side of pan. Place fish in the pan and turn heat to medium. Sprinkle fish lightly with tamari, lemon and spearmint leaves. Add more butter, if needed, and cook for about 3 minutes. Turn fish over and sprinkle again with tamari, lemon and mint. Cook until done, about 1 minute longer. Remove fish and keep warm on a platter. Add honey to pan sauce. Stir and pour over fish. Serve immediately. Makes 2 servings.

Terry Byrne (Mrs. Gerald)
Mother of Tricia Nance
Carmel, California

BAKED FILLET OF SOLE

2 pounds fillet of sole   ½ teaspoon basil leaves
½ cup mayonnaise   ¼ teaspoon dry mustard
½ cup chopped onion   2 tablespoons fine dry bread
¼ cup dry white wine   crumbs
½ teaspoon salt   ½ teaspoon paprika

Preheat oven to 400°. Pat fish dry; place in a buttered shallow baking dish. Combine the mayonnaise, onion, wine, salt, basil and mustard. Spread mixture over fillets. Sprinkle with bread crumbs and paprika. Bake 40 minutes or until fish flakes easily. Serves 4.

Gigi Vincenz Eastman (Mrs. Samuel)
Class of '58
Salinas, California

"This dish is simple to prepare and delicious. I particularly like to serve it to guests as I can get all of the preparation done early and refrigerate until ready to bake."

SOLE FLORENTINE

3 (10 ounce) packages frozen spinach
2 cups sour cream
3 tablespoons flour
½ cup chopped green onions, including tops

Juice of 1 lemon
½ teaspoon salt
1½-2 pounds fillet of sole (Petrale, if available)
2 tablespoons butter
Paprika

Cook spinach and drain thoroughly. Blend the sour cream with the flour, green onions, lemon juice and salt. Combine half of this mixture with the drained spinach and spread evenly in the bottom of a buttered shallow baking dish (about 10 x 15 inches). Arrange the sole on the spinach, overlapping as needed. Dot with butter and spread the remaining sour cream mixture over the sole. Dust lightly with paprika and bake in a 375° oven for 25 minutes. Serves 8.

Pat Near (Mrs. F. James)
Mother of Nancy '84
Saratoga, California

"This is a great 'diet' dinner. The vegetables retain their crunchiness and fresh taste because of the short cooking time."

FILLET OF SOLE BONNE FEMME

1½ pounds fillet of sole
¾ cup chopped green pepper
¾ cup chopped onion
¾ cup chopped tomato
½ cup dry white wine
¼ cup water

Salt
Pepper
¼ teaspoon basil
¼ teaspoon tarragon
1 tablespoon butter

Place the chopped vegetables in the bottom of an ungreased 8 x 8 inch baking pan. Place the fillet of sole over the vegetables. Pour white wine and water over the sole and sprinkle with seasonings. Cover with a buttered sheet of wax paper, pressing down to cover the sole completely. Bake 20 minutes at 350°.

Mary Munhall Holl (Mrs. Stephen)
Class of '70
San Bernardino, California

FILLETS OF SOLE DUGLERE

Salt
1 cut clove of garlic
Freshly ground pepper
½ teaspoon sugar
Onions
Mushrooms
Tomatoes
Oregano

Marjoram
Parsley
1 cup white wine
Fillets of sole
Lemon juice
Butter
1 cup heavy cream
1 egg yolk

Salt a large skillet and rub with the cut side of the garlic clove; sprinkle evenly with the pepper and sugar. Thinly slice the onions and layer them in the skillet; finely slice the mushrooms and layer them over the onions; peel, seed, and thinly slice the tomatoes and layer them over the mushrooms. Season with oregano, marjoram, and parsley; add the white wine. Sprinkle the fish fillets with lemon juice, salt and pepper; fold in thirds and place on the bed of vegetables. Cut a circle of waxed paper slightly larger than the skillet, butter it, and place on top of the fish, buttered side down. Cover the skillet (the paper will make a tight seal) and put on a high flame. As soon as it boils, reduce heat and cook for 5 minutes. Remove fish with a slotted spoon and place on a heated serving platter, keeping warm. Once the fish has been removed, turn the heat to its highest point and reduce the vegetable mixture completely. When all liquid has evaporated, add the heavy cream and cook only until warm. Beat an egg yolk with a small amount of the warmed cream and add to the sauce in the skillet. Cook for 2 minutes on low heat; correct seasoning. Pour sauce over the fish and garnish the platter with parsley, lemon slices and tomatoes.

Pauline Cantin (Mrs. Giles)
Music Department
Mother of Marie '70
Monterey, California

POACHED SALMON

2 pounds salmon
1 cup sherry
Juice of 1 lemon

¼ cup olive oil
Salt
Pepper

Mix together the sherry, lemon juice, olive oil, salt and pepper. Pour over the salmon in a shallow baking dish and bake in a 400° oven for 30 minutes.

Polly Reese (Mrs. Bob)
Mother of Heather
Monterey, California

BARBECUED STUFFED WHOLE FISH

8-10 pounds whole fish (salmon,
   cod, tuna, etc.)
Salt
Pepper
Salad oil

½ cup butter
½ cup lemon juice
Garden vegetable stuffing (recipe
   follows)
Mustard Butter (recipe follows)

Wash fish quickly in cold water and pat dry with paper towels. Rub the cavity of the fish with salt and pepper. Stuff with garden vegetable stuffing. Close opening with skewers; lace. Brush fish with salad oil. Mix the butter and lemon juice; set aside. Place fish in a wire basket on grill about 4 inches from medium coals. Cook for approximately 45 minutes, or until fish flakes easily with a fork, turning 3 times and basting with butter mixture. Serve with mustard butter or lemon-parsley butter. Makes 12 servings. NOTE: If a fish basket is unavailable, improvise by forming one with chicken wire.

GARDEN VEGETABLE STUFFING

1 cup finely chopped onion
¼ cup butter
2½ cups dry bread cubes
1 cup shredded carrot
1 cup sliced fresh mushrooms
½ cup snipped fresh parsley

1½ tablespoons lemon juice
1 egg
1 clove garlic, minced
2 teaspoons salt
¼-½ teaspoons marjoram
¼ teaspoon pepper

Saute the onion in butter until the onion is tender. Lightly mix the remaining ingredients with onion and butter. If you have extra stuffing, place in an aluminum foil pan; cover and heat on grill 20 minutes before serving. NOTE: I generally make a double recipe to insure the extra pan of stuffing as it goes very quickly.

MUSTARD BUTTER

½ cup butter
¾ teaspoon salt
2 teaspoons lemon juice

1 teaspoon prepared mustard
Dash pepper

In a sauce pan over low heat melt the butter. Add the remaining ingredients. You may experiment with various kinds of mustard such as Dijon to vary flavor. Serve with barbecued or grilled fish. The mustard sauce is especially good with fresh Monterey Bay salmon.

John H. Brazinsky
Father of April
Carmel, California

SALMON IN SORREL SAUCE

2 carrots, sliced
3 stalks celery, sliced
1 large onion, chopped
1 bouquet garni (large bunch
  parsley and ½ bay leaf)
4 cups water
2 cups J. Lohr Johannisberg
  Riesling

1 pound salmon, center cut
4 ounces fresh sorrel
1 cup heavy cream
Few drops lemon juice
Salt
Pepper
1 tablespoon butter

Boil carrots, celery, onion and bouquet garni in water until the water is reduced to 2 cups. Strain, add Johannisberg Riesling, and poach the salmon in the liquid for 5 minutes. Set salmon aside. Reduce the broth to 1/3 its volume over low heat. Remove the stems from the sorrel leaves and add to the broth. Pour in cream and reduce until the mixture is thick, being careful not to boil. Add the lemon juice and salt and pepper. Swirl in butter. Place the salmon in the sauce long enough to heat. Serves 2.

Turgeon & Lohr Winery
San Jose, California

BAKED SALMON LOAF

1 (16 ounce) can salmon
1½ cups fine breadcrumbs
2 large eggs, beaten
½ cup milk
½ cup finely chopped green
  pepper
1 cup finely chopped celery
¼-½ cup finely diced onion

1 teaspoon salt
Freshly ground black pepper
½ teaspoon cayenne pepper
½ teaspoon dill weed
Nutmeg
Pinch of dry English mustard
2 tablespoons melted butter
2 tablespoons lemon juice

Drain and flake the salmon, removing all skin and bones. Stir in the breadcrumbs, eggs, milk, green pepper, celery and onion. Add seasonings, butter and lemon juice and mix thoroughly. Spoon into a lightly greased 8 x 4 x 3 inch loaf pan and bake in a preheated 375° oven for approximately 1 hour or until lightly browned and firm. Unmold and serve hot with a mushroom sauce or chilled and sliced for salad. Serves 4-6. NOTE: A mushroom sauce can be made from cream of mushroom soup undiluted, or with just a small portion of milk added.

Latchmee A. Schults (Mrs. Rolf)
Mother of Melanie and Debbie
Salinas, California

CLAM LOAF WITH SHERRY SAUCE

2 (7 ounce) cans minced clams
½ pound lean pork sausage
1 cup bread or cracker crumbs
1 onion, minced
Minced parsley
2 eggs, beaten

Tabasco or Worcestershire sauce
Salt
Pepper
1 teaspoon baking powder
¾ cup clam juice and milk
Sherry Sauce (recipe below)

Drain the clams, reserving liquid; combine with the sausage, crumbs, onion, parsley, and eggs. Mix well and season with the tabasco or Worcestershire sauce, salt and pepper; add baking powder. Add enough milk to the clam juice to make ¾ cup and stir into the clam-sausage mixture. Place in a loaf pan or casserole dish and bake in a 350° oven for 1 hour. Serve with Sherry Sauce.

SHERRY SAUCE

1 (3 ounce) can mushrooms
4 tablespoons butter
1 teaspoon paprika
1 onion, minced
1 teaspoon flour

Mushroom liquor
1 cup cream
1 teaspoon Worcestershire
Dash Tabasco
3 tablespoons sherry

Saute the mushrooms in the butter until brown; add remaining ingredients and cook, stirring constantly until thickened. Serve over the Clam Loaf.

Mrs. Powell Harrison Taylor
Norfolk, Virginia

OYSTER LOAF

1 large round loaf of sourdough
  french bread
½ cup butter
2 (10 ounce) jars oysters
Salt

Pepper
Fine dry bread crumbs
½ cup lemon juice
1 bunch parsley, finely chopped

Cut off top 1/3 of bread and hollow out the bottom 2/3, leaving 1 inch of crust all around. Melt butter and brush generously inside of loaf. Place loaf, including lid, in a 400° oven for about 5 minutes. Drain oysters, salt and pepper lightly, and coat with crumbs; fry in butter until just golden and plump. Layer oysters in loaf, sprinkle each layer with lemon juice and chopped parsley, repeating layers until all oysters are used. Replace lid, brush outside of loaf with melted butter and warm in a 400° oven for 5 - 8 minutes. Cut in wedges to serve, or if you are truly barbaric, pull off chunks of bread and divide oysters among diners. Serves 6-8.

Mary Ann Taylor (Mrs. James)
Mother of James, Katie, and Asher
Monterey, California

OYSTER LOAF

1 large round loaf sour dough
bread
Butter
1 (10 ounce) package frozen
chopped spinach
3 eggs, beaten
½ cup mayonnaise
Salt

Pepper
Sprinkle of nutmeg
15 medium sized raw oysters
2 medium tomatoes, cut in
wedges
Grated Swiss or Parmesan cheese
Bread crumbs

Cut a thin slice off the top of the round loaf to use as a lid; hollow out loaf, being careful not to cut into sides or bottom of crust. (Save the bread removed from the loaf for toasted crumbs). Butter the inside of the loaf. Thaw the spinach and drain thoroughly; combine with the eggs and mayonnaise (and some bread crumbs if needed to extend the spinach mixture). Season with salt, pepper, and nutmeg. Layer in order the interior of the loaf with oysters, spinach, tomatoes, cheese, and bread crumbs; repeat until loaf is filled, ending with a layer of bread crumbs. Wrap loaf in foil, leaving top uncovered. Bake in a 350° oven until spinach mixture is set, about 30 - 40 minutes. Remove foil, replace lid and cut in wedges. Delicious with Wente Brothers Pinot Blanc. Serves 4-6.

Jean Wente
Wente Brothers Vineyards and Winery
Livermore, California

Under the auspices of the L.S B. Leakey Foundation, the Maasai warrior, Tepilit Ole Saitoti, presented a lecture slide-show on "Maasai: The Land and the People" on September 22, 1980 to the student body, faculty and members of the Monterey community at the Performing Arts Center, just prior to publication of his best-seller, "Maasai."

BOUILLABAISSE

¼ cup butter
¼ cup olive oil
½ cup flour
1 cup chopped onion
1 tablespoon minced garlic
3 tablespoons chopped celery
1 cup coarsely chopped tomatoes
3 bay leaves, broken
2 tablespoons minced parsley
1 pint oysters, liquor reserved
½ cup dry white wine
2 pounds redfish filets

1 pound trout filets
2 quarts cold water
2 teaspoons salt
½ teaspoon pepper
1/8 teaspoon cayenne
1/8 teaspoon saffron
2 tablespoons lemon juice
¾ cup lump crabmeat
1 cup crawfish tails (in season)
1 pound fresh shrimp, peeled and
  deveined
8 (½" thick) slices of stale
  French bread

In a heavy 7-quart pot, melt the butter over low heat. Mix in the oil, gradually stir in the flour and cook over low heat, stirring constantly, until a light brown roux is formed. When the roux reaches the desired color, about 25 minutes, quickly add the onion, garlic and celery. Continue cooking over low heat, stirring constantly, until the vegetables begin to brown, about 8 minutes. Add tomatoes, bay leaves, parsley, oyster liquor, wine, ½ pound of the red fish and ¼ pound of the trout. Raise the heat, bring to a boil, lower heat and simmer for 20 minutes. Gradually add water, remaining seasonings and lemon juice. After 20 additional minutes, add the remaining filets, crab and crawfish tails. Cook for 8 minutes, then add the shrimp and oysters and cook for 6 more minutes. Remove pot from the stove and let stand for 5 minutes. Place bread, 1½ cups fish and 1 cup liquid in each of 8 bowls.

Mara P. Reardon (Mrs. John)
Class of '78
Houston, Texas

BOUILLABAISSE

4 tablespoons olive oil
1 cup onions, thinly sliced
½ cup celery, julienned
1 bay leaf
½ teaspoon thyme
4 cloves garlic, mashed
1 cup clam juice
1 cup dry white wine
1/8 teaspoon saffron

1 cup fresh tomatoes, peeled
  and diced
2 tablespoons cornstarch
½ cups water
3 pounds fish (cod or halibut)
1 pound shrimp
2 dozen clams or mussels
1 pound scallops
Garlic Croutons

Saute the vegetables in the olive oil over low heat until tender. Add all other ingredients except fish and shellfish and simmer for 15-20 minutes. Thicken the mixture with the water and cornstarch. Cut the fish into 2-inch cubes or pieces. Put all fish and shellfish, except the scallops, into a 5 quart casserole pan. Pour broth over fish and bake uncovered in a preheated 400° oven for 10 minutes. Remove from oven and add scallops. Wait two minutes and serve with garlic croutons. NOTE: Garlic croutons may be made by tossing 4 cups bread cubes with ½ cup butter mixed with 4 cloves crushed garlic.

Carolyn Wuerflein
Mother of Marlene Wakefield '84
Los Gatos, California

LOBSTER – STUFFED TROUT

1 lobster tail, diced
1 cup Weibel White Cabernet
Sauvignon
¼ cup minced onion
½ cup chopped parsley

4 trout, dressed and boned
3 lemons, sliced
Salt
Parsley Butter (recipe below)
4 slices bacon

Marinate the diced lobster in the White Cabernet Sauvignon in the refrigerator for approximately 1 hour. Remove lobster from wine (reserve liquid and use to baste trout while baking), add minced onion, sprinkle with parsley and set aside. Make 3-4 diagonal cuts into side of trout, cutting from tail towards head. Rub inside of trout and inside of cuts of skin with slices of lemon and dust lightly with salt. Stuff each trout with 2 tablespoons lobster mixture, add 2-3 dollops Parsley Butter and wrap with bacon. Bake in a 425° oven for 10-15 minutes, or until trout is tender.

PARSLEY BUTTER

½ cup softened butter
¼ teaspoon finely chopped
parsley

1 clove garlic, minced

Whip the butter and fold in the chopped parsley and the minced garlic.

Weibel Champagne Vineyards
Mission San Jose, California

ROBERT PRESTONS SCAMPI

½ cup butter
2 teaspoons Worcestershire sauce
¼ cup sherry
1 clove garlic, crushed
Juice of ½ lemon
1 tablespoon sugar

2 tablespoons chopped fresh or
dried dill
1 pound raw shrimp, shelled and
deveined
¼ cup minced parsley
2 cups hot cooked rice
Parmesan cheese

In a shallow pan, melt the butter over low heat. Add the Worcestershire sauce, sherry, lemon, sugar and dill; mix well. Arrange the shrimp in a single layer on top of the sauce. Spoon some sauce over the shrimp. Broil in oven on low heat for 8 minutes. Remove from broiler and let stand for 15 minutes. Garnish with parsley and broil on high heat for 3 minutes. Place rice on serving platter and cover with the sauce; arrange shrimp on top and sprinkle with Parmesan cheese. Serve with a crisp green salad, French bread and white wine.

Liz Holt Protell (Mrs. Robert)
Class of '64
Tucson, Arizona

SHRIMP MACADAMIA

1 pound potatoes
24 jumbo shrimp, shelled and
deveined
Cold clarified butter
3 ounces Macadamia nuts,
finely chopped

1 clove garlic, crushed
2 ounces sherry
¼ cup butter
Juice of ½ lemon
Parsley sprigs
Paprika

Boil potatoes; drain and mash them with a little butter and milk and season with white pepper and salt. Set aside. Coat shrimp with cold clarified butter and roll in chopped nuts. In just enough clarified butter to cover the bottom of a frying pan, saute the garlic clove for about 2 minutes. Carefully place the coated shrimp in the pan and remove the clove of garlic. Cook the shrimp for about 2 minutes on each side. Add the sherry and flambe. Stir in the ¼ cup butter and the lemon juice. Fit a pastry bag with a rosette tip. Fill the pastry bag with the mashed potatoes and pipe a decorative border around the rim of each of 2 scallop shells. Pour the shrimp into the center of the shells, decorate with a sprig of parsley and dust lightly with a little paprika. Makes 2 generous servings.

Latchmee A. Schultz (Mrs. Rolf)
Mother of Melanie and Debbie
Salinas, California

SHRIMP ALMONDINE

1½ cups small curd cottage
  cheese
1½ tablespoons dry sherry
2 tablespoons grated Parmesan
  cheese
1 tablespoon Worcestershire sauce
1½ tablespoons lemon juice

¼ teaspoon white pepper
2 pounds cooked prepared
  shrimp
½ cup fine bread crumbs
6 tablespoons butter
1/3 cup blanced sliced almonds

In a bowl, mix together the cottage cheese, sherry, Parmesan cheese, Worcestershire sauce, lemon juice and pepper. Place shrimp into 4 individual oiled casseroles. Cover with the cottage cheese mixture and sprinkle with the bread crumbs. Saute the almonds in the butter and spoon over bread crumbs. Bake in a 350° oven for 15-20 minutes. Serves 4.

Margery Bobbs Johnson (Mrs. Robert)
Class of '65
Eagle, Colorado

SHRIMP WITH SNOW PEAS

2/3 pound fresh shrimp
1½ teaspoons dry sherry
¾ teaspoon salt
½ teaspoon minced fresh ginger
  root
2 teaspoons cornstarch
1 teaspoon sesame oil

1 tablespoon chicken broth
3 tablespoons water
3 tablespoons oyster sauce
½ cup vegetable oil
1 garlic clove, crushed
½ pound fresh snow peas

Shell and devein the shrimp; rinse and pat dry with paper towels. Make a marinade by combining the sherry, ½ teaspoon of the salt, the ginger root, 1½ teaspoons of the cornstarch and the sesame oil. Add the shrimp, mix well and marinate for 30 minutes; drain and pat dry with a paper towel. In a small bowl, combine the chicken broth, water, the remaining ½ teaspoon cornstarch and the oyster sauce, mixing well to make a seasoning sauce. Heat the oil in a wok for 30 seconds over high heat; stir-fry the garlic until golden. Add the shrimp and stir-fry until the shrimps are pink, about 30 seconds; remove from wok with a slotted spoon, draining well over wok. Add the remaining ¼ teaspoon salt and the snow peas to the oil in the wok. Stir-fry over high heat for 30 seconds. Add the seasoning sauce and stir until the sauce thickens slightly. Return shrimp to wok and stir-fry until coated with sauce. Serves 4.

Julie Nebreda
Marina, California

SHRIMP-ARTICHOKE CASSEROLE

3 tablespoons butter
3 tablespoons flour
½ teaspoon salt
Dash white pepper
½ teaspoon paprika
1-2/3 cup milk
½ cup dry white wine
¾ cup Swiss cheese, shredded
1 tablespoon catsup

2¼ cups cooked rice
½ teaspoon dried basil
½ teaspoon oregano
16 ounces shelled shrimp
1 (9 ounce) package frozen
  artichoke hearts
2 tablespoons fine dry bread
  crumbs, buttered
Paprika

Melt the butter over low heat; blend in the flour, salt, pepper and paprika. Add the milk all at once; cook and stir until the mixture is thickened and bubbly. Stir in the wine and heat through. Add the cheese and catsup and cook, stirring until the cheese is melted; set aside. In a small bowl, combine the rice, basil and oregano and place in a casserole. Drop the shrimp into boiling salted water, return to a boil, lower heat and simmer until pink, 1-3 minutes, and drain. Cook the artichoke hearts according to package directions and combine with the shrimp; stir into the rice mixture. Blend in the sauce, sprinkle with paprika and top with buttered crumbs. Bake in a 350° oven for 20-25 minutes. NOTE: Mushrooms may be added to this casserole, if desired.

Sondra Shapiro
Detroit, Michigan

SEAFOOD PILAF WITH GARLIC BUTTER

1 (9 ounce) box rice pilaf mix
3 cloves garlic, crushed
2 tablespoons butter
1 (12 ounce) package frozen or
  cooked crabmeat (or shrimp or
  lobster)

1 tablespoon chopped fresh
  parsley
1 tablespoon lemon juice

Prepare pilaf as directed on box. Saute garlic in butter over low heat; add seafood which has been cut in chunks, and add the parsley and lemon juice. Heat, uncovered, over low heat. Add the prepared pilaf and mix well. Serve immediately or refrigerate to heat later. To reheat, cover and place in a 275° oven 45-60 minutes until hot. Garnish with lemon wedges and parsley. Serves 4-5.

Margaret Brooks (Mrs. Chester)
Aunt of Kim Bowden '87
West Dennis, Massachusetts

"This is great for picnics on the beach. Eat the crab with your fingers and dunk the French bread in the broth."

CRAB IN WINE AND GARLIC BROTH
"WOKING THE CRAB"

¼ cup butter
1 large yellow onion, cut in rings
2 cloves garlic, minced
½ teaspoon liquid hot pepper
* seasoning*
1/8 teaspoon cayenne
¼ cup chopped parsley

1 bay leaf
2-3 (14 ounce) cans regular
* strength chicken broth*
1 (4/5 quart) bottle dry white
* wine*
2-3 Dungeness crabs, cooked,
* cracked and cleaned (2*
* pounds each)*
French sourdough bread

Place wok over fire. When the wok is hot, add butter, onion and garlic, stirring until onion is limp, approximately 2 minutes. Add hot pepper seasoning, cayenne, parsley, bay leaf, 2 cans of chicken broth and wine. Heat to simmering. Add the crab and simmer for about 10 minutes or until crab is thoroughly heated. Add more broth, if needed. Serves 4.

Kathy Anderson
San Jose, California

DEVILED CRAB

3 tablespoons butter
2 tablespoons onion, grated
3 tablespoons flour
1¾ cup milk
2 tablespoons sherry
1 tablespoon minced parsley
½ teaspoon dry mustard
3 drops tabasco sauce

Dash cayenne pepper
Dash grated nutmeg
Salt
Pepper
Parmesan cheese
Paprika
Lemon slices
1 pound fresh crab

Melt the butter and saute the onion. Add flour to make a roux. Slowly add the milk and cook, stirring constantly until thickened. Add the sherry, parsley, mustard, tabasco, cayenne, nutmeg, salt and pepper. Add the crab and blend well. Place in individual baking dishes or a shallow baking pan. Top with grated Parmesan cheese, lemon slices and paprika. Bake in a 400° oven until bubbly and slightly brown.

Helen L. Howard (Mrs. Charles)
Mother of Elinor Howard Franchetti '54,
Jane Howard Goodfellow '56, Katherine, Howard McGrath '58
Grandmother of Michele McGrath '79,
Joan Goodfellow '80, Kathleen McGrath '81
Walnut Creek, California

"If you like lobster Newburg, you will probably enjoy this interesting variation."

PETONCLES A LA NEWBURG
(Scallops Newburg)

1 quart scallops
1 cup dry wine
½ cup + 3 tablespoons butter
¼ teaspoon salt
¼ teaspoon pepper

¼ teaspoon paprika
1 cup dry sherry
1½ cups heavy cream
4 egg yolks, slightly beaten
¼ teaspoon cayenne pepper

Poach scallops in white wine for 5 minutes. Remove with a slotted spoon and set aside to keep warm. Add ½ cup of the butter, the salt, pepper, paprika, sherry and ¾ cup of the cream to the poaching liquid; cook 5 minutes over medium heat. Remove sauce from heat and stir a little of it into the egg yolks. Slowly stir egg yolk mixture back into the sauce. Return to heat and add the remaining ¾ cup cream. When hot, but not boiling, slowly add the remaining 3 tablespoons butter, and then the scallops. Heat gently for 3 minutes, add cayenne and serve in a chafing dish. Serves 4.

Velva Garrihy (Mrs. Michael)
Mother of Suzanne and Michelle
Pebble Beach, California

CAPE COD CASSEROLE

¾ pound lobster meat (2 or 3
lobsters)
1 pound fresh scallops, sauteed in
butter
1 pound shrimp, precooked

1 (10¾ ounce) cream of shrimp
soup
1 pint sour cream
¼ cup sherry
¾ cup unseasoned bread crumbs
¼ pound butter or margarine

Cut the lobster in bite-sized pieces and put the seafood in a 9 x 13 inch baking dish. Combine the soup, sour cream and sherry and pour over the seafood. Mix crumbs with melted butter and sprinkle on the top. Bake ½ hour at 350°. Serves 6-8. Serve with rice and a green vegetable or salad. Follow with a simple dessert.

Margaret Brooks (Mrs. C. W.)
Aunt of Kim Bowden '87
West Dennis, Massachussetts

LOBSTER THERMIDOR

4 tablespoons butter, melted   ½ teaspoon salt
1 cup sliced mushrooms   ½ teaspoon nutmeg
½ small onion, minced   ½ teaspoon cayenne
1 tablespoon minced green pepper 2 cups diced lobster
1 tablespoon minced parsley   ¾ cup broth, mushroom juice or
1 tablespoon minced pimento   cream
2 tablespoons flour   2 egg yolks, beaten
1¾ cup canned milk   ½ cup warm sherry
                                Buttered bread crumbs

Saute the mushrooms, onion, green pepper, parsley and pimentos in the melted butter in the top of a double boiler. Blend in the flour; add the milk gradually. Season with the salt, nutmeg and cayenne. Stir in the lobster, and thin with the broth. Just before serving, add the beaten egg yolks and the warm sherry. Fill the lobster shells or small ramekins with the mixture, top with buttered bread crumbs, and warm in a 300° oven.

Joan Hunter (Mrs. F. R.)
Mother of Jane
Pebble Beach, California

On Monday, June 4, 1951, twelve eighth graders received their diplomas from Monsignor Dowling on the Chapel lawn and became the first graduating class.

Vegetables and Accompaniments

"Since long before the American Revolutionary War, the Pennsylvania Dutch (who came from Germany, not Holland, and whose name is derived from the word Deutsch) have been setting standards for good food. The farms of southeastern Pennsylvania are among the finest in the world, and farming families deliver their own produce and tend market stalls in agricultural centers such as Lancaster, which is a few miles west of Philadelphia."

PENNSYLVANIA DUTCH FRIED CUCUMBERS

2 cucumbers, 7-8 inches long
Salt
Freshly ground pepper
1 egg, beaten
1 cup fresh bread crumbs

¼ teaspoon dried savory
¼ teaspoon dried thyme
6 tablespoons corn oil
Juice of ½ lemon

Peel the cucumbers and cut into ¼ inch slices. Let them steep with a sprinkling of salt for about 20 minutes; drain and pat dry. Dip the cucumber slices in the beaten egg, then in the bread crumbs well mixed with the herbs, salt and pepper. Fry the slices in oil for about 15 minutes, turning once to give them an even color. Sprinkle with lemon juice and serve with a flank steak. Serves 4.

Nancy Rembert (Mrs. Paul)
Mother of Grey '81
Concord, Massachusetts

STUFFED MUSHROOMS

16 large fresh mushrooms
2 cloves garlic
2 sprigs fresh parsley
½ cup dry bread crumbs
½ cup grated Romano cheese

¼ teaspoon oregano
¼ teaspoon salt
1/8 teaspoon freshly ground
* pepper*
4 teaspoons olive oil

Wash the mushrooms and remove the stems. Chop the stems, garlic and parsley in a blender or food processor. Combine the mixture with the dry bread crumbs, cheese, oregano, salt and pepper; stuff into the mushroom caps. Drizzle the olive oil over each mushroom; place on a cookie sheet and bake in a preheated 350° oven for 40 minutes. Serves 8.

Teresa Stevens
Class of '81
Hollister, California

"This is an adaptation of a recipe of my mother's from the late 1800's. It was a family favorite."

GREEN ONIONS AND MUSHROOMS

4 slices of bacon
1 bunch green onions

1 (4 ounce) can mushrooms
or fresh mushrooms

Fry the bacon until crisp; remove and set aside. Cut the onions into 1 to 2 inch pieces, and place in a skillet with 2 tablespoons of the bacon drippings. Add the mushrooms and ½ cup water and cook to desired doneness, adding the crumbled bacon the last few minutes of cooking. Serves 2-3.

Mrs. Julia Brazinsky Goulden
Great aunt of April Brazinsky
Shenandoah, Pennsylvania

ONION CELESTE

8 slices sourdough French
bread, cubed
2 large yellow onions, cut in
chunks
2 tablespoons butter

½ pound Swiss cheese, grated
1 (10 ounce) can cream of
chicken soup
½ cup milk

Butter a casserole dish and cover the bottom with half of the French bread. Saute the onions in the 2 tablespoons butter until soft and distribute over the French bread in the casserole. Sprinkle half of the cheese over the onions; combine the soup and the milk and pour over the cheese layer. Evenly distribute the remaining bread chunks over the soup layer and top with the remaining cheese. Bake in a 350° oven for 30 minutes. Serves 5.

Mary Jean Quinlan Cling (Mrs. Michael)
Class of '65
Salinas, California

GREEN BEAN CASSEROLE

3 (9 ounce) packages frozen
French style green beans
1 (5 ounce) can sliced water
chestnuts
2 (10 ounce) cans cream of
celery soup

1/8 teaspoon pepper
½ cup milk
1 or 2 (3 ounce) cans French
onion rings

Cook beans in boiling salted water until thawed and slightly crisp, approximately 4 minutes; drain. Layer the beans and the water chestnuts in a 2 quart casserole. Combine the soup and milk and season with pepper. Pour over the beans and bake in a 350° oven approximately 35 minutes. Top with the onions and bake an additional 10 minutes. Serves 10.

Nancy Weight
Director of Development
Mother of Katharine
Carmel Valley, California

"This is a mild and an unusual accompaniment."

EGGPLANT CASSEROLE

1 eggplant	*½ onion, chopped*
4 eggs	*Salt*
½ cup canned or fresh milk	*Pepper*
¼ pound crackers, crumbled	*Pinch of rosemary*
1½ cups cheese, grated	*Pinch of sage*

Peel the eggplant, cut into chunks, and cook until tender. Drain and rinse in cool water. Beat together the eggs and milk and combine with the eggplant; season with salt and pepper, stir in the crackers, cheese, onion, rosemary and sage. Top with additional cheese and bake for 30 minutes in a 350° oven. Serves 12.

Margaret Ann Frick (Mrs. Kenneth)
Mother of Linda '66 and Gail '69
Arvin, California

BAKED BEETS

2 (16 ounce) cans Julienne beets	*Salt*
½ pint sour cream	*Pepper*
2 tablespoons grated onion	*½ cup bread crumbs*
2 tablespoons lemon juice	*3 tablespoons melted butter*
¼ teaspoon seasoning salt	

Drain the beets and reserve ¼ cup of the juice. Mix the juice with the sour cream, lemon juice, onion and seasonings. Stir in the drained beets and pour into a buttered casserole. Mix the bread crumbs with the melted butter and sprinkle over the casserole. Bake in a 375° oven about 25 minutes. Serves 6.

Teisah Miller
Monterey, California

JILL'S VEGETABLE PIE

3 eggs, beaten
1½ cups soft bread crumbs
1½ cups cheddar cheese or a
   mixture of cheddar and jack
½ cup milk
1 teaspoon salt

½ teaspoon pepper
1½ teaspoons French blend herbs
3 different colored vegetables,
   cooked and chopped
Pastry for 2 crust pie

Combine the eggs, bread crumbs, cheese, milk and seasonings; divide into 3 equal parts. Add a different color vegetable to each portion. Line a 10-inch pie plate with the pastry. Place each vegetable mixture in 1/3 of the pie plate. Do not mix vegetables. Top with a lattice of pastry and bake in a 375° oven for 45 minutes. Serves 6-8. NOTE: Examples of vegetables to use are beets, carrots, and broccoli or cauliflower, spinach and well drained tomatoes, or use your imagination.

Marie Cressey Belden (Mrs. Lester)
Mother of Cressey Joy '87
Santa Rosa, California

TOMATO SANDWICHES BUDACH

12 (½ inch) slices ripe tomatoes
2 (3 ounce) packages cream
   cheese
2 tablespoons cream
1 garlic clove, minced

1 egg, slightly beaten
1 tablespoon water
1 cup fresh bread crumbs
2 tablespoons butter
Salt

Drain the tomatoes on paper towels for 5 minutes. In a bowl, combine the softened cream cheese, cream and garlic. Spread the mixture evenly over six slices of tomato, and top each slice with a remaining slice. Add the water to the beaten egg and dip the sandwiches into the mixture. Coat with the bread crumbs and let stand for 15 minutes. Dip again in the egg and coat again with the crumbs. In a skillet, saute the sandwiches in the butter over moderately high heat for 3 minutes on each side or until golden. Season with salt and transfer to a platter. Serve as a vegetable or a first course.

Mrs. Lee B. Price
Monterey, California

Santa Catalina offers computer classes in the summer for beginning, intermediate, and advanced students, using a variety of computers. In these classes, students design and execute their own programming project.

"A family favorite for years. I can never make enough to see us through until the next tomato season."

GRANDMOTHER'S TOMATO RELISH

10 pounds ripe tomatoes
2 pints vinegar
3 pounds brown sugar

1 tablespoon salt
¼ teaspoon red pepper
Spice Bag

SPICE BAG:
1 tablespoon whole cloves
1 tablespoon whole allspice

1 tablespoon cracked cinnamon

Peel the tomatoes by submerging them in boiling water for about 1 minute, then cooling slightly; the skin can then be pulled off easily. Leave the tomatoes whole and place in a large bowl; pour 1 pint of the vinegar over them and let stand overnight. Drain, reserving 1½ cups of the liquid. Make a syrup by combining the reserved liquid, the remaining 1 pint vinegar, the brown sugar, salt and red pepper in a large kettle; heat. Add the tomatoes and the spice bag. Boil slowly for 3 hours or until the mixture is thick and dark. Pour into sterilized pint jars and seal. Makes 5 pints. NOTE: The spice bag may be removed after 2½ hours if desired, according to taste.

Eleanor Winans (Mrs. W. E.)
Mother of Martha '74
La Jolla, California

SWEET PICKLED CARROTS

6 pounds carrots (about 36)
3 cups sugar
3 cups vinegar
3 cups water

1/3 cup mustard seed
6-8 inches of stick cinnamon
6-8 whole cloves

Cut carrots lengthwise into quarters and cook in boiling, salted water just until tender, 7-8 minutes; drain. In an 8 to 10 quart kettle, combine all ingredients except the carrots. Bring to a boil and simmer 20 minutes. Remove cinnamon and cloves. Pack carrots into hot jars, leaving ½ inch headspace. Cover with the vinegar mixture, and adjust the lids. Process in a boiling water bath for 5 minutes. NOTE: This recipe may be easily halved and instead of canning, kept in the refrigerator and given as hostess gifts at Christmas time.

April Anderson Bettencourt (Mrs. Jerry)
Aunt of April Brazinsky
Meadow Vista, California

GOOD CARROTS

8-10 medium carrots, sliced
2 tablespoons butter
2 tablespoons light brown sugar

2 tablespoons bourbon
Dried dill

Scrub and slice the carrots and cook just until tender; drain and set aside. In a small saucepan, combine the butter and brown sugar and cook over a low heat until the butter melts, stirring constantly. Add the bourbon and cook an additional minute. Gently stir the carrots into the butter/bourbon mixture. Garnish with a sprinkling of dried dill.

Ellen Christie (Mrs. Ivan)
Mother of Linda '81
Aptos, California

CARROT RING MOLD

2 cups cooked carrots, sieved
1 cup bread crumbs
1 (3 ounce) package slivered
  almonds
1 cup milk

2 eggs, beaten
Salt
Pepper
Seasoned salt

Combine all ingredients and spoon into a buttered ring mold. Place the mold in a pan partially filled with hot water and bake for 1 hour in a 350° oven. To serve, unmold on a large platter and fill the center with hot, cooked peas. Serves 6-8.

Mrs. Frank H. Pierce
Carmel, California

BROCCOLI CASSEROLE SUPREME

4 cups cooked broccoli
  (1½ pounds) cut into 1 inch
  pieces
1 (10½ ounce) can cream of
  mushroom soup
1 (2 ounce) jar sliced pimiento,
  drained

¾ cup sour cream
1 cup sliced celery
½ teaspoon salt
¼-½ cup grated cheddar cheese

In a large mixing bowl, blend together all the ingredients except the cheese. Put in a 1½ quart oiled casserole. Top with cheese. Bake in a 350° oven for 20-25 minutes. Makes 6 servings. NOTE: Slightly under-cook the broccoli as it will continue cooking in the oven.

Mr. and Mrs. James Manassero
Parents of Tori '84
Salinas, California

"This dish rates high in flavor. It can be made into a main dish by adding browned ground beef to the sauce."

BROCCOLI ESPANOL

1 bunch broccoli
3 tablespoons butter
2 tablespoons minced onion
2 tablespoon minced green
  pepper
2½ cups tomato pieces, drained
1 teaspoon chili powder, optional

1 pinch cayenne pepper
1 teaspoon salt
1/8 teaspoon pepper
1 teaspoon sugar
½ cup Parmesan cheese

Cut broccoli stalks into ¼ inch slices and cut large flowerets in half. Cook in ½ cup boiling water and ½ teaspoon salt, covered, until tender crisp. Drain. Put in a 1½ quart casserole and set aside. Brown the onion and green pepper in butter and add tomatoes and seasonings. Mix together. Pour over the broccoli. Sprinkle with cheese. Cover and bake in a 350° oven for about 20 minutes. Serves 6.

Mr. and Mrs. James Manassero
Parents of Tori '84
Salinas, California

BROCCOLI ITALIAN STYLE

1 bunch broccoli
4-5 tablespoons olive oil
1 clove garlic, peeled and chopped
3 tablespoons onion, minced

3 tablespoons water
¾ teaspoon salt
Pinch cayenne pepper
½ teaspoon oregano

Wash the broccoli. With a vegetable peeler, remove the thin layer of skin on the stems. Split each stem lengthwise, quarter and cut into 1 inch pieces. Cut flowerets into coarse pieces. Heat oil in a large skillet and add the garlic and onion; cook slowly until tender. Add the broccoli, water, salt, pepper and oregano. Cover tightly and cook slowly for about 15 minutes or until broccoli is tender. Serves 5-6.

Mr. and Mrs. James Manassero
Parents of Tori '84
Salinas, California

"Change plain broccoli to fancy."

BROCCOLI WITH ALMOND LEMON BUTTER

1 bunch broccoli
½ cup butter

½ cup toasted slivered almonds
3 tablespoons fresh lemon juice

Melt the butter in a heavy skillet, heat slowly until golden brown. Add the almonds and lemon juice. Serve over cooked broccoli. Serves 4.

Mr. and Mrs. James Manassero
Parents of Tori '84
Salinas, California

TANGY MUSTARD CAULIFLOWER

1 medium cauliflower
½ cup mayonnaise
1 tablespoon minced onion

1 teaspoon prepared mustard
½ cup cheddar cheese, grated

Wrap the whole cauliflower in plastic wrap or wax paper and place on a serving plate. Cook on high in a microwave oven for 5-7 minutes. Let stand 4 minutes. Combine the mayonnaise, mustard and onion and spread on the cauliflower. Sprinkle with cheese and heat for 1 minute on high. Serves 6-8.

Brenda Guy (Mrs. Michael)
Mother of Jennifer
Pebble Beach, California

FRENCH FRIED ZUCCHINI (OR CAULIFLOWER)

1 (12 inch) zucchini, 2 inches in
*   diameter*
1 egg, beaten
¼ teaspoon salt

¼ teaspoon pepper
½ cup milk
½ cup flour
Oil for frying

Slice the zucchini into ¼-½ inch slices. Mix the egg, salt, pepper, milk and flour. Add flour, if necessary, so that the mixture will be the consistency of pancake batter. Dip the zucchini slices one at a time into the batter, and fry in oil until golden brown on both sides. Drain. Serve hot or cold as an accompaniment, or as an hors d'oeuvre. Serves 4-6. NOTE: These make delicious sandwiches when served cold. Parboiled flowerets of cauliflower may be substituted for the zucchini.

Elaine Scaccia (Mrs. Sam)
Mother of Yolanda '67
Cloverdale, California

ZUCCHINI PANCAKES

3 cups grated zucchini   1 teaspoon onion powder
1 egg   ½ cup flour
Salt   1 teaspoon baking powder
Pepper

Combine the zucchini, egg, salt, pepper and onion powder. Sift the flour and baking powder over the zucchini mixture and combine the ingredients thoroughly. Drop the mixture by ¼ cupfuls on to a lightly oiled griddle or skillet and cook the pancakes until they are brown on both sides. Serve with melted butter and Parmesan cheese, if desired. Delicious!

Mrs. Lee B. Price
Monterey, California

STUFFED ZUCCHINI

4 zucchini   ½ cup cream
½ cup onions, finely chopped   1 cup Swiss cheese
2 cloves garlic, minced   Salt
3 tablespoons butter   White pepper
½ cup ground blanched almonds   Pinch of ground cloves
½ cup chopped parsley

Remove the stem ends and cut the zucchini in half lengthwise. Scoop out the pulp, chop and set aside. Salt and pepper the shells and place in a buttered baking dish. In a skillet, saute the onions and garlic in the butter until softened. Add the chopped zucchini pulp and cook until the moisture has evaporated from the squash; remove from heat. Stir in the almonds, parsley and cream; season with salt, pepper and cloves. Add half of the cheese and mix well. Spoon the stuffing into the shells; top with the remaining cheese. Bake for 20-25 minutes in a 350° oven until bubbling hot and brown on top. Serve from a baking dish or arrange around a meat platter. Serves 8.

Gloria Didion (Mrs. James)
Mother of Lori
Pebble Beach, California

ZUCCHINI CASSEROLE

2 pounds zucchini, cubed
4 eggs, beaten
½ cup milk
1 pound cheddar cheese,
  shredded
1 teaspoon salt
2 teaspoons baking powder

3 teaspoons flour
½ cup parsley, chopped
1 (4 ounce) can diced green
  chiles
2 cups bread crumbs
4 tablespoons butter

Cook the squash in salted water until tender, drain well and cool. Mix the eggs, milk, cheese, salt, baking powder, flour, parsley and chiles; fold in squash. Butter a casserole dish, sprinkle bread crumbs on the bottom and sides, pour in the squash mixture and sprinkle with the remaining bread crumbs; dot with butter. Bake in a 350° oven for 30 minutes. Serves 12.

Linda Ann Frick
Class of '66
Washington, D.C.

ZUCCHINI-CHEESE CASSEROLE

2 tablespoons butter
4 eggs
8 ounces jack cheese with
  jalapeno peppers, grated
8 ounces Cheddar cheese, grated

½ cup dry, seasoned bread
  crumbs
2 cloves garlic, minced
2 tablespoons onion, grated
4 cups zucchini, grated
1/3 cup Romano or Parmesan
  cheese, grated

With the 2 tablespoons of butter, butter a 2-quart baking dish; set aside. Beat the eggs in a large mixing bowl; stir in the jack cheese, cheddar cheese, bread crumbs, garlic and onion. Mix well. Fold in the zucchini. Place the squash mixture into the buttered baking dish and smooth the top; sprinkle with the Romano or Parmesan cheese. Bake, uncovered, in a 350° oven until the top is browned and the center is firm, about 45 minutes. Cool 5-10 minutes before serving. Serves 8.

Candy Hazard Ducato (Mrs. John)
Class of '60
Mother of Caroline '85
Hillsborough, California

"This makes an excellent side dish with ham, turkey or pork. It can also be served as an appetizer with unsalted wheat crackers."

ARTICHOKE CASSEROLE

2 (14 ounce) cans artichoke   ½ cup grated Parmesan cheese
hearts packed in water   1 cup mayonnaise

Drain the artichokes well. Mix with mayonnaise and cheese and place in a 1-quart casserole. Cover and bake in a 350° oven for 20-30 minutes. Serves 4.

Yolanda Scaccia Manuel (Mrs. Chris)
Class of '67
San Mateo, California

ARTICHOKE BOTTOMS AND SPINACH WITH HOLLANDAISE SAUCE

2 (10 ounce) packages frozen   1 clove garlic, minced
chopped spinach   2 (20 ounce) cans artichoke
½ pound fresh mushrooms   bottoms
6 tablespoons butter   1 cup sour cream
1 tablespoon flour   ¼ cup lemon juice
½ cup milk   1 cup mayonnaise
½ teaspoon salt

Cook the spinach as directed on the package; drain thoroughly. Remove the stems from 14 mushrooms, setting the caps aside. Chop the stems and saute in 2 tablespoons of the butter. Saute the 14 caps separately in 2 tablespoons of butter. Make a cream sauce with the remaining butter, flour and milk; season with salt and garlic. Add the spinach and sauteed chopped mushrooms. Lay the artichoke bottoms in a 9 x 13 inch baking dish. Fill and cover with the spinach mixture. Make a sauce by combining the sour cream, mayonnaise and lemon juice; heat slowly. Spoon over the filled artichoke bottoms and top with the mushroom caps. Heat in a 375° oven for 15 minutes. Serves 7-14. NOTE: If this is prepared in advance, cover with foil to prevent drying.

Marilyn Brown Wykoff (Mrs. Victor C.)
Class of '59
Mother of Wendy '86
Stockton, California

"The amount of vegetables used depends on the number of guests invited. It is easy, different, delicious and perfect for a summer barbecue."

EXPANDABLE VEGETABLE CASSEROLE

Sliced eggplant　　　　　　*Broken soda crackers*
Chopped onions　　　　　　*Sliced cheddar cheese*
Chopped tomatoes　　　　　*Beer*
Sliced zucchini, optional　　*Tomato sauce*

Layer all ingredients, except the beer and tomato sauce, in the order given in a buttered casserole dish. Pour the beer and tomato sauce over all and bake in a 350° oven for 1½ hours.

Mrs. Francis E. Sammons, Jr.
Menlo Park, California

SPINACH-ARTICHOKE CASSEROLE

2 (6 ounce) jars marinated　　*3 (3 ounee) package cream*
artichoke hearts　　　　　　　*cheese*
3 (10 ounce) packages frozen　*4 tablespoons soft butter*
spinach, *thawed*　　　　　　*6 tablespoons milk*
　　　　　　　　　　　　　　1/3 cup Parmesan cheese

Line the bottom of a 1½ quart casserole with the drained artichoke hearts. Squeeze excess liquid from the spinach and spread over the artichokes. With a mixer, blend the butter and cream cheese; add the milk and spread over the spinach. Sprinkle with the Parmesan cheese and bake, uncovered, for 40 minutes in a 375° oven. Serves 8. NOTE: This may be refrigerated for up to 24 hours.

Charlotte Daniel (Mrs. Donald)
Upper School Faculty
Pacific Grove, California

UNCLE EDDIE'S SPINACH CASSEROLE

1 (10 ounce) package frozen　*½ cup shredded cheddar cheese*
spinach　　　　　　　　　　*1 egg*
1 (10 ounce) can cream of　　*Salt*
mushroom soup　　　　　　　*Pepperidge Farm dressing*

Thaw and drain the spinach; mix with the soup, egg, cheese and salt. Place in a small buttered casserole and sprinkle with Pepperidge Farm dressing. Bake in a 350° oven for 1 hour. Serves 2-3.

Mollie Love (Mrs. Richard J.)
Mother of Victoria '84
San Francisco, California

CLAM AND SPINACH SHELLS

1 green onion, finely chopped
2 tablespoons butter
2 (7½ ounce) cans minced clams
1/3 cup dry white wine
1 (10 ounce) package frozen
  spinach, thawed

2 tablespoons cornstarch
¼ cup heavy cream
¼ teaspoon salt
1/8 teaspoon nutmeg
6 tablespoons grated Romano
  cheese
½ cup shredded Swiss cheese

Saute the green onion in the butter until limp. Drain the clams, reserving the juice, and add to the onion, stirring until well coated. Add the dry white wine and cook until the liquid is reduced by half. Drain well the thawed chopped spinach, and add to the clam and onion mixture. Place the cornstarch in a small pan and blend in the clam juice and heavy cream. Stir and cook until thickened. Season with salt and nutmeg. Combine with the spinach and clam mixture and spoon into 6 buttered scallop shells. Combine the cheeses and sprinkle over the mixture. Bake in a 400° oven for 15 minutes.

Patricia Allen Sparacino (Mrs. Robert)
Class of '65
San Mateo, California

"This recipe is quick and easy to prepare and compliments any meal."

SPINACH DELUXE

2 (9 ounce) packages frozen
  creamed spinach
½ cup sliced mushrooms
½ cup chopped onion

2 slices bacon, cooked and
  crumbled
2 tablespoons butter
6 eggs, beaten
½ cup white cheddar cheese

Cook the spinach according to package directions; set aside. Saute the mushrooms and onions with the crumbled bacon in the butter until the onions are soft but not browned. Add the spinach and heat until warm; stir in the eggs and cook until set. Pour into a buttered 13 x 9 x 2 dish, cover with the cheese, adding more if desired, and broil until the cheese melts. Cut into squares and serve.

Linda Kuenzli Theiring (Mrs. James)
Class of '58
Aptos, California

"A touch of the Italian-Swiss who first brought dairy farms to Greenfield is found in this subtle blending of spinach, cream, wine, Parmesan cheese and, of course, olive oil."

SPINACH GREENFIELD

3 slices bacon
1 pound chopped spinach
1 tablespoon olive oil
2 cloves garlic, crushed

1 onion, finely chopped
½ cup J. Lohr Johannisberg
* Riesling*
3 tablespoons Parmesan cheese
Sour cream or whipping cream

Fry the bacon until crisp; drain, reserving the drippings. Cook the spinach and drain well, set aside. In a skillet, add the olive oil, 1 tablespoon of the bacon drippings, the garlic, onion, salt and pepper; saute until the onions are golden brown. Add the wine and simmer until reduced. Stir in the spinach and 2 tablespoons of the Parmesan cheese and cook, stirring constantly, until thoroughly heated. Add the crumbled bacon and the remaining Parmesan. Remove from the heat and blend in the sour cream or whipping cream to desired consistency. Serves 4-6.

Turgeon and Lohr Winery
San Jose, California

SPINACH-RICE CASSEROLE

1 cup raw rice
1 (10 ounce) package frozen
* chopped spinach*
1 pound sharp Cheddar cheese,
* grated*

1 (10 ounce) can cream of
* mushroom soup*
1 pint half and half
Paprika

Cook the rice and the spinach according to package directions. Spread the rice evenly on the bottom of a buttered large shallow baking dish. Cover with half the grated cheese, then all of the well drained spinach; sprinkle with the remaining cheese. Combine the soup and the cream and pour evenly over the casserole. Shake the pan to settle. Garnish with paprika and bake slowly for 1½ hours in a 275° oven. Serves 6-8. NOTE: This casserole can be made ahead and cooked the next day quite easily.

Chris Sullivan (Mrs. Ray)
Aunt of Kim Bowden '87
San Mateo, California

LEEKS WITH RICE

2 pounds fresh leeks
2 tablespoons olive oil
¾ cup finely chopped onions
1 teaspoon flour

1 teaspoon salt
½ teaspoon sugar
1½ cups water
3 tablespoons Uncle Ben's rice

Cut the roots from the leeks, remove all but 2 inches of green tops, and wash well under cold water to remove grit. Slice the leeks crosswise in about 1 inch sections and set aside. Heat the oil in a heavy casserole; add the onions and stir for 5 minutes or until limp and transparent but not brown. Stir in the flour, salt and sugar, cook for about a minute, add the water and raise the temperature to high, stirring constantly until the mixture comes to a boil and thickens slightly. Add the rice and leeks, stir to cover with the sauce, reduce heat, cover tightly and simmer for 30 minutes, or until the leeks and rice are tender but still intact. This can be served warm or at room temperature. Serve with lemon wedges.

Kate Craft (Mrs. Jack)
Mother of Lisa '69
Carmel, California

RICE PILAF WITH CASHEWS

½ cup butter
1 (8 ounce) package fine noodles
1 cup raw rice
2 cups chicken broth

4-5 bouillon cubes
1½ cups boiling water
½ pound unsalted cashews

In a large saucepan or skillet, melt the butter. Add the noodles and saute over low heat, stirring constantly until lightly browned. (Be careful as they burn easily.) Add the raw rice and chicken broth to the sauteed noodles and mix well. Dissolve the bouillon cubes in boiling water and add to the rice mixture. Cover the pilaf and cook over low heat until all of the liquid is absorbed, about 30 minutes. Sprinkle cashews on the top before serving. Serves 4-6. NOTE: This may be made a day ahead and reheated in a low oven, adding extra chicken broth if it gets too dry.

Joanne Cohen (Mrs. Sheldon)
Mother of Poppy '86
Fresno, California

SPICY RICE

1¼ cups uncooked rice · Salt
8 ounces sour cream · 3 tablespoons butter
1 (4 ounce) can diced green chiles · ½ pound Monterey jack cheese

Cook the rice according to package directions, and combine with the sour cream and green chiles. Salt as desired. Place half of the mixture in a buttered 2-quart baking dish; dot with butter and layer with thin slices of the cheese. Repeat the process. Cover the casserole and bake in a preheated 350° oven for 40 minutes. Serves 4.

Laurie McWhorter Kehl (Mrs. James)
Class of '72
Farmington, New Mexico

"Very easy and a delicious accompaniment to beef or fish."

CHILI CHEESE RICE

2 cups cooked medium or long · ½ pound Monterey jack cheese,
  grain rice ·   grated
2 cups sour cream · 2 (4 ounce) cans diced green
·   chiles

Combine all ingredients and place in a 2-quart buttered baking dish. Bake in a 375° oven for 45 minutes or until brown. Serves 8-10.

Sheila Mathews (Mrs. Charles)
Mother of Christine, '83
Marysville, California

CHEESE GRITS

1½ cup hominy grits · 2 teaspoons salt
6 cups water · 2 drops Tabasco
1 pound grated cheddar cheese · 3 eggs, beaten
¾ cup butter · 3 teaspoons seasoning salt,
·   optional

Cook the hominy grits in the six cups of boiling water until thick and dry. Add the cheese, butter, salt, Tabasco, eggs and seasoning salt, if desired. Place in an oblong shallow baking dish and bake in a 350° for 1-1½ hours. This is excellent served with chicken or pork.

Mrs. Price Berrien
Santa Barbara, California

MOTHER'S HOMINY GRITS

1 cup hominy grits
4 cups milk
½ cup butter
½ teaspoon salt

2 cups grated cheddar cheese
1 tablespoon butter
½ cup Parmesan cheese

Combine the hominy grits with the milk and butter over medium heat, stirring constantly until thick. Add the salt and cheddar cheese and place in a buttered 2-quart casserole. Spread with the 1 tablespoon butter and top with the Parmesan cheese. Bake, uncovered, 1 hour in a 350° oven. NOTE: This can be made ahead and refrigerated, unbaked.

Beezie Leyden Moore (Mrs. H. Walker)
Class of '53
Clovis, California

HOMINY DISH

2 large yellow onions, chopped
2 green bell peppers, chopped
2 (29 ounce) cans yellow hominy

2 (10 ounce) cans mushroom
  soup
1 pound sharp cheddar cheese,
  grated
Paprika

In a skillet, saute the onions and bell pepper until the onion is translucent. Combine with the remaining ingredients and place in a large oiled casserole. Garnish with a sprinkling of paprika and bake, uncovered, for 1 hour in a 325° oven. Serves 12.

Janet Bruno (Mrs. Frank)
Mother of Michael and Christopher
Monterey, California

DELUXE BAKED BEANS

1 onion, chopped
1 green pepper, chopped
2 stalks celery, chopped
2 tablespoons molasses
½ cup catsup
2 drops Tabasco

1 teaspoon dry mustard
1 (16 ounce) can pork and beans
1 (16 ounce) can B & M baked
  beans
Bacon or Polish sausages or
  frankfurters or ham slices

Combine all ingredients and bake in a 375° oven for 25-30 minutes, or place in a crock pot on high for 1 hour and low for 4-6 hours. Serves 6.

Amy Kajikuri
Class of '80
Carmel, California

BUFFALO BAKED BEANS

1 pound dried lima beans   1 cup brown sugar
1 cup butter   1 cup catsup
1 cup chili sauce

Soak beans and cook according to package directions; drain and set aside. Combine the butter, chili sauce, brown sugar and catsup in a medium bowl to make a sauce. In a bean pot or roaster, combine the beans and sauce. Bake for 3½ hours in a preheated 250° oven. Serves 4. NOTE: Slices of hot dogs may also be added for extra flavor.

Joanne Cohen (Mrs. Sheldon)
Mother of Poppy '86
Fresno, California

SPANISH BEANS WITH RUM AND SOUR CREAM

1 pound dried black beans   1 teaspoon pepper
1 onion, finely chopped   3 tablespoons butter
3 ribs celery, chopped   2 jiggers dark rum
1 carrot, diced   Cold sour cream
2-3 teaspoons salt   Chopped green onions

Soak the beans overnight; drain. Cover the beans with water in a large pot or kettle. Add the onion, celery, carrot, salt and pepper; bring to a boil and simmer for 2 hours. Place in a bean pot with the butter, add 1 jigger of rum, mixing well. Cover and bake in a 325° oven until tender. Stir in the remaining rum. Serve in bowls and garnish with sour cream and chopped green onion.

Jennifer English (Mrs. John)
Mother of Lauren '85 and Alison, Summer Camp
Lafayette, California

"This is a garni for Bar-B-Q leg of lamb, lamb chops, rack of lamb, or any place a chutney or mint jelly is needed. These are beautiful on the plate."

MINT JELLY CRESCENTS

1 tablespoon gelatin   1 (12 ounce) jar mint jelly
2 tablespoons cold water

Dissolve the gelatin in the cold water. In a saucepan, melt the jelly; do not boil. Add the gelatin and cook until dissolved; skim, Cool. Pour into small orange juice cans and refrigerate until set. Remove from cans by opening the bottoms and pushing the jelly out. Dip a sharp kitchen knife in warm water and slice into 1 inch slices. Cut the slices into crescent shapes. NOTE: Small cookie cutters may be used to make other shapes.

Susan Grupe Smith (Mrs. Wilbur)
Class of '66
Stockton, California

DRESSING FOR RACK OF LAMB

6 slices of white bread
6 slices of whole wheat bread
4 tablespoons butter
2 ounces dark rum
3 firm, sour apples
6 ounces cooked ham, finely diced

2 teaspoons sugar
Salt
Pepper
2 teaspoons dried sweet basil
6 teaspoons fresh parsley

Trim crusts from bread and cut into cubes; brown on a baking sheet in the oven. Melt the butter in a pan with the dark rum; add the apples, ham, sugar, salt and pepper. Stir briefly and remove from heat. Combine with the bread cubes, basil and parsley. Heat thoroughly in a buttered casserole. Serve with rack of lamb, boiled potatoes, glazed baby carrots and a good red wine.

Latchmee Schultz (Mrs. Rolf)
Mother of Melanie and Debbie
Salinas, California

BUTTER-CRUMB HERB DUMPLINGS

2 cups flour
4 teaspoons baking powder
½ teaspoon salt
1 teaspoon poultry seasoning
1 teaspoon celery seed
1 teaspoon onion flakes

1 teaspoon poppy seeds, optional
¼ cup salad oil
1 cup milk
¼ cup melted butter
1 cup fine bread crumbs

Sift together the flour, baking powder and salt; add the poultry seasoning, celery seed, onion flakes and poppy seeds if desired. Add the salad oil and the milk, stirring until just moistened. Drop rounded teaspoonful of dough into the melted butter and coat well before rolling in the bread crumbs. Place the dumplings on a hot stew. Bake, uncovered, for 20-25 minutes in a 425° oven or until a deep golden brown.

Kathi Bowden
Mother of Kim '87
Monterey, California

HEAVENLY POTATOES

6 medium potatoes, parboiled
and grated
¾ cup grated yellow cheese
2 green onions, finely chopped
1 (10 ounce) can cream of
chicken soup

1 (8 ounce) package cream
cheese, softened
Parsley, chopped
Paprika

In a buttered 9 x 13 inch glass baking dish, layer half of the potatoes, the yellow cheese and the onions. Repeat. Blend together the soup and the cream cheese and pour over the casserole. Garnish with the parsley and paprika. Bake in a 350° oven until hot and bubbly. Serves 8. NOTE: May be assembled ahead and heated before serving.

Ellen Van Der Plas (Mrs. Gerry)
Mother of Joanne, '84
Arcadia, California

CREAMED POTATOES

5 tablespoons butter
5 tablespoons flour
2 cups half and half
2/3 cup chicken broth
5 tablespoons Parmesan cheese,
grated
1 teaspoon salt

½ teaspoon white pepper
2 pounds potatoes, cooked,
peeled and diced
2 tablespoons Roquefort cheese,
crumbled, optional
2 or more teaspoons melted
butter
2 teaspoons paprika

Melt the 5 tablespoons butter in a saucepan; add the flour and cook over low heat, stirring for 2 minutes. Remove from the heat and gradually stir in the cream; add the chicken broth. Cook, stirring until thick. Add the cheese, salt and pepper, fold in the potatoes. Divide the mixture evenly among 6-8 buttered ramekins or place in a buttered 2-quart casserole. Sprinkle with the Roquefort, if desired, the melted butter and paprika. Bake in a 425° oven for 12-14 minutes or until bubbly. Serves 6-8.

Kristin Searle (Mrs. Dan)
Mother of Danny
Salinas, California

"This can be baked while the meat is being carved and the gravy made!"

FESTIVE POTATO CASSEROLE

2 pounds potatoes   1 egg
1 medium onion, finely chopped 1 (4 ounce) package whipped
                                                          cream cheese

Boil and mash the potatoes as usual, omitting butter in the preparation. Combine with the remaining ingredients and place in a buttered casserole; bake in a 350° oven for 30 minutes. Serves 6. NOTE: This may be prepared a day ahead, and the oven time can be varied according to what else is in the oven.

Margaret Brooks (Mrs. Chester)
Aunt of Kim Bowden '87
West Dennis, Massachusetts

SWEET POTATO BALLS

1 (16 ounce) can sweet potatoes, ½ cup light brown sugar, packed
   drained   6 large marshmallows
1 teaspoon vanilla   Crushed cornflakes

Mash the sweet potatoes thoroughly; add the brown sugar and vanilla and blend well. Wrap enough of the sweet potato mixture around each marshmallow to cover well, forming in a ball. Roll in the crushed cornflakes and bake in a shallow baking dish for 6-10 minutes in a 350° oven. Serves 6.

Shirley Becker (Mrs. Arthur)
Mother of Brianna, Summer Camp
Calabasas Park, California

Fathers have come from as far away as Saudi Arabia and Hong Kong to attend the Annual Father-Daughter Weekend at Santa Catalina School. The festivities begin on a Friday with a reception for the fathers followed by dinner in restaurants on the Monterey Peninsula, and dancing. Saturday is a day for sports and a steak barbeque on campus. There are awards for sports as well as awards for fathers who have come the farthest and attended the most years. In the evening, the fathers are entertained by their daughters with a musical, such as Gigi or Hello Dolly!, and the fathers, in turn, entertain their daughters with skits. Mass is followed by brunch on Sunday morning. It is the most fun filled, appreciated, looked-forward-to weekend of the year.

LAYERED SWEET POTATOE AND CRANBERRY CASSEROLE

4 large sweet potatoes
½ cup packed light brown sugar
2 tablespoons butter

1 cup fresh cranberries
½ cup fresh orange juice

WALNUT TOPPING:
½ cup chopped walnuts
2 tablespoons melted butter

1 tablespoon brown sugar
½ teaspoon cinnamon

Place the sweet potatoes in a saucepan and add water to cover; boil 30-40 minutes or until tender. Drain, cool slightly, peel and cut into ¼ inch slices. Arrange ½ of the sliced sweet potatoes in an oiled 1½ quart casserole and sprinkle with ¼ cup of the brown sugar. Dot with butter and sprinkle ½ cup of the cranberries over the top. Cover with the remaining potatoes, sprinkle with the remaining brown sugar, add the remaining cranberries and pour the orange juice over all. Cover and bake in a 350° oven for 45 minutes. Make the WALNUT TOPPING by combining all ingredients in a small bowl. Uncover the casserole and distribute the walnut topping over the casserole. Bake 10 minutes more. Serves 6-8.

April Anderson Bettencourt (Mrs. Jerry)
Aunt of April Brazinsky
Auburn, California

CRANBERRY FLUFF

1 (16 ounce) package fresh
  cranberries
1 cup sugar
3½ cups small marshmallows

3-4 cups diced apples
¾ cup chopped nut meats
¼ teaspoon salt
1 cup whipping cream, whipped

In a blender or food processor, process the fresh cranberries; add the sugar and marshmallows and chill overnight. Just before serving, add the apples, nuts and salt and gently fold in the whipped cream. Serves 12-15. NOTE: Do not use whipped topping in this recipe as a substitute for the whipping cream.

Marie Cressey Belden (Mrs. Lester)
Mother of Cressey Joy '87
Santa Rosa, California

BLACK BANANAS

6 bananas   Oil

Rub the skins of the bananas with cooking oil. Bake in a preheated 325° oven for 45 minutes. To eat, peel 1 strip off banana and eat out of the skin. Serve with roast duck, goose, ham or pork.

Libby Warner (Mrs. Silas)
Cousin of Margaret Skillicorn '86
Gladwyne, Pennsylvania

APPLE ONION PIE

1 (21 ounce) can apple pie filling   3 tablespoons melted butter
1/3 cup minced onion   ½ cup bread crumbs
1 (9-inch) pie crust, unbaked

Combine the pie filling and minced onion and pour into an unbaked pie shell. Toss the crumbs with the melted butter and evenly distribute over the pie filling. Bake 25-35 minutes in a 425° oven. Serve hot as an accompaniment to meat. Serves 6-8. NOTE: This is scrumptious with pork. For a less rich meal, cook in a casserole, omitting the pie crust.

Margaret Brooks (Mrs. Chester)
Aunt of Kim Bowden '87
West Dennis, Massachusetts

CURRIED FRUIT

1 (16 ounce) can peach halves   1/3 cup butter
1 (16 ounce) can pear halves   ¾ cup brown sugar, packed
1 (16 ounce) can pineapple   4 teaspoons curry powder (or to
   chunks   taste)
5 maraschino cherries

Drain the fruit, pat dry and layer in a buttered casserole dish. In a saucepan, melt the butter; add the sugar and curry powder and stir until dissolved. Pour the sauce over the fruit in the casserole and bake in a 325° oven for 1 hour. Serve warm. Makes 4-6 servings.

Mrs. Lee B. Price
Monterey, California

"This is delicious with lamb and with curry dishes, and it is a nice hostess or holiday gift."

OLD FASHIONED NECTARINE CHUTNEY

2 cups cider vinegar
1 pound light brown sugar
1½ teaspoons salt
1 teaspoon ground ginger
¼ teaspoon cayenne
2 cups pared, diced apples OR
*   canned, drained pineapple tidbits*

1 cup thinly sliced onion
1 cup raisins
½ lemon, thinly sliced
3 cups sliced nectarines

Combine the vinegar, brown sugar, salt, ginger and cayenne in a large saucepan and cook over low heat until reduced to about half. Add the apple, onion, raisins and lemon and cook 10 minutes longer. Stir in the nectarines and bring just to a boil. Chill well. This chutney will keep for months tightly covered in the refrigerator.

Kit Nelson Bedford (Mrs. Peter)
Class of '56
Mother of Laura '85
Lafayette, California

"This condiment is always appreciated and it goes well with lamb or fowl."

PEACH CHUTNEY

½ to 1 pound raisins
½ cup chopped onion
1 clove garlic
4 pounds fresh peaches, sliced
2/3 cup fresh ginger, peeled and
*   shredded*

2 tablespoons red chili pepper
2 tablespoons mustard seeds
1 tablespoon salt
2 cups vinegar
1½ cups brown sugar

Combine all ingredients in a large pan and bring to a boil, uncovered, stirring constantly. Simmer 1-2 hours or longer until it is rather thick and a rich brown color. Pour into sterilized jars and seal. NOTE: Correct for flavor, adding a little sugar or more chopped raisins, if neeeded, as it is cooking.

Jeanne Adams (Mrs. Michael)
Mother of Sarah '83
Fresno, California

MANGO CHUTNEY

6 cups granulated sugar
2 teaspoons ground cinnamon
1 teaspoon ground cloves
1 teaspoon ground allspice
2 teaspoons chili powder
3 teaspoons curry powder
Juice and grated rind of 1 lime
3 cups vinegar

1 small hot green or Jalapeno
  pepper, minced
½ cup ginger root, finely sliced
1 clove garlic, finely chopped
1 medium onion, finely chopped
12 cups diced green, or part ripe,
  peeled mangoes
3 cups seedless raisins

Mix together the sugar and spices in a large pot or kettle. Stir in the lime juice, grated lime and vinegar. Add remaining ingredients except for the mangos and raisins. Bring to a boil and boil for 2 minutes; add the diced mangos. Simmer for ½ hour, stirring occasionally. Add the raisins and simmer 15 minutes more. Put into sterilized glass jars and cover with melted paraffin; cool. Put lids on the jars and store in a cool place.

Priscilla Hathorn
Monterey, California

INDIAN CHUTNEY

2 pounds sultanas
2 pounds dates
1 pound dried apricots
2 pounds green tomatoes
½ pound dried peaches
5 large green apples
4 large red chiles

½ pound green ginger
2 pounds brown sugar
¼ pound salt
4 pints vinegar
1 dessert-spoon allspice
1 dessert-spoon cloves

Finely mince the sultanas, dates, dried apricots, tomatoes, dried peaches, apples and ginger and combine in a bowl with the brown sugar. Add the salt, vinegar, allspice and cloves and simmer for 2 hours in an enameled pot. Spoon into sterilized jars and seal.

Margaret Blackwell
Mother of Stella '73
Santa Cruz, California

STRAWBERRY BUTTER

½ cup butter   Pinch of salt
2½ cups powdered sugar   ½ cup crushed strawberries
1 teaspoon vanilla

Beat the butter until light and fluffy and then gradually beat in the sugar, vanilla and salt; add the crushed strawberries. Serves 5. NOTE: Keep refrigerated and use the strawberry butter as a jam.

Sally Post (Mrs. Roger)
Mother of Shelley '79, Jennifer '82
and Stefanie '85
Pacific Grove, California

"For those on salt-free diets, and for those who prefer as little salt in their diets as possible, these herb blends are offered."

HERB BLENDS

BLEND I (for vegetables and meat)
1 teaspoon thyme   ¾ teaspoon rosemary
1 teaspoon marjoram   ½ teaspoon sage

BLEND II (for vegetables, poultry and meat)
¾ teaspoon marjoram   ½ tablespoon sage
½ teaspoon thyme   ½ teaspoon rosemary
½ teaspoon oregano

BLEND III (for fish)
¾ teaspoon parsley flakes   ¼ teaspoon marjoram
½ teaspoon onion powder   ¼ teaspoon paprika
½ teaspoon sage

BLEND IV (for meat, potatoes and vegetables)
1 teaspoon dry mustard   ½ teaspoon thyme
½ teaspoon sage   ¼ teaspoon marjoram

John H. Brazinsky, M.D.
Father of April
Carmel, California

"I sometimes use salt substitutes and give as gifts to people on low-salt diets."

SEASONED SALT

4 tablespoons salt
1 tablespoon sugar
1 tablespoon Accent (MSG)
1 tablespoon paprika
1 tablespoon celery seed
1 teaspoon mace

1 teaspoon nutmeg
1 teaspoon curry powder
1 teaspoon garlic powder
1 teaspoon onion powder
1 teaspoon dry mustard

Mix well. These ingredients may be varied to taste and used in cooking and on the table for seasoning instead of plain salt.

Jeanne Adams (Mrs. Michael)
Mother of Sarah '83
Fresno, California

Desserts

JUSTICE LILLIE'S CHOCOLATE MOUSSE PIE

CHOCOLATE CRUST:
2/3 of an 8½ ounce package   *2 tablespoons butter, melted*
chocolate wafers

MOUSSE:
8 eggs, separated   *10 ounces unsweetened*
1½ cups plus 3 tablespoons sugar   *chocolate*
2 teaspoons vanilla   *2 ounces semi-sweet chocolate*
¼ teaspoon salt   *¾ cup butter, softened*
½ cup brandy   *½ cup coffee*
     1½ cups whipping cream

For the crust: Place the wafers in a blender and process until the crumbs are very fine. Combine with the butter and pat into the sides and bottom of a buttered 9 x 2½ inch springform pan. Bake in a 325° oven for 10 minutes. Remove from oven and cool completely. For the mousse: Beat the egg yolks in the top of a double boiler with 1½ cups of the sugar, the vanilla, salt and brandy over simmering water until pale yellow and thick, about 8 to 10 minutes. Remove from water and set aside. Melt both types of the chocolate in the top of a double boiler over hot water. When melted, remove from water and beat in the butter, a bit at a time; gradually beat the chocolate into the egg yolk mixture until smooth (chocolate will congeal and become very stiff). Beat in the coffee. In a separate bowl, beat the egg whites into soft peaks; gradually beat in 3 tablespoons sugar until stiff peaks form. Beat 1 cup of beaten egg whites into chocolate mixture, then carefully fold in remaining egg whites until thoroughly incorporated. Whip cream until stiff and gently fold into chocolate mixture. Pour into crust and chill overnight. Garnish with Cherry Cordials. Serves 6-9.

CHERRY CORDIALS

13 maraschino cherries with   *½ cup brandy*
steams, drained   *5 ounces semi-sweet chocolate*

Soak the cherries in brandy and place in the freezer. Melt the chocolate over hot water. When the cherries are frozen, dry on a paper towel; quickly dip, one at a time, into the chocolate, swirling around by the stem, until completely covered. Place on a wax paper lined rack in the refrigerator until ready to use.

Mr. Cary Grant, Father of Jennifer '83
Beverly Hills, California

"Very, very rich and fattening."

CHOCOLATE MOUSSE

8 ounces pastry chocolate
3 ounces unsalted butter
4 egg yolks
1 cup heavy cream, whipped

2 tablespoons sugar
1 tablespoon vanilla
1 tablespoon dark rum
4 egg whites, optional

Melt the chocolate with the butter in the top of a double boiler. Add the egg yolks, beating well after each addition. Whip the cream with the sugar, vanilla and rum, and fold into the chocolate mixture. If desired, fold in the stiffly beaten egg whites for a much lighter mousse. Chill at least 6 hours before serving. Serves 6-10.

Louise Harris (Mrs. Joseph)
Mother of Gingy '83
San Francisco, California

CHOCOLATE MOUSSE

2 tablespoons sweet butter
24 lady fingers
4 square semi-sweet baking
   chocolate
1 square unsweetened chocolate
2/3 cup plus 3 tablespoons
   superfine sugar

2-4 tablespoons powdered
   instant coffee
1/3 cup warm water
2 cups heavy cream
¾ cup sweet butter
9 egg yolks
9 egg whites
Pinch of cream of tartar

Butter a springform pan with the 2 tablespoons of sweet butter. Line with ladyfingers and place in the refrigerator. Melt all the chocolate in a double boiler. Add 2/3 cup of the sugar and blend in the instant coffee and water; cool. Whip the cream and refrigerate. Cream the butter with an electric mixer and beat in the egg yolks, one at a time. When the chocolate mixture cools and begins to harden, stir into the egg yolk mixture. Beat the egg whites with the cream of tartar; add the remaining sugar and continue to beat until stiff, but not dry. Alternately blend the whipped cream and the stiffly beaten egg whites into the chocolate. Pour into the prepared pan and refrigerate or freeze. If frozen, remove from the freezer 6 hours prior to serving and refrigerate. Chill plates and platter. Unmold and frost, if desired, with whipped cream flavored with Swiss mocha, vanilla and sugar. Garnish with ½ cup toasted almonds. NOTE: The amount of coffee may be varied from 2 to 4 tablespoons, according to taste.

Mary Jane Wesson (Mrs. W.P.)
Mother of Jameen '77
Modesto, California

CHOCOLATE MOUSSE CAKE

1 cup butter
2 cups powdered sugar
8 eggs, separated
1 teaspoon vanilla

3 tablespoons brandy
8 squares unsweetened chocolate
1 cup whipping cream, whipped
2 dozen ladyfingers

Cream the butter and sugar; beat in the egg yolks, vanilla and brandy. Melt the chocolate over hot water and add to the creamed mixture. Whip the cream and add to the chocolate mixture. Beat the egg whites until stiff. Line a springform pan with a portion of the ladyfingers. Layer the chocolate alternately with the remaining ladyfingers. Best made 1-2 days ahead of serving. Serves 8 generously.

Nina Davis Gray (Mrs. Elisha)
Class of '62
Winnetka, Illinois

CHOCOLATE MOUSSE CAKE

7 ounces semi-sweet chocolate
¼ pound unsalted butter
7 eggs, separated

1 cup sugar
1 teaspoon vanilla
1/8 teaspoon cream of tartar

WHIPPED CREAM FROSTING:
1 cup whipping cream
1/3 cup powdered sugar

Vanilla

In a small saucepan, melt the chocolate and butter over low heat. In a large bowl, beat the egg yolks and ¾ cup of the sugar until very light and fluffy, about 5 minutes. Gradually beat in the warm chocolate mixture and the vanilla. In another large bowl, beat the egg whites with the cream of tartar until soft peaks form. Add the remaining ¼ cup sugar, 1 tablespoon at a time, and continue beating until stiff. Fold the egg whites carefully into the chocolate mixture. Pour ¾ of the batter into an ungreased 9-inch springform pan. Cover the remaining batter and refrigerate. Bake the cake 35 minutes in a preheated 325° oven. Prepare the whipped cream frosting by beating the cream until soft peaks form; add the powdered sugar and vanilla and beat until stiff; set aside. Remove the cake from the oven and cool (the cake will drop as it cools). Remove outside rings from the springform pan. Stir the refrigerated batter to soften lightly and spread over the cake; refrigerate until firm. Spread the whipped cream frosting over the top and sides. Garnish with shaved chocolate, if desired. Refrigerate several hours or overnight. This may be frozen. Serves 8-10.

Mrs. Donald J. Atha
Mother of Abigail, Summer Camper
Hillsborough, California

CHOCOLATE CHEESECAKE

CRUST:
1½ cups zweiback crumbs   *1/3 cup melted butter*
3 tablespoons sugar

CHEESECAKE:
3 (8 ounce) packages cream   *1 cup sugar*
*   cheese*   *1 ounce unsweetened chocolate,*
1 tablespoon vanilla   *   melted*
½ teaspoon salt   *1 teaspoon instant coffee powder*
4 large eggs

Make the crust by blending together the crumbs, sugar and butter and pressing over the bottom and sides of an 8 or 9 inch springform pan. Set aside. Blend the softened cream cheese with the vanilla and salt. In a separate bowl, beat the eggs until thickened and blend in the sugar gradually until the mixture is lemon colored. Continue beating while adding the cream cheese mixture, a little at a time, blending until smooth. Stir in the melted chocolate and the instant coffee powder, mixing well. Pour into the prepared pan and bake in a 350° oven for 25-30 minutes. Cool and garnish with whipped cream and chocolate curls as desired. Serves 8.

Sandra Smith (Mrs. Stanley)
Mother of Laura
Pebble Beach, California

CHOCOLATE CHEESECAKE

1½ cups fine graham cracker   *3 tablespoons heavy cream*
*   crumbs*   *2 cups sour cream*
½ cup butter   *½ cup dark rum*
2 cups sugar   *¾ teaspoon cinnamon*
3 (8 ounce) packages cream   *¾ teaspoon almond extract*
*   cheese*   *1 cup confectioners' sugar*
3 eggs   *1 cup fresh strawberries*
½ pound semi-sweet chocolate

Mix together the graham cracker crumbs with the butter and 3 table-spoons of the sugar, blending well. Press the mixture evenly onto the bottom of a 10-inch springform pan. Beat the cream cheese until light; gradually beat in the remaining sugar and the eggs and continue beating until the mixture is perfectly smooth. In a small saucepan, melt toge-ther the chocolate and the heavy cream and beat into the cream cheese mixture along with 1 cup of the sour cream. Add the rum, cinnamon and almond extract and beat a few minutes more. Pour into the prepared pan and bake in a preheated 350° oven for 55 minutes to 1 hour. Allow the cake to cool before frosting. Blend together the remaining 1 cup sour cream and the confectioner's sugar and spread it over the top of the cake. Slice each strawberry in half lengthwise and arrange, cut side down and tips pointing toward the center around the edge of the cake. Chill at least 1½ hours before serving. Serves 12-14. NOTE: If a smooth top is desired, remove the pan side and slice the uneven edges carefully from the top with a sharp knife; smooth the cut area with a butter knife.

Pamela Wilson
Class of '84
San Diego, California

GERMAN CHOCOLATE CHEESECAKE

CRUST:
1 cup chocolate wafer crumbs
3 tablespoons butter, melted
2 tablespoons sugar

FILLING:
3 (8 ounce) packages cream cheese
¾ cup sugar
¼ cup cocoa
2 teaspoons vanilla
3 eggs

TOPPING:
2 tablespoons butter
¼ cup evaporated milk
2 tablespoons brown sugar
1 egg, beaten
½ teaspoon vanilla
½ cup chopped pecans
½ cup flaked coconut

For crust, combine the crumbs, melted butter and sugar and press onto the bottom of a 9-inch springform pan. Bake in a 250° oven for 10 minutes. Remove and increase the oven temperature to 350°. For filling, combine the softened cream cheese, sugar, cocoa and vanilla, mixing at medium speed in the electric mixer until well blended. Add the eggs, one at a time, mixing well after each addition. Pour mixture over the crust. Bake in a 350° oven for 35 minutes. Loosen cake from the rim of the pan, cool before removing the rim. Chill. For the topping, melt the butter in a saucepan over low heat. Blend in the milk, brown sugar, egg and vanilla. Cook, stirring constantly until thick. Stir in the nuts and coconut; cool. Spread over the cheesecake.

Joanne May
Class of '71
Oakland, California

"This is an absolute chocolate lover's delight. It freezes well and can be thawed for 'special company'. Cheesecake improves with ripening after baking, so if possible, make it the day before you plan to serve it. Enjoy! But be careful, this recipe is addicting!"

CHOCOLATE ESPRESSO CHEESECAKE

4 tablespoons ground espresso
  coffee
2/3 cup boiling water
3 (8 ounce) packages cream
  cheese
1 cup sugar
2 eggs

1 cup sour cream
8 ounces semi-sweet chocolate
  (melted)
1 teaspoon vanilla
Chocolate crust
Chocolate curls for garnish,
  optional

Brew a strong extract of espresso with the boiling water and ground coffee in any coffee maker or place the coffee in a cheesecloth-lined strainer over a bowl. Moisten evenly with boiling water, press and squeeze to extract the concentrate. Measure ½ cup of the extract and set aside to cool. Beat the cream cheese, sugar and eggs in a large bowl until blended. Beat in the sour cream, melted chocolate, espresso concentrate and vanilla. Pour into a crust-lined 8-inch springform pan and bake in a 350° oven for 45 minutes (the soft center will firm up during cooling). Cool, then chill 3 hours or more until firm in the center. Remove side of pan and garnish with chocolate curls, if desired. To make the chocolate curls, draw a vegetable peeler across the surface of a warm (slightly warmer than room temperature) chocolate square.

CHOCOLATE CRUST

24 Nabisco's Famous Chocolate
  Wafers

½ cup soft butter
½ teaspoon cinnamon

Crush the chocolate wafers between sheets of wax paper to make fine crumbs. Mix with the soft butter and cinnamon until crumbly. Press evenly into an ungreased 8-inch springform pan.

Teresa Rothe
Class of '74
San Diego, California

All nine members of Santa Catalina's first graduating class attended their 30th reunion in 1983. Alumnae reunions are held in March of every year and the classes specially honored are those who are celebrating their 5th, 10th, 15th, 20th, 25th, and 30th year reunions.

KAHLUA CHEESECAKE

CRUST:
1½ cups fine zwieback crumbs 1/3 cup melted butter
1/3 cup sugar

CHEESECAKE:
2 envelopes unflavored gelatin 1/8 teaspoon salt
½ cup Kahlua 2 (8 ounce) packages cream
½ cup water cheese
3 eggs, separated 1 cup whipping cream
¼ cup sugar Shaved or curled semi-sweet
chocolate pieces

For crust, blend together the crumbs, sugar and melted butter, and press firmly over the bottom and half-way up the sides of a 9-inch springform pan. Bake in a 350° oven for 8-10 minutes. Cool. For more flavor, spoon a little Kahlua over the crust. For the cheesecake, in the top of a double boiler, soften the gelatin in Kahlua and water. Beat in the egg yolks, sugar and salt. Cook over boiling water, stirring constantly. until slightly thickened. Beat the cream cheese until fluffy; gradually beat in the Kahlua mixture and cool. Beat the egg whites until stiff but not dry; whip the cream. Fold the egg whites and whipped cream into the cheese mixture. Pour into the prepared crust and chill 4 to 5 hours or overnight. Remove from the refrigerator 15 minutes before serving. Decorate with the chocolate. Serves 10-12.

Jennifer Michaels (Mrs. Paul)
Mother of Chrissy
Salinas, California

"This recipe is a 'second generation' Santa Catalina. My mother baked it for the 'old ladies' class of 1960, and I make it for my girls, Ann, an alum, and Peggy, class of '84."

MRS. MILLER'S CHEESECAKE

½ pint whipping cream 1 tablespoon vanilla
1 (8 ounce) package cream 1 graham cracker crust for a
cheese 9-inch pie
¾ cup powdered sugar 1 (20 ounce) can cherry pie
filling

Whip the cream; set aside. Cream the cheese, sugar and vanilla; fold in the whipped cream and pour into the crust. Chill for 1 hour; top with the cherry pie filling and chill again. Serves 8.

Wendy Miller Frasse (Mrs. I. Benjamin)
Class of '60
Mother of Ann, '82 and Wendy, '84
San Francisco, California

"I ordered this at Lindy's in 1952 and enjoyed it so much I asked for the recipe which they brought me along with my bill for 25 dollars".

LINDY'S FAMOUS CHEESECAKE
(From the old Lindy's Restaurant in New York)

CRUST:
1 cup sifted flour
¼ cup sugar
1 teaspoon grated lemon peel

½ teaspoon vanilla
1 egg yolk
¼ cup butter

FILLING:
5 (8 ounce) packages cream cheese
1¾ cup sugar
3 tablespoons flour
1½ teaspoons grated lemon peel

1½ teaspoons grated orange peel
¼ teaspoon vanilla
5 eggs
2 egg yolks
¼ cup heavy cream

For crust: Mix all ingredients until crumbly. Sprinkle ¾ of the dough over the bottom of a 9-inch springform pan; press to form a crust, being careful to seal the seam where the bottom and sides join. (Remaining dough may be discarded.) Bake in a preheated 400° oven until lightly brown, about 10 minutes. Remove from oven and increase temperature to 500°. For filling: In a mixing bowl, combine the cream cheese with the sugar, flour, lemon and orange peels, and vanilla. Add the eggs and yolks, one at a time, beating after each addition. Beat until the mixture is well combined and smooth; beat in the cream. Pour filling into the prepared pan and bake in a 500° oven for 10 minutes; reduce heat to 250° and continue baking for 50-60 minutes or until firm. Chill 3 hours or overnight. Top with a fruit topping or serve "Plain Jane". Freezes beautifully. Serves 16-20.

Nancy Deliantoni
Pebble Beach, California

THE BEST CHEESECAKE

CRUST:
2 cups graham cracker crumbs
1 cup sugar

¾ cup butter, melted
Cinnamon

FILLING:
3 (8 ounce) packages cream cheese
1 cup sugar

4 eggs
1 tablespoon vanilla

TOPPING:
12-16 ounces sour cream
½ cup sugar

Vanilla

For the crust: Combine the graham cracker crumbs, sugar, melted butter and cinammon to taste, mixing well; press into a 10-inch springform pan. Bake in a 375° oven for 10 minutes; cool. For filling: Cream together the cream cheese and sugar; add the eggs, one at a time, beating well after each addition. Blend in the vanilla. Pour into the springform pan and bake in a 350° oven for 30-35 minutes. Cool 10-20 minutes. For topping: Blend the sour cream, sugar and vanilla and spread over the cheesecake. Bake in a 400° oven for 10 minutes. Chill for 24 hours. NOTE: Gina Marie or other deli brands of cream cheese are the best.

Theresa May
Class of '69
Tahoe Vista, California

CLASSIC CHEESECAKE

CRUST:
1½ cups graham cracker crumbs   *½ teaspoon cinnamon*
½ cup butter, melted   *1 tablespoon sugar*

FILLING:
3 (8 ounce) packages cream   *1½ teaspoons vanilla*
*   cheese*   *2 teaspoons lemon juice*
¾ cup sugar   *1 teaspoon finely grated lemon*
5 eggs   *   peel*

TOPPING:
1 pint sour cream   *1 tablespoon vanilla*
4 tablespoons sugar

For crust: Combine the graham cracker crumbs, the melted butter, the cinnamon and the sugar, mixing well. Press into the bottom of a 9-inch springform pan and chill while the cake is being assembled. For filling: Combine all ingredients in a large mixing bowl and blend until smooth with an electric mixer. Pour filling into the crust and bake in a 325° oven for 50 minutes or until the center of the cake is set. For topping: Blend together the sour cream, sugar and vanilla and spread on the cheesecake while the cake is still warm. This cheese cake is best chilled for 8-24 hours before serving. Serves 8-12. NOTE: This recipe is equally good made with 3 (8 ounce) packages Neufchatel cheese in place of the cream cheese and makes for a slightly "thinner" cheesecake.

Janice Koht Marasco (Mrs. Matthew)
Class of '76
Carmel Valley, California

PUMPKIN PIE CHEESECAKE

CRUST:
6 tablespoons butter

2 cups finely crushed ginger cookies

CHEESE CAKE:
2 (8 ounce) packages cream cheese
1 cup canned pumpkin
1 cup brown sugar (lightly packed)
¼ cup flour
1 teaspoon cinnamon

1 teaspoon ginger
1 teaspoon allspice
½ teaspoon salt
1½ teaspoons vanilla
¾ cup milk
4 eggs, slightly beaten

TOPPING:
1 cup sour cream
2 tablespoons sugar

1 teaspoon vanilla

Melt the butter and blend with the ginger cookies. Using a metal spatula, press crust halfway up the sides and over the bottom of an ungreased 9 or 10 inch springform pan. Bake in a 350° oven for 10-12 minutes or until the edges are well browned; cool. Using an electric mixer, beat the cream cheese until smooth. Add the pumpkin and brown sugar and beat 3-5 minutes or until light and fluffy. Beat in the flour and spices. In a separate measuring cup, mix milk, vanilla and slightly beaten eggs. Pour into the cream cheese mixture and beat until blended. Pour into the cooled crust and bake in a 350° oven for 1¼ to 1½ hours or until a knife inserted into the cake halfway between the center and the edge comes out clean. Turn off the oven, set door slightly ajar and leave the cheesecake in the oven for 1 hour; remove to a wire rack. Cool for 2 hours and then blend together the sour cream, sugar and vanilla and spread over the cake. Serve at room temperature or chilled. Serves 10-12.

Terri Brazinsky (Mrs. John)
Mother of April
Carmel, California

AUTUMN CHEESECAKE

1½ cups graham cracker crumbs
½ cup ground walnuts
7 tablespoons butter, melted
4 (8 ounce) packages cream cheese
1½ cups sugar
1/3 cup flour
2 teaspoons cinnamon

1 teaspoon nutmeg
½ teaspoon ground cloves
¼ teaspoon ground allspice
5 extra large eggs (or 6 large)
1½ cups pumpkin puree
Whipped cream

Prepare pan: Butter sides and bottom of a 9-inch springform pan. Combine the graham cracker crumbs, walnuts and melted butter and press up the sides and bottom of pan; chill. In a large bowl, beat the cream cheese until light; gradually add the sugar, flour, cinnamon, nutmeg, cloves and allspice and blend well. Beat in the eggs, one at a time, blending well after each addition. Add the pumpkin puree, mixing well. Pour the batter into the chilled pan and bake in the center of a preheated 325° oven for 90 minutes. Turn off heat and let cake stand for 30 minutes with the oven door open. Cool on rack and then chill for 2 hours. Serve with whipped cream. Serves 10-12.

Mary Romano
Director of Activities
Santa Catalina School
Monterey, California

"This recipe is so popular at the Thanksgiving and Christmas season that I no longer have to bake pumpkin pies."

PUMPKIN LOG

3 eggs
1 cup sugar
2/3 cup pumpkin
1 teaspoon baking soda

½ teaspoon cinnamon
¾ cup flour
½ cup chopped walnuts

FILLING:
2 tablespoons butter
¾ teaspoon vanilla

1 (8 ounce) package cream
cheese
1 cup powdered sugar

Combine the eggs, sugar, pumpkin, soda, cinnamon and flour and mix well. Line a 10 x 15½ inch cookie sheet with greased wax paper. Pour the batter onto the wax paper and sprinkle with the walnuts. Bake in a 375° oven for 15 minutes; turn out onto a sugared towel. Cool 20 minutes before removing wax paper. Prepare the filling by beating the butter, vanilla, cream cheese and powdered sugar until smooth. Spread on the cake and roll up (be sure the cake is cooled completely before rolling or it will crack). Refrigerate until ready to serve. Serves 8-10.

B.J. Burton Szemborski (Mrs. Stanley)
Class of '66
Sandbank, Scotland

BRANDIED-PUMPKIN PIE

ALMOND PASTRY:
1 cup sifted flour
½ teaspoon salt

1/3 cup shortening
½ cup ground blanched almonds
2 tablespoons ice water

FILLING:
1 cup canned pumpkin
1 cup evaporated milk
1 cup light brown sugar, firmly
packed
3 eggs, slightly beaten

¼ cup brandy
1 teaspoon pumpkin pie spice
¾ teaspoon salt

For pastry, sift the flour with the salt in a large bowl. With a pastry blender, cut in the shortening until the mixture resembles coarse cornmeal. Stir in the almonds, and sprinkle the ice water, 1 tablespoon at a time, over all of the mixture, tossing lightly with a fork after each addition; shape into a ball. Roll between 2 sheets of wax paper into an 11-inch circle. Refrigerate 15 minutes or until ready to use. Line a 9-inch pie plate, forming a neat rim (not crimped) around the edge of the pie plate. For the filling, combine the pumpkin, milk and sugar in a large bowl, blending until well mixed. Stir in the eggs, brandy, pumpkin pie spice and salt; mix well. Pour the filling into the prepared pie shell and bake in a preheated 450° oven for 10 minutes. Reduce oven temperature to 325° and bake 30 minutes longer or until the filling is set in the center when the pie is gently shaken. Cool on a wire rack. Garnish the pie with whipped cream before serving. Serves 6-8.

Julianna Kleppe (Mrs. John)
Mother of Johanna '82 and Judy '84
Reno, Nevada

Speakers who have appeared at the Performing Arts Center since 1980 under the auspices of the L.S.B. Leakey Foundation are, among others, Richard Leakey, Dr. Thor Heyerdahl, and Jane Goodall, as well as Roger Payne, who first recorded the "Songs of the Humpback Whale," and archeologist Dr. Donald C. Johanson who discovered "Lucy" in 1974.

"An absolutely light and wonderful pumpkin pie that our family has used for many years!"

PUMPKIN CHIFFON PIE

½ cup brown sugar
1½ cups canned pumpkin
½ cup milk
3 eggs, separated
2 teaspoons cinnamon
½ teaspoon ginger

¼ teaspoon allspice
½ teaspoon salt
1 tablespoon unflavored gelatin
¼ cup cold water
2 tablespoons white sugar
1 (10 or 11 inch) baked pie shell

Combine the brown sugar, pumpkin, milk, egg yolks (slightly broken), spices and salt. Cook in the top of a double boiler until the mixture begins to thicken, about 5 minutes. Soak the gelatin in the water and add to the pumpkin mixture; cool. Beat the egg whites until stiff but not dry; beat in the granulated sugar. Fold into the pumpkin mixture when cooled and partly congealed. Pour into a baked pie shell and chill for 1 or 2 hours, or until stiff enough to cut and hold its shape. Garnish with whipped cream and toasted coconut, if desired. Serves 8-10.

Jan Gryp (Mrs. Firmin A.)
Mother of Melinda '70
Salinas, California

PUMPKIN OR SWEET POTATO PIE

1 cup sugar
1 teaspoon salt
¼ teaspoon cloves
¼ teaspoon nutmeg
¼ teaspoon ginger
2 cups cooked pumpkin or
  sweet potatoes

3 tablespoons melted butter
1 cup milk
2 tablespoons flour
1 cup coconut
3 egg whites
1 (9 inch) unbaked pie shell

Mix together all ingredients except the egg whites and coconut; set aside. Beat the egg whites until stiff and fold carefully with the coconut into the pumpkin mixture. Pour into the pie shell and bake in a 450° oven for 10 minutes. Reduce the heat to 350° and bake an additional 30 minutes.

Sadie Sharpe Correll (Mrs. E. T.)
Great-grandmother of April Brazinsky
Woodleaf, North Carolina

PECAN PIE

4 eggs, slightly beaten
1 cup light corn syrup
2 teaspoons vanilla
1 cup sugar
½ teaspoon salt

3 tablespoons melted butter
1 (9-inch) unbaked pie shell
1½ teaspoons flour
1¼ cups coarsely chopped pecans

Beat together the eggs, syrup, vanilla, sugar and salt; add the melted butter. Line a 9-inch pie plate with the pastry and sprinkle the flour over the pastry. Arrange the pecans on the bottom of the pie shell and slowly pour in the filling. Place in a 450° oven and bake for 10 minutes. Reduce heat to 350° and continue baking for 1 hour longer. Remove from heat while filling quivers a little. Do *not* bake until completely firm. Serves 8.

Sue Pinckney
Upper School Faculty
Carmel Valley, California

"My mother, Viola Hintze Cressey, made this pie quickly and often. She substituted chopped walnuts from the farm at times."

PECAN PIE

1 cup white corn syrup
1 cup dark brown sugar
1/3 teaspoon salt
1/3 cup melted butter

1 teaspoon vanilla
3 eggs
1 (9 inch) unbaked pie shell
1 heaping cup pecan halves

Mix together the syrup, sugar, salt, butter, vanilla; add the slightly beaten eggs and pour into a 9-inch unbaked pie shell. Sprinkle the pecans over the filling. Bake in a 350° oven for about 45 minutes.

Marie Cressey Belden (Mrs. Lester M.)
Mother of Cressey Joy '87
Santa Rosa, California

Copies of the inaugural ball gowns of America's first ladies, on loan from the Smithsonian Institution, were modeled Friday, March 14, 1980 at the Performing Arts Center by members of the Service League and Board members and members of their families. This fund-raising event was followed by a dinner dance in Santo Domingo Hall.

WALNUT PIE

½ cup brown sugar, packed
2 tablespoons cake flour
3 tablespoons butter
¼ teaspoon salt

1¼ cups light corn syrup
1½ teaspoons vanilla
3 eggs, beaten
1 cup large pieces and halves of
    walnuts
1 (9 inch) unbaked pie shell

Combine the brown sugar and cake flour in a saucepan. Add the butter, salt and corn syrup, and heat slowly until the butter is melted. Add the vanilla to the beaten eggs and blend into the slightly cooled syrup mixture. Bake in a 375° oven for 40-45 minutes or until the mixture is set in the center.

Nancy Crane (Mrs. Bert)
Mother of Karen '83
Merced, California

WALNUT PIE

2 tablespoons butter
½ cup granulated sugar
½ cup brown sugar
3 eggs, beaten

½ cup dark corn syrup
10 ounces walnuts
1 (9-inch) unbaked Basic Pie
    Crust

Cream by hand the butter and sugars; beat in the eggs and the syrup and stir in the walnuts. Pour into the pie crust and place in a preheated 400° oven. Immediately reduce the heat to 350° and bake 30 minutes or until set.

BASIC PIE CRUST

½ cup butter
1 tablespoon sugar

1 cup plus 2 tablespoons flour

Melt the butter; add the sugar and flour and mix well. Pat into a 9-inch pie pan. No rolling necessary.

Jill Shoemake Vogel (Mrs. Fred)
Class of '64
Modesto, California

MOCHA ANGEL PIE

3 egg whites
¼ teaspoon cream of tartar
FILLING:
1 (12 ounce) package semi-sweet chocolate
1 tablespoon instant coffee granules

Dash salt
¾ cup granulated sugar

1 cup heavy cream, whipped
1 teaspoon vanilla

Preheat the oven to 275°. Beat the egg whites until stiff; gradually add the cream of tartar, salt and sugar, beating until stiff and satiny. Spread about 2/3 of the meringue over the bottom and sides of a well greased 8-inch glass pie plate. Drop the remaining meringue in mounds along the rim of the plate, pulling each mound up into points. Bake 1 hour. Cool on a wire rack away from drafts. For the filling, melt the chocolate pieces in a double boiler over hot, but not boiling water. Combine the instant coffee and ¼ cup boiling water and stir into the melted chocolate. Cool 5 minutes, stirring occasionally. Fold in the whipped cream and vanilla. Pour into the cooled meringue shell and refrigerate.

Linda Hall (Mrs. John, Jr.)
Mother of Amy '86
San Francisco, California

CHOCOLATE ANGEL PIE

2 eggs white
1/8 teaspoon cream of tartar
1/8 teaspoon salt
½ cup sugar
½ cup walnuts or pecans, chopped

1 teaspoon vanilla
4 ounces Baker's German sweet chocolate
3 tablespoons water
1 cup whipping cream

Combine the egg whites, salt and cream of tartar and beat until foamy. Add the sugar, 2 tablespoons at a time, beating well after each addition. Continue beating until very stiff peaks form. Fold in the nuts and ½ teaspoon of the vanilla. Spoon into a lightly greased 9-inch pie pan and form a nest-like shell, building up the sides of the pan to about ½ inch above the pan. Bake in a slow oven (300°) 50-55 minutes. Cool. Melt the chocolate in the water over low heat, stirring constantly. Cool until thick. Add the remaining ½ teaspoon vanilla and then whip the cream and fold in the chocolate mixture. Spoon into the meringue shell. Chill 2 hours. Serves 6. NOTE: Many times I double the meringue recipe in order to make a more luscious shell. This may be made ahead at least 1 day and kept in the refrigerator.

Christa Chamlian (Mrs. Dikran)
Mother of Yvette '84
Truckee, California

COFFEE SILK PIE

COCONUT CRUST:
1½ cups shredded coconut
½ cup ground pecans

¼ cup melted butter

FILLING:
1 cup butter
1¼ cups sugar
2 ounces unsweetened chocolate
2 tablespoons brandy

2 tablespoons instant coffee
2 eggs
1 teaspoon vanilla
1 cup heavy cream, whipped and
    slightly sweetened

For the crust, mix together the coconut, pecans and melted butter and press into a slightly oiled 9-inch pie pan. Bake 50-60 minutes at 250° until golden. For the filling, thoroughly cream the butter and slowly add the sugar. Melt chocolate squares over boiling water or in the microwave. Stir in the brandy and the coffee granules. Cool. Blend the butter and sugar mixture into the chocolate mixture and add the vanilla. Add the eggs, one at a time, beating *five minutes* after *each* one. Pour into the crust and chill at least 6 hours. Top with the sweetened whipped cream and chocolate curls, if desired. Serves 8-10.

Carolyn Estrada (Mrs. Marshall)
Aunt of Kim Bowden '87
Whittier, California

MOCHA PIE WITH RAISINS

1 cup seedless raisins
½ cup sugar
2 tablespoons cornstarch
¼ teaspoon salt
2 teaspoons instant coffee
    granules
1 envelope unflavored gelatin

1 cup milk
2 eggs, separated
1 teaspoon vanilla
1 cup whipping cream, whipped
1 (9 inch) pie shell, baked

Chop the raisins coarsely, set aside. Blend together ¼ cup of the sugar, the cornstarch, salt, coffee and gelatin; stir in the milk. Cook, stirring constantly, over moderate heat until gelatin dissolves and the mixture thickens. Beat the egg yolks and carefully blend into the filling. Cook 2 to 3 minutes longer. Remove from heat, stir in the vanilla and raisins. Cool until the filling begins to thicken. Beat the egg whites to soft peaks, gradually add the remaining ¼ cup sugar and continue beating until stiff. Fold the beaten egg whites and whipped cream into the raisin custard. Pour into the baked pie shell; chill until firm. If desired, garnish with additional whipped cream.

Emiko Johnson (Mrs. William)
Mother of Susan '76 and Barbara '83
Marina, California

KEY LIME PIE

CRUST:
¼-½ cup sugar
¼ cup crushed almonds

1¼ cups graham cracker crumbs
¼ cup melted butter

FILLING:
6 egg yolks
1 (14 ounce) can sweetened
  condensed milk

¾ cup lime juice
2 teaspoons grated lime peel

TOPPING:
1 cup whipping cream
1 teaspoon vanilla

2½ tablespoons sugar

For the crust, combine the sugar, almonds, graham cracker crumbs and the melted butter and press into a 10-inch pie pan. Bake 10 minutes in a 375° oven. For the filling, beat the yolks until light yellow and add the milk, stirring constantly. Blend in the lime juice and peel and pour into the pie crust. Bake in a 350° oven for 30-40 minutes; cool. For the topping, whip the cream with the vanilla and sugar and spread over the cooled pie. Chill.

Kristin Johnson
Class of '78
Sacramento, California

LEMON MERINGUE PIE

1 cup sugar
1/3 cup cornstarch
¼ teaspoon salt
1½ cups water
3 egg yolks

2 tablespoons butter
1/3 cup lemon juice
1½ teaspoons grated lemon rind
1 baked (8 or 9 inch) pie shell
Meringue

MERINGUE:
3 egg whites
6 tablespoons sugar

¼ teaspoon cream of tartar

Combine ½ cup of the sugar, the cornstarch and salt in the top of a double boiler; blend in the water gradually. Cook until thickened, stirring constantly. Cover and cook 10 minutes longer. Beat together the remaining ½ cup sugar and the egg yolks. Blend a little of the hot mixture into the egg yolk mixture, then stir into the remaining hot mixture; cook for 2 minutes. Remove from heat and add the butter, lemon juice and rind. Cool; pour into the baked pie shell. Make a meringue by beating the egg whites until fluffy. Gradually add the sugar and cream of tartar and continue beating until stiff. Spread evenly over the pie filling. Bake in a 350° oven for 15-20 minutes, until the meringue is browned. Cool and refrigerate several hours before serving. NOTE: Eggs are much easier to separate when they are cold. Let eggs come to room temperature before beating as they will yield more volume. For a really tart pie, increase the amount of lemon juice, but remember to increase the amount of cornstarch accordingly.

Barbara Jo Burton Szemborski (Mrs. Stanley)
Class of '66
Sandbank, Scotland

MINT PIE

24-30 creme filled chocolate
   cookies, crushed
¼ cup butter, melted
2 (7 ounce) jars marshmallow
   creme

½ cup green creme de menthe
2 pints heavy cream, whipped
Chocolate shavings

Combine the cookies and the butter; press into the bottom of a 9-inch springform pan. Blend the marshmallow creme and the creme de menthe and fold in the whipped cream; pour over the cookies in the pan. Garnish with the shaved chocolate and freeze.

Susan Grupe Smith (Mrs. Wilbur)
Class of '66
Stockton, California

EMERALD CLOUD PIE

1 envelope unflavored gelatin
¼ cup The Monterey Vineyard
   Classic White Wine
4 eggs, separated

1 cup sugar
½ teaspoon salt
2 teaspoons grated lime rind
1/3 cup fresh lime juice
1 (9 inch) pie shell, baked

Stir the gelatin into the wine; set aside. Beat egg yolks in the top of a double boiler and gradually beat in ½ cup of the sugar until the mixture is light and fluffy. Place over heat. Stir in the salt, lime rind and juice. Cook, stirring constantly until the mixture thickens and coats the spoon well; remove from heat. Add the softened gelatin and stir until dissolved. Cool to room temperature. Beat the egg whites until soft peaks form; gradually beat in the remaining ½ cup sugar and continue beating until very stiff. Fold in ¼ of the beaten egg whites into the lime mixture. Pour in the remaining whites and fold to combine. Spoon into a baked pie shell. Refrigerate 3 to 4 hours or until firm. Garnish with whipped cream and thin slices of lime. Serves 8.

Monterey Vineyards
Hayward, California

AVOCADO PIE

2 medium or 3 small avocados
1/3 cup lemon juice
1 (8 ounce) package cream cheese

1 (14 ounce) can sweetened
condensed milk
1 (8 or 9 inch) graham cracker
crust

TOPPING:
1 cup whipping cream
1 teaspoon vanilla

Light brown sugar to taste
¼ cup chopped nuts

Peel and slice the avocados and place in a mixing bowl with the lemon juice, softened cream cheese and condensed milk. Beat 5-10 minutes until thick and fairly smooth. Pour into the graham cracker crust. Whip the cream with the vanilla and brown sugar and spread over the pie filling. Sprinkle with nuts.

Dorita Jean Jud
Seaside, California

PEACH GLAMOUR PIE

CRUST:
1 cup blanched almonds
1 cup flaked coconut

¼ cup sugar
¼ cup soft butter

FILLING:
4 cups fresh or 1 (29 ounce) can
peach slices
Pinch salt
¼ cup superfine sugar

1 teaspoon orange juice
1 teaspoon coarsely grated
orange rind
1 teaspoon vanilla
1 cup sour cream

Put the almonds through a food chopper, using a medium blade. Then chop the coconut and combine with the chopped almonds. Work in the sugar and butter. Press the mixture evenly on the bottom and up the sides of a 9-inch pie pan, reserving 2-3 tablespoons for topping. Bake in a 375° oven for 12-15 minutes until a light golden brown. Put the topping crumbs in a shallow pan and toast in the oven at the same time for about 5 minutes. Cool thoroughly. For the filling: About 1 hour before serving time, drain the peach slices on paper towels. Blend the salt, sugar, orange juice, orange rind and vanilla into the sour cream. Spread this mixture on the bottom and sides of the pie shell. Top with drained peaches. Sprinkle with the reserved topping crumbs. Chill. Serves 8.

Jeanne Adams (Mrs. Michael)
Mother of Sarah '83
Fresno, California

APPLE PIE

2/3 cup sugar
2 tablespoons flour
1 teaspoon cinnamon

4-5 cups peeled, thinly sliced
   apples
½ cup sour cream
1 (9 inch) unbaked pie shell

TOPPING:
¾ cup flour
½ cup brown sugar, firmly
   packed

½ teaspoon cinnamon
1/3 cup butter softened

Combine the sugar, flour and cinnamon and toss with the apples; stir in the sour cream, mixing well. Place in the pie shell. Combine the topping ingredients and sprinkle evenly over the apples. Bake in a 350° oven for 40-45 minutes or until the topping is golden brown.

Jane McFarlane Gamble (Mrs. Barrett)
Mother of Alison
Pacific Grove, California

FRENCH APPLE PIE

4 cups sliced Gravenstein apples
¾ cup sugar
2 tablespoons flour

¼ teaspoon salt
1 unbaked (9 inch) pastry shell

TOPPING:
½ cup dry bread crumbs
½ cup brown sugar
½ teaspoon cinnamon

2 tablespoons chopped walnuts
2 tablespoons melted butter

Peel, core and slice the apples and toss with a mixture of the sugar, flour and salt. Fill the pastry shell with the apples and cover with a sheet of heavy paper to prevent apples from drying out. Bake in a 450° oven for 20 minutes; reduce heat to 350° and continue baking about 30 minutes longer, or until the apples are tender. Make a topping by combining the bread crumbs, brown sugar, cinnamon, walnuts and melted butter. Remove the heavy paper and evenly distribute the topping mixture over the pie. Bake 10 additional minutes, or until nicely browned. Serve warm with whipped cream. Serves 6.

Gail Wagner (Mrs. Charles)
Mother of Beth '86
Stockton, California

WINE APPLE PIE

Pastry for 2-crust (10 inch) pie
¾ cup sugar
3 tablespoons cornstarch
Pinch salt
¼ teaspoon cinnamon

¾ cup The Monterey Vineyard
 Gewurztraminer
1 egg beaten
1 tablespoon butter, melted
¾ cup boiling water
2 cups thinly sliced apples

Roll out pastry for the bottom crust to less than 1/8 inch thickness; fit loosely into a 10-inch pie pan. Combine the sugar, salt, cornstarch and cinnamon; add the wine and blend well. Mix in the egg and melted butter and stir in the boiling water. Spread the apples in the bottom of the pastry-lined pie pan and add the mixture. Roll out the top crust. Moisten the edge of lower crust and set the top crust in place; crimp or flute the edge and cut slashes in the top. Bake in a 425° oven for 40-50 minutes. Cool before serving.

Monterey Vineyard
Hayward, California

"A creamy delicious version of the old fashioned fruit pie."

RHUBARB CREAM PIE

Pie Pastry
3 cups cut rhubarb
1½ cups sugar
3 tablespoons flour

½ teaspoon nutmeg
1 tablespoon butter
2 well beaten eggs

Using a basic pastry recipe, prepare and line a 9-inch pie pan, reserving any dough scraps to be used later. Place the cut rhubarb in the pie shell. Blend together the sugar, flour, nutmeg and butter; add the eggs and beat until smooth. Pour over the rhubarb. Top with pastry cut in fancy shapes. Bake in a 450° oven for 10 minutes, reduce the heat to 350° and continue baking about 30 minutes longer.

Shirley Anderson (Mrs. Russell)
San Jose, California

FRENCH CHERRY PIE

1 (3 ounce) package cream
 cheese
½ cup powdered sugar
½ teaspoon vanilla
1 cup whipping cream

1 (9 inch) pastry shell
1 (20 ounce) can cherry pie
 filling
Dash of lemon juice

Blend together the cream cheese, powdered sugar and vanilla until smooth. Whip the cream and fold into the cream cheese mixture. Pour into the pastry shell and cover with the cherry pie filling and lemon juice which have been blended together. Chill thoroughly.

Polly Reese (Mrs. Bob)
Mother of Heather
Monterey, California

STRAWBERRY PIE

1 cup sugar
2 tablespoons cornstarch
1 cup water
3 tablespoons strawberry gelatin
mix

2 pints fresh strawberries
1 baked pie shell
½ pint whipping cream, whipped
and sweetened

Combine the sugar and cornstarch in a small saucepan; add the water and cook over medium heat, stirring until clear and slightly thickened. Remove from heat and stir in the 3 tablespoons strawberry gelatin. Place the strawberries in the pie shell and pour the gelatin mixture over the berries. Chill for 3-4 hours. Before serving, cover the entire pie with the sweetened whipped cream. Place 1 large pretty strawberry on top. Serves 8.

Susan Durney Mickelson (Mrs. Lon)
Class of '65
La Canada, California

STRAWBERRY CREAM PIE

1 (8 ounce) package cream cheese
¼ cup sugar
½ teaspoon vanilla
Dash nutmeg

1 cup sliced strawberries
1 cup whipping cream
¼ cup sifted confectioner's sugar
1 (9 inch) graham cracker crust

Combine the softened cream cheese, sugar, vanilla and nutmeg, mixing until well blended. Mash ¾ cup of the strawberry slices and stir into the cream cheese mixture. Whip the cream with confectioner's sugar until stiff peaks form and fold into the cream cheese mixture. Fold the remaining strawberries into the cream cheese mixture and spoon into the crust. Chill several hours or overnight. Garnish with additional strawberries if desired. Serves 6.

Nicola Latham
Class of '77
Santa Barbara, California

GLACE STRAWBERRY PIE

1 quart strawberries   1½ cups juice
1 (3 ounce) package cream cheese 1 cup sugar
1 (9 inch) baked pie shell   3 tablespoons cornstarch

Wash, drain and hull the strawberries. Spread the softened cream cheese evenly over the bottom of a 9-inch cooled baked pie shell. Cover with the choicest half of the berries. Mash and strain the remaining berries until juice is extracted; add enough water to make 1½ cups liquid. Bring the juice to a boil and gradually stir in the sugar and cornstarch; cook over low heat, stirring constantly for 1 minute. Cool and pour over the berries in the pie shell. Chill until set and garnish with whipped cream. Serves 5-6.

Katherine Nomellini (Mrs. John)
Mother of Angela '71, Elizabeth '74,
Sara '78, and Nancy '81
Stockton, California

STRAWBERRY LADY FINGER CAKE

4 cups crushed strawberries   4 cups heavy cream
2 tablespoons lemon juice   3 (3 ounce) packages lady fingers
½ cup sugar   2 teaspoons vanilla
¼ teaspoon salt   6 tablespoons powdered sugar
2½ tablespoons gelatin   Red food coloring
5 tablespoons cold water

Stir together the strawberries, sugar, lemon juice and salt. In a small saucepan, soften the gelatin in the cold water for about 5 minutes. Simmer over medium heat just long enough to dissolve; stir into the strawberry mixture and chill until slightly thickened. Whip 2 cups of the heavy cream and fold into the strawberry mixture. Place lady fingers on the bottom and sides of a buttered springform pan. Pour half of the mixture into the pan, add another layer of lady fingers; top with the remaining strawberry mixture. Freeze. Remove from the freezer and spingform pan 6 hours before serving. Whip the remaining 2 cups of heavy cream with the vanilla and powdered sugar. Tint with a few drops of red food coloring to make the cream a light pink. Cover the top with the whipped cream and garnish with fresh strawberries.

Mary Jane Wesson (Mrs. W.)
Mother of Jameen '77
Modesto, California

STRAWBERRY SUPREME

1 pound fresh strawberries
1¾ cup sugar
2 envelopes unflavored gelatin
¼ cup water

6 egg whites
1 pint whipping cream
2 teaspoons vanilla

Place the strawberries in a 9 x 12 inch serving dish, sprinkle with ½ cup of the sugar, and press with a fork; refrigerate for about 1 hour. Meanwhile, soften the gelatin in the water for about 5 minutes, then heat to dissolve completely; set aside. Beat the egg whites to soft peaks; add the remaining 1¼ cups sugar a little at a time, beating constantly. Add the chilled whipping cream and continue beating for an additional minute. Beat in the gelatin mixture and the vanilla. Spread the cream mixture evenly over the crushed strawberries and refrigerate until set. Serves 12.

Patricia C. de Astivia (Mrs. Lorenzo)
Mother of Claudia and Gabriela, Summer Campers
Naucalpan, Mexico

LIME DELIGHT

1 (14½ ounce) can evaporated
   milk
2 cups chocolate wafer crumbs
½ cup melted butter
1 (3 ounce) package lime gelatin
1¾ cup hot water

1 cup sugar
¼ cup lime juice
2 teaspoons lemon juice
½ cup creme de menthe
Semi-sweet chocolate shavings

Chill the evaporated milk in the freezer until partially frozen. Meanwhile, combine the chocolate crumbs and the melted butter and press into a 9 x 13 inch pan; set aside. Dissolve the gelatin in the hot water and chill until partially set; beat until fluffy, adding in the sugar and fruit juices. Whip the chilled evaporated milk and fold into the gelatin mixture. Add the creme de menthe. Pour the whipped mixture into the crust and garnish with the shaved chocolate and chill until firm. Serves 10-12. NOTE: The longer the filling is beaten, the larger the dessert and the better it will be.

Cleo Devoto (Mrs. Ralph)
Grandmother of Ulrike Devoto '86
Lakeport, California

MANDARIN ORANGE DESSERT

1 (6 ounce) package orange
  gelatin
1 cup orange sherbert

1 (11 ounce) can mandarin
  oranges
1 pint whipping cream, whipped

Dissolve the gelatin in 2 cups boiling water; add the sherbert and chill until slightly thickened. Fold in the drained oranges and the whipped cream. Chill until set. Serves 6.

Tina Tomlinson Del Piero (Mrs. Marc)
Class of '73
Salinas, California

LEMON FLUFF CAKE

1 (12 ounce) package vanilla
  wafers
½ cup butter, melted
6 egg yolks
½ cup sugar

Juice and rind of 2 lemons
1 envelope unflavored gelatin
½ cup water
6 egg whites
1 pint whipping cream, whipped

Crush the vanilla wafers and combine all except ½ cup with the melted butter; press into a springform pan. Beat the egg yolks with the sugar and add the lemon juice and rind. Cook in the top of a double boiler until thickened; cool. Dissolve the gelatin in the water and add to the cooked mixture. Fold in the stiffly beaten egg whites, then the whipped cream. Pour the mixture over the crust and cover with the reserved crumbs. Chill several hours before serving.

Mrs. William Zeff
Mother of Ann '67
Modesto, California

LEMON SNOW BAVARIAN CREAM

8 eggs, separated
2 cups sugar

2½ tablespoons unflavored
  gelatin
2 lemons

Soak gelatin in ¼ cup cold water and dissolve in ½ cup boiling water. Cool. Beat the egg yolks until thick and lemon colored. Add the gelatin solution, the juice of 2 lemons and the grated rind of one. Fold in the beaten egg whites. Chill until firm. Serve with whipped cream or slightly thickened fruit juice. Decorate with silver candy pearls.

Marlene Kellogg (Mrs. Clarence)
Mother of Kellene '79 and Christina '85
Pacific Grove, California

"This is a good summertime dessert."

MOLDED LEMON DESSERT

12 lady fingers
1 (13 ounce) can evaporated milk
1 (3 ounce) package lemon
 gelatin

½ cup hot water
½ cup fresh lemon juice
¾ cup sugar

Chill the can of milk in the refrigerator for 24 hours before using, and chill a bowl and beater. Line the sides of a 2-inch high springform mold with the lady fingers (cut off the bottoms to make them stand up). Dissolve the lemon gelatin in the hot water. When thoroughly dissolved, add the lemon juice. Whip the chilled milk thoroughly in a large bowl; continue beating, adding the sugar and then the cooled gelatin mixture until well blended. Pour into the springform mold and chill in the refrigerator overnight. Before serving, mask with whipped cream slightly sweetened and flavored with dark Jamaica rum and garnish with fresh strawberries.

Anne Treadway (Mrs. Frederick)
Monterey, California

LEMON FROMAGE WITH STRAWBERRIES

3 whole eggs
2 egg yolks
½ cup sugar
Grated rind of 1 lemon

¾ tablespoon unflavored gelatin
¼ cup lemon juice
2 cups heavy cream
1 pint strawberries or blueberries

Beat together the eggs and egg yolks until lemon colored and frothy; continue beating, adding the sugar in a slow stream until the mixture is thickened. Add the grated rind. Combine the gelatin and lemon juice in a heat-proof measuring cup over hot water and stir until the gelatin dissolves. Add to the egg mixture and beat well. Whip the cream until stiff and fold it gently into the egg mixture. Pour the mixture into a 1-quart mold and chill 4 hours. Unmold and serve with strawberries or blueberries which have been sweetened to taste. Serves 6-8.

Mrs. Bill Butterfield
Mother of Nina Peck '83
Sun Valley, Idaho

ORANGE SOUFFLES

BASIC SOUFFLE MIXTURE

3 ounces bread flour   *3 ounces unsalted butter*
3 ounces sugar

Rub all ingredients together to form a smooth paste. This can be made ahead and placed in a refrigerator for several days. The proportion is always 9 ounces of this mixture to 1 pint of milk.

GRAND MARNIER SOUFFLE

1 pint milk   *8 egg yolks*
9 ounces Basic Souffle Mixture   *10 egg whites*
Grand Marnier   *3 ounces sugar*

For Orange Shells:
15 large perfect oranges   *Sugar*
Unsalted butter

Boil the milk; remove from heat and add the Basic Souffle Mixture. Blend well, stirring until smooth. Return to heat and cook for 1-2 minutes. Place in a round bowl and add the egg yolks little by little while stirring briskly. Mix well after each addition. Add Grand Marnier to taste. At this point, cut off the top 1/3 of a large perfect orange. Scoop out the center very well. Rub the inside of the orange with unsalted butter and dredge with sugar. When ready to cook the souffles, beat the egg whites and sugar until stiff and immediately fold into the creamy mixture. Fill the oranges to within ½ inch of the rim. Sprinkle with powdered sugar. Place these in a Bain Marie. This consists of bringing water, in a pan large enough to hold the oranges with an inch space between each other, to just short of a boil. Place in a 425° oven for 25 minutes. Makes 15 servings.

Virginia Adams (Mrs. Ansel)
Grandmother of Sarah Adams '83
Carmel, California

On Saturday, February 20, 1983, more than 200 friends and admirers from all over the world gathered in Santo Domingo Hall to celebrate master photographer Ansel Adams' 80th birthday at a black-tie dinner that featured a birthday cake in the shape of Yosemite's Half Dome. On this occasion, Ansel Adams received an award from the French government through the French consul from New York City.

GRAND MARNIER DESSERT SAUCE

1 (16 ounce) carton sour cream   3-4 tablespoons Grand Marnier
1 (7 ounce) jar marshmallow
  creme

Thoroughly blend all ingredients. Use as a dip for fresh strawberries or other fruits; or as a dessert sauce. Delicious served over strawberry crepes, pound cake or as an ice cream topping.

Louise Beardsley
Monterey, California

COEUR A LA CREME

2 (8 ounce) packages cream   ½ cup sour cream
  cheese, softened
1 cup heavy cream, whipped

Blend the softened cream cheese with the whipped cream and mix in the sour cream, making sure there are no lumps. Line china heart molds with damp cheesecloth and fill with the cheese mixture. Place the molds in the refrigerator on a cookie sheet for several hours before serving. Unmold onto a dessert plate. Remove the cheesecloth and outline the heart of cheese with strawberries. Pass a melted currant jelly sauce laced with Kirsch. NOTE: Do not use a blender or food processor as this must be done by hand. The creme mixture may be forced through a sieve to avoid lumps.

Virginia Stanton (Mrs. Robert)
Carmel Valley, California

"This dessert always gets raves and makes a nice presentation when served with fruit as a topping. A dietician friend reduced this recipe for me when I enjoyed it in the hospital after Sarah was born."

RUSSIAN CREME

2 tablespoons unflavored gelatin   2 cups cream or half and half
1/3 cup cold water   2 cups sour cream
2/3 cup hot water   2 teaspoons vanilla
1-1/3 cups sugar

Soften the gelatin in the cold water for about 5 minutes. Dissolve the sugar and the softened gelatin in the hot water; combine with the remaining ingredients and chill until ready to serve. Serves 12.

Jeanne Adams (Mrs. Michael)
Mother of Sarah '83
Fresno, California

"This is very rich so I recommend the smaller portions, but it is so good you'll think you've died and gone to heaven when you taste it."

CREME BRULE (BURNT CREME)

1 pint whipping cream
4 egg yolks
½ cup granulated sugar

1 teaspoon vanilla extract
Granulated sugar for topping
(about 8 tablespoons)

Heat the whipping cream until scalded; set aside. Beat the egg yolks and the ½ cup sugar until thick, about 3 minutes. Gradually stir in the scalded cream; add the vanilla. Pour into 4 6-ounce custard cups or 8 3-ounce cups or individual souffle dishes. Place the custard cups in a baking pan and add boiling water into the pan, enough to come up 2/3 to the top of the dish. Bake in a preheated 350° oven until set, about 45 minutes. Remove the cups from the hot water and refrigerate until well chilled. Sprinkle each custard with enough sugar to cover. Place under preheated broiler and brown, watching carefully. Refrigerate until ready to serve.

Anne Berolzheimer (Mrs. Philip)
Mother of Caroline '85
Stockton, California

CREPES A L'ORANGE

1½-2 cups flour
Pinch of salt
4 eggs
3 cups milk
½ cup water

4 tablespoons sugar
3 tablespoons melted butter or
oil
1 teaspoon vanilla
Orange peel and juice from 1
small orange
1-2 tablespoons Grand Marnier

Sift the flour into a mixing bowl; add a pinch of salt, the eggs and half of the milk. Stir with a wire whip until smooth. Add the remainder of the milk and the water, the sugar, butter or oil, vanilla, orange peel, orange juice and the liqueur. All of the ingredients may be put in the blender for 10 seconds. If the batter is made in the blender, it may be used immediately; if prepared by hand, allow it to rest for at least an hour. Grease a 6-inch skillet or crepe pan lightly. Pour 3-4 tablespoons of batter into the skillet. Tip the pan to spread the batter around evenly. Cook until lightly browned.

Juliette Piercy (Mrs. George)
Mother of Veronique
Carmel, California

CARAMEL PEARS

6 firm pears
12 teaspoons butter

Brown sugar
¾ cup heavy cream

Preheat oven to 500°. Peel, halve and core the pears. Arrange the pear halves close together in a shallow baking dish and sprinkle them generously with brown sugar; place 2 teaspoons of butter in the hollow of each pear. Bake the pears, basting frequently for about 20 minutes or until the fruit is tender and the sugar is caramelized. Stir the cream into the pan juices and serve warm or at room temperature.

Kathleen McPharlin Fischer (Mrs. Louis)
Class of '60
Washington, D.C.

POACHED PEARS BOURGOGNE

6 small Bartlett pears, not too
ripe
Juice of 1 lemon
2 cups red burgundy

2 cups sugar
2 cinnamon sticks
4 cloves
Mint leaves

Peel the pears, leaving the stems intact. As the pears are peeled, put them in a mixture of 1 quart water and the juice of 1 lemon. Cut a slice from the bottom of each pear so they will stand upright. In a large saucepan, combine the wine, sugar, cinnamon, cloves and enough water to cover the pears. Cover and simmer gently for 30 minutes. Add pears and poach until tender, about 30 minutes (the length of time will depend on the ripeness of the fruit). Remove from heat and cool in the poaching syrup. To serve, drain and decorate with fresh mint leaves.

Mr. Paul Anka
Father of Alexandra, Alicia, Amanda, Anthea, Amelia
Monterey, California

Paul Anka has given three benefit concerts for Santa Catalina School at our Performing Arts Center, each one a sell-out: January 14, 1978, February 21, 1981, and January 15, 1983.

SHANNON'S SATURDAY NIGHT FONDUE
(Fruit Fritters)

Strawberries
Bananas
Apples
Peaches
Lemon juice
1 egg
1 cup milk
¼ cup sugar

1 tablespoon melted butter
1 teaspoon vanilla
1½ cups flour
3 teaspoons baking powder
Salt
Cooking oil
Sweetened whipped cream
Powdered sugar

One, or a combination of fruits, may be used. Clean and prepare fruit by cutting into bite-sized pieces; sprinkle bananas, apples and peaches with lemon juice to keep fruit from darkening. Cover and chill. Prepare the batter by beating the egg with the milk; stir in the sugar, butter and vanilla. Combine the flour, baking powder and salt and stir into the egg mixture. Beat until smooth and creamy. Fill a metal fondue pot ½ full with cooking oil. Heat the oil to 350°. Arrange fruit on a platter surrounding the batter. Spear a piece of fruit with a fondue fork, dip into batter, drain well, and place in hot oil until golden brown, about 2-3 minutes. Remove from oil and cool slightly. Dip in powdered sugar or whipped cream. NOTE: A dash of cinnamon added to the batter is especially delicious when apples are used.

Laura Nyman
Mother of Shannon Nicholson '86
Corona del Mar, California

"This is a fun recipe. We love the delicious aroma that permeates as you take the lid off the crock. It's amusing to see how friends are curious about it and sample it spot on! Feel free to add more good brandy, and to choose the name you like."

BRANDIED FRUIT OR ROM TOPF
TUTTI-FRUITTI OR FERMENTED FRUIT
FRUITES AVEC OR L'EAU DE VIE

1 quart brandy
1 quart raspberries
1 quart cherries
1 quart strawberries
1 quart currants

1 quart gooseberries
1 quart peeled and sliced apricots
1 quart peeled and sliced peaches
1 quart peeled and sliced
   pineapple
Sugar

Pour the brandy into a large sterile stone crock with a lid (at least 2 gallons). As generously as fruits come into season, add to the pot. With each addition of fruit, add half the amount of sugar (for a sweeter taste, add the same amount of sugar). Stir carefully every day until the last fruit has been added. Cover the crock and keep in a cool place. The mixture will keep indefinitely and improves with age. NOTE: This is good as an accompaniment to a meal or as a dessert served over ice cream, puddings, or cake.

Marie Cressey Belden (Mrs. Lester M.)
Mother of Cressey Joy '87
Santa Rosa, California

"This recipe is a fine winter dessert."

HOT RUMMED FRUIT

Rind of 4 oranges
1-1½ cups sugar syrup (recipe
* follows*
1 (16 ounce) can apricot halves
1 (16 ounce) can pineapple pieces

1 (16 ounce) can pears
½ cup dark rum
1 (16 ounce) can dark bing
* cherries*

Finely julienne the rind of four oranges and put into a saucepan with 1-1½ cups of sugar syrup for each quart of fruit to be used. Simmer the sugar syrup for 2 hours or more. Add the cans of apricots, pineapple and pears with some but not all of their juices. Add the rum and cook for a few minutes until the fruit is heated thoroughly. Stir in the drained cherries and heat until piping hot. Serve from a deep serving dish or a chafing dish and accompanied by a thin ginger cookie or a chocolate florentine. NOTE: Use fresh seasonal fruit instead of canned if possible. Grapes are delicious too, but be very careful not to over-cook them.

Katie Clare Mazzeo (Mrs. Rosario)
Upper School Faculty
Carmel, California

SUGAR SYRUP

5 cups Light Syrup:
2 cups sugar
4 cups water

5½ Medium Syrup:
3 cups sugar
4 cups water

6½ cups Heavy Syrup:
4¾ cups sugar
4 cups water

Combine the sugar and water in a saucepan and cook over medium heat until all the sugar is dissolved. Sugar syrup may be used as a base for a recipe or for canning or freezing fruits to help retain their shape and color. Each quart of fruit used requires approximately 1-1½ cups of sugar syrup. NOTE: For some or all of the water, fruit juice may be substituted.

"When my father comes to visit, he usually brings fresh fruit by the crate, all of it ripe right now! Rather than watch all that beautiful summer fruit go to waste, I get busy and make as many of these as I can. You can make these in the summer when fruit is cheap and good, freeze them, and then bring them out in the winter when you'll really appreciate them."

DAD'S-IN-TOWN COBBLER

FILLING:
5-6 cups sliced fresh fruit
1/3 cup brown sugar
1/8 teaspoon salt
1-1½ tablespoons cornstarch
¼ teaspoon cinnamon

1/8 teaspoon nutmeg
1 tablespoon lemon juice
½ teaspoon lemon peel
1 teaspoon vanilla
Butter

TOPPING:
1¾ cup buttermilk baking mix
2 tablespoons sugar

2 tablespoons melted butter
1/3 cup milk

Combine all the filling ingredients in a saucepan and heat to boiling. Butter an 8 x 8 inch pan or, if cobbler is to be frozen, line pan with foil with enough overlapping to cover the entire cobbler. Pour filling into the pan and dot with butter. Mix together the topping ingredients and spread evenly over the filling. Bake in a 425° oven for 30 minutes.

Julie Bisceglia
Class of '64
Manhattan Beach, California

"This is a great dessert that really wows guests."

APPLE DUMPLINGS

Pastry for a 2 crust (10 inch) pie
6 pippin apples
½ cup sugar

2 tablespoons cinnamon
3 tablespoons butter

SYRUP:
1 cup sugar
¼ teaspoon salt

4 tablespoons butter
2 cups water

Divide the pastry into 6 equal portions. Roll out each portion into a square large enough to encircle the apple when placed in the middle of the square. Core apples, and place each in the middle of a pastry square. Combine the sugar and cinnamon and fill the cavity of each apple with the mixture. Dot each with ½ tablespoon of the butter. Pull corners of pastry up and tuck into the cavity of each apple, enclosing the apple. Press the seams together with a fork. (If desired, scraps of dough may be cut into leaf shapes and placed on top of the dumplings. A little water brushed on will make them stick.) Place in a baking pan 2 inches apart and refrigerate overnight. When ready to bake, make a syrup by combining the sugar, salt, butter and water in a saucepan; bring to a boil. Pour the hot syrup in the pan with the apples (NOT on the apples but around the chilled apple dumplings). Bake in a preheated 450° oven for 30 minutes; reduce heat to 350° and bake an additional 20-30 minutes. Apples are done when you can carefully insert a straw. Place each dumpling on a dessert plate and pour the syrup over the top. Serve with whipped cream and grated nutmeg.

Elizabeth Holt Protell (Mrs. Robert)
Class of '64
Tucson, Arizona

"These are a traditional dessert served at the US Naval Academy in Annapolis, Maryland, my husband's alma mater."

CANNON BALLS

Pie dough
6 apples, cored and peeled
Cinnamon sugar

½ pound confectioner's sugar
½ cup butter, softened
Vanilla or rum flavoring

Roll out 6 (1 ounce) pieces of pie dough into 6-inch circles. Place 1 apple on each circle of pie dough. Fill the center of each apple with cinnamon sugar. Fold the pie dough up around the apple and place on a greased sheet pan. Bake in a 400° oven for approximately 25 minutes or until the apple is soft. Make a hard sauce by combining the confectioner's sugar and the butter in a mixing bowl, beating until light. Add vanilla or rum flavoring and serve over the warm apples. Serves 6.

B. J. Burton Szemborski (Mrs. Stanley)
Class of '66
Sandbank, Scotland

APPLE PUDDING CRISP

4-5 cups sliced apples
1 teaspoon cinnamon
½ cup water
1 cup sugar

¾ cup flour
½ cup butter
Vanilla ice cream or whipped cream

Place the apples in a buttered 1½ quart casserole. Mix the cinnamon with the water and pour over the apples. Combine the sugar and flour and cut in the butter with a pastry blender or 2 knives. Spread this mixture over the apples and bake in a 350° oven for 1-1½ hours. Serve warm or cold with whipped cream or vanilla ice cream. Serves 6.

Helen O'Hara
Mother of Catherine '60, Mary '66, Virginia '72
San Francisco, California

CRANBERRY CASSEROLE

1 (1 pound) bag fresh
  cranberries
4-5 apples, chopped
1½ cups sugar
½ cup butter, melted

½ cup brown sugar
½ cup flour
1 cup quick oats
Chopped pecans

Combine the cranberries, apples and sugar and press into a buttered oblong flat baking dish. Mix together well the butter, brown sugar, flour and oats and evenly distribute over the fruit mixture. Sprinkle with chopped pecans. Bake for 1 hour in a 350° oven.

Mrs. Powell Harrison Taylor
Norfolk, Virginia

PRUNE TORTE

½ cup butter
½ cup light brown sugar
1 cup sifted flour
½ cup chopped nuts
4 egg whites
Pinch of salt
½ tablespoon lemon juice

¼ cup plus 2 tablespoons sugar
½ cup cooked, pitted prunes,
  chopped
1 cup heavy cream
Garnish: 10 pitted prunes
¼ cup chopped nuts
3 cherries

Cream the butter with the brown sugar; thoroughly mix in the flour and stir in the nuts. Pat dough into the bottom of a 9-inch cake pan with removable sides that has been lined with heavy aluminum foil. Bake 20 minutes in a 350° oven. Beat the egg whites with the salt and lemon juice until stiff; slowly beat in the sugar. Fold in the prunes and pour over the cooked crust. Bake for 1 hour in a 300° oven; cool. Whip the cream and sweeten as desired; spread over cooled torte. Garnish with the cooked prunes, nuts and cherries. Serves 10.

Pauline Cantin (Mrs. Giles)
Music Department
Mother of Marie '70

In 1976, we inaugurated our Theater Trips to San Francisco, which may include a production of A.C.T., the Civic Light Opera, a Symphony, a Ballet, or whatever is current in the world of theater that would offer an evening of entertainment for the student body and their faculty chaperones. Attendance has steadily increaed over the years in this most popular of our many activities offered.

BLUEBERRY TORTE DESSERT

20 graham cracker squares
½ cup melted butter
½ cup brown sugar
1 (8 ounce) package cream
  cheese, softened
½ cup sugar

2 eggs
2 tablespoons lemon juice
1 (20 ounce) can blueberry
  pie filling
½ pint whipping cream, whipped

Crush the graham crackers, combine with the melted butter and brown sugar, and pat firmly into a 9 x 13 inch pan. Cream together the cream cheese and sugar; add the eggs one at a time, beating well after each addition. Add the lemon juice. Pour over the graham cracker crust and bake 20 minutes in a 350° oven; cool. Spoon the blueberry filling over the top and cover with the whipped cream. Chill overnight. Serves 12-16.

Sue Pinckney
Upper School Faculty
Carmel Valley, California

"This torte is elegant looking and rich in taste. It is perfect to top off a light lunch, an afternoon tea, or for coffee and dessert."

DOBOSCH TORTE

1 (12 ounce) Sara Lee pound
  cake
8 (1 ounce) squares sweet
  German's chocolate

¼ cup strongly brewed coffee
2 tablespoons cognac
1½ cups whipping cream

While partially frozen, slice the cake lengthwise into 6 layers using a serrated knife. In the top of a double boiler, melt the chocolate; add the coffee and cognac and mix well; cool. Whip the cream in a chilled bowl and fold into the cooled chocolate mixture. Frost each layer, the top and sides of cake. Chill several hours before serving. Serves 10. NOTE: Serve thinly sliced as this is very rich. Recipe can be doubled easily using the family size Sara Lee pound cake.

Nancy Weight
Director of Development
Mother of Katharine
Carmel, California

GATEAU NICOISE

1 (10 ounce) package frozen
  puff pastry shells

FILLING:
1 (2 ounce) envelope whipped
  topping mix
½ cup milk
¼ teaspoon almond extract

1 egg white
3 tablespoons sugar

¼ teaspoon orange extract
¾ cup chopped candied ginger
Almonds

Press pastry shells together and form 3 balls of dough. Roll out each ball into a 9 inch circle and trim edges evenly. Place each on an un-greased cookie sheet and brush with the lightly beaten egg white. Sprinkle each with 1 tablespoon of the sugar. Bake one at a time in a 400° oven for 18-20 minutes or until golden brown (Each circle will shrink to 6 inches). Cool on a wire rack. For filling: Beat the whipped topping mix with the milk, and flavor with the extracts. Fold in all but 1 tablespoon of the candied ginger. Top each pastry round with the fil-ling and garnish with the remaining candied ginger and the almonds. Stack and chill. To serve, cut each layer into fourths with a serrated knife. Serves 12.

Cleo Devoto (Mrs. Ralph)
Grandmother of Ulrike Devoto '86
Lakeport, California

QUEEN MOTHER TORTE
(Chocolate Almond Torte)

¾ cup unsalted butter
¾ cup sugar
6 ounces (1¼ cup) finely ground
  blanched almonds
6 ounces semi-sweet chocolate,
  melted

6 large eggs, separated
1/8 teaspoon salt
Cream of tartar
Dry bread crumbs

In a large bowl, beat the softened butter until fluffy; add the egg yolks one at a time, beating well after each addition. Beat in the sugar and almonds and stir in the cooled chocolate. In another large bowl, beat the eggs whites with the salt and a pinch of cream of tartar until they hold soft peaks. Fold into the chocolate mixture in 3 parts. Butter an 8-inch springform pan and line with wax paper. Butter the paper and sprinkle with the dry bread crumbs. Pour batter into the pan, spreading the top evenly. Place pan 1/3 up from the bottom of the oven which has been preheated to 350°. Bake for 15 minutes and then reduce the heat to 325° and bake for 35 minutes or until a tester inserted in the center comes out clean. The cake should be moist. Allow the cake to cool in the pan on a rack for 45 minutes. Run a knife around the edge of the pan and release the sides. Transfer to a serving dish and cool completely. Sprinkle the top with powdered sugar and serve with whipped cream or frost with chocolate icing. Serves 8.

CHOCOLATE ICING

½ cup heavy cream
8 ounces semi-sweet chocolate

2 teaspoons instant coffee

In a saucepan or top of double boiler, combine the cream and the coffee. Bring to a boil, stirring constantly until the coffee is dissolved. Remove the pan from the heat and add the chocolate, cut into ¼ inch pieces. Whisk until melted. Spread on top and sides of cake. Chill until set. Serve at room temperature.

Earlene Merriman (Mrs. John)
Mother of Jennifer '84
Boonville, California

"Elegant, but nothing to it! My sister gave me this recipe fifteen years ago and it is still one of our favorite desserts."

CHOCOLATE LADYFINGER TORTE

1 (8 ounce) bar semi-sweet
   chocolate
3 tablespoons water
4 eggs, separated
½ cup butter, softened

1 teaspoon vanilla
¼ cup sugar
2 cups whipping cream
10 double ladyfingers (20 halves)

Using a vegetable peeler, make chocolate curls with about 1 ounce of the chocolate. Let the curls drop on to wax paper lined pan and refrigerate until ready to garnish the torte. Melt the remaining 7-ounces chocolate with water in a mixing bowl placed over hot water. Remove from heat and beat in the egg yolks, one at a time. Beat in the butter, a small amount at a time, and add the vanilla. Beat the egg whites until soft peaks form and gradually beat in the sugar; fold into the chocolate mixture, which should be cooled to room temperature. Whip 1 cup of the cream until stiff and fold in. Separate the ladyfingers and stand, rounded side out, around the inside of a buttered 9-inch springform pan. Spoon in the chocolate filling, spreading evenly. Chill thoroughly, overnight, if desired. Several hours before serving, whip the remaining cup of cream and sweeten with sugar; spread over the torte. Garnish with the chocolate curls. Serves 8.

Marilyn B. Wykoff (Mrs. Victor C.)
Class of '59
Mother of Wendy '86
Stockton, California

CHOCOLATE DECADENCE

1 pound bittersweet chocolate
4 ounces unsalted butter
1½ teaspoons flour
1½ teaspoons sugar

1 teaspoon water
4 eggs, separated
Raspberry puree, optional
Whipped cream, optional

Grease the bottoms and sides of an 8-inch round pan and line the bottom with wax paper. Melt the chocolate and unsalted butter in a double boiler; add the flour, sugar and hot water and blend well. Beat in the egg yolks, one at a time. Beat the egg whites until stiff and fold into the chocolate mixture. Pour into the prepared pan and bake in a 375° oven for 15 minutes (the center will look very uncooked). Cool and then freeze. When frozen, place in the refrigerator. Bring almost to room temperature before serving. This is best served with raspberry puree made from fresh or unsweetened frozen berries, strained through a sieve. Or with whipped cream or both! Serves 12.

Janine A. Heymann (Mrs. Michael)
Mother of Simone '84
San Francisco, California

BLACK BOTTOM CUPCAKES

FILLING:
1 (8 ounce) package cream cheese
1/3 cup sugar

1 egg
1 cup semi-sweet chocolate chips

CUPCAKES:
1½ cups unsifted flour
1 egg
1 cup water
1 cup sugar
¼ cup cocoa

1/3 cup cooking oil
1 teaspoon soda
½ teaspoon salt
1 tablespoon vinegar
1 teaspoon vanilla

For filling: In a small mixing bowl, combine the cream cheese, sugar and egg and beat with an electric mixer until well blended. Stir in the chocolate chips; set aside. For cupcakes: Combine all ingredients in a mixing bowl and beat on low speed with an electric mixer or stir well with a wire whisk until mixture is well blended. Line muffin tins with cupcake papers; fill liners ½ full with the cupcake batter. Top each with a heaping teaspoonful of the filling and bake in a preheated 350° oven for 20-25 minutes. Cool. Yields 18 cupcakes.

Pamela Rowe (Mrs. Dennis)
Mother of Larissa
Salinas, California

"In this era of instant cake mix, a scratch cake is something of a rarity. Here's one that's easy, and every chocolate lover in your life will tell you that it's worth the little extra effort."

HARRY'S CAKE

3 squares baking chocolate　　*1-3/8 cups sifted flour*
6 tablespoons butter　　*¾ teaspoon baking soda*
¾ cup boiling water　　*5/8 teaspoon salt*
1½ cups sugar　　*2 eggs*
3/8 cup sour milk or buttermilk

WHITE FROSTING:
1 cup sugar　　*2 unbeaten egg whites*
¼ teaspoon salt　　*3 tablespoons water*
½ teaspoon cream of tartar　　*1 teaspoon vanilla*

Cut chocolate into small pieces and place in a bowl with the butter. Pour the boiling water over and melt. Stir in the sugar and the milk. Add remaining ingredients all at once and stir to blend. Add unbeaten eggs and beat 2 minutes. Grease and flour a 9 x 13 inch sheet pan or 2-9 inch layer pans. Pour in the batter and bake in a preheated 350° oven for 25 minutes. NOTE: Do not substitute sweet milk for the sour or buttermilk. For the frosting, place all ingredients in the top section of a double boiler; place over boiling water and beat with a rotary mixer for 3 minutes or until the frosting peaks. Spread on the cooled cake.

Robert G. Beaumont
San Carlos, California

CHOCOLATE CAKE "PAUL"

2 cups sugar　　*2½ cups flour*
1 cup margarine　　*¼ teaspoon soda*
4 eggs　　*2 teaspoons vanilla*
1 (5 ounce) bar Cadbury　　*1 (16 ounce) can Hershey*
chocolate　　*chocolate syrup*
1 cup buttermilk

In a large mixing bowl, beat the sugar and margarine until fluffy. Add the eggs, one at a time, beating well after each addition. Melt the chocolate in a double boiler and add to the creamed mixture. Add the buttermilk, flour, soda, vanilla and lastly the chocolate syrup. Pour into a greased and floured bundt pan and bake in a 325° oven for 1 hour 15 minutes. Cool on rack. Dust with powdered sugar.

Dr. Tom McGuire
Oakland, California

CHOCOLATE DELIGHT

1 cup cake flour
1¼ cups sugar
1 teaspoon baking powder
½ teaspoon salt
6 eggs, separated

1 teaspoon vanilla
1 teaspoon lemon extract
¼ cup water
¼ teaspoon cream of tartar

Sift together the cake flour, 1 cup of the sugar, the baking powder and salt; set aside. In a bowl, slightly mix the egg yolks, vanilla, lemon extract and water; add the flour mixture and beat for 1 minute. In a separate bowl, beat the egg whites and cream of tartar until foamy; gradually add the remaining ¼ cup sugar and beat until stiff. Fold the egg yolk mixture into the egg whites. Grease and flour a 10-inch tube pan, a 9 x 13 inch baking dish or two 8 x 8 inch pans. Pour batter into desired pan and bake in a 350° oven for 35-40 minutes if a tube pan is used, or for 30 minutes if other pans are used. When cool, frost with Chocolate Marshmallow Icing as follows: If a *tube pan* is used, slice the cake into 3 layers and frost each layer, top and sides of cake. If a *9 x 13 inch pan* is used, slice cake into 2-9 x 13 x 1 inch layers and frost bottom layer, top and sides of cake. If *8 x 8 inch pans* are used, frost as you would a normal layer cake.

CHOCOLATE MARSHMALLOW ICING

1 (6 ounce) package chocolate
  chips
16 large marshmallows

½ cup milk
½ pint whipping cream

Combine the chocolate chips, marshmallows and milk in the top of a double boiler until the chocolate chips and marshmallows are melted, blending well. Remove from heat and set aside to cool for at least an hour. Whip the cream until thick and fold in the chocolate mixture.

Dorothy Limov (Mrs. Nicholas)
School Nurse
Carmel, California

BOX TREE INN CAKE

1 cup butter
2 cups sugar
4 eggs
3 cups flour

4 teaspoons baking powder
¼ teaspoon salt
1 teaspoon vanilla
½ cup milk

Cream the butter and sugar; add the eggs. Sift together the dry ingredients and add to the creamed mixture alternately with the milk and vanilla. Pour into 2 greased and floured pans and bake for 30 minutes or until done. Bake in a 375° oven for layer cakes or in a 350° oven for a sheet cake.

BOX TREE INN ICING

4 (1 ounce) squares baking
  chocolate
2 cups sugar

1 cup milk
½ cup butter
½ teaspoon vanilla

In a saucepan, combine the chocolate, sugar, milk and butter; boil, stirring constantly until thick. Add the vanilla and beat until thick enough to spread.

Melanie Dugan
Director of Lower School
Monterey, California

"This cake is easy, quick, rich and good — a standby treat for 4H or FFA meetings or a quick dessert with sliced oranges or ice cream."

CHOCOLATE SHEET CAKE

2 cups flour
2 cups sugar
¼ teaspoon salt
1 cup butter
¼ cup cocoa

1 cup water
½ cup buttermilk
1 teaspoon baking soda
2 eggs
1 teaspoon vanilla

ICING:
½ cup butter
3½ tablespoons cocoa
1/3 cup buttermilk

1 pound confectioners' sugar
½ cup chopped nuts

In a large bowl, sift together the flour, sugar and salt. Set aside. In a saucepan, bring to a boil the butter, cocoa and water; remove from heat, pour over the dry ingredients and mix well. Thoroughly blend in the buttermilk, soda, eggs and vanilla. Pour into a greased 18 x 27 inch cookie sheet and bake in a 350° oven for 20 minutes. For the icing, combine in a saucepan the butter, cocoa and buttermilk; bring to a boil, remove from heat and add the confectioner's sugar and nuts, mixing well. Frost while the cake is still warm.

Olive Beacham Lansburgh (Mrs. Larry)
Mother of Jennifer Wright '79
Eagle Point, Oregon

GRANDMA'S CHOCOLATE CAKE

1/3 cup cocoa
Cooled coffee
1 teaspoon baking soda
½ cup butter
2 cups brown sugar

½ cup granulated sugar
3 eggs, separated
½ cup sour cream
2 cups flour

FROSTING:
2 tablespoons butter, melted
2 tablespoons cocoa

Milk
2 cups powdered sugar
1 teaspoon Kahlua, optional

Place the cocoa in a liquid measuring cup and add enough cooled coffee to equal 1 cup; stir in the baking soda and set aside. Cream the butter, brown sugar, and ¼ cup of the sugar and egg yolks. Add the sour cream and blend in the cocoa-coffee mixture and the flour. Beat the egg whites with the remaining ¼ cup sugar until stiff. Fold into the batter and pour into a greased and floured 13 x 9 inch baking pan. Bake in a 350° oven for 30-40 minutes or until done. Frost when cool. For frosting: In a mixing bowl, combine the butter and cocoa and beat in the powdered sugar a little at a time, adding enough milk for a smooth consistency. Blend in the Kahlua, if desired. Serves 10-12.

Diana King
Mother of Darren and Meredith
Pebble Beach, California

WALDORF ASTORIA RED VELVET CAKE

½ cup shortening
1½ cups sugar
2 ounces red food coloring
2 eggs
1 teaspoon vanilla
2 cups flour

1 teaspoon salt
1 tablespoon cocoa
1 cup buttermilk
1 teaspoon soda
1 teaspoon vinegar

ICING:
1 cup milk
¼ cup flour
Salt

1 cup shortening
1 cup sugar
2 teaspoons vanilla

Cream together the shortening and sugar; add the red food coloring and beat in the eggs, one at a time, beating well after each addition. Add the vanilla. Sift together 3 times the flour, salt and cocoa and add alternately with the buttermilk; beat until smooth. Mix together the soda and vinegar and fold gently into the batter. *Do not beat.* Pour into 2 greased and floured 9-inch pans and bake in a 350° oven 35-40 minutes. For icing: In a saucepan, combine the milk, flour and salt and cook until thick, stirring constantly; cool for 1 hour. Beat the shortening and sugar until very fluffy. Add the vanilla. Frost the cake and garnish with red coconut.

Nancy Deliantoni
Pebble Beach, California

"This is the richest, most chocolate-y" chocolate cake I've know. It's expensive to make, but deliciously worth it."

JUSTIN'S DOUBLE CHOCOLATE FUDGE CAKE

3 squares unsweetened chocolate
½ cup butter
2¼ cups firmly packed brown
    sugar
3 eggs
1½ teaspoons vanilla

1 cup sour cream
2¼ cups sifted cake flour
2 teaspoons baking soda
½ teaspoon salt
1 cup boiling water

Melt the chocolate and set aside to cool. In a large bowl, cream the butter; add the sugar and eggs and beat with a mixer at high speed until light and fluffy, about 5 minutes. Beat in the vanilla and cooled melted chocolate. Combine the flour, soda and salt and stir alternately into the batter with the sour cream. Beat with a wooden spoon after each addition until batter is smooth. Stir in the boiling water (batter will be thin). Pour at once into 2 greased and floured 9-inch cake pans. Bake in a 350° oven for about 35 minutes. Serves 10.

FUDGE FROSTING

½ cup butter
4 squares unsweetened chocolate
1 pound powdered sugar

2 teaspoons vanilla
½ cup milk

Melt the butter and chocolate over low heat; set aside. In a medium sized bowl, combine the powdered sugar, vanilla and milk and stir until smooth; add the chocolate mixture. Place bowl in a pan of ice and water and beat with a wooden spoon until frosting is thick enough to spread and hold its shape.

Ethelyne Hughes
Upper School Faculty
Monterey, California

"This is Chanel's father's favorite cake."

CHOCOLATE CHERRY SHEET CAKE

1 (1 pound 2½ ounce) package
   chocolate fudge cake mix
2 eggs, beaten

2 teaspoons almond extract
1 (20 ounce) can cherry pie
   filling

EASY CHOCOLATE FROSTING:
1 cup sugar
1/3 cup milk
5 tablespoons butter

1 (6 ounce) package semi-sweet
   chocolate chips
1 teaspoon vanilla

Mix together the cake mix, eggs and almond extract with a fork. Stir in cherry pie filling (do not beat with a mixer). Lightly grease and flour a 10 x 15 inch pan. Spread the mixture evenly in the pan. Bake in a 350° oven for 30 minutes. Cool ½ hour in the pan. For the frosting, combine the sugar, milk and butter in a saucepan; bring to a boil and boil for 1 minute. Remove from heat and stir in the chocolate chips until smooth; add the vanilla. Spread on cake immediately.

Pat DeLaney (Mrs. L. B.)
Mother of Chanel '84
Reno, Nevada

"Jessica found this one in one of her children's cookbooks when she was about eight years old. It's still my favorite!"

JESSICA'S HOT FUDGE CAKE

1 cup flour
2 tablespoons unsweetened cocoa
2 teaspoons baking powder
½ teaspoon salt
½ cup milk
½ cup corn syrup

2 tablespoons cooking oil
1 teaspoon vanilla
¾ cup brown sugar, packed
¼ cup cocoa
1½ cups boiling water

Combine the flour, 2 tablespoons cocoa, baking powder and salt, mixing well with a fork. Combine the milk, corn syrup, oil and vanilla and add to the dry ingredients, mixing until smooth. Spread the batter evenly into a greased 9 x 9 inch pan. Using your fingers, mix together the brown sugar and ¼ cup cocoa in a small bowl and sprinkle over the batter. Pour the boiling water over all; do not stir. Bake in a 350° oven for 35-40 minutes; let stand 15 minutes. Serve warm with French vanilla or Jamoca ice cream. Serves 6-8.

Mr. Gill M. Girard III
Father of Jessica '83
Dhahran, Saudi Arabia

MRS. REES' CHOCOLATE CAKE

1 cup butter
2 squares unsweetened chocolate
2 beaten eggs
2 cups brown sugar
1 cup buttermilk

1½ cups cake flour
1 teaspoon baking soda
½ teaspoon salt
2 teaspoons vanilla

ICING:
5 squares unsweetened chocolate
½ cup butter
1½ pounds powdered sugar
1 egg yolk

Salt
2 teaspoons vanilla
Coffee

Melt the butter and chocolate in the top of a double boiler; combine in a large bowl with the eggs, brown sugar and buttermilk. Add the flour, baking soda and salt; blend in the vanilla and beat for 1 minute. Pour into 3 greased and floured cake pans and bake in a preheated 350° oven for 20 minutes. Frost when cool with an icing made by melting the chocolate and the butter in the top of a double boiler. Combine with the powdered sugar, egg yolk, salt and vanilla. Thin to desired consistency with coffee.

Donna Robbins
Mother of Sky '86
Piedmont, California

WACKIE CAKE

1½ cups flour
¼ cup cocoa
1 teaspoon soda
½ teaspoon salt
1 cup sugar

1 tablespoon vinegar
1 tablespoon vanilla
1/3 cup salad oil
1 cup cold water

Sift together the flour, cocoa, soda and salt; add the remaining ingredients and beat until smooth. Pour into a 9-inch square baking pan and bake in a 350° oven for 30-35 minutes. Serves 6-8. Sprinkle powdered sugar on the top or frost with your favorite frosting.

Marlene Kellogg (Mrs. Clarence)
Mother of Kellene '79 and Christina '85
Pacific Grove, California

"This is almost every year's request for birthdays. It is especially good since not all of the chocolate melts and there are bits of 'chips' here and there."

DARK CHOCOLATE CAKE

5 ounces unsweetened chocolate
  chopped
¾ cup butter
2 cups hottest tap water
2 cups sugar
2 teaspoons baking powder

2 teaspoons baking soda
½ teaspoon salt
2 1/3 cups unsifted flour
2 eggs
1 teaspoon vanilla

FROSTING:
3 ounces unsweetened chocolate
  squares, chopped
3 tablespoons butter

1/3 cup water
3 cups unsifted powdered sugar

Place the chocolate and the butter which has been cut in small pieces into a mixing bowl. Pour the hot water over the chocolate and butter and stir until almost melted. Stir together in a separate bowl the sugar, baking powder, baking soda, salt and flour; set aside. Beat the eggs with the vanilla into the chocolate mixture. Stir in the dry ingredients and beat until smooth and blended. Pour into a greased 9 x 13 inch pan. Bake in a preheated 350° oven for 45 minutes or until the cake begins to pull slightly away from the sides of the pan. Cool. *For Frosting:* combine together in a small saucepan the chocolate, butter and the water. Heat gently until the chocolate and the butter are melted and the mixture is smooth. Remove from heat and beat in the powdered sugar. Spread evenly over the cooled cake. Cut into squares to serve.

Mary Ann Taylor (Mrs. James)
Mother of James, Katie, and Asher
Monterey, California

Prize Day is held every year on the day before graduation. On this occasion, students are recognized for excellence in all areas of school life; among them are academics, sports, the performing arts, school support, service to their community, and consistent participation and contribution to a range of school activities. Veritas is the highest award and is given for qualities of character, leadership, and scholarship. The Alumnae Award is given to the student who gives the most notable support of school traditions and activities and who carries out all that alumnae have fostered in their years at School. The Munras Courtesy Award is the oldest award and was established by Lady Antonia Field of the Munras family of Monterey. The Christopher Award is given for leadership and example in the religious life of School. The highest academic award is given to the Senior who has the highest cumulative GPA for the four years of high school.

CHOCOLATE CAKE

2 cups sugar
2 cups flour, sifted
½ teaspoon salt
½ cup butter
½ cup oil

3 tablespoons cocoa
1 cup water
2 eggs
½ cup buttermilk
1 teaspoon baking soda
1 teaspoon vanilla

FROSTING:
½ cup butter
2 tablespoons cocoa
1/3 cup milk

1 teaspoon vanilla
1 pound powdered sugar, sifted
1 cup nuts, optional

In a large bowl, mix together the sugar, flour and salt. Set aside. In a saucepan, bring to a boil the butter, oil, cocoa and water; stir into the flour mixture. Add the eggs, buttermilk, soda and vanilla, blending well. Pour into a greased and floured 13 x 9 inch metal baking pan and bake in a 350° oven 25-30 minutes. For the frosting: In a saucepan, heat the butter, cocoa, milk and vanilla until the butter is melted. Add the sugar and nuts, stirring well. Frost cake when cool.

Lynne Howard (Mrs. Stephen)
Mother of Trent
Monterey, California

SWEET BUTTER FROSTING

2/3 cup sugar
¼ cup flour
¼ teaspoon salt

¾ cup milk
½ pound unsalted butter (cold)
1 teaspoon vanilla

Measure the sugar, flour and salt into a saucepan and mix thoroughly; stir in the milk until smooth. Place over medium heat and cook, stirring constantly, until very thick (If not smooth when partially cooked, beat with a rotary beater, then continue cooking and stirring). Remove from heat and pour into a 2 or 3 quart mixing bowl. Cool to room temperature by placing the bowl in cold water. The mixture should not be warm enough to melt the butter. Remove a stick of butter one at a time from the refrigerator, cut in half lengthwise and then crosswise into ½ inch pieces. With an electric mixer, beat in the firm butter, about 2 tablespoons at a time, beating until smooth after each addition. When all the butter has been added, beat in the vanilla. NOTE: The entire beating time is 8-10 minutes. The frosting will spread more evenly if chilled 5-10 minutes after mixing. Refrigerate cake after frosting.

Chuck Jones
Seattle, Washington

"A handsome garnish for ice cream, puddings, cakes or fresh fruit. Instead of using chocolate curls, these leaves are magnificent and so easy to make. My children have such fun making these."

CHOCOLATE LEAVES

1 (14 ounce) milk chocolate   6 ounces semi-sweet chocolate
bar, coarsely chopped

Choose any thick, textured leaf with an attractive pattern on the underside, such as camellia or magnolia. Leave on a section of stem. Wash well and dry thoroughly. Heat water to simmering in the bottom of a double boiler and put the chocolates in the top. Reduce the heat to the lowest setting, just to keep the water hot. Stir occasionally until the mixture is melted and smooth. Brush the chocolate on the underside of a leaf in a layer about ¼-½ inch thick, using a small brush. Leave a tiny margin around the edge of the leaf. Coat well along the heavy central vein. Place on a pan, chocolate side up and chill. Carefully peel the real leaf from the chocolate one. Remove one leaf at a time from the refrigerator to peel. Store the chocolate leaves in an airtight container in the refrigerator until just before serving.

Marilyn Brown Wykoff (Mrs. Victor C.)
Class of '59
Mother of Wendy '86
Stockton, California

ANGEL FOOD-CHOCOLATE CHIP CAKE

1 (12 ounce) package chocolate   1 cup walnuts
  chips   1 teaspoon vanilla
4 eggs, separated   1 large angel food cake
¼ teaspoon salt
1 envelope prepared Dream Whip topping

Melt the chocolate chips in the top of a double boiler; add the eggs and salt. When the mixture is partially cooled, add the stiffly beaten egg whites, nuts and vanilla. When entirely cooled, fold in the Dream Whip. Break the cake into bite-sized pieces and place half of the pieces into the bottom of a 13 x 9 x 2 inch dish; pour half of the chocolate mixture on top, add the remaining angel food cake pieces and top with the remaining chocolate mixture. Store in the refrigerator.

Eileen C. Sullivan (Mrs. Richard T.)
Mother of Erin '85
Monterey, California

TOFFEE TRIFLE

1 (5-3/8 ounce) package vanilla
  instant pudding
3 cups half and half
6 cups angel food or pound cake,
  cut into 1½ inch pieces
¾ cup Kahlua

1 pint whipping cream
2 tablespoons instant coffee,
  powder or granules
2 tablespoons sugar
1 teaspoon vanilla extract
½ pound English toffee, broken
  and coarsely crushed

Prepare pudding according to package directions, substituting half and half for the milk. Sprinkle the cake with Kahlua and let set 5 minutes. Mix the pudding and cake together; set aside. Pour the whipping cream and coffee into a mixing bowl; let stand 1 minute. Beat until the mixture begins to thicken; add sugar and vanilla and continue beating until the mixture forms soft peaks. Set aside approximately 1½ cups of the whipped cream for garnish. In a pretty 2-quart serving bowl, layer half the cake-pudding mixture, half the coffee flavored whipped cream and half the English toffee. Repeat with the remaining pudding and cream. Using a star tip, pipe the reserved whipped cream around the outer edge of the bowl. Sprinkle with the remaining English toffee. Serves 8-10.

Joanne Cohen (Mrs. Sheldon)
Mother of Poppy '86
Fresno, California

ANGEL BERRY CAKE DESSERT

2 (10 ounce) packages frozen
  raspberries
2 (3 ounce) packages raspberry
  gelatin

½ angel food cake loaf
1 (8 ounce) container whipped
  topping

Thaw and drain the raspberries, reserving the juice. Combine enough hot water with the juice to equal 2 cups; dissolve the gelatin in this liquid and chill until partially set. Fold in the raspberries, whipped topping and angel food cake which has been broken into bite-sized pieces. Place in an oiled 8-inch round mold and chill overnight. Before serving, unmold and garnish with fresh raspberries. Serves 10.

Mary Ann Dickie (Mrs. Ernest)
Mother of Laura '86
Pebble Beach, California

The Performing Arts Center was completed in its Phase I and dedicated during the school's celebration of its 25th anniversary in December, 1975.

STRAWBERRY FLUFF CAKE

1 package yellow cake mix with   *1 cup strawberries*
   pudding   *1 egg white, stiffly beaten*
1 egg
1 cup sugar

Prepare the cake according to package directions, adding an extra egg. Combine the sugar, strawberries and egg white to make a topping. Top each cake slice before serving.

June and Virginia Boyle
Aunts of Sister Mary Ellen and
Kathleen Ryan
San Mateo, California

THE THREE MILKS CAKE

CAKE:
4 eggs   *2 cups sifted flour*
2 cups sugar   *2 teaspoons baking powder*
1 cup milk   *Salt*
2 tablespoons butter

MILK MIXTURE:
1 (14 ounce) can sweetened   *1½ cups whole milk*
   condensed milk   *½ teaspoon vanilla*
1 (12 ounce) can evaporated milk *3 egg yolks*

TOPPING:
3 egg whites   *6-7 tablespoons sugar*

For the cake: Beat the eggs for 5 minutes; gradually add the sugar and beat 5 more minutes. Scald the milk with the butter and blend into the egg-sugar mixture. Sift together the flour, baking powder and salt and fold gently into the batter; pour into a buttered 9 x 12 inch glass pan and bake in a 350° oven for 30-40 minutes or until a toothpick inserted in the center comes out clean. For the milk mixture: Blend the milks, vanilla and egg yolks. After the cake cools, pierce all over with a fork and pour the milk mixture over the cake. For the topping: Beat the egg whites until fluffy, add the sugar and beat until stiff. Frost the top of the cake with this meringue and broil until lightly browned. This cake may be served cold or at room temperature. Serves 15.

Pilar Salido (Mrs. Ildefonso)
Mother of Maria Pilar, Summer Camper
Los Mochis, Sinaloa, Mexico

THE NEXT BEST THING TO ROBERT REDFORD

1 cup flour
½ cup softened butter
1 cup finely chopped pecans
1 (8 ounce) package cream
  cheese, softened
1 cup sugar
1 pint whipping cream, whipped

1 (6¾ ounce) package instant
  vanilla pudding mix
1 (6¾ ounce) package instant
  chocolate pudding mix
4 cups cold milk
Grated chocolate Hershey bar

Prepare bottom crust by mixing together the flour, butter and pecans until crumblike. Press the mixture into a greased 13 x 9 inch baking pan. Bake in a preheated 350° oven for 15-20 minutes until lightly golden. Cool. Beat the cream cheese with the sugar until smooth; fold in half of the whipped cream. Spread this mixture over the cooled crust. Combine the vanilla and chocolate pudding mixes; beat in the milk until smooth and thickened. Evenly spread over the cream cheese layer. Top with the remaining whipped cream and garnish with the grated chocolate bar, if desired. Cover and refrigerate overnight. Makes 16 servings.

Joanne Cohen (Mrs. Sheldon)
Mother of Poppy '86
Fresno, California

AUNT SALLY'S CHOCOLATE PUDDING

Per Serving:
1 square unsweetened chocolate
1 teaspoon sugar

1 egg, separated
Vanilla

Melt the chocolate over hot water. Beat the egg whites and set aside. Beat together the egg yolks and sugar until thick; beat in the chocolate. Beat the mixture into the egg whites. Pour into a serving dish and refrigerate for at least 2 hours. Garnish with whipped cream, if desired. NOTE: As you increase portions, decrease chocolate. 7 eggs take 6 chocolate squares.

Penelope Douglas
Class of '69
San Francisco, California

ROSE'S WHIPPED CREAM PUDDING

1 large egg
1 cup sugar
1 cup milk
1 envelope unflavored gelatin

½ cup cold water
1 teaspoon vanilla
1 pint whipping cream, whipped
Macaroon crumbs

Lightly beat the egg, add the sugar and beat until pale and thick, add the milk and whisk well. Dissolve the gelatin in the water and set aside. Heat the egg-milk mixture to just under boiling point. Do not boil. Stir in the gelatin, add the vanilla and cool. When almost set (it will be a syrupy consistency), fold in the whipped cream. Pour into an oiled mold and chill until set. Unmold and garnish with toasted macaroon crumbs. Serve with fruit or a raspberry or bitter chocolate sauce.

Norma Eversole (Mrs. Henry)
Mother of Alexandria '65, Gillian '69, Helena '70, Melina '79
La Canada, California

DATE PUDDING

1 cup dates
1 cup sugar
¾ cup soft bread crumbs
¾ cup chopped nuts

1 egg
1 cup milk
½ teaspoon vanilla

Combine all the ingredients in the top of a double boiler and cook for several hours until stiff. Serve with whipped cream.

Lucia de Guajardo (Mrs. Carlos)
Mother of Gabriela '84
Monterey, Mexico

CRANBERRY STEAMED PUDDING

2 cups raw cranberries
1-1/3 cups flour
½ teaspoon salt
1 teaspoon baking soda
¼ teaspoon cinnamon

¼ teaspoon cloves
¼ teaspoon mace
1/3 cup hot water
½ cup dark molasses

SAUCE:
1 cup white sugar
1 cup half and half

1/3 cup butter
Vanilla, rum or brandy to taste

Coarsely chop the cranberries in a food processor; add the flour, salt, baking soda, cinnamon, cloves, mace, hot water and molasses and process no longer than 1 minute. Place in a well greased pudding mold and steam for 2 hours. Serve hot with the sauce. For the sauce, combine all the ingredients and cook, stirring constantly, until the sugar is dissolved and the butter is melted (stir before serving to keep the butter from rising to the top). Serves 4. NOTE: Never double the recipe — make two.

Caroline Lord Mackenzie (Mrs. Gordon)
Class of '65
Singapore

CARROT PUDDING

1½ cups shortening	*1 teaspoon salt*
1 cup brown sugar	*2 tablespoons water*
2 eggs	*2 tablespoons lemon juice*
2½ cups flour	*2 teaspoons vanilla*
1 teaspoon baking soda	*6 cups grated carrots*
2 teaspoons baking powder	

Cream together the shortening and sugar; add the remaining ingredients in the order given and mix well. Bake in a greased bundt pan in a 350° oven for 1 hour. Serves 10-12. NOTE: This is a pudding, not a cake, and can be served with your favorite sauce, e.g. lemon, vanilla or hard sauce.

Sheila Lamson (Mrs. Perry)
Upper School Faculty and Administration
Pebble Beach, California

VERY BEST CARROT CAKE

1½ cups safflower oil	*1 teaspoon salt*
2 cups brown sugar	*3 teaspoons cinnamon*
4 eggs	*3 teaspoons vanilla*
2 cups flour	*3 cups grated carrots*
2 teaspoons baking soda	*Walnuts, optional*
FROSTING:	
1 (3 ounce) package cream cheese	*8 ounces powdered sugar*
½ cup butter	*2 teaspoons vanilla*

Combine all the cake ingredients in a large bowl, mixing well. Pour into a greased 9 x 11 inch baking pan, and bake in a 350° oven for 45 minutes. Cool for 1 hour before frosting. Make the frosting by blending the cream cheese, butter, sugar and vanilla until smooth. Frost the cake liberally. Serves 10.

Cherie Pettit Arkley (Mrs. Robin)
Class of '74
Arcata, California

"As advisor to the Catalinan, our school year book, I sometimes bring food to staff meetings for the girls. This carrot cake is easy to make and quick to disappear."

CATALINAN CARROT CAKE

2 cups flour
2 tablespoons cinnamon
1 teaspoon baking powder
½ teaspoon soda
2 cups sugar
¼ cup oil

2 eggs
2 cups shredded carrots
1 cup crushed pineapple
1 cup chopped apple
1 cup chopped walnuts
1 cup raisins

FROSTING:
2 tablespoons butter
2 (3 ounce) packages cream cheese

12 ounces powdered sugar

Sift together the flour, cinnamon, baking powder and soda and mix well; add the sugar, oil and eggs. Fold in the remaining ingredients and pour into a greased and floured 9 x 12 inch pan. Bake in a 350° oven for 40-60 minutes. Frost the cake when cool. Make the frosting by creaming together the butter, cream cheese and powdered sugar. Serves 12.

Barbara Blevens (Mrs. Mel)
Upper School Faculty
Carmel Valley, California

"My grandmother called this recipe 'Skillet Cake' sometimes. It's a popular Happy Birthday request in our family. On special occasions pop candles in the pineapple centers! This is the very first recipe that my grandmother shared with my mother after she married my dad. This upside down cake was my Uncle Charlie's very favorite."

MY GRANDMOTHER'S PINEAPPLE UPSIDE DOWN CAKE

1/3 cup butter
1 cup brown sugar, packed
1 (8 ounce) can sliced pineapple
6 tablespoons pineapple juice
Pecans/ walnuts/ almonds or
    cherry halves

1 cup flour
1 teaspoon baking powder
¼ teaspoon salt
2 eggs
2/3 cup granulated sugar
1½ teaspoons vanilla

Melt the butter in a 10-inch cast-iron skillet. Sprinkle the brown sugar over the melted butter and stir to remove lumps. Drain the pineapple, reserving the juice. Arrange the pineapple slices in a single layer in the skillet. Put either cherries or nutmeat halves in the center of each pineapple ring. Sift together the flour, baking powder, and salt; set aside.

Beat the eggs until thick and lemon colored; slowly add the granulated sugar. Combine the pineapple juice with the vanilla and add to the egg mixture. Blend in the dry ingredients until smooth; pour into the skillet and bake in a 350° oven for 40-50 minutes. Turn out on a cake platter and let the skillet sit to allow the syrup to drain onto the cake. Serve with whipped cream or ice cream. Serves 6-8.

Cressey Joy Belden
Class of '87
Santa Rosa, California

INGRID'S GERMAN APPLE CAKE

1 cup unsalted butter, melted	*2 teaspoons baking powder*
3 cups sugar	*2 teaspoons vanilla*
4 eggs	*1 tablespoon cinnamon*
2 cups flour	*5 large apples*

Grease an 11 x 16 x 1 inch jelly roll pan. Combine the butter, 2 cups of the sugar and the eggs in a mixing bowl; add the flour, baking powder and vanilla, and beat until well blended. Spread the mixture evenly in the prepared pan. Combine the remaining 1 cup sugar and the cinnamon. Peel, core and slice the apples; mix with the sugar and cinnamon and arrange on top of the batter. Bake in a preheated 350° oven for 45 minutes to 1 hour. Makes 18 servings. NOTE: Granny Smith apples are excellent.

Nancy Beaumont McNeil
Clovis, California

FRESH APPLE CAKE

1¼ cups oil	*¼ teaspoon nutmeg*
2 cups sugar	*½ teaspoon salt*
2 eggs	*2 tablespoons vanilla*
3 cups flour	*3 cups chopped apples*
1 teaspoon baking soda	*1 cup chopped pecans*
1 teaspoon cinnamon	

Cream together the oil, sugar and eggs; add the dry ingredients and vanilla and blend well. Stir in the apples and nuts. Pour into a greased and floured 13 x 9 x 2 inch pan and bake in a 350° oven for 1 hour. Serves 12.

Susan Kendall (Mrs. Scott)
Lower School Faculty
Pacific Grove, California

"This recipe comes from my Swedish aunt."

APPLE CAKE

4 cups apples, grated
½ cup vegetable oil
2 cups sugar
2 eggs
2 teaspoons vanilla

2 cups flour
2 teaspoons baking soda
2 teaspoons cinnamon
½ teaspoon salt
1 cup chopped nuts

In a bowl, combine the grated apples, the oil, sugar, eggs and vanilla. Sift together the flour, baking soda, cinnamon and salt; add to the apple mixture and blend for approximately 2 minutes. Fold in the chopped nuts. Pour into a greased 9 x 13 inch pan and bake in a 325° oven for 55 minutes.

Jane Day (Mrs. Donald)
Mother of Kelly
Pebble Beach, California

APPLE CAKE

2 cups sugar
3 eggs
1¼ cups oil
¼ teaspoon salt
¼ cup orange juice
3 cups sifted flour

GLAZE:
½ cup butter
1 cup sugar

1 teaspoon baking soda
1 teaspoon cinnamon
1 teaspoon vanilla
1 cup apples, peeled and
   chopped
1 cup coconut
1 cup chopped walnuts

½ teaspoon baking soda
½ cup buttermilk

Combine all cake ingredients in the order given, mixing well; bake in a greased and floured bundt pan for 1½ hours in a 325° oven. For the glaze. Melt the butter and blend in the remaining ingredients; bring to a rolling boil. Pour over the hot cake in the pan. Let stand 1 hour; remove from pan. Serves 12.

Phyllis Burnette Gambill (Mrs. Denman, Jr.)
Class of '55
Claremont, California

"This is a Southern family recipe I got from my Louisiana mother, Mrs. J. F. Rosett."

APRICOT CAKE

1 package yellow cake mix
1 (3 ounce) package lemon
   gelatin
¾ cup apricot nectar
2/3 cup Wesson oil or melted
   margarine

1 teaspoon vanilla
1 teaspoon lemon extract
¼ teaspoon salt
4 eggs
¼ cup water

ICING:
½ cup margarine
3 tablespoons lemon juice

1½ cups powdered sugar

In a large bowl, mix together the cake mix and gelatin; add the apricot nectar and oil or melted margarine. Blend in the vanilla, lemon extract and salt. Beat in the eggs, one at a time, add the water with the last egg. Pour the batter into a greased and floured tube pan and bake in a 300° oven for 1 hour. Ice the cake while still warm with an icing made by combining the margarine, lemon juice and powdered sugar. NOTE: If desired, prick the top of the cake before frosting to allow icing to penetrate the cake.

Jacqueline Dickman (Mrs. Gerald)
Lower School Faculty
Carmel, California

"This is easy to assemble and is a refreshing, light dessert."

ORANGE CAKE

1 (3 ounce) package orange
   gelatin
1 package yellow cake mix

Orange rind
1 large orange
2 cups powdered sugar

Combine the gelatin and the cake mix and stir in the grated rind of 1 orange. Prepare and bake the cake mixture according to the directions on the cake mix package, using a 9 x 13 inch pan. When the cake is cool, pierce all over with a fork and top with a mixture of the juice and rind of 1 large orange and the powdered sugar. Serves 12.

Sally Nagle (Mrs. Robert)
Mother of Wendy Waldo '69 and Carolyn Kimble '85
Fresno, California

ORANGE-DATE CAKE

4 cups flour
1 teaspoon baking soda
1 teaspoon baking powder
¼ teaspoon salt
1 cup shortening

2 cups sugar
4 eggs, separated
1½ cups buttermilk
2½ cups chopped pecans or
   walnuts
1 (12 ounce) package dates,
   chopped

ORANGE GLAZE:
½ cup confectioners' sugar
2 tablespoons grated orange rind

1 cup orange juice
1 tablespoon apricot brandy

Sift together 3½ cups of the flour, the baking soda, baking powder and salt; set aside. Beat the shortening, sugar and egg yolks in a large bowl with an electric mixer at high speed until light and fluffy. Beat in the flour mixture alternately with the buttermilk at low speed, beginning and ending with the flour mixture, until the batter is smooth. Toss the nuts and dates with the remaining ½ cup flour and fold into the cake batter. Beat the egg whites until stiff; fold gently into the cake batter until no white streaks remain. Pour into a greased and floured 10 inch tube pan. Bake in a preheated 300° oven for 1 hour and 45 minutes, or until a toothpick inserted in the top comes out clean. Remove from oven; cool in pan on a wire rack for 10 minutes. Prepare the orange glaze by combing the confectioners sugar, orange rind, orange juice and apricot brandy, blending until smooth. Loosen cake around edges with a metal spatula; turn out on rack. Prick the cake all over with a skewer. Brush glaze over cake. Let cool. Refrigerate overnight. Garnish with orange slices, whole dates and pecans, if desired.

Shirley Anderson (Mrs. Russ)
San Jose, California

WINE CAKE

1 package yellow cake mix
1 (3¾ ounces) package vanilla or
   lemon instant pudding
4 eggs

1 teaspoon nutmeg
¾ cup salad oil
¾ cup sherry

Combine all ingredients and beat for about 4 minutes. Pour into a greased and floured tube pan and bake in a 350° oven for 45 minutes.

Virginia West (Mrs. Thomas)
Mother of Tanisha
Seaside, California

MILKY WAY CAKE

6 Milky Way bars, large size
1 cup butter
2 cups sugar
4 eggs
2½ cups sifted flour

½ teaspoon baking soda
1¼ cups buttermilk
1 teaspoon vanilla
1 cup chopped nuts

Combine the Milky Way bars with ½ cup of the butter in a saucepan, and melt over low heat. While the candy is melting, prepare the batter by creaming the remaining ½ cup butter and the sugar until light and fluffy; add the eggs, one at a time, beating well after each addition. Add the flour and baking soda alternating with the buttermilk, stirring until smooth. Add the melted candy, mixing well. Stir in the vanilla and nuts. Pour batter into a greased and floured bundt pan and bake in a 350° oven for 1 hour 20 minutes.

Joanne Cohen (Mrs. Sheldon)
Mother of Poppy '86
Fresno, California

WATERGATE CAKE

1 package white cake mix
1 (3 ounce) package pistachio
  pudding

WATERGATE ICING:
2 envelopes Dream Whip
1½ cups cold milk

1 cup oil
1 cup club soda
3 eggs

1 (3¾ ounce) package
  instant pistachio pudding

Combine the cake mix and the pudding; add the oil, club soda and eggs and blend well. Pour into a greased and floured tube pan and bake in a 350° oven for 50 minutes. Frost with Watergate icing made by whipping the Dream Whip with cold milk and gradually beating in the pudding until mixture is thickened. Garnish with cherries and nuts. Serves 10-12.

Christina M. Kellogg
Class of '85
Pacific Grove, California

POPPY SEED CAKE

1 cup poppy seeds
1/3 cup honey
¼ cup water
1 cup softened butter
1½ cups brown sugar
4 eggs, separated

1 cup sour cream
1 teaspoon vanilla
2½ cups flour
1 teaspoon salt
1 teaspoon baking powder
Powdered sugar

Simmer the poppy seeds, honey and water in a small saucepan for 5 minutes. Cream the butter and sugar in a large bowl, then add the poppy seed mixture. Add the egg yolks, one at a time, blending well after each addition. Add the sour cream and vanilla, mixing well. Stir in the flour, salt and baking powder. Beat the egg whites until stiff and fold into the batter. Pour into 4 floured medium loaf pans (or 1 bundt pan and 1 medium loaf pan) and bake in a 350° oven for 60 minutes. Cool and dust with powdered sugar before serving, if desired.

Julie A. Lambert
Class of '80
Corvallis, Oregon

"This is Helen Walton's cake, grandmother of Heather and Tracy."

COCONUT CAKE

2 cups sugar
1 cup oil
5 eggs
1 teaspoon coconut flavoring
1 teaspoon vanilla

½ cup milk
2 cups flour
1½ teaspoons baking powder
½ teaspoon salt
1-1/3 cup coconut

GLAZE:
1 cup sugar
½ cup water

¼ cup butter
1 teaspoon coconut flavoring

Mix the sugar and oil. Add the eggs one at a time, beating after each addition. Add the flavorings to the milk and add alternately with the flour, baking powder and salt; stir in the coconut. Bake in a greased and floured tube pan for 1 hour in a 350° oven, and then add the glaze to the hot cake. To make the glaze, bring to a boil the sugar, water, butter and coconut flavoring. Leave the cake in the pan to cool.

Jean Walton (Mrs. John)
Mother of Heather and Tracy
Pebble Beach, California

"This recipe is an old Miller favorite, especially around the Christmas holiday time. If we didn't have a Gum Drop cake then it just wasn't Christmas! Children especially love this treat because it is so colorful and also good to eat."

GUM DROP CAKE

1 cup vegetable shortening
1 cup white sugar
1 cup brown sugar
2 eggs
4 cups flour
¼ teaspoon cloves
1 teaspoon cinnamon
¼ teaspoon nutmeg

1 teaspoon salt
1 cup walnuts or pecans
1 pound white raisins
1 pound gum drops (except
   black), thinly sliced
2 cups applesauce
1 teaspoon soda
1 teaspoon vanilla

Toss the gumdrops, raisins and nuts with ½ cup of the flour; set aside. Cream the shortening and sugar; add the eggs and vanilla. Sift together the remaining flour, the spices and salt; add to the creamed mixture with the applesauce. Dissolve the soda in 1 tablespoon hot water and add to the mixture. Add the fruit, gumdrops and nuts and mix well. Bake in a 300ᵛ oven in 2 loaf pans or a bundt pan which have been well greased. Loaf pans bake in about 1 hour, and the bundt pan takes slightly longer.

Cameron Miller Menghetti (Mrs. Charles)
Class of '76
Long Beach, California

WHITE CHRISTMAS CAKE

1 cup butter
1 pound confectioner's sugar
½ teaspoon salt
½ teaspoon vanilla
6 eggs
1 cup cold water

3 cups flour
1 teaspoon baking powder
1 (8 ounce) jar maraschino
   cherries, drained
1 cup chopped walnuts
1 (14 ounce) package flaked
   coconut

Cream the butter and sugar. Beat 2 whole eggs into the creamed mixture; separate the remaining 4 eggs and beat in the yolks, salt and vanilla. Add the water alternately with the unsifted flour and baking powder. Stir in the cherries, nuts and coconut with a spoon. Beat the 4 egg whites until stiff; fold into the batter. Bake in 2 greased loaf pans in a 325ᵛ oven for 1 hour 10 minutes.

Kathi Bowden
Mother of Kim '87
Monterey, California

"This recipe is an heirloom and is wonderful at Christmas time."

PECAN CAKE

1 scant pound butter (no
   substitute)
1 pound sugar
6 eggs
2 ounces lemon extract

1 pound flour
2 teaspoons baking powder
1 to 1½ pounds pecans
Crystallized pineapple, diced
Crystallized cherries, sliced

Cream the butter and sugar and add the eggs one at a time, beating well after each addition; add the lemon extract. Blend in the flour and baking powder and stir in the pecans, pineapple and cherries. Let stand overnight. Pour into a tube pan lined with brown paper which has been greased. Bake in a 250° oven for 3 hours. Serves 12 or more.

Alice Cloran
Upper School Staff
Carmel, California

"This is a nice addition to a coffee or a holiday dessert tray."

STRUDEL

1½ cups flour
¼ cup plus 2 tablespoons orange
   juice
Pinch of salt
½ teaspoon vanilla
½ cup butter
1½ teaspoons oil

½ cup pineapple/apricot jam
½ cup chopped nuts
½ cup coconut
½ cup raisins
Powdered sugar

Mix together well the flour, orange juice, salt, vanilla, butter and oil. Form into 2 balls and wrap individually in plastic wrap. Refrigerate a few hours for use on the same day, or freeze for future use. Roll out each ball separately as thin as possible. Spread each with ¼ cup jam and then sprinkle each with ¼ cup each of chopped nuts, coconut and raisins. Roll up and seal edges well. Sprinkle each roll with powdered sugar and place on an ungreased baking sheet, sealed side down. Bake in a 400° oven for 15 minutes, reduce oven to 350° and continue to bake about 30 additional minutes, or until golden brown. Remove from the oven and place on a cooling rack. Slice when cold in pieces about 1 inch thick. Serves 12-16.

Brenda Guy (Mrs. Michael)
Mother of Jennifer
Pebble Beach, California

SWEDISH PASTRY

1 package dry yeast
¼ cup warm water
¾ cup milk
1 egg
3 cups flour

2 tablespoons sugar
½ teaspoon salt
1 cup butter
Blackberry jam

Mix the yeast in ¼ cup of warm water and add to the milk, egg, flour, sugar and salt to make a dough. Roll out to approximately 24 x 12 inches, spread the butter on half of the dough. Fold in half and roll out again. Fold dough in thirds and then in half. Refrigerate for 30 minutes. Repeat rolling, folding and refrigeration procedure 2 more times. Roll out to 24 x 12 inches and cut into strips about ½ inch wide. Twist the strips into rolls and place a teaspoon of jam in the center of each. Bake on a cookie sheet in a preheated 375° oven for 10-11 minutes. Glaze with a powdered sugar glaze while still warm.

Helen Uhrig
Mother-in-law of Sandra Chappe Swenson '75
Lebanon, Oregon

PAT'S OATMEAL CAKE

1 cup oatmeal
1 cup sugar
1 cup brown sugar
1-1/3 cups flour
½ teaspoon salt
1 teaspoon soda

1 teaspoon cinnamon
1 teaspoon nutmeg
2 eggs
½ cup butter
1½ cups boiling water

TOPPING:
1 cup chopped walnuts
½ cup brown sugar
½ cup granulated sugar
¼ cup cream (or half and half)

6 tablespoons melted butter
1 cup shredded coconut
1 teaspoon vanilla

Place the oatmeal and the sugars in a large bowl. Sift together the dry ingredients and add to the oatmeal and sugars; blend well. Add the eggs, butter and *boiling* water and mix until blended (the batter will be thin). Pour into a greased 13 x 9 inch baking pan. For topping, combine the walnuts, sugars, cream, melted butter, coconut and vanilla. Drop in small portions evenly over the batter. Bake in a 350° oven for 45 minutes. Serves 8-10.

Renee Perrault-Perry (Mrs. Drew)
Lower School Faculty
Monterey, California

SCHAUM TORTE (MERINGUES)

4 egg whites   1 teaspoon white vinegar
1 cup sugar   1 teaspoon vanilla·

Beat the egg whites until stiff; beat in the sugar, vinegar and vanilla. Drop by tablespoonfuls on plain brown paper on a cookie sheet. Bake in a 275° oven for 1 hour. Remove at once. Meringues may be served with whipped cream, sweetened mashed strawberries or chocolate sauce.

Helen L. Howard (Mrs. Charles)
Mother of Elinor Howard Franchetti '54
Jane Howard Goodfellow '56,
Katherine Howard McGrath '58
Grandmother of Michele McGrath '79
Joan Goodfellow '80, Kathleen McGrath '81
Walnut Creek, California

"This is a kid pleaser as well as an adult pleaser!"

PEANUT BRITTLE WHIP

2 cups whipped cream   1/8 teaspoon almond extract
1½ cups peanut brittle

Fold the peanut brittle into the whipped cream, reserving some for garnish; add the almond extract and place in the freezer. When it is firm, sprinkle additional brittle on top and return to the freezer. Cut and serve. This could also be placed into individual sherbert glasses for a more elegant presentation. Adults might like it with a tablespoon of almond flavored liqueur poured over it! Other garnish potentials: whipped cream, a cherry, hot caramel sauce.

Diane Ortner (Mrs. Paul)
Mother of Kristin '85 and Stephanie '85
Hillsborough, California

The first Santa Catalina was founded in 1850 by a French Dominican, Mother Mary Goemaere, who came to California from Paris. The school was located in an old adobe near the Presidio of Monterey, and the first students were daughters of the Spanish families from the neighboring areas.

"This is an excelllent 'do ahead' dessert for a large group."

MOCHA ICE CREAM DESSERT

24 Oreo cookies, crushed
1/3 cup melted butter
½ gallon coffee ice cream
3 ounces unsweetened chocolate
2 tablespoons butter
1 cup sugar

2 (6 ounce) cans evaporated milk
½ teaspoon vanilla
1½ cups heavy cream, whipped
1½ ounces Kahlua
Powdered sugar
Chopped nuts

Combine the cookie crumbs and the melted butter and press into the bottom of a buttered 9 x 13 inch pan; refrigerate. When chilled, spread the softened ice cream over the crust and freeze. Melt together the chocolate and butter; add the sugar and milk. Bring to a boil, stirring until thickened. Remove from heat and add the vanilla; cool. Spread over the ice cream and return to the freezer. Whip the cream, add the Kahlua and powdered sugar to taste; spread over the chocolate layer and sprinkle with the chopped nuts. Serves 15. NOTE: This is also good with peppermint stick ice cream and garnished with cookie crumbs or chocolate shavings.

Susan Hull (Mrs. Cordell)
Mother of Pamela '86
Atherton, California

MONTEREY MUD PIE

2 cups chocolate wafer crumbs
6 tablespoons butter
½ gallon vanilla ice cream

½ cup Kahlua
1 (16½ ounce) jar thick fudge
  topping
Whipped cream

Combine 1½ cups of the wafer crumbs with the butter and press into the bottom of an 8 x 11 inch pan. Freeze until firm. Combine the softened ice cream and the Kahlua and pour over the crust; freeze until firm. Mix the remaining ½ cup wafer crumbs with the fudge topping. Spread over the ice cream and freeze for 8 hours or overnight. Serve cut into squares and topped with whipped cream. Serves 12.

Kay Covert (Mrs. Robert)
Mother of Robin '86
Salinas, California

"This is an elegant, but embarrassingly simple dessert. Perfect for the busy hostess."

KAHLUA SUNDAE

Coffee ice cream   *Kahlua*
Heath bars

Scoop ice cream into dishes. Crumble Heath bars over each serving and top with 1 ounce of Kahlua. That's it!

Suzanne Townsend Finney (Mrs. J.P.)
Class of '60
Hillsborough, California

VANILLA ICE CREAM

6 eggs, beaten   *1¾ cup sugar*
2 tablespoons vanilla   *3 pints half and half*
1 (13 ounce) can evaporated milk *Dash of salt*

Combine all ingredients and make in ice cream maker. NOTE: If fruit is desired, add 3 cups of fruit and reduce the amount of half and half to 2 pints. For an even richer ice cream, substitute extra rich whipping cream for 1 or 2 pints of the half and half. This is a great base for any flavoring.

Margaret Rosenberg Duflock (Mrs. William)
Class of '59
Mother of Melissa '85
San Ardo, California

FAMOUS PIE

1 cup mini-marshmallows   *1 (8½ ounce) package Nabisco*
1 cup semi-sweet chocolate chips   *Famous Wafers*
1 cup evaporated skim milk   *Vanilla ice cream*

In the top of a double boiler, combine the marshmallows, chocolate and milk. Cook until the marshmallows and chocolate have melted; cool. Line a pie plate with the whole chocolate wafers. Spoon a layer of softened ice cream over the cookies, then a layer of chocolate sauce, a second layer of the ice cream, and top with the remaining chocolate sauce. Freeze for at least 2 hours.

Grace Beacham (Mrs. Richard)
Mother of August and Amy
Carmel, California

Cookies, Candies, and Snacks

AUNT MARGARET'S OATMEAL COOKIES – Circa 1890

1 cup unsalted sweet butter
1 cup brown sugar
1 cup white sugar
2 extra large eggs
2 teaspoons vanilla
2 cups sifted flour

1 teaspoon soda
1/8 teaspoon salt
1 cup quick oats
½ cup chopped walnuts
½ cup flaked coconut

Cream the butter and sugars well; beat in the eggs one at a time. Blend in the vanilla. Add the flour, soda and baking powder and salt, mixing well. Stir in the walnuts, oats and coconut. For each cookie, drop 1 teaspoon of dough, 2 inches apart, on a greased cookie sheet. Bake in a 350° oven, preheated, for 14-15 minutes. Cool on a rack. NOTE: These are very crunchy cookies.

Dr. Tom McGuire
Oakland, California

"These good and spicy cookies are very easy to make."

GRANDMA'S OATMEAL COOKIES

2 cups flour
1 teaspoon salt
½ teaspoon cloves
1 teaspoon baking soda
1 teaspoon cinnamon
1 teaspoon nutmeg
1 cup white sugar
1 cup brown sugar

1 teaspoon vanilla
2 eggs
¼ cup milk
1 cup shortening, melted
3 cups oats
1 cup raisins
½ cup nuts

In a large bowl, mix together the dry ingredients. Beat the eggs with the milk and vanilla and stir into the dry ingredients; add the melted shortening and mix well. Stir in the oats, raisins and nuts. Drop onto ungreased cookie sheets and bake in a preheated 350° oven for about 12 minutes. Makes 4 dozen cookies.

Pati Foster (Mrs. Gregory)
Pre-school Faculty
Pebble Beach, California

OATMEAL COOKIES

2 cups shortening
2 cups dark brown sugar
2 cups white sugar
2 teaspoons vanilla
4 eggs
2½ cups sifted flour

2 teaspoons salt
2 teaspoons baking soda
5 cups oatmeal
Raisins and/or nuts and/or
Chocolate chips

Beat together the shortening, sugars, vanilla and eggs; gradually add the flour, salt and baking soda. Stir in the oatmeal, raisins and/or nuts and/ or chocolate chips by hand. Drop by teaspoonful onto a cookie sheet and bake in a 350° oven for 10 minutes. Makes 6 dozen cookies. NOTE: For variety, cereal or chinese noodles may be substituted for the oatmeal.

Dianne King (Mrs. Don)
Mother of Jeanne
Salinas, California

"This has been a favorite dessert of Santa Catalina students."

COWBOY COOKIES

1 pound 2 ounces shortening
1 pound 2 ounces sugar
13 ounces brown sugar
4 eggs
1 tablespoon vanilla

1 pound 3 ounces flour
1 teaspoon baking powder
2½ teaspoons baking soda
1 teaspoon salt
14 ounces rolled oats
1 (12 ounce) bag chocolate chips

Cream the shortening with the sugars; add the eggs and vanilla and beat until light and fluffy. Sift together the flour, baking powder, baking soda and salt; blend into the creamed mixture. Add the oats and chocolate chips. For best results, let the dough rest for 2 hours before baking (if cookies are baked right away, the volume will not be as great). Using 1 tablespoon of dough for each cookie, place 2 inches apart on a greased cookie sheet. Bake in a 375° oven for 15 minutes. Makes 10 dozen.

Mr. and Mrs. Jerry Munckton
Saga Corporation
Santa Catalina School

MINCEMEAT COOKIES

1 cup shortening
1½ cups sugar
3 eggs, beaten
1 teaspoon soda
3¼ cups flour

2 teaspoons baking powder
1 teaspoon salt
1 cup chopped walnuts
1 pint mincemeat

Cream the shortening and sugar well; add the beaten eggs. Add the soda dissolved in a small amount of hot water. Add half of the flour sifted with salt and baking powder. Add the nuts and mincemeat and remaining flour; mix well. Drop from a teaspoon onto a greased baking sheet. Bake in a 350° oven until golden brown. Remove while warm. Makes 6 dozen cookies.

Lucille Bowman (Mrs. Merle F.)
Alumnae Secretary
Mother of Barbara '66 and Melinda '67
Monterey, California

CLOVE COOKIES

4 cups flour
1½ cups sugar
1½ tablespoons ground cloves

4 teaspoons baking powder
¾ cup butter
5 large eggs, beaten

Mix together the flour, sugar, cloves and baking powder; cut in the butter until the mixture resembles coarse crumbs. Add the beaten eggs, stirring until moistened. Add a small amount of milk, if necessary. Turn out on a well-floured surface and knead until smooth. Roll 1-inch thick, 2 inches wide and as long as the pan you will be using. Bake on a cookie sheet in a 400° oven until light brown. Remove to rack; cool. Cut at an angle approximately ¾ inch wide and bake again until the cut sides are brown. Yields about 100 cookies.

Mrs. William S. Blackwood
Mother of Irene '75
Pacific Grove, California

Santa Catalina's Christmas traditions include the Christmas mimes, the Candlelight Mass, and the collection of food baskets for the needy, as well as other activities sponsored by the various classes and the student body as a whole. The Lower School presents a Christmas Concert and the Pre-school presents a pageant.

GINGER COOKIES

¾ cup Crisco
1 egg
2 cups flour
1/8 teaspoon salt
1 teaspoon cinnamon

1 cup sugar
4 tablespoons molasses
2 teaspoons soda
1 teaspoon cloves
1 teaspoon ginger

Cream together the shortening, sugar, eggs and molasses; combine with the remaining ingredients. Chill the dough for about an hour. Form into balls and place on a cookie sheet. Flatten with a fork, leaving a criss-cross design on each cookie. Sprinkle with sugar. Bake in a 350° oven for approximately 10 minutes.

Jameen Wesson
Class of '77
Modesto, California

CINNAMON ALMOND COOKIES

1 cup brown sugar
1 tablespoon molasses
1 cup whole wheat pastry flour
2/3 cups slivered almonds

¼ cup oil
2 teaspoons cinnamon
¼ teaspoon salt
¼ cup water

In a bowl, blend the sugar and molasses; stir in the flour, almonds, oil, cinnamon and salt. Add sufficient water to make a stiff dough. Spoon onto a cookie sheet in large drops. Bake in a 300° oven for 15-20 minutes. Cool on a rack. Makes 1 dozen cookies.

Margery Bobbs Johnson (Mrs. Robert)
Class of '65
Eagle, Colorado

RUM BALLS

¼ cup rum
1½ tablespoons corn syrup
1 cup vanilla wafer crumbs

1 cup finely chopped pecans
1 cup sifted powdered sugar
2 tablespoons cocoa

Mix together the rum and corn syrup; set aside. Combine the remaining ingredients and stir in the rum mixture, blending well. Form into balls and roll in additional powdered sugar. Store in an airtight container. The taste improves with age. Makes about 6 dozen.

Marianne McFadden
Class of '62
Salinas, California

VERY DELICATE BUTTER COOKIES

1 cup butter
1 cup sugar
½ teaspoon salt
1 teaspoon vanilla

2 well beaten eggs
1½ cups flour
½ cup chopped walnuts

Cream the butter, gradually add the sugar, then the salt, vanilla and eggs. When fluffy, stir in the flour and then the nuts. Drop from a spoon onto a lightly greased cookie sheet. Bake in a 350° oven for 10 minutes until golden brown around the edges.

Nancy Barg (Mrs. Irwin)
Mother of Elizabeth '77, Jocelyn '81, and Meredith '85
Fresno, California

RICH BUTTER COOKIES

½ cup butter
2 tablespoons powdered sugar
½ teaspoon vanilla

1 cup sifted flour
2½ ounces walnuts, chopped

In a small bowl, cream the butter; add the sugar and vanilla and beat for 2 minutes. Add the flour and then the walnuts, beating until mixed. Roll dough into 1 inch balls and place an inch apart on an ungreased cookie sheet. Bake in a 350° oven for 10-15 minutes until lightly browned. When cool, sprinkle with colored sugar. NOTE: This recipe may be doubled.

Susan Verble Gantner (Mrs. John)
Class of '57
San Francisco, California

MELT AWAYS

1 cup butter, softened
½ cup powdered sugar, sifted

¾ cup cornstarch
1 cup flour

FROSTING:
2 tablespoons melted butter
1 cup powdered sugar

1 teaspoon lemon juice

Cream the butter and sugar; add the cornstarch and flour and chill slightly. Roll into balls and place on a cookie sheet. Bake in a 350° oven for 15-20 minutes or until lightly brown. Frost when cool with a frosting made by combining the melted butter, powdered sugar and lemon juice.

Mary Jane Wesson (Mrs. W. P.)
Mother of Jameen
Modesto, California

"Here is a cookie recipe that I enjoyed as a student at Santa Catalina when I would spend an afternoon at my grandmother's, Mrs. C. P. Holt, in Pebble Beach. Now my children love them."

GUMDROP COOKIES

1 cup butter
1 cup granulated sugar
1 cup brown sugar
2 eggs
2 cups flour
2 teaspoons baking powder

1 teaspoon baking soda
½ teaspoon salt
½ pound gumdrops
2 cups quick oats
1 cup coconut, optional

Cream the butter with the sugars; add the eggs one at a time, beating well after each addition. Set aside. Sift the flour, measure, then sift again. Add the baking powder, soda and salt to the flour and stir into the creamed ingredients, mixing well. After removing the black ones, chop the gumdrops and add to the mixture along with the oatmeal and coconut. Roll teaspoonsful of dough into balls and place on a greased baking sheet, leaving room for the cookies to spread. Bake in a 350° oven for 15 minutes.

Liz Holt Protell (Mrs. Robert)
Class of '64
Tucson, Arizona

"It looks as if some ingredients have been omitted, but I guarantee this recipe works and tastes as good as the ones calling for 10 or 12 ingredients. Better make a double batch!"

EASY PEANUT BUTTER COOKIES

1 cup crunchy peanut butter
1 cup sugar

1 egg
1 teaspoon vanilla

Blend the peanut butter, sugar and egg in a medium-sized bowl; add the vanilla and mix well. Form into 1-inch balls and place on an ungreased cookie sheet about 3 inches apart. Flatten with a fork, leaving a criss-cross design on each cookie. Bake in a 350° oven for 8-10 minutes. Remove from cookie sheet carefully as these cookies are very fragile when they are warm. They need to rest for several minutes before they can be eaten.

April Brazinsky
Lower School Student
Carmel, California

DIANNE'S EASY NO BAKE COOKIES

1 (12 ounce) package chocolate
  chips
½ cup butter

½ cup peanut butter
3 cups quick cooking oats
½ cup coconut, optional

In a saucepan, melt the chocolate chips and the butter. Stir in the peanut butter, oats and, if desired, the coconut. Drop by spoonfuls onto wax paper and cool.

Dianne Kletch Saugier (Mrs. Joseph)
Class of '72
Shawnee, Kansas

CHOCOLATE PEANUT BUTTER BARS

½ cup peanut butter
1/3 cup butter
¾ cup brown sugar
¾ cup granulated sugar
2 eggs

2 teaspoons vanilla
1 cup flour
1 teaspoon baking powder
¼ teaspoon salt
1 (12 ounce) package chocolate
  chips

Cream together the peanut butter, butter and sugars; beat in the eggs and vanilla. Fold in the flour, baking powder and salt; blend well and spread in a lightly greased and floured 13 x 9 x 2 inch pan. Sprinkle with chocolate chips. Bake in a preheated 350° oven for 5 minutes. Swirl through the mixture with a knife to create a marbleizing effect. Continue baking for 20-25 minutes. Cool and cut into bars.

Margie Missig
Pacific Grove, California

BABY RUTH COOKIES

6 cups Special K cereal
1¼ cups sugar
¼ cup light corn syrup

1½ cups peanut butter
6 ounces butterscotch morsels
6 ounces chocolate morsels

Place the Special K in a large bowl and set aside. Bring to a boil the sugar and corn syrup; add the peanut butter. As soon as the peanut butter is melted, pour over the Special K and mix quickly. Press into a greased 9 x 13 inch dish and top with the butterscotch and chocolate morsels. Place in a warm oven until the morsels are melted.

Virginia Boyle
Aunt of Sister Mary Ellen and Kathleen Ryan
San Mateo, California

"These 'cookies' are a chocoholic's delight and are sure to be popular."

HELLO DOLLIES

1 cup butter
1 cup graham cracker crumbs
1 cup shredded coconut
1 cup semi-sweet chocolate chips

1 cup butterscotch chips
1 (14 ounce) can condensed
   milk, sweetened
1 cup chopped walnuts

Melt the butter in a 13 x 9 inch baking pan. Layer in order over the butter, the graham cracker crumbs, shredded coconut, chocolate chips, butterscotch chips, sweetened condensed milk and walnuts. Bake in a 350° oven for 30 minutes (If a glass pan is used, reduce heat to 325°). Cool and cut into squares.

Kathy Trafton
Class of '74
Menlo Park, California

"Yummie!"

CHOCOLATE CHIP ANGEL BARS

CRUST:
1/3 cup sweet butter
½ cup brown sugar, packed

1 cup flour

TOPPING:
2 eggs, beaten
1 cup brown sugar
1 teaspoon vanilla
2 tablespoons flour

½ teaspoon baking powder
½ teaspoon salt
1 cup chopped walnuts or pecans
1 (16 ounce) package chocolate
   chips

For crust: Cream the butter and sugar and stir in the flour; press and flatten with hand to coat the bottom of an ungreased 13 x 9 inch pan. Bake in a 350° oven for 10 minutes. For topping: Combine the eggs, sugar and vanilla; mix with the flour, baking powder and salt. Stir in the nuts and chocolate chips. Spread over the crust and return to the oven for 15-20 minutes.

Linda Kuenzli Theiring (Mrs. James)
Class of '58
Aptos, California

"Sinfully delicious!"

YUM YUM COOKIES

1 package German chocolate
  cake mix
¾ cup melted butter
1/3 cup milk
1 (14 ounce) bag of caramels
  (about 50)

1/3 cup evaporated milk
1 (6 ounce) package chocolate
  chips
1 cup chopped nuts

Mix together the cake mix, melted butter and milk. Pour half of this mixture into a greased and floured 13 x 9 inch pan and bake in a 350° oven for 6 minutes. Melt the caramels with the evaporated milk in the top of a double boiler; set aside. Sprinkle the chocolate chips and the nuts over the baked cake mixture and spread the melted caramel mixture over the nuts and chips. Pour the rest of the cake mixture evenly over the caramel mixture and bake at 350° for 15-20 minutes. Cool and cut. Makes 2-3 dozen.

Suzanne Talbot
Class of '64
Carmel, California

"These cookie squares are very rich and habit-forming."

NANAIMO BARS

COOKIE LAYER:
¼ cup sugar
½ cup butter
1 square unsweetened chocolate
1 teaspoon vanilla

1 egg, beaten
2 cups graham cracker crumbs
1 cup shredded coconut
½ cup walnuts, chopped

FILLING LAYER:
½ cup butter
3 tablespoons milk

3 tablespoons (1 envelope) Bird's
  Custard Powder
2 cups powdered sugar

ICING LAYER:
2 squares unsweetened chocolate
¾ cup semi-sweet chocolate chips

2 tablespoons butter

Cookie layer: In the top of a double boiler, mix the sugar, butter, chocolate and vanilla. Cook over boiling water until the chocolate melts, stirring constantly. Add the egg and cook, stirring, 5 minutes. Mix in the graham cracker crumbs, coconut and nuts and press into a buttered pan. Chill. For the filling layer: Cream all ingredients and spread over the chilled cookie layer. Refrigerate. For the icing layer: Place all ingredients in the top of a double boiler and stir over boiling water until melted. Spread carefully over the chilled filling layer. Chill until firm. Cut into squares.

Linda Johnson (Mrs. Jay)
Mother of Erin
Monterey, California

ROCKY ROAD BARS

¾ cup butter
1 ounce dark chocolate
1½ cups sugar
3 eggs
1½ teaspoons vanilla
1 teaspoon baking powder

1 cup plus 2 tablespoons flour
6 ounces cream cheese
1 cup chocolate chips
1 cup chopped walnuts, optional
2 cups mini-marshmallows

FROSTING:
¼ cup butter
1 ounce semi-sweet chocolate
2 ounces cream cheese

¼ cup milk
3 cups powdered sugar
1 teaspoon vanilla

Melt together ½ cup of the butter and the dark chocolate; set aside. Cream 1 cup of the sugar and 2 of the eggs; combine with the melted butter-chocolate mixture. Add 1 teaspoon of the vanilla, the baking powder and 1 cup of the flour; mix well and pour into a greased 13 x 9 inch pan. Combine the cream cheese, ½ cup sugar, 2 tablespoons flour, ¼ cup butter, 1 egg and ½ teaspoon vanilla. Mix well and spread over the chocolate mixture in the pan. Sprinkle with the chocolate chips and walnuts. Bake 25 minutes in a 350° oven; remove from oven and top with the mini-marshmallows. Bake for 2 minutes. Remove from oven and frost immediately. For the frosting: In a saucepan, heat the butter, chocolate, cream cheese and milk until smooth. Remove from the heat and add the powdered sugar and vanilla. Spread and swirl lightly over the rocky road bars in the pan.

Mallory Vail Weymann (Mrs. Conrad)
Class of '65
Darien, Connecticut

October 6, 1979 was groundbreaking day for the two-story dormitory that houses 40 seniors, provides two lounges, and offers accommodations for faculty families. Music, balloons, a song of dedication written by students and refreshments made a festive occasion for the beginning of the new dormitory.

GOOEY BROWNIES

2 squares bittersweet chocolate   ½ teaspoon vanilla
½ cup sweet butter   ¼ cup flour
1 cup sugar   ½ teaspoon salt
2 eggs   1 cup chopped nuts, optional

Melt the chocolate squares and butter in a heavy saucepan; remove from heat and stir in the sugar. Add the eggs and vanilla and beat hard. Stir in the flour, salt and nuts, if desired, and mix well. Pour into a buttered 8 x 8 inch pan. Bake in a preheated 325° oven for 20 minutes. Turn off oven and let sit for 5 minutes. Cool in pan on a rack. Cut into 15-20 squares when cool. NOTE: Triple the ingredients to make a 13 x 9 inch pan of brownies.

Lani Le Blanc
Class of '60
Sausalito, California

THUMPER'S FAMOUS BROWNIES

1 cup margarine   2 cups sugar
4 squares unsweetened chocolate   4 eggs, slightly beaten
1½ cups plus 2 tablespoons sifted   1 teaspoon vanilla
   flour   ¾ cup chopped walnuts
½ teaspoon baking powder
1 teaspoon salt

Melt the margarine and chocolate over very low heat; cool. Sift together the flour, baking powder and salt; set aside. Gradually add the sugar to the eggs, mixing thoroughly. Add the vanilla and the cooled chocolate mixture, blending well. Stir in dry ingredients; blend in the nuts. Bake in a greased 9 x 13 inch pan at 375° for 30-35 minutes. Makes 3 dozen.

FUDGE FROSTING

2 squares unsweetened chocolate   1/8 teaspoon salt
3 tablespoons butter   ½ teaspoon vanilla
5 tablespoons milk   3 cups sifted powdered sugar

Combine the chocolate, butter and milk in the top of a double boiler. Cook over hot water until the chocolate and butter melt. Stir to blend thoroughly. Add the salt and vanilla and mix well. Remove from heat and stir in enough powdered sugar to make a smooth spreading consistency. Spread quickly over the brownies.

Kathleen "Thumper" Rosenauer
Class of '76
Reno, Nevada

STONECROFT BROWNIES

¾ cup butter, melted
2/3 cup evaporated milk
1 German chocolate cake mix

½ cup chopped walnuts
1 (6 ounce) package chocolate chips
1 (14 ounce) package Kraft caramels

Combine the melted butter and 1/3 cup of the evaporated milk and beat into the cake mix. Stir in the nuts. Pour half of this mixture into the bottom of a greased 7 x 12 inch pan and bake in a 350° oven for 10 minutes. Remove and sprinkle with the chocolate chips. Melt the caramels with the remaining evaporated milk in the top of a double boiler. Pour over the chocolate chips. Pour the remaining cake mixture over the caramel layer. Bake for 20-25 minutes. Cool and cut into 50 squares.

Mrs. Roger S. Vail, Jr.
Mother of Mallory '65
Wayne, Illinois

BROWNIES

1 cup sugar
1 cup butter
4 eggs
1 (16 ounce) can Hershey syrup

1 cup plus 1 tablespoon flour
½ teaspoon baking powder
½ teaspoon salt
1 teaspoon vanilla

Cream together the butter and sugar; add the eggs and beat well. Add the syrup, then the flour, baking powder, salt and vanilla. Pour the batter into a greased 11 x 13 inch pan and bake in a 350° oven for 20 minutes.

FROSTING:
6 tablespoons butter
6 tablespoons milk or half and half
1½ cups sugar

1 (6 ounce) package chocolate chips
1 teaspoon vanilla
1 cup chopped walnuts

Bring to a boil the butter, milk and sugar. Remove from heat, add the chocolate chips and stir until melted. Beat in the vanilla and stir in the walnuts. Spread over the brownies.

Peggy Rhoads
Monterey, California

LEMON SQUARES

1 cup plus 2 tablespoons flour
¼ cup powdered sugar
½ cup butter
2 eggs
1 cup sugar

1 tablespoon grated lemon rind
(or more)
2 tablespoons lemon juice
(ore more)
½ teaspoon baking powder

In a large bowl, combine 1 cup of the flour and the powdered sugar and cut in the butter until crumbly; press into an ungreased 8 or 9 inch square pan. Bake 15 minutes in a preheated 350° oven. In a small bowl, beat the eggs and sugar until light-colored; stir in the remaining 2 tablespoons flour, the lemon juice and rind and the baking powder. Pour over the partially baked crust; return to oven and bake 18-25 minutes or until just golden. Cool completely. Sprinkle with powdered sugar and cut into small squares. Makes 24 bars. NOTE: This recipe freezes well.

Lucille Bowman (Mrs. Merle F.)
Alumnae Secretary
Mother of Barbara '66 and Melinda '67
Monterey, California

"This recipe was given to me by a lovely lady and wonderful neighbor. The cookies are easy, delicious and freeze well."

CELESTE PODESTA'S COCONUT SQUARES

1¼ cups flour
½ cup butter
2-3 tablespoons cold water
2 eggs

½ cup sugar
1 (7 ounce) package flaked
coconut
1/3 cup raspberry preserves (or
other flavor)

Using a pastry blender, cut the butter into the flour to form a coarse, crumbly mixture. Add the water, a small amount at a time, until particles cling together. Press into a 9-inch ungreased pan. Bake in a 350° oven 15-20 minutes. Beat the eggs until thick and lemon colored; add the sugar gradually, beating until thick and ivory colored. Fold the coconut into the egg mixture; set aside. Spread preserves over the baked pastry, leaving ¼ inch space around the edges. Carefully spread coconut mixture over the preserves. Bake in a 375° oven for 20-25 minutes. Cool before cutting.

Susan Parodi (Mrs. John)
Mother of Terri, Summer Camper
Modesto, California

WALNUT SQUARES

1 cup plus 2 tablespoons flour
½ cup butter
1½ cups brown sugar
FROSTING:
2 cups powdered sugar
2 tablespoons orange juice

½ teaspoon vanilla
2 beaten eggs
1 cup chopped walnuts

2 teaspoons lemon juice
2 tablespoons melted butter

Mix together 1 cup of the flour and the butter and pat into a greased 8 x 8 inch baking pan. Bake in a 325° oven for 15 minutes. Combine the brown sugar, the remaining 2 tablespoons flour, the vanilla, eggs and the walnuts; pour over the baked crust and return to oven for approximately 20 minutes. Cool and frost with a mixture of the powdered sugar, orange juice, lemon juice and melted butter. Cut into 16 squares.

Mrs. Donald McNeely
Mother of Nora '78
Pebble Beach, California

APRICOT KOLACHES

1 package yeast
¼ cup warm milk
1 cup shortening
2 eggs

2-3 cups flour
1 pound small dried apricots
½ cup water
¼ cup granulated sugar

Dissolve yeast in the warm milk; add the shortening, eggs and 2 cups of the flour. Mix well, adding more flour as needed for a pie dough consistency. Refrigerate overnight. Cook the apricots in the water and sugar until soft and plump. Roll the dough 1/8 to 1/4 inch thick on a board covered with granulated sugar. Cut into 3-inch diamond shapes; place 1 apricot in the center of each. Overlap and seal the 2 long points over the apricot. Bake until lightly browned in a 375° oven. While warm, sprinkle with powdered sugar.

Elaine Scaccia (Mrs. Sam)
Mother of Yolanda '67
Cloverdale, California

September 10, 1950 was the official opening day of the Fall semester. Thirty-two students were enrolled in the 5th through 8th grades, and eight in the Freshman and Sophomore classes of the high school, a capacity enrollment of 40, of which 14 were boarders and 26 were day students.

"I'm sure this recipe has another name, but I never bothered to ask. My grand-mother used to make them all the time, hence the name."

GRANNY'S TARTS

1 cup butter
¾ cup sugar
2 eggs, beaten
2 cups flour

2 teaspoons baking powder
¾ teaspoon salt
Seedless raspberry jam
Whipped cream

Cream the butter and sugar; add the beaten eggs. Combine and add dry ingredients. Press the mixture into greased tart pans. Make an indentation in the center of each for the jam and add 1 teaspoon of jam. Bake in a 375° oven for 12 minutes until golden brown. Serve with a dollop of whipped cream, if desired.

Marian Guiry Impey (Mrs. Guy)
Class of '72
Richmond, British Columbia
Canada

TERESA'S ONLY RECIPE
(INDIVIDUAL CHERRY CHEESE CAKES)

20 vanilla wafers
2 (8 ounce) package cream cheese
4 eggs

½ cup sugar
1 teaspoon vanilla
1 (20 ounce) can cherry pie
   filling

Line 20 muffin cups with paper baking liners. Place a vanilla wafer in the bottom of each paper liner. Beat together the cream cheese, eggs, sugar and vanilla. Spoon over the vanilla wafers in the paper liners. Bake in a 375° oven for 15 minutes until lightly browned and puffed. While still warm, top with the cherry pie filling. Refrigerate. NOTE: These also freeze well.

Teresa Estrada
Cousin of Kim Bowden '87
Whittier, California

PUDDING-WICHES

1½ cups cold milk
½ cup creamy peanut butter

1 (3 ounce) package chocolate
   instant pudding mix
1 package oatmeal cookies

Add the milk gradually to the peanut butter in a deep, narrow-bottomed bowl, blending until smooth. Add the pudding mix and beat slowly with a hand beater or at lowest speed of the electric mixer until well blended, about 2 minutes. Let stand 5 minutes. Spread filling ½ inch thick on ½ of the cookies. Top with the remaining cookies and freeze until firm, about 3 hours. NOTE: Use any hard cookies or any flavor pudding mix. This is especially easy and stores in the freezer for at least a month so it is ready at a moment's notice.

Bonnie McWhorter Bertelsen (Mrs. Jeffrey)
Class of '63
Foster City, California

PEANUT BUTTER FUDGE

2 cups sugar
2/3 cup milk
1 (7 ounce) jar marshmallow
*   creme*

1 cup chunk-style peanut butter
1 (6 ounce) package semi-sweet
*   chocolate*
1 teaspoon vanilla

Butter the sides of a heavy 2-quart saucepan. Combine the sugar and the milk in the buttered saucepan and stir over medium heat until sugar dissolves and the mixture boils. Cook to softball stage (234°). Remove from heat; quickly add the marshmallow creme, peanut butter, chocolate chips and vanilla; blend. Pour into a buttered 9 x 9 x 2 inch pan. Score; cut when firm.

Suzanne Byers
Sister of Jenny '85 and Sally Evenson
Sacramento, California

"If you like Reeses' Peanut Butter Cups, you'll love these."

CHRISTMAS BUCKEYES

1 pound peanut butter
1½ pounds powdered sugar
1 cup melted butter

1 (12 ounce) package chocolate
*   chips*
¼-½ sheet paraffin

Combine the peanut butter, powdered sugar and melted butter; knead until a smooth dough is formed. Roll into ¾ inch balls; chill. Melt the chocolate chips and the paraffin in the top of a double boiler. Using a toothpick, dip the balls one at a time, covering ¾ of each ball with the chocolate. It will resemble a buckeye. Serve on a platter. NOTE: The recipe may be halved. Leftover dough may be refrigerated for later use.

April Brazinsky
Lower School Student
Carmel, California

315

ENGLISH TOFFEE

1 cup chopped almonds
1 (8 ounce) Hershey bar or
  6 (1.4 ounce) Hershey bars

½ cup butter
1 cup sugar

Spread ½ cup of the almonds in the bottom of a greased 8 x 8 inch baking dish. Break half of the chocolate into small pieces over the almonds. In a heavy saucepan, combine the butter and sugar; cook slowly over medium heat for 5 minutes, stirring constantly with a wooden spoon. Increase heat and cook until the mixture registers 290° on a candy thermometer. Pour over the broken chocolate pieces in the pan. Break the remaining chocolate over the hot toffee. Cover with the remaining almonds, and press lightly into the chocolate. Cool; break into chunks.

Jeanette Nordstrom (Mrs. Gerald)
Mother of Adrienne '85
Fresno, California

"This is based on a recipe given to me in 1960 by Maria Berde, a Hungarian refugee; the basics are hers, the variations mine."

SWEET SALAMI

8 ounces semi-sweet chocolate
Unsalted butter
Powdered sugar

8 ounces chopped walnuts
4 ounces chopped candied fruit

Soften the chocolate (add butter, if necessary for a mixing consistency). Add sugar to taste, and fold in the nuts and candied fruit. Shape into a log and, if desired, roll the log in finely ground nutmeats; refrigerate. Slice into thin rounds. NOTE: Very little sugar is needed with unsweetened chocolate and if sweet chocolate is used, omit the sugar entirely.

Marilyn Rappaport (Mrs. James)
Mother of Mary Lynn '81
Dhahran, Saudi Arabia

"A recipe from my childhood that I still enjoy!"

ALMOND ROCA

2 cups butter
2 cups sugar

6 (1.4 ounce) Hershey chocolate
  bars
1 cup chopped almonds

Melt the butter and add the sugar; cook over low heat, stirring constantly, until the "hard crack" stage (300-310°) on a candy thermometer. Pour into a greased 9 x 13 inch metal pan or a 10 x 15 inch jelly roll pan. When the mixture begins to harden, but is still warm, lay the chocolate bars on top to melt. Sprinkle the chopped almonds over the chocolate and cool in the refrigerator for 15-30 minutes. Crack or break into chunks.

Nancy Christofaro
Class of '78
Oakland, California

ALMOND ROCA

¾ cup butter
2 cups sugar
2 cups whole almonds

1 (12 ounce) package semi-sweet chocolate chips
1/3 cup finely chopped almonds

Combine the butter, sugar and whole almonds in a heavy frying pan. Cook over high heat, stirring constantly, for about 10 minutes (do not let caramelize). When the mixture reaches the liquid stage, pour onto a greased cookie sheet and spread. Do not try to cover the entire cookie sheet. Immediately top with the chocolate chips. When soft, spread smoothly over the candy layer and immediately sprinkle with the chopped almonds. Cool completely and break into pieces.

Elizabeth Crawford
Class of '84
Tracy, California

CARAMEL CORN

2 cups brown sugar
1 cup butter
½ cup corn syrup
1 teaspoon salt

1 teaspoon baking soda
6 quarts popped corn
Nuts, optional

Boil the brown sugar, butter, syrup and salt for 5 minutes; remove from heat and add the baking soda. Stir well over the popped corn and add nuts, if desired. Spread on cookie sheets and place in a 200° oven for 1 hour, stirring at 15 minute intervals. Remove from oven and let cool. Store in a covered container.

Velma Leist (Mrs. F. F.)
Monterey, California

TOASTED WALNUT HALVES

Walnut halves 　　　　　　*Worcestershire sauce*

Place walnut halves on a cookie sheet under the broiler (low heat setting for broiler, or adjust rack to lower level), leaving the door open. Turn the halves several times until they are lightly browned. Sprinkle with Worcestershire sauce and toast a minute or two longer. Cool on paper towels and store in a covered jar or refrigerate. These are good served with ice cold Wente Brothers Le Blanc de Blanc.

Jean R. Wente
Wente Brothers
Vineyard and Winery
Livermore, California

"This is a great gift idea — tie a ribbon or wrapping paper around the jar and bring to your hostess. It is a good snack food while on long trips too."

SPICED NUTS

2-2/3 cups nuts 　　　　　*¾ cup sugar*
1 egg white 　　　　　　　*1 tablespoon pumpkin pie spice*
1 teaspoon water

Beat the egg white and the water with a fork until frothy; add the nuts. Mix together the sugar and spice and add to the nuts. Toss to coat evenly. Spread in a single layer on a lightly greased cookie sheet. Bake in a 300° oven for 20 minutes. Cool on wax paper and break up large clusters. Store in an airtight container. NOTE: Either peanuts or mixed nuts may be used.

Basia Belza Tack (Mrs. Charles)
Class of '73
McLean, Virginia

Two alumnae of Santa Catalina, TV actress Sharon Gless and A.C.T. stage actress Barbara Dirickson, addressed the student body about careers in the theatre world in one of a series of seminars on careers sponsored by the School on Sunday, October 21, 1973.

"This recipe is a pre-school favorite. We usually make it on our first cooking day each year."

ANTS ON A LOG

32 (3 inch log) celery pieces   *1 cup raisins*
3 cups peanut butter

Fill each piece of celery with the peanut butter — the "log". Put 6 raisins — the "ants" — on each.

Santa Catalina Pre-School
Santa Catalina School
Monterey, California

"I selected this simple recipe with the hope of helping mothers answer the dilemma of 'what can I mail to my daughter besides cookies?' It packs easily and will keep a long time."

BEEF JERKEY

1 flank steak   *1/8 teaspoon garlic salt*
¼ teaspoon lemon pepper   *½ cup soy sauce*

Remove all visible fat from the flank steak; slice into long strips ¼ inch thick with the grain. Combine the lemon pepper, garlic salt and soy sauce and pour over the flank steak, thoroughly coating each slice with the spiced sauce. Lay the strips of meat on a rack which has been placed on a cookie sheet. Place in a 140° oven for 10 hours.

Gretchen de Baubigny (Mrs. Andre)
Mother of Helene '85
San Francisco, California

International

BLANQUETTE DE VEAU
(Veal In White Sauce)

Prenez une livre de petite poitrine de veau que vous faites couper en morceaux; mettez ces morceaux dans un vase quelconque et versez dessus de l'eau bouillante, de maniere a ce que le tout soit couvert; ajoutez du sel. Au bout de vingt minutes, retirez vos morceaux de l'eau, laissez-les egoutter et faites une blanquette de la facon suivante. Mettez dans la casserole un morceau de beurre gros comme la moitie d'un oeuf; lorsqu'il est fondu, ajoutez deux cuilleres de farine; melez bien avec une cuillere de bois sans laisser roussir; ajoutez deux verres d'eau, sel, poivre et bouquet de laurier, persil, et thym. Lorsque votre sauce est bien liee, ajoutez vos morceaux de veau et quelques petits ognons et champignons; seulement ces derniers ne doivent etre mis que trois quarts d'heure avant de servir. Lorseque votre blanquette est cuite, placez vos morceaux de veau dans un plat creux et servez avec la sauce autour; vous pouvez ajouter quelque croutons frits dans le beurre.

VEAL IN WHITE SAUCE

1 pound breast of veal	Salt
Boiling water	Pepper
Salt	Bouquet garni (Bay leaf, parsley,
1 tablespoon butter	thyme)
2 tablespoons flour	Small onions
2 cups water	Small mushrooms
	Croutons

Cut the veal into cubes. Place in a container and cover with boiling water; add salt to taste. After 20 minutes, drain the veal and make a sauce in the following manner: Put butter in a pan and allow to melt on low fire; add flour, mix well with a wooden spoon without allowing to brown; add water, salt, pepper and bouquet garni. When the sauce has thickened, add veal, onions and mushrooms; the last 2 ingredients should be added only 45 minutes before serving. When your blanquette is ready, put the veal in a serving dish and pour sauce around. Croutons which have been fried in butter may be added if desired.

Doris R. Hale
Carmel, California

LUMPIA

4 cloves garlic, finely diced
2 tablespoons sesame oil
1 pound ground beef
1 pound ground pork
1-2 large onions, finely diced
1 grated carrot
1 small bell pepper, finely diced

¼ cup soy sauce
1 tablespoon salt
¼ teaspoon pepper
½ teaspoon MSG
50 lumpia or spring roll wrappers
Peanut oil

Saute the garlic in the sesame oil; add the ground beef and pork and brown. Add the onions, carrot and bell pepper and cook until just tender. Stir in the soy sauce, salt, pepper and MSG. Strain thoroughly and cool completely. Separate the wrappers and cover with damp paper towels to prevent them from drying out while working. Place approximately 1 tablespoon of the filling in the center of each wrapper. Roll up, envelope style, using flour paste to seal. Fry in the hot peanut oil until golden brown; drain. Serve with *Sweet and Sour Sauce*.

SWEET AND SOUR SAUCE

½ cup vinegar
1 cup water
1 cup sugar
2 tablespoons cornstarch

2 tablespoons catsup
½ teaspoon salt
½ teaspoon crushed dried red
   chiles
½ teaspoon minced garlic

Combine all ingredients in a saucepan and stir until the cornstarch is dissolved. Bring to a boil over medium heat; cook until thickened, stirring constantly.

Debby Sather
Cousin of Kim Bowden '87
Canyon Country, California

"This recipe can be used as an hors d'oeuvre or as a vegetable serving for a meal."

SPANAKOPETA
(Greek Spinach Pie)

1 cup butter
3 cups flour
¼ cup water (or more)
3 (10 ounce) packages frozen
   chopped spinach
3 eggs, beaten
1 small onion, chopped

Olive oil
6 ounces feta cheese
6 ounces cottage cheese
Salt
Pepper
Butter
Parmesan cheese

Cut the 1 cup butter into the flour; moisten with the water to make a smooth dough and refrigerate overnight. Cook and drain the spinach and add the beaten eggs. Saute the onion in olive oil. Combine the feta and cottage cheeses and add to the spinach mixture along with the sauteed onions. Season with salt and pepper; set aside. Roll out half of the dough and place on the bottom of a 9 x 13 inch pan. Spread the filling over the dough, dot with butter and sprinkle with Parmesan cheese. Roll out the remaining dough and place over the filling to make a top crust, and place in a 350° oven. Bake for approximately 45 minutes or until a beautiful crispy crust is formed. Let stand a few minutes before cutting into squares; serve while hot. NOTE: This recipe may be made ahead and frozen for later use.

Rose Marie Ansel
Santa Catalina School Staff
Monterey, California

SPANAKOPITA

4 bunches fresh spinach
6 shallots
1 small yellow onion
1 bunch scallions
3 tablespoons butter
2 cups feta cheese
1 cup cottage cheese

1 cup tofu, mashed
1 teaspoon basil
1 teaspoon oregano
½ teaspoon vegetable salt
½ teaspoon pepper
5 eggs, beaten
1 (1 pound) package phyllo
  dough, prebuttered

Clean and chop the spinach and steam lightly, about 2 minutes. Finely chop the shallots, onion and scallions and saute in the butter until soft; combine with the spinach in a large bowl. Add the feta and cottage cheeses, the tofu, the seasonings and the eggs. Place 8 layers of the pre-buttered phyllo leaves in the bottom of a 9 x 13 inch pan, letting the ends drape over the sides of the pan. Cover with half of the spinach filling. Place 8 more layers of phyllo over the spinach, then the remaining filling. Tuck in the phyllo dough and top with as many more layers as will fit. Bake, uncovered, in a 375° oven for about 45 minutes, until golden brown.

Dolores Berta Ransom
Class of '65
Carmel Valley, California

FOCACIA (ITALIAN BREAD)

2½ cups water (115° - 120°)
4-5 cups flour
1 package dry yeast

1 teaspoon sugar
1 tablespoon salt

TOPPING:
About ¼ cup olive oil
1 bunch green onions with tops
¼-½ teaspoon oregano

3-4 shakes crushed red pepper
Coarse salt (ice cream salt)

Combine flour, yeast, sugar and salt in a large bowl. Add hot water and stir vigorously with a spoon; dough will be very sticky. Cover with wax paper which has been coated with Pam or oil. Let rise until doubled. Spread dough into a greased jelly-roll pan. Cover with greased wax paper and let rise again until doubled. While dough is rising, prepare topping by sauteeing green onions, oregano and crushed red pepper in the olive oil until onions are slightly browned. Cool. Spread topping evenly over dough after it has risen; indent into dough by pressing lightly with fingertips. Sprinkle lightly with rock salt. Bake in 350° oven for 35-45 minutes, until golden brown.

Camille Annotti Stevens
Class of '57
Mother of Teresa '81
Hollister, California

"This is a traditional Yucatan recipe. It takes time to prepare, but it is absolutely delicious, fresh and substantial. Have a Mayan holiday!"

SOPA DE LIMA
(Lime and Chicken Soup)

1 (2½-3 pounds) broiler-fryer
   chicken with giblets
1½ teaspoons salt
4 chicken livers
4 chicken gizzards
1 small onion, thinly sliced
1 small green pepper, thinly sliced
3 large cloves garlic, minced
¼ teaspoon oregano

2 medium tomatoes, peeled
   and chopped
Juice of 2 sweet limes
2 (1 x 2 inch) pieces grapefruit
   rind
Salt
Pepper
Stale tortillas, thinly sliced in
   strips
Lime wedges

Remove giblets from chicken, reserving the liver and gizzard. Cut the chicken in half and put in a soup pot with 2½ quarts water. Heat to boiling and add the salt. Cover and simmer until chicken falls from the bone, about 2 hours. Strain off the broth and chill. Remove the meat from the bones. When the fat has set on top of the chilled broth, remove and save for sauteeing. Put all the chicken livers and gizzards in the broth and heat to boiling. Simmer for 15 minutes; remove with a slotted spoon. Trim gristle from the gizzards and chop with the liver into small pieces and return along with the chicken meat to the soup pot. Add 2 cups of water. In the hot chicken fat, saute the onion with the green pepper, garlic and oregano until the onion is limp. Add to the soup pot along with the tomatoes, lime juice, and grapefruit rind. Simmer, covered, 1 hour and season with salt and pepper. Just before serving, fry tortilla strips in hot fat until crisp. Divide the strips among 4-6 bowls and cover with hot soup. Serve with lime wedges.

Dr. Danielle Chavy Cooper
Upper School Faculty
Pacific Grove, California

"The fourth grade class, while studying the tribes of Africa, enjoyed a Mossi feast. This is one of the many dishes served."

MOSSI MEAL CORN SOUP

4 slices bacon	*4 cups water*
2 medium onions, finely chopped	*1 teaspoon salt*
2 ribs celery and leaves, chopped	*4 cups milk*
4 medium potatoes, peeled and diced	*2 cups corn kernels*

Fry bacon until crisp, remove from the pan and brown the onions and celery in the fat. In a large soup pot, place the potatoes, water, salt, onions, celery and crumbled bacon. Cover the pot and bring to a boil; reduce the heat and simmer until the potatoes are soft. Stir in the milk and corn and correct seasoning. Cover the pot and simmer until the corn is tender. Serves 4-6.

Fourth Grade Class
Santa Catalina Lower School
Monterey, California

During the year, the Mothers' Service League hosts a pot-luck in honor of the faculty and administration of the Upper School, Lower School, and Pre-school to show their appreciation for all their hard work and thoughtfulness on behalf of the students.

"My husband is Colombian-born and this is one of the favorite recipes of the capital of Colombia, Bogota, therefore the name, Ajiaco Bogotano."

AJIACO BOGOTANO
(Creamed Chicken and Potato Soup with Avocado, Corn and Capers)

3-3½ pound chicken, cut into 6
    pieces
2 quarts cold water
1 large onion, peeled
1 small bay leaf
1/8 teaspoon dried thyme
1 tablespoon salt
¼ teaspoon white pepper

4 medium boiling potatoes,
    peeled and sliced ¼ inch thick
3 ears corn, cut into 2-inch
    rounds
1 cup plus 2 tablespoons heavy
    cream
2 tablespoons capers, drained
1 avocado, peeled, pitted, thinly
    sliced

In a heavy 5-quart casserole, combine the chicken and water. The water should cover the chicken by about an inch; if necessary, add more water. Bring to a boil over high heat, skimming off the scum that rises to the surface. Add the onion, bay leaf, thyme, salt and pepper. Reduce the heat to low, cover for 30 minutes or until the chicken is tender. Transfer the chicken to a platter. Pick out and discard the bones and onion, strain the stock through a fine sieve and return it to the casserole. Remove the skin from the chicken with a small knife or your fingers. Cut or pull the meat away from the bones; discard the skin and bones. Cut the chicken meat into strips ¼ inch wide and 1 inch long. Return the stock in the casserole to a boil over moderate heat and drop in the potatoes. Cover and cook for 30 minutes, or until the potatoes are soft, then mash them against the sides of the pan with a spoon until the soup is thick and fairly smooth. Add the corn and chicken and simmer, uncovered, for 5-10 minutes, depending on the tenderness of the corn. To serve: Pour 3 tablespoons of cream and 1 teaspoon of capers into each of 6 deep soup bowls. Ladle the soup into the bowls and float the sliced avocado on top.

Penelope Corey Arango (Mrs. Jorge)
Class of '61
Coconut Grove, Florida

"This soup is easy to make and assembled in a jiffy."

PAVESE
(Italian Egg Soup)

6 cups Basic White or Chicken
    stock (see page 50)
1 tablespoon minced parsley

3 eggs
3 tablespoons grated Parmesan
    cheese

Bring stock to a boil; season to taste. Beat parsley, eggs and cheese together. Stir into the broth and cook, stirring for a few seconds, or until eggs are set. Makes 1½ quarts, or 4 to 6 servings.

Pauline Cantin (Mrs. Giles)
Music Department
Mother of Marie '70
Monterey, California

ZUCCHINI TIMBALES WITH SMOKED SALMON SAUCE

375 grams (12 ounces) zucchini *1 medium onion, diced*
½ teaspoon salt *1½ ounces butter*

EGG MIXTURE:
6 large eggs *Salt*
2 ounces milk *1½ ounces butter, melted*

Grate the zucchini with salt. Allow the zucchini to drain for 1 hour; squeeze to remove any remaining liquid. Cook the onion in butter until soft. Add the zucchini and stir about 3-4 minutes; cool. For the egg mixture: Beat 4 of the eggs with the milk and salt. Add to the melted butter and cook to the consistency of creamy scrambled eggs. Beat in the remaining 2 eggs and add the zucchini. Pour into buttered timbales which have been lined with foil. Place in a dish with water halfway up the sides of the timbales and bake in a 350° oven 25-30 minutes or until set. Unmold. This may be served hot or cold. Serves 6-8.

SMOKED SALMON SAUCE

4 ounces sour cream *2 tablespoons mayonnaise*
2 teaspoons grated white onion *Pepper*
1 teaspoon horseradish *3 ounces smoked salmon*

Combine all ingredients in a blender or food processor and pour over the timbales.

Denise LeBlanc de Forest (Mrs. Lockwood)
Class of '57
Melbourne, Australia

COQUILLES SAINT JACQUES

8 scallop's meat
1 handful crab meat
1 handful shrimp meat
1 glass dry white wine (1 cup)
Juice of 1 lemon

SAUCE MORNAY:
30 grams butter (2 tablespoons)
30 grams flour (about ¼ cup)
½ liter milk (2 cups)

200 grams mushrooms (about ½ pound)
2 shallots
Butter
Chopped parsley

60 grams grated Swiss cheese (2 ounces)
Salt
Pepper

Cut scallops in half and simmer with the crab and shrimp in the wine and lemon juice for about 5-10 minutes. Saute the minced mushrooms and shallots in a small amount of butter for approximately 8 minutes. Prepare the Sauce Mornay by placing the butter in a saucepan, melt but do not allow to become too hot. Add the flour at once while stirring rapidly with a wooden spoon. Remove from heat and stir constantly while adding the milk. Blend in the grated cheese and season with salt and pepper. Assemble by combining the drained scallop mixture and mushroom mixture with the Sauce Mornay. Fill scallop shells and sprinkle with chopped parsley. Broil until golden and serve immediately. Serves 4-6.

Michele Neisess
Mother of Aimee '84
Pacific Grove, California

BAKED PRAWNS (GREEK STYLE)

2 pounds large uncooked prawns
1 medium onion, chopped
½ cup olive oil
1 cup green onions, chopped
2 cloves garlic, crushed
2 cups peeled tomatoes, chopped

½ cup dry white wine
¼ cup parsley, chopped
½ teaspoon dried oregano
Salt
Pepper
4 ounces feta cheese

Shell the prawns, leaving the last segment of the shell and tail intact. Devein and rinse; drain and dry with paper towels. Refrigerate. Heat the oil in a pan and gently fry the onion until transparent. Add the green onion and garlic and cook 2 minutes longer. Add the tomatoes, wine, most of the parsley, oregano, salt and pepper to taste. Cover and simmer gently for 30 minutes, until thick. Spoon half the tomato sauce into 6 individual dishes or 1 large one. Add the prawns and spoon the remaining sauce over them. Coarsely crumble the feta cheese over the top. Place in a 500° oven for about 12 minutes until the prawn tails are pink, the meat is firm and the feta cheese has melted and is lightly browned. Sprinkle with the remaining parsley and serve with crusty bread.

Barbara Mahaney (Mrs. Robert J.)
Mother of Molly '75, Susan '79, Kate '81
Monterey, California

SHRIMP CURRY

2 tablespoons oil
½ teaspoon fenugreek
1 teaspoon mustard seed
1 teaspoon jeera
1 medium onion, chopped
1 tablespoon green ginger,
  crushed

3 cloves garlic, crushed
2 tablespoons curry powder
1 pound green shrimp, shelled
  and deveined
2 large tomatoes, coarsely
  chopped

Heat the oil enough so that the spices pop; do not burn. Add the fenugreek, mustard, jeera and stir just until you get their aroma. Add a few teaspoons of onion to cool the oil a little, then add the ginger and garlic. Stir a few seconds; add the remainder of the onion. Stir until the onion is soft and then add the curry powder. When it is well mixed, add the shrimp. Stir until the shrimp is pink. Reduce the heat to low; add the tomatoes and simmer until the sauce is thick. Serve over rice with a few condiments such as: chopped cucumber, sliced banana, mango chutney, chopped hard cooked eggs, chopped peanuts, chopped parsley. NOTE: If this curry is too hot, use chopped cucumber to make it seem less hot. If it is not hot enough, add a few drops of tabasco.

Lois Hickey (Mrs. Carl)
Mother of Sandra '84
West Truckee, California

Each year, just before first semester finals, the faculty give a Finals Party for the students to help ease the tension and give the students a study break. It is a dinner with a surprise theme, but the dessert is always the traditional ice cream pie.

POULET AU VINAIGRE DE FRAMBOISES
(CHICKEN IN RASPBERRY VINEGAR)

3 tablespoons butter
1 pound onions, cut into fine
  circles
2 medium tomatoes
2 garlic cloves, peeled and slashed
1 small bouquet garni
1 (3 inch) piece celery, cut roughly

Salt
Pepper
1 chicken, cut in 4 pieces
1 cup raspberry vinegar
1 cup red wine
1 basket fresh raspberries

In a skillet, melt 1 tablespoon of the butter; add the onion rings and toss. Add 2 tablespoons water, cover and cook slowly for about 30 minutes, adding an additional 2 tablespoons water if the onions start to brown. Peel and chop the tomatoes; add to the onions and cook 5 minutes. Add the garlic, bouquet garni and celery; toss about 2 minutes and remove. While onions are cooking, salt and pepper the chicken. Melt 1 tablespoon of the butter in a saucepan and brown the chicken quickly; remove. Place the onion mixture in the bottom of the saucepan and arrange the chicken pieces on top; cover tightly and steam for 25 minutes until the chicken is tender. Remove the chicken and vegetables. Discard fat from saucepan, add the vinegar and deglaze, allowing to reduce. Add the wine and reduce by half. Return chicken to pan and cover. Puree onion mixture and add to chicken; boil for about 5 minutes. Correct seasonings. Mix the remaining 1 tablespoon butter with a little of the sauce and add to the chicken. Reheat and serve, garnishing with raspberries. Serves 4.

Cri Cri Solak-Eastin (Mrs. Richard Eastin)
Class of '71
Pasadena, California

"My husband's mother is Hungarian. This is the first recipe she gave me as a 'must do'. I shuddered, but to my complete surprise, I loved it! My family used paprika as a garnish for deviled eggs and veal kidneys for the dogs. This is a birthday dinner request from all three children."

KIDNEY OR CHICKEN PAPRIKASCHE

1-1¼ pounds veal kidney or
2 whole chicken breasts
1 large onion, sliced
1½ tablespoons bacon drippings

1 tablespoon Hungarian paprika
Salt
1 cup chicken broth
1 cup sour cream

Soak the kidney for 30 minutes in cold salted water; cut into small pieces. If chicken is used, debone, skin and cut into cubes. Brown the onion lightly in the bacon drippings, add the paprika and kidney or chicken; stir quickly and add the broth. Season with salt. Cover and simmer for 30 minutes; do not allow pot to boil dry. Cool slightly and blend in the sour cream. Serve over hot wide noodles or spaetzle. Serves 6.

Mary Ann Taylor (Mrs. James)
Mother of James, Katie and Asher
Monterey, California

"A hearty, healthy meal. Leftover broth is a delicious soup at the end of the meal."

MIZUTAKI
(Japanese Pot-au-feu)

1 (12 ounce) package tofu
1 large nappa cabbage
1 bunch scallions
Shiitake (dried black mushrooms)
*   or regular mushrooms*
½ daikon (Japanese radish)

1 chicken, boned
Lemon juice
Soy sauce
1 carrot, sliced
1-1½ cups short grain rice

Cut the vegetables and the meat into bite-sized pieces and arrange decoratively on a platter, reserving some of the daikon to grate (grated ginger may be substituted). Individually, in small dishes, place the grated daikon, lemon juice and soy sauce. Fill an electric wok or fry pan 1/3-1/2 full with water. Add chicken bones and bring to a boil to make "instant stock", skim the froth and simmer for 20-30 minutes; remove bones. While the stock is simmering, cook the rice Japanese style: Place the rice in a pot and add water to a level about 1 inch above the level of the rice. Soak for 15 minutes; cover and bring to a high boil, reduce heat and simmer gently for 20 minutes. Do not lift lid. Let stand for 10 minutes. This will make a sticky Japanese rice (if rice seems too firm, add 1-2 tablespoons water and simmer a bit longer; if rice seems too wet, remove cover and place over very low heat for 3-5 minutes). Add the vegetables and chicken to the broth according to the length of cooking time (carrots, daikon, shiitake and chicken take longer, the cabbage and the scallions take about 1-2 minutes). Each person makes his/her own dipping sauce by combining the soy sauce, lemon juice and grated daikon to taste. As the food is cooked, each person serves herself from the wok. Serve the rice in small individual bowls. Serves 6. NOTE: Table setting for each person consists of 1 pair of chopsticks, 1 rice bowl, 1 serving spoon and 1 sauce bowl.

Piper McNulty
Class of '70
Santa Clara, California

CHINESE ALMOND CHICKEN

2 chicken breasts	½ cup sliced water chestnuts
3 tablespoons oil	½ cup toasted, blanched almonds
3 tablespoons soy sauce	1 cup chicken broth, heated
1 cup diced celery	2 tablespoons cornstarch
½ cup sliced green onions	2 tablespoons water
1 cup sliced fresh mushrooms	1 cup Chinese snow peas

Cook, skin and bone the chicken and cut into small strips. Heat the oil in a wok and add the chicken, soy sauce, green onions, water chestnuts, mushrooms and almonds. Stir and cook for 2 minutes. Add the chicken broth. Cover the wok and simmer for 4 minutes. Mix the cornstarch and water into a paste, stir into the wok. Add the snow peas, stir and cook for 1 minute until the sauce is slightly thickened. Serve with or over rice. Serves 4.

Margery Bobbs Johnson (Mrs. Robert)
Class of '65
Eagle, Colorado

"This is a marvelous recipe to assemble early in the day. Dinner is ready with just a few minutes in the kitchen."

CHICKEN ALMOND

3 whole chicken breasts, boned	2 green onions
1 carrot	½ bell pepper
2 cups broccoli tops	Peanut oil
1 rib celery	½ cup blanched almonds
8 medium mushrooms	1 cup water
1 (8 ounce) can sliced water	1 bouillon cube
chestnuts	1 tablespoon cornstarch
1 cup pea pods	

Slice the chicken and all of the vegetables on the diagonal, Chinese style. pour a small amount of peanut oil in a wok and lightly brown the almonds. Add the chicken and cook until no longer pink. Add the vegetables according to length of cooking time, the firmer ones first, and stir-fry. Mix together the water, bouillon cube and cornstarch; add to the wok, cover and simmer 5 minutes. Serve with rice and condiments such as freshly grated ginger, soy sauce and grated coconut. NOTE: Cubes of tofu may be added just before simmering.

Mrs. Caleb Alldrin
Mother of Laura
Modesto, California

SOY CHICKEN

2 pounds chicken thighs
1 slice ginger
½ cup sake

5 tablespoons Aji-mirin (sweet
cooking rice wine)
6 tablespoons soy sauce
1½ cups water

Cook the chicken over medium heat until browned on all sides. Remove the pieces to a cooking pot. Mix the remaining ingredients and pour over the chicken. Cover and bring to a boil; lower the heat and simmer for 1 hour or until the chicken is tender. Serves 6.

Susan Johnson
Class of '76
Marina, California

BULGOGI (KOREAN BEEF)

1-2 tablespoons sugar
½ cup soy sauce
2 cloves garlic, minced
2/3 cup chopped scallions
½ teaspoon black pepper
2 tablespoons white sesame seeds,
toasted

1½ tablespoons sesame oil
2 pounds round steak, thinly
sliced
2-3 carrots, thinly sliced
Optional: Chopped onions,
Dry Japanese mushrooms,
soaked and sliced

Combine the sugar, soy sauce, garlic, scallions, pepper, sesame seeds and sesame oil and pour over the meat and marinate for 30 minutes. Cook the carrots and onions until tender; set aside. Grill the meat and mix with the vegetables. Serve with rice. Serves 6-8.

Piper McNulty-Leung
Class of '70
Carmel, California

SOSATIES

Mutton, cut into 1½ inch cubes
1 onion
Oil
2 ounces curry powder
½ cup wine vinegar or lemon juice

1 tablespoon sugar
Salt
Pepper
1 cup milk
Lemon or bay leaves, broken

Lace the mutton onto metal skewers. Finely chop the onion and saute in a small amount of oil until limp and transparent; pour over the meat. Combine the remaining ingredients to make a marinade and pour over the meat. Cover and leave in a cool place for several days, turning occasionally. Grill over an open fire.

Joy De la Porte
Salisbury, Zimbabwe
Africa

BABOTIE

1 large slice white bread
1 onion, chopped
Butter
2 tablespoons curry powder
2 teaspoons sugar
Salt

Juice of 1 lemon
2 pounds minced meat (mutton
  or beef)
4 eggs
1 cup milk
Lemon or bay leaves
Chutney

Soak the bread in water and squeeze dry. Saute the onion in butter. Mix the curry powder, sugar, salt and lemon juice with the meat and the bread; add the onions. Beat 3 of the eggs with the milk and add to the meat mixture. Mix well and place in a round baking dish. Beat the remaining egg with a tablespoon of milk and brush over the top of the meat. Top with a few lemon or bay leaves. Bake in a 350° oven for 30-45 minutes. Serve with chutney.

Joy De la Porte
Salisbury, Zimbabwe
Africa

"This was the first recipe I learned from my mother-in-law when I married my Polish husband."

GOLUMKE
(Polish Stuffed Cabbage)

1 large head green cabbage
2 pounds lean hamburger
1 pound ground pork
2 onions, chopped

1 cup cooked rice
Garlic powder
Salt
Pepper
Marinara sauce

Remove leaves from the cabbage head by removing the core and covering with cold water. Let stand about 10 minutes and remove leaves. Cover the leaves with boiling water and let stand for 10 minutes until limp; drain well. Mix together the hamburger, pork, onions and rice in a large bowl. Season with the garlic powder, salt and pepper. Place ¼ cup of the meat mixture near the stem end of a cabbage leaf. Roll the leaf around the meat mixture, tucking in the sides. Place the cabbage rolls, seam side down, in a large pan and cover with the marinara sauce. Cook, covered, over lowest heat possible for 3-4 hours. NOTE: This is best if refrigerated overnight and reheated.

B.J. Burton Szemborski (Mrs. Stanley)
Class of '66
Sandbank, Scotland

COPENHAGEN CASSEROLE

2 pounds zucchini
2 or 3 large tomatoes, peeled
  and sliced
1 cup diced cooked ham
3 tablespoons butter
2 cups half and half
Salt

Pepper
1 cup shredded Danish Havarti
  cheese
1 egg yolk
Dash cayenne
Chopped parsley

Trim the zucchini and parboil whole in salted water for 5 minutes; drain, cool, and then cut into ¼ inch slices. Arrange zucchini, ham and tomatoes in layers in a greased 7 x 12 inch baking dish. Melt 2 tablespoons of the butter and drizzle over the casserole. Bake in a 400° oven for 20 minutes. While the casserole is in the oven, melt the remaining butter in a saucepan; blend in flour to a smooth paste, and gradually add half and half, stirring constantly with a wire whip. Cook over medium heat until the mixture thickens; add shredded cheese, salt and pepper. Bring just to a boil. Stir a small amount of the sauce into the egg yolk, and slowly stir the egg yolk mixture back into the sauce. Heat just to boiling, stirring constantly. Remove from heat, add cayenne and spoon over the zucchini casserole. Garnish with parsley and serve over a bed of rice. Serves 4-6.

Latchmee A. Schultz (Mrs. Rolf)
Mother of Melanie and Debbie
Salinas, California

TOURTIERS
(French Canadian Meat Pie)

Pastry for 2 crust (9-inch) pie
1 pound lean pork, ground
1 medium onion, chopped
½ small garlic clove, minced
¼ teaspoon savory
½ teaspoon parsley

Pinch oregano
Salt
Pepper
2 tablespoons flour
1 rib fresh celery

Cook the meat in a skillet with ½ cup water until the meat is white, about 20 minutes. Add the onions, garlic, savory, parsley, oregano, salt, pepper, flour, and celery and cook an additional 20 minutes. Remove the celery stalk, and skim the fat, if necessary; cool. Pour into an uncooked 9-inch pastry shell. Adjust top crust, cut vents and flute edges. Bake in a 400° oven for about 30 minutes. Serves 6-8. NOTE: This freezes well and is good for a holiday dinner with turkey.

Arliene Beesley (Mrs. John)
Mother of Jennifer '84
Monterey, California

"This is a family recipe from England."

STEAK AND KIDNEY PIE

2 pounds rump or chuck roast   1½ teaspoons salt
3-4 lamb kidneys   1 teaspoon pepper
1 cup flour   Pie pastry

Cut the beef into approximately 1¼ inch cubes. Devein the kidneys and cut into small pieces. Place the meat in a brown paper bag with the flour, salt and pepper. Coat the meat by shaking the bag. Remove the meat and place in a round 2-quart casserole dish; add enough boiling water to barely cover the meat. Place the casserole into a larger pan or baking dish and surround with boiling water, making sure the water level is lower than the casserole dish. Bake in a 375° oven for 2-3 hours, stirring occasionally. Remove from pan of water and place pie pastry over the top of the casserole. Increase the oven temperature to 425° and bake for 20 minutes until the crust is lightly browned. Serve over riced potatoes. NOTE: If desired, onion can be added with the meat and ¼ cup red wine with the liquid.

Jane Buffington (Mrs. John)
Mother of Jamie '85
Sherman Oaks, California

"I always make sure to prepare Adobo on open weekends for my daughters. They love it!"

ADOBO

½ cup vinegar   1 bay leaf
½ cup soy sauce   1 (2 pound) chicken, cut in
3 garlic cloves, crushed   serving pieces
½ teaspoon whole peppercorns   1 pound pork butt, cut in pork
    chop size

Combine the vinegar, soy sauce, cloves, pepper and bay leaf and pour over the meat in a large pot. Let stand for 1 hour. Cook, covered, on medium heat until the mixture boils. Reduce heat to simmer, turn the meat and cook, covered, for 1 hour or until meat is tender. Serve with plain boiled rice. Serves 6. NOTE: Chicken or pork may be used individually.

Lilia Ferrer-Ibabao (Mrs. Florentino)
Mother of Cheryl '82 and Emily '84
Orinda, California

"This Swedish dish has been enjoyed by my family for years. We make a big batch and serve what we need for dinner and then freeze the rest."

KALDOLMAR

2 pounds ground pork
2 pounds ground veal
2 pounds ground beef
2 cups cooked rice
2 eggs
1 small onion, chopped
1 cup canned milk
1 tablespoon salt

½ tablespoon white pepper
½ tablespoon mace
½ tablespoon nutmeg
½ tablespooon allspice
½ tablespoon Accent
2-3 large cabbages
½ cup butter
Brown sugar

Combine the meat, rice, eggs, onion, milk and seasonings. Place the whole cabbage in boiling water to soften. Remove the outer leaves as they become soft and drain on paper towels. Put 1-2 tablespoons of the meat mixture inside of each cabbage leaf; roll up and secure with toothpicks. Brown the cabbage rolls, a few at a time, in about 2 tablespoons each butter and brown sugar, adding more butter and brown sugar as needed. Bake 2 hours in a 325° oven after browning. Makes about 52 meat rolls.

Marian Anderson (Mrs. Kenneth)
San Jose, California

"This Mexican stew is my father's creation. He's a wonderful inprovisational cook."

POZOLE

2 pounds pork (1 inch cubes)
2 pounds beef (1 inch cubes)
3 onions, chopped
4 cloves garlic, minced
3 bell peppers, chopped
1 (29 ounce) can tomatoes, chopped with juice
1 (29 ounce) can red beans
1 (29 ounce) can hominy
1 (29 ounce) can pinto beans

1 (15 ounce) can tomato paste
5 tablespoons chili powder
2 teaspoons cumin
3 tablespoons oregano
1 (7 ounce) can chopped green chiles
2 tablespoons flour
¼ cup water
Salt
Pepper

Brown the cubed beef and pork in a large pot; add the onions, garlic and bell pepper and saute. Add the remaining ingredients, except for the flour and water, to the meat and vegetable mixture. Simmer 3-4 hours and season with salt and pepper. Thicken with a mixture of the flour and water and simmer about 20 minutes more.

Linda Nelson
Mother of Kelly, Summer Camper
Santa Cruz, California

STUFFED MUSHROOMS IN BATTER

24 dried mushrooms
2 teaspoons white wine
1/3 teaspoon salt
3½ teaspoons light soy
½ tablespoon cornstarch
½ egg
Dash pepper

Sesame oil
½ pound pork, minced
6 water chestnuts, diced
2 spring onions, chopped
½ cup flour
½ cup stock
Dash MSG

Clean and soak the mushrooms; set aside. Combine 1 teaspoon of the white wine, the salt, 1 teaspoon of the light soy, the cornstarch, egg, pepper, and a dash of sesame oil and mix well; combine with the minced pork, diced water chestnuts, and chopped spring onions. Squeeze the mushrooms dry and remove the stems. Divide the pork mixture evenly among 12 of the mushrooms, topping with the remaining 12. Sift the flour into a bowl, adding enough water to form a thin batter. Dip mushrooms to coat. Bring to a boil 2 tablespoons oil in a shallow frying pan; fry the mushrooms until golden brown on both sides. Sprinkle the remaining 1 teaspoon wine in the pan; add the stock, remaining soy and MSG. Simmer over low heat until liquid is evaporated. Sprinkle with a dash of sesame oil and serve.

Mrs. Raymond Koo
Mother of Dorothea '84
Hong Kong

PANSIT (PHILIPPINE SPAGHETTI)

1 pound boneless chicken
1 pound boneless pork
¼ cup vegetable oil
2 garlic cloves, crushed
1 onion, chopped
1/3 pound medium shrimp,
    shelled, slit in middle
2 tablespoons soy sauce
1 cup green beans, French cut
1 cup cabbage, shredded

1 carrot, sliced into thin strips
½ cup celery, cut into thin strips
1 teaspoon Accent
½ teaspoon salt
1/8 teaspoon pepper
Chicken broth
1 (1 pound) package rice sticks,
    softened
Hard cooked eggs
Scallions

Slice the chicken and pork in small pieces. Ready all the other ingredients on a tray. In hot oil, brown the garlic, add the onions, saute until transparent; add the meats and stir-cook for 5 minutes. Add the shrimp and soy sauce and stir-cook for 5 minutes. Add all the green beans, cabbage, carrots and celery; season with accent, salt and pepper. Pour in 1 cup of chicken broth and stir-cook for 2 minutes. Add the drained rice sticks, which have been soaked in hot water for 15 minutes, and cook over low heat for 3 minutes while stirring (If the mixture is too dry, moisten with more broth). Transfer to a platter and garnish the top with slices of hard-cooked eggs and finely cut scallions. Serve with lemon wedges and soy sauce. Serves 10. NOTE: Snow pea-pods, sliced Chinese sausage and mushrooms may be included. A chinese wok is a good pan to cook in.

Lilia Ferrer-Ibabao (Mrs. Florentino)
Mother of Cheryl '82 and Emily '84
Orinda, California

"Black beans and rice are the staple foods of my husband's home, Honduras. Carlos eats them with every meal, even breakfast."

FRIJOLES NEGROS
(Honduran Black Beans)

1 pound dried black beans
4 cups cold water
2 large cloves garlic, crushed
¼ cup diced salt pork
2 tablespoons virgin olive oil
1 large onion, diced
1 large green pepper, diced

1 bay leaf
1 tablespoon dried oregano
Salt
Pepper
2 tablespoons red wine vinegar
1 large cooked Polish or other smoked sausage, optional

Cull and wash beans in cold running water. Put beans and water in a large kettle or dutch oven. Bring to a boil; boil 2 minutes. Remove from heat and let stand, covered, for 1 hour. Add 1 clove garlic and bring to a boil; lower heat and simmer, covered, 1½ hours. Meanwhile, fry salt pork in a small skileet to render all fat; add olive oil and heat. Add remaining clove of garlic, onion and green pepper; saute until onions are tender. After beans have cooked 1½ hours, add the sauteed onion mixture, bay leaf, oregano and mix well. Continue cooking about 30 minutes or until beans are very tender. Remove half the beans and puree in blender or food processor; return to kettle and mix with remaining beans. Add the salt, pepper and vinegar. Cut the sausage into 2-inch pieces and stir into beans. Simmer until sausage is heated through and swollen. Remove from heat and discard the bay leaf. Serve with cooked white rice, sour cream and Parmesan cheese. NOTE: Add water as needed throughout cooking process if beans get too dry; beans should always be at least half-covered with water.

Margaret Donlin Bonilla (Mrs. Carlos)
Class of '76
Chevy Chase, Maryland

GEVETCH
(Bulgarian Vegetable "Stew")

1 large eggplant, cubed
2-3 bell peppers, cubed
3-4 tomatoes, chopped
String beans, cut
Carrots, sliced

Zucchini, sliced
2-3 large onions
2-3 cloves garlic, minced
4 tablespoons salad oil
Thyme

This dish is best when cooked in a covered earthenware baking dish, but it can be baked in a covered casserole. Arrange the vegetables in layers with the slowest cooking on the bottom and the eggplant and tomatoes on the top. Drizzle the salad oil over the vegetables and season with thyme. Cover the casserole and put in a 325° oven for at least 3-4 hours. Peek from time to time and if the vegetables are becoming too "soupy", remove the lid to reduce. This dish is served warm, traditionally, with crusty French bread and white wine; however, a more modern way of serving is as a cold side dish to replace salad. NOTE: Vegetables can vary with individual tastes and amounts can be adjusted according to the capacity of the vessel.

Dr. Ivan T. Christie
Father of Linda '81
Aptos, California

"This is a pretty dish to serve on a buffet table. By altering the ingredients, it can be spicy or mild. It is lovely on a hot summer day with BBQ meats, especially chicken."

CHINESE SZECHUAN SESAME NOODLES

1 pound fresh pasta, linguini
cut
2 tablespoons vegetable oil
2 tablespoons soy sauce
3 tablespoons black vinegar
1 tablespoon sesame oil

1 tablespoon chili oil
2 cloves garlic
1 slice ginger
1-2 tablespoons sesame paste
½ cup sesame seeds, toasted
2 scallions

Cook the noodles in boiling water until done (1-2 minutes); rinse in cold water. Pour the vegetable oil over the noodles and toss. Transfer to a large pan. Mix in a blender the soy sauce, vinegar, sesame oil, olive oil, garlic, ginger and sesame paste; pour over the noodles. Add the sesame seeds and the scallions cut in ¼ inch slices; toss well. Chill several hours until very cold. Serves 6.

Catherine Josi-Langer
Mother of Erica, Summer Camper
Hartsdale, New York

RICE PILAF

2 tablespoons butter
1 onion, finely chopped
1 cup long grain rice
2 bouillon cubes
1-1/3 cups hot water
¼ teaspoon salt

¼ teaspoon pepper
¼ teaspoon fine herbs
¼ teaspoon curry powder
2 tablespoons raisins
2 tablespoons bacon bits

Saute the onion in the butter until limp; add the rice and stir until opaque. Stir in the remaining ingredients and heat to boiling. Bake in a covered casserole in a 325° oven for 25-30 minutes. Serves 4.

Mary Kay Sanders (Mrs. Jack)
School Nurse
Grandmother of Kim Ward '83
Seaside, California

"In Indonesia, Nasi Goreng Istimewa (Fried Rice Special) is fried rice topped with a fried egg."

NASI GORENG
(Fried Rice, Indonesian style)

2 cups long grain rice
2 teaspoons salt
2½ cups water
1 chicken breast, diced
2 tablespoons margarine or
  vegetable oil
2 large onions, sliced
2 cloves garlic, chopped

½ teaspoon coriander
½ teaspoon laos (ginger)
Sliver of shrimp paste
1 red chile, crushed
2 tablespoons sweet soy sauce
1 cup cooked shrimp
1 fried egg, optional

Cook the rice with the salt in the usual manner with the 2½ cups water. After rice is cooked, set aside to cool. Fry the diced chicken in margarine or oil until light brown. Add the sliced onions and saute the chicken until the onions are brown. Lower heat and add the chopped garlic, coriander, laos and shrimp paste. Stir well and add the crushed red chile. Fry for about 1 minute; add the soy sauce and shrimp, mixing thoroughly. Stir in the cooled rice. Maintain a low steady heat; stir constantly until rice turns a light brown. NOTE: Though chicken and shrimp are used in this recipe, any kind of meat or fish will do as well, as long as it is properly diced.

Jeanette Eppler (Mrs. Charles)
Mother of Stephanie '86
Sumatra, Indonesia

"This recipe from County Galway and County Mayo is over 100 years old."

IRISH POTATO CAKE

6 good sized potatoes   Salt
Butter   3 cups flour

In a large kettle with water, boil the potatoes with their jackets on; while hot, remove skins and put through a ricer. Add the butter and season with salt as potatoes are put through the ricer. Cool slightly. Knead while gradually adding the flour. Shape the cakes into 1-inch thick squares or rectangles, about the size of a small to medium potato. Place on a greased baking sheet and bake in a slow oven about an hour or until cakes are golden brown. Serve with butter.

Sister Carlotta
Principal, Santa Catalina School
Monterey, California

"This is delicious as an accompaniment with lunch or dinner instead of mashed potatoes."

KUGEL
(Lithuanian Potato Pudding)

6 large potatoes, grated   1 cup milk
4 eggs   ¼ cup butter, melted
1 onion, grated

Drain excess moisture from potatoes, and mix with remaining ingredients. Pour into a buttered casserole and bake in a 375° oven for 1 hour. Serve with sour cream or cream cheese. NOTE: Kugel may be baked in a loaf pan instead of a casserole dish. Leftover kugel may be cut into thick slices and fried.

Julia Brazinsky Goulden
Great Aunt of April Brazinsky
Shenandoah, Pennsylvania

Parents Weekend at Santa Catalina occurs in November of every year. It is a time for parents to meet with one another and faculty members, talk with representatives of colleges and universities, and learn more about the curriculum, activities, and life at School.

LITHUANIAN BLEENI
(Grated Potato Pancakes)

6 large potatoes, grated　　1 medium onion, grated
3 eggs　　3 tablespoons flour
½ cup milk

Drain excess moisture from potatoes, and mix with remaining ingredients in a large bowl. Heat cooking oil in a frying pan (oil should be ½ inch deep) and drop batter by large mixing-spoonfuls into the hot oil. Cook until pancakes are golden on each side; drain on a paper towel. Serve hot with sour cream or cream cheese. Makes about 1 dozen. NOTE: 1 teaspoon of baking powder may be added to the batter to make the pancake higher.

Julia Brazinsky Goulden
Great Aunt of April Brazinsky
Shenandoah, Pennsylvania

"This may be served over scrambled eggs, omelets, tacos, or as an accompaniment to barbecued meat."

FRESH SALSA

6 tomatoes, chopped　　1 clove garlic, minced
6-8 green onions, finely chopped　Salt
1 (7 ounce) can diced green chiles　Pepper
¼ cup salad oil　　1 tablespoon dried oregano OR
¼ cup fresh lime juice　　fresh minced cilantro (NOT
　　BOTH)

Combine the tomatoes, green onions and diced chiles in a deep bowl, add the oil; then add the remaining ingredients. Mix well.

Ellen Christie (Mrs. Ivan)
Mother of Linda '81
Aptos, California

The Cake Auction as a fund-raiser by students was first used in May 1977, and the proceeds were donated that year to the Carmelite Nuns in the Monastery in Carmel for their special needs. This "fun" raiser has become an annual event.

SCOTTISH TEA SCONES

2 cups unsifted flour
½ cup sugar
2 teaspoons cream of tartar
1 teaspoon baking soda
¾ teaspoon salt

½ cup shortening
½ cup raisins
2 eggs, slightly beaten
¼ cup milk

Sift dry ingredients together; blend in shortening with pastry blender until mixture resembles fine bread crumbs. Add remaining ingredients and mix with a fork. Divide in 2 parts and turn each part out on a floured board. Do not handle. Flatten with a rolling pin into a circle about ½ inch thick. Cut in triangles and place on a greased baking sheet. Bake in a 400° oven for 15 minutes or until golden. Serve warm with butter. Makes about 16.

Ella Nicklas
College Counselor
Monterey, California

"When the grey mountain mists swirl thickly around the Welsh hills, the sheep farmers spend many wet miserable hours herding the animals to lower, safer pastures. This cake is served then in thick slabs with steaming mugs of hot tea. It's substantial enough for the husky shepherds, but thinly sliced, it's also a hit with the 'shepherdesses' at their dainty porcelain high teas."

WELSH FARM CAKE

3¼ cups self-rising flour
¾ pound butter
1½ cups sugar
3 eggs, lightly beaten

½ cup milk, approximately
1¾ cup raisins
1 cup nuts, optional
1 cup brown sugar

Cut the butter into the flour; mix in the sugar and add the eggs and enough milk to form a stiff batter. Stir in the raisins and nuts. Pour into a greased and floured round cake tin. Sprinkle the top with brown sugar and bake in a 350° oven for approximately 1¾ hours until done. Serves 12. NOTE: Black currants may be substituted for the raisins.

Olivia Morgan (Mrs. Kelly)
Lower School Faculty
Monterey, California

"These cakes are light and fluffy and are traditionally served at most school functions. They are known as 'happy cakes' in many parts of the country. When they are given as small prizes in schools, they usually have happy faces decorated on them."

CHILDREN'S SCHOOL CAKES

½ cup butter
¾ cup sugar

2 eggs
1¼ cups self-rising flour

Cream the butter and sugar. Add the eggs, one at a time, adding 1 tablespoon of the flour with each addition. Fold in the remaining flour. Pour into greased muffin pans and bake in a 375° oven for 20-25 minutes. Cakes can be glazed with icing when cool.

Olivia Morgan (Mrs. Kelly)
Lower School Faculty
Monterey, California

CYXAPUKU
(Russian Cookies)

½ pound butter
1 cup sugar
4 eggs
¼ cup currants
¼ cup raisins

½ cup chopped almonds
1 teaspoon vanilla
1 teaspoon baking soda
2 tablespoons boiling water
5 cups flour (approximately)

Cream together the butter and sugar; add the eggs, currants, raisins, almonds, vanilla and the baking soda which has been dissolved in the boiling water. Add the flour, a cup at a time, until the dough is easy to handle. Shape dough into rolls about 1 inch thick and the length of your cookie sheet. Bake in a 350° oven for 30 minutes until lightly browned. While still hot, slice diagonally in ¾ inch pieces, about 2 inches long. Place in a 325° oven for 15 minutes until the cut edges are lightly brown and dry. Cool.

Faina Holodiloff
Grandmother of Anastasia
San Francisco, California

GERMAN CHRISTMAS COOKIES

1 cup finely minced almonds	¾ cup sugar
1 package vanillensucer	2-2/3 cups flour
1 cup plus 2 tablespoons butter	Milk
5 egg yolks	Black currant jelly

Combine the finely minced almonds and ½ tablespoon of the vanillensucer; set aside. Mix together the butter, 4 of the egg yolks, the sugar, flour and the remaining vanillensucer. Form into 1½ inch diameter cookies and place on a cookie sheet. Make a thumb print deep in the dough. Combine the remaining egg yolk with a small amount of milk and brush on each cookie. Sprinkle with the almonds and fill the indentation with the jelly. Bake in a 325° oven for 14 minutes until lightly browned. NOTE: Vanillensucer is available through German delicatessens or specialty shops.

Myrna Mink (Mrs. Ronald)
Mother of Matthew
Carmel Valley, California

"These cookies have become a Christmas favorite, tinted pink or green. Other shapes and colors can be used for teas, showers and receptions."

SWEDISH CREAM WAFERS

1 cup butter	2 cups flour
1/3 cup heavy whipping cream	Sugar

CREAM FILLING:

¼ cup soft butter	1 teaspoon vanilla
¾ cup powdered sugar	1 egg yolk

Mix the butter, cream and flour thoroughly and chill for 1 hour. Roll the dough 1/8 inch thick on a lightly floured board. Cut into 1½ inch rounds or shapes with scalloped edges. Transfer to wax paper heavily covered with granulated sugar; coat both sides well. Place on an ungreased cookie sheet and prick 3-4 times with a fork. Bake in a 375° oven 7-9 minutes or until lightly browned and slightly puffy. Make a filling by blending all ingredients until smooth. Put 2 cooled cookies together with the cream filling.

Yolanda Scaccia Manuel (Mrs. Chris)
Class of '67
San Mateo, California

KOEKSESTERS

½ cup sugar
½ cup butter
2 eggs
7 cups flour

SYRUP:
3 cups sugar
3 cups water

2½ teaspoons baking powder
1 teaspoon salt
½ cup milk
4 tablespoons cream

¼ teaspoon cream of tartar

Cream together the butter, sugar and well beaten eggs; set aside. Sift together the flour, baking powder and salt and add alternately to the creamed mixture with the milk and the cream. Toss onto a board, sprinkle lightly with flour and roll to a ¼ inch thickness. Cut into strips about 4 inches long and plait. Fry in deep fat or oil at 360° until golden brown. Drain and dip into a thick syrup made by dissolving the sugar in the water with the cream of tartar. Bring to a boil and simmer for about 5 minutes. Dip the pastries in the syrup and then drain well before serving.

Joy De La Porte
Salisbury, Zimbabwe
Africa

BAKLAVA

1½ pounds walnuts, chopped
¾ cup sugar
2 teaspoons cinnamon

SYRUP:
1 cup sugar
1 cup water

1 teaspoon allspice
1½ cups melted butter
1 pound phyllo pastry sheets

1½ cups honey
2 teaspoons vanilla

Mix together the walnuts, sugar and spices. Butter an 11 x 17 inch pan. Place 6 phyllo sheets in the pan, brushing each with melted butter. Sprinkle with the walnut mixture and continue alternating with the buttered sheets until all the mixture is used and 6 sheets remain. Butter and top with the remaining 6 sheets. With a sharp knife, cut in a diamond pattern and pour remaining melted butter into the slits. Bake 1 hour in a 300° oven. Combine all ingredients for syrup and bring to a boil; slowly pour half of the syrup over the baklava and place in a 400° oven for 3 minutes. Pour remaining syrup over the baklava and let stand, covered, preferably 1 day before serving. NOTE: For a lighter and less sinful baklava, half of the melted butter may be substituted with vegetable oil.

Amy Crawford (Mrs. Henry)
Mother of Elizabeth '84
Tracy, California

"A creative cook will enjoy this recipe. It is both beautiful and delicious, and it has been a favorite in our house for many years. Its name comes from being white, big, rectangular and soft looking as a pillow. The pillow torte is not a rich dessert, and that makes it an ideal cake for weight watchers too.

JASTUK TORTA
(MAMA'S PILLOW TORTE)

1 large sponge cake	*Syrup*
1 small sponge cake	*12 ounces frozen raspberries or*
Custard	*strawberries*
	Meringue

One to three days in advance, make the 2 sponge cakes, the custard and the syrup; assemble the torte. On the day the torte is to be served, make the meringue and frost the torte.

FOR LARGE SPONGE CAKE:

8 eggs
1 cup sugar
2 cups sifted cake flour
½ teaspoon salt
2 teaspoons vanilla OR
   1 teaspoon lemon zest

FOR SMALL SPONGE CAKE:

4 eggs
½ cup sugar
1 cup sifted cake flour
¼ teaspoon salt
1 teaspoon vanilla OR
   ½ teaspoon lemon zest

Mix and bake each cake separately in a 13 - 9 inch pan which has been lined with wax paper and greased well. Place the eggs, which have been warmed to room temperature, in a large mixing bowl and beat at high speed until thick. Add the sugar gradually, continuing to beat until very thick and light. Using a rubber spatula or spoon, fold in the flour, salt and vanilla. Turn into the pan and spread evenly. Bake 10 minutes, or until surface springs back when gently pressed with fingertips. Cool slightly; carefully turn out of pan; remove wax paper at once; cool completely.

CUSTARD:

6 egg yolks (reserve egg whites)
2 cups hot milk
½ cup sugar

½ cup plus 2 tablespoon all
   purpose flour
3 tablespoons butter
1 teaspoon vanilla

Beat the egg yolks and sugar until thick; add the flour and mix well. Gradually beat in hot milk. Stir over moderate heat until thick. Remove from heat, stir in the butter and vanilla; cool.

1 (12 ounce) package frozen   ¼ cup water
   pitted sour cherries   3 tablespoons Jamaica rum
1 cup sugar   2 tablespoons lemon juice

Thaw and strain the cherries; set aside. Cook the sugar with the water for about 5 minutes; add the cherries and boil to 225°F. Remove the cherries from the syrup and reserve. Add the rum and lemon juice to the syrup. (This will make about ¾ cup of syrup.) TO ASSEMBLE THE TORTE: Thaw the raspberries, reserving juice; set aside. Slice the larger sponge cake into 10 slices lengthwise to obtain slices about 13 inches long and about 1 inch thick. Using 5 of the slices, lay the cut sides flat on a large tray. The slices are touching each other with their crust sides. After arranging this layer, sprinkle it with 1/3 of the syrup, ½ of the cooked cherries and ½ of the raspberries. Spread half of the custard over the fruits. Slice the smaller sponge cake crosswise into 12 slices to obtain slices about 9 inches by ½ inch. Using the 12 slices, make the second layer of the torte going crosswise over the first layer. These slices are also arranged with the cut side down. Sprinkle the layer with 1/3 of the syrup and the remaining cherries and raspberries; top the fruits with the remaining custard. The third and last layer is arranged the same as the bottom layer, using the remaining 5 slices of the larger sponge cake. Soak it with the remaining syrup and the juice from the thawed raspberries. Refrigerate overnight.

MERINGUE:
1-1/3 cups sugar   6 egg whites
½ cup water   ½ teaspoon cream of tartar

Cook the sugar and water to a temperature of 238°F. Beat egg whites with the cream of tartar, then pour the hot sugar syrup into the egg whites using thin stream and beating continuously until cool. Frost the cake with the meringue. To serve, cut the cake into 2-3 inch squares. Serves 15-18.

Ljubinka Milovanovic
Grandmother of Laura Haney
Monterey, California

Marcia Farrell Hart built and furnished the Chapel on the Santa Catalina campus in memory of her father, James C. Farrell, in 1954. The architect was Germano Milono who later did many buildings, among them the Library, Science Building and the Study Hall.

KARIDOPITA
(Greek Walnut Cake)

9 egg yolks
1 cup sugar
3 cups finely ground walnuts
½ cup soft bread crumbs
2 teaspoons grated lemon zest
1 heaping tablespoon grated
　orange zest

¼ cup fresh orange juice
3 tablespoons brandy
1 teaspoon cinnamon
½ teaspoon cloves
2 teaspoons baking powder
9 egg whites

Beat the egg yolks with the sugar until pale and thick. Mix the walnuts with the bread crumbs, lemon and orange zest. Fold thoroughly into the yolk mixture. Stir in the orange juice and brandy. Add the spices and baking powder. Beat the egg whites until stiff but not dry, and fold into the batter gently. Be sure to incorporate the whites thoroughly. Pour into a buttered and floured pan and bake in a preheated 350° oven for about ½ hour, or until the center of cake is set. Serve plain, covered with sweetened whipped cream, or glazed with a good apricot jam and then a shiny bitter chocolate icing.

Norma Eversole (Mrs. Henry)
Mother of Alexandra '65, Gillian '69,
Helena '70, Melina '79
La Canada, California

"This recipe was given to me by my Indonesian cook, Rabaion."

HOLLAND CAKE

1 cup shortening
1 cup brown sugar
1 cup granulated sugar
2 eggs, slightly beaten
3 cups flour
1 teaspoon salt
1½ teaspoons baking soda

¼ teaspoon nutmeg
1 teaspoon vanilla
1 cup fresh pineapple pieces
1 cup fresh papaya pieces
1 cup banana slices
1 cup chopped nuts

Cream together the shortening and sugars; add the beaten eggs, mixing well. Stir in the flour, salt, soda, nutmeg and vanilla and mix well. Blend in the fruits and fold in the nuts. Bake in a greased and floured loaf pan in a 350° oven approximately 40 minutes or until done. NOTE: If desired, cup cakes may be made. Bake approximately 20 minutes.

Jeanette Eppler (Mrs. Charles)
Mother of Stephanie '86
Sumatra, Indonesia

For Middle Europeans and etymologists it might be of interest to know the origin of the word "palatschinken." It was introduced by the Romans who occupied central and eastern Europe until the third century, and in its original form it was simply "placenta" or "flat cake." The Rumanians pronounced it "placinta" and the Hungarians turned that into "palacsinta." The Czechs adopted it from the Hungarians, changing the word slightly into "palacsinta." Finally this delicious dish reached Vienna, where it has remained a favorite dessert for centuries. It is often served after a soup only, without any entree."

TOPFENPALATSCHINKEN
(Crepes with Creme Cheese Filling)

1 cup plus 1 tablespoon flour
1¼ cups milk
2 eggs

1 egg yolk
Pinch of salt
5 tablespoons sugar

FILLING:
16 ounces cream cheese
1 cup sugar (or to taste)
2 eggs
Pinch salt

Lemon rind of 1½ lemons
Lemon juice of ½ lemon
2/3 cup golden raisins

TOPPING:
2 cups sour cream
3 egg yolks
1 cup sugar (or to taste)

Lemon rind of ½ lemon
Lemon juice of ¼ lemon

Blend all batter ingredients until smooth; let stand for at least ½ hour. The batter should be thin, just thick enough to coat a spoon dipped in it. If the batter is too thick, add a little milk. Heat a 5-6 inch frying pan. Grease lightly with a mixture of melted butter and salad oil. Pour in just enough batter to cover the pan with a thin layer. Tilt the pan so the batter spreads evenly. Cook on one side until it has golden spots, then turn with a spatula and cook briefly on the other side until it is golden yellow. Repeat until all the batter is used. For the filling, cream the ingredients (except for the raisins) until smooth. Spread about 3 tablespoons on each palatschinke and roll up. Put several layers of the filled crepes into a buttered, oven-proof dish and heat at 300° for about 20 minutes. Meanwhile prepare the topping. After the palatschinken has been in the oven for 20 minutes, add the topping mixture and bake for another 20 minutes or until the sour cream mixture is hot, slightly thickened, but not set. Makes 5-6 portions.

Monika Howell (Mrs. Ned)
Upper School Faculty
Mother of Naomi '84
Monterey, California

PAVLOVA

6 egg whites
Pinch salt
2 cups sugar

1½ teaspoons vinegar
1½ teaspoons vanilla

Preheat oven to 300°. Beat the egg whites with the salt until stiff peaks form. Gradually beat in the sugar, a tablespoon at a time. Fold in the vinegar and vanilla. Place a sheet of foil, approximately 8-10 inches long on a cookie sheet. Draw a circle 7 inches in diameter on the foil. Spoon the egg white mixture onto the circle and build up the edges with a spatula. Make a well in the center. Bake in the coolest part of the oven 45-60 minutes. Turn off the oven, but do not remove the pavlova until the oven is cooled. (The center of the Pavlova should be slightly marshmallowy.) Transfer to a serving plate and, just before serving, top with whipped cream and sliced fruit. Strawberries and kiwis are very decorative. If passion fruit is available, this, to an Australian, is the piece de resistance.

Ursula Medanich (Mrs. James)
Mother of Valerie '85
Piedmont, California

KNEGGELAVERR
(Danish Lemon Pudding)

1 package unflavored gelatin
½ cup cold water
5 eggs, separated
¾ cup sugar

Juice of 1 lemon
1 teaspoon grated lemon rind
Pinch of salt

Soak gelatin in the cold water 5 minutes. Dissolve over boiling water; cool to lukewarm. In a large mixing bowl, beat the egg yolks well; add the sugar a bit at a time, beating constantly. Add the lemon juice and rind and continue beating. Pour in the cooled gelatin mixture and beat again. Add salt to the egg whites and beat until stiff; fold into the yolk mixture. Pour into a 1½ quart bowl and chill. Serve with whipped cream and maraschino cherries. Serves 6-8 hungry Danes.

Linda Madsen
Wife of Roy, Upper School Faculty
Marina, California

MELK TERT
(MILK TART)

3 cups milk
1 tablespoon butter
6 tablespoons sugar
3 tablespoons cornflour
   (cornstarch)
2 eggs, separated

1 teaspoon vanilla
1 teaspoon almond extract
Cinnamon
1 pre-baked tart crust

Boil the milk in the top of a double boiler with the butter. Add 4 table-spoons of the sugar and mix well. Mix together the remaining 2 table-spoons sugar and the cornflour and add enough additional cold milk to make a smooth consistency; blend in the egg yolks. Slowly stir the cornflour mixture into the boiled milk, stirring constantly; add the vanilla and almond extracts. In a small bowl, beat the egg whites until stiff. Remove the milk mixture from the heat and fold in the egg whites. Pour into a tart or pie crust and garnish with cinnamon. Bake in a 300° oven for 20 minutes.

Joy De la Porte
Salisbury, Zimbabwe
Africa

"Bread is used to accompany every meal in Italy and is bought daily. The practical reason for this recipe is to utilize leftover bread."

DOLCE DI PANE SECCO
(Old Dried Bread Dessert)

Butter
Dried French bread
Milk
Marmalade or sugar

Raisins
Fruit
2 eggs

Generously spread a layer of butter on the bottom and sides of a baking dish. Line the baking dish with the pieces of bread. Cover with enough warm milk to saturate the bread; let stand until the milk is absorbed. Spread with marmalade or sprinkle with sugar according to taste. Add raisins and fresh or dried fruits as desired. Beat the eggs, pour into the dish and combine with the other ingredients. Bake in a 350° oven for about 35 minutes until golden.

Guilia Gaglioti Fly
Mother of Gregory
Monterey, California

AUSTRALIAN LAMINGTONS

4 ounces butter
1 cup sugar
½ teaspoon vanilla
2 eggs

2 cups self rising flour
Pinch salt
1 cup milk

ICING:
12 tablespoons powdered sugar
2 tablespoons cocoa
1 dessert-spoon butter

1-2 tablespoons hot water
Dessicated coconut

Grease a cake tin and line the bottom with greased paper. Cream the butter with the sugar and vanilla until soft, white and fluffy. Add the eggs, one at a time, beating until well mixed. Fold in the sifted flour and salt alternately with the milk, then pour into the prepared tin. Bake in a moderate oven 35-40 minutes. Remove from tin and cool. When cool, cut into small blocks and cover as follows: Sift the powdered sugar and cocoa well. Melt the butter in the hot water, and add a little at a time to the sugar and cocoa until the mixture is thin enough to pour easily. Place one square of cake on the prongs of a fork and dip in chocolate icing, coating well. Drain, toss in coconut, then place on a plate until the icing is set. Repeat until cakes are covered. If the icing begins to set, warm slightly. NOTE: These squares can be cut in half and filled with cream and jam before coating for a more exotic sweet-meat.

Margaret Blackwell
Mother of Stella '73
Santa Cruz, California

On March 3, 1981, Malcolm Miller, official English guide-lecturer to Chartres Cathedral, addressed the student body at the Performing Arts Center on the art and architecture of Chartres Cathedral and the significance of both to the spiritual life.

Gourmet Cooking Seminar

One of the Senior Independent Seminars, led by Katie Clare Mazzeo, is the Gourmet Cooking Seminar, a two week survey of various aspects of cooking. The girls were presented with a variety of cuisines: French, Middle Eastern, Indian, Japanese, "Nouvelle Cuisine" Italian, diet menus and quite a few examples of clever home entertaining. Cooking is shown to be not only an art in itself, but a part of a way of living. Each person must create for herself and her family a type of space and a style of cooking — which may in fact be a combination of many types of menus — that fits her own lifestyle. No one kind of cooking is right or proper for everyone.

As a final product, the girls were asked to prepare and serve a dinner to the faculty members who had not only given generously of their time to this particular program, but who had advised girls in the Senior Independent Study Program. A sit-down, four course dinner was prepared and served for about 25 guests. Following is the menu for this dinner and the recipes of the dishes served.

****

Spinach Borek
Sushi
Hot Almonds
Marinated Olives

Grandmother Roy's Deviled Crab

Coq au Vin
Potato Baskets with Vegetables
Whole Wheat or White Rolls

Salad Raspberry Vinaigrette

Cream Puffs
Baklava
Cold Rum Souffle with Cherries
Fruit Macedoine in Pineapple

BOREK

1 pound phyllo leaves

¾ pound sweet butter

FOR A SPINACH FILLING:
2 (10 ounce) packages frozen
   chopped spinach
1 pound feta cheese
1 large onion, chopped
2-3 eggs, beaten

Pepper
Oregano, optional
Nutmeg, optional

FOR A CHEESE FILLING:
¾ pound feta cheese
2 cups ricotta or cottage cheese

1 egg, beaten
Pepper

FOR A MEAT FILLING:
1 pound ground beef
2 large onions, chopped
½ cup chopped parsley

3 teaspoons cumin
Salt
Pepper

For SPINACH FILLING, cook the spinach and drain well; combine with the cheese, onion, eggs, pepper, and, if desired, oregano and nutmeg. For CHEESE FILLING, combine the cheeses with the egg and season with pepper. For MEAT FILLING, saute the ground beef and onions; add the parsley and season with cumin, salt, and pepper. Drain well. TO ASSEMBLE, cover the bottom of a large cookie pan with 1/3 of the phyllo leaves, brushing each leaf with the melted butter. Spread the desired filling evenly over the buttered phyllo. Brush the remaining 2/3 phyllo leaves with butter and layer over the filling. Bake in a 350° oven for 45-60 minutes, until the pastry is crispy and slightly browned. Cut into small squares to serve. NOTE: For individual pastries, cut phyllo sheets into long strips, approximately 3-4" wide. Brush each strip with melted butter and place a small amount of filling at one end; fold in the long edges ½" or so to enclose the filling. Begin folding in triangles by bringing the bottom edge of the strip to meet the left side, forming a right angle. Continue folding back at right angles, buttering as you fold. When the end is reached, butter and tuck in remaining phyllo. Other individual shapes to fold are squares or rolls, which are less time consuming than triangles. Bake these 20-25 minutes in a 350° oven. You may also roll the full sheet of phyllo, forming a long "cigar", which may be cut into finger-size pieces after baking.

Perihan Shefik

In October, Santa Catalina hosts a sanctioned tennis tournament for Independent Schools of California girls' tennis teams. About 15 to 20 teams participate every year.

NORIMAKI-SUSHI

2 cups short-grain rice
¼ cup Sushi-Su (seasoned
  rice vinegar)
½ ounce dried mushrooms
4 tablespoons sugar
4 tablespoons soy sauce

4 tablespoons water
Salt
2 strips kompyo (dried gourd)
2 eggs, beaten
4 to 5 pieces nori (seaweed)
Pickled red ginger, optional

Cook the rice according to package directions. Turn the cooked rice immediately into a large bowl and carefully fold in the vinegar while fanning the rice to cool it quickly to prevent the rice from becoming soggy. Soak the mushrooms in water to cover until soft. Rinse, drain and cut into long, thin strips, discarding the stems. Put the sliced mushrooms into a small pan with 2 tablespoons each of the sugar, soy sauce, and water, and ½ teaspoon salt. Cover the pan and simmer until the water is evaporated and mushrooms are tender, about 5 minutes. Soak the kompyo in water to cover until soft. Rinse and drain. Put kompyo into small pan with the remaining sugar, soy sauce, and water, and a pinch of salt. Cover the pan and simmer until water is evaporated and kompyo is tender. Preheat frying pan to medium low, grease it well, pour in the eggs. When slightly browned, carefully turn to cook the other side. When done, remove to a piece of paper towel to absorb any excess grease. Cut into long, thin strips. Put about 1 cup of the rice on a piece of nori, which has been placed on a bamboo mat; with moist hands, pat down to about ½" thickness, spreading rice to edges of nori. Leave a border of 1" of the nori on the side closest to you and 1½" on the farthest side. In the middle of the rice mixture arrange a horizontal row of the cooked mushroom strips, kompyo, egg, and if desired, pickled red ginger. Holding the center ingredients down with fingers, lift the mat with thumbs and roll over until the near edge of the nori wrapper meets the far edge of the rice (not the edge of the wrapper). Pull mat away as you roll the nori and rice — use a little pressure to tighten roll. Press in any loose ingredients at ends of roll. Use a sharp, moistened knife to cut into slices about 1½" thick.

Barbara Johnson
Class of '83

HOT ALMONDS

Unblanched, unsalted almonds

Spread out the almonds on a cookie sheet and place in a very low pven for 2-3 hours. Cool slightly; serve while still warm.

Katie Clare Mazzeo

MARINATED OLIVES

Minced parsley
Fresh rosemary
2-3 tablespoons olive oil

Lemon juice
1 clove garlic, minced
1-2 (7 ounce) cans green olives

Combine the parsley, rosemary, olive oil, lemon juice and garlic. Mix vigorously and pour over the drained olives. Marinate at least 2 hours.

Katie Clare Mazzeo

GRANDMOTHER ROY'S DEVILED CRAB

3-4 slices of bacon
1 onion, finely chopped
½ cup celery, finely chopped
2-3 tablespoons butter
2-4 tablespoons flour
2-4 cups milk
Dash Worcestershire sauce
Pinch curry
Cayenne pepper

4 tablespoons tomato catsup
  or tomato paste
2 (6½ ounce) cans crab meat
1 cup small shrimp, optional
Fine breadcrumbs
Parmesan cheese
Butter
Paprika
Parsley for garnish

Saute the bacon slowly, remove, and drain on a paper towel; crumble. Saute the onions in the bacon drippings until transparent; add the celery and saute for 5 additional minutes. Drain and set aside. Make a white roux with the butter, flour and milk (substituting canned milk for 1 cup fresh makes a very creamy sauce). Flavor to taste with Worcestershire sauce, curry, pepper and catsup or tomato paste. Blend in the onions, celery, and bacon; add the crab meat, which has been rinsed with cold water, and the shrimp, if desired. Heat in the top of a double boiler; do not boil. Fill large clam shells or individual ramekins with the slightly cooled crab mixture. Cover completely with fine breadcrumbs and sprinkle with grated Parmesan cheese; dot with tiny pieces of butter. These can be refrigerated for several hours or overnight. Heat on a cookie tray in a 375° oven for 15-20 minutes and serve piping hot. Place on heat-proof pottery plates and garnish with paprika and a sprig of parsley. NOTE: This recipe may be served from a chafing dish with rice on the side as a main dish, in which case the sauce should be thinner. It can also be placed in a baking dish, covered with crumbs, and heated as a casserole. This recipe is for 6 people and uses canned crab, but fresh crab may be used. Tiny shrimps may be substituted for some of the crab.

Katie Clare Mazzeo

"This is an excellent dish for a large group of guests. It is started the day before and is easy to serve."

COQ AU VIN

16 chicken thighs, skinned	*4 tablespoons oil*
3 strips bacon	*2 cloves garlic*
½ cup small round white onions	*1-2 cubes sugar*
1 cup small round mushrooms	*Salt*
1 large "bouquet garni"	*Pepper*
1 tablespoon minced parsley	*1 bottle red wine (Beaujolais or*
4 tablespoons butter	*Burgundy)*
	2 tablespoons brandy

Salt, pepper and flour the chicken lightly; let stand. In a dutch oven, saute the bacon until crisp; cool and break into pieces. Pour the fat out of the dutch oven and replace with half the butter and half the oil. Saute the onions until transparent; remove and keep warm. Saute the mushrooms lightly; remove and keep warm. Use the other half of the butter and the oil and saute the thighs until lightly brown on both sides. (For that number it will have to be done in 2 batches.) Return the ingredients to the pan, add the bouquet garni and the garlic, cover and cook slowly for 30 minutes. Remove the meat and vegetables; keep warm. Bring all the juices to a fast boil. Flambe the 2 tablespoons brandy and pour in with the wine. Add the sugar and let boil for a few minutes until reduced by half. Taste the sauce and verify the seasoning. Return the meat and vegetables to the pan. Let cool and keep refrigerated until the next day. About 45 minutes before serving, place in the oven at 350° to warm. Serves 8.

Janine McGregor

POTATO BASKETS

Potatoes	*Oil*

Peel and grate the potatoes; cover with cold water. Heat the oil in a deep fat fryer. Drain and pat the potatoes dry with a paper towel. Separate a bird's nest frying basket. Line the larger basket with grated potatoes, replace the smaller basket and clip together to hold firmly. Fry in hot oil for several minutes until brown; drain. Repeat until all potatoes are used and the desired amount of baskets have been made. Fill baskets with vegetables of your choice.

Janine McGregor

SALAD WITH RASPBERRY VINAIGRETTE

Red cabbage
Head lettuce

Spinach
½ cup coarsely chopped walnuts

DRESSING:
4 tablespoons olive oil
2 tablespoons raspberry vinegar
1 egg

½ teaspoon Dijon mustard
Salt
Pepper

Use equal amounts of cabbage, lettuce and spinach. Shred the cabbage and lettuce and chop the spinach. Make a dressing by combing all the dressing ingredients; stir with a whisk just before serving and add the walnuts; pour over the salad.

Paola Berthoin

DINNER ROLLS

2 packages active dry yeast
1½ cups lukewarm milk
½ cup sugar
2 teaspoons salt

2 eggs
½ cup soft shortening
7-7½ cups sifted flour

Soak the yeast in ½ cup lukewarm water for 5 minutes without stirring. Mix together the milk, sugar and salt. Stir the yeast well and add to the milk mixture. Stir in the eggs and shortening. Mix in 3 cups of the flour, first using a spoon, then working with hands. Add the remaining flour, using the amount necessary to make it easy to handle. When the dough begins to leave the sides of the bowl, turn it out onto a lightly floured board to knead. Knead dough until it is smooth, elastic and doesn't stick to the board. Place in a greased bowl, turning once to bring the greased side up. Cover with a damp cloth and let rise in a warm, draft free spot until double. Punch down: Thrust fist into dough, pull edges into the center and turn completely over in the bowl. Let rise again until almost double in bulk. After the second rising, round up, cover and let rest 15 minutes, so the dough is easy to handle. Shape into balls. Place in greased pans. Let rise until light (15-20 minutes). Bake in a preheated 425° oven 12-20 minutes until golden brown.

Barbara Johnson
Class of '83

Austin Fagothey, S.J., Chairman of the Philosophy Department at University of Santa Clara, addressed the Philosophy seminar of senior students at Santa Catalina School on May 2, 1983, delighted that the subject had been introduced in the School curriculum.

WHOLE WHEAT DINNER ROLLS

2 cups water
¾ cup shortening or cooking oil
2 tablespoons molasses
3¾-4¼ cups all purpose or
    unbleached flour
3 cups whole wheat flour

½ cup sugar
2 teaspoons salt
2 packages active dry yeast
2 eggs

In a small saucepan, heat the water, shortening and molasses until very warm (120° - 130° F). In a large bowl, combine the warm liquid, 1 cup of the all-purpose flour, 1 cup of the whole wheat flour, and the remaining ingredients; beat 4 minutes at medium speed. By hand, stir in the remaining whole wheat flour and enough all-purpose flour to make a stiff dough. On a well-floured surface, knead the dough until smooth and elastic, about 5 minutes. Place in a greased bowl. Cover; let rise in a warm place until light and doubled in size, 45-60 minutes. Generously grease three 8-inch square pans or one 13 x 9-inch pan and one 8-inch square pan. Punch down dough. Divide dough into 36 pieces; shape into balls and place in the greased pans. Cover; let rise in a warm place until light and doubled in size, 30-45 minutes. Bake in a preheated 375° oven 15-20 minutes until golden brown. Immediately remove from pan. If desired, brush with melted butter.

Barbara Johnson
Class of '83

PATE A CHOUX
(Cream Puffs shaped like swans)

1 cup water
4 ounces butter
1 cup unbleached flour

4 eggs
Whipped cream flavored with
    vanilla

Bring the water and butter to the boiling point and add the flour all at once. Reduce heat and stir rapidly until the dough forms a ball. Remove from heat and let cool about 5 minutes. Transfer to a food processor equipped with the steel blade. Add the eggs and mix; cool. Fill a pastry bag with the dough. Use a 9 plain tip for the body and Number 1 for the necks. Squeeze the dough out, resting the tip on a cookie sheet, and end in a point to form the tail. The same technique is used for the necks on another baking sheet. Just draw the shape of the neck, starting with the part which is attached to the body. Bake the puffs in a preheated oven at 400° for 10 minutes; 375° for 10 minutes; 350° for another 10 minutes. Turn the oven off and let stand for another 10 minutes. Bake the necks for only 10 minutes or until lightly brown. Baking time is important. Cream puff dough will expand with heat and create a vacuum, which is filled with different possibilities, but if the crust is not hard enough it will collapse when cooling. To assemble the swans, saw off the top third of the swan body and fill the center with whipped cream flavored with vanilla. Cut the removed top in half lengthwise to make 2 wings. Insert the wings and the neck in the whipped cream.

Janine McGregor

BAKLAVA

1 pound sweet butter, melted
1 pound phyllo
4 cups finely chopped nuts
  (almonds, pistachio or walnuts)
4 cups sugar

¼ teaspoon cardamon
1½ cups water
Juice of ½ lemon
2 tablespoons rosewater

With a pastry brush, grease the bottom of a large deep cookie sheet. Fold or cut 4 layers of phyllo to fit the bottom of the pan, brushing each layer with butter as it is placed in the pan. Mix together the nuts, 1 cup of the sugar and the cardamon. Continue to butter and layer the sheets of phyllo dough, sprinkling each layer with a small amount of the nut mixture. Generously butter the top layer. Using a sharp knife, cut into a diamond pattern and bake slowly in a 275° oven for 1½ hours. While the baklava is baking, prepare a syrup by combining the water, the remaining sugar and lemon juice. Bring to a slow boil and cook until thickened, about 20 minutes. Cool and add the rosewater. After it is baked, pour the syrup over the baklava and let stand.

Perihan Shefik

The Santa Catalina Service League was formed in 1973 under the inspiration and guidance of Gloria Jansheski, class of 1954, to perform services for the school as proposed by the school administration. Blanche Brown, mother of Roe Brown, class of 1975, was the first president.

COLD RUM SOUFFLE

7 teaspoons gelatin	1¼ cups sugar
½ cup cold water	1-1/3 cups dark rum
11 eggs	4 cups whipping cream, whipped

Soften the gelatin in the cold water; set aside. Beat the eggs and the sugar until very white and fluffy and almost stiff. Add the rum to the softened gelatin and stir with a wisk. Fold the eggs into the whipped cream; fold in the rum-gelatin mixture. Place into 25 (6 ounce) dishes, tightly wrap and store in the refrigerator for a day. The souffle will keep for 10 days. Serve with cherry sauce.

CHERRY SAUCE

1 (29 ounce) can cherries	¼ cup cherry wine
½ cup sugar	2 tablespoons cornstarch
Cherry brandy	

Drain the cherries, reserving the juice; set cherries aside. Combine the juice with the sugar and some cherry brandy in a saucepan; bring to a boil. In a separate saucepan boil the cherry wine. Dissolve the cornstarch in a little water until smooth. Combine with the wine and pour into the brandy mixture. Add the cherries and bring to a second boil. Add additional brandy if the sauce is too thick. Cool.

Triples Restaurant
Monterey, California

The first "Daddy Dinner" was held in 1972 for Pre-school children and their fathers, and has been a tradition ever since, complete with a traditional menu, entertainment by the fathers and songs by the children.

Restaurants

"These may seem a little extravagant, but this recipe feeds from two to forty, and it is as much fun at a party as Western Onion. And it's worth the trouble to find a fresh truffle if you haven't had one."

MICHAEL'S EGG SALAD SANDWICHES

4 extra large Carmel Valley eggs
2 quarts boiling water
½ cup extra virgin California olive oil
½ lemon
Pinch cayenne pepper
2 egg yolks

1 medium truffle (fresh in late fall and winter)
1 chopped medium shallot
¼ cup chopped parsley
1 baguette sweet Monterey Baking Company Bread
¼ pound fresh Beluga Malossol caviar

Gently lower the 4 eggs into the boiling water, let boil 13 minutes, drain and cool under cold running water; peel. Make the dressings by whisking the egg yolks in a small bowl. Slowly dribble the oil, making sure it is completely absorbed before adding more. Whisk in a few tablespoons of lemon juice and the cayenne. Finely chop the truffle, the shallot and the parsley. Cut thin slices from the baguette and lightly toast under the broiler. Chop the eggs and toss gently in a bowl with the shallot, parsley and truffle. Cover and refrigerate for half an hour to let the flavors mingle. To serve, gently fold in the dressing, spoon onto the bread, and top with the caviar. Makes at least 36 heaping-tablespoon size sandwiches.

Michael Jones
A Moveable Feast Caterers
Carmel Valley, California

SMOKED SCOTTISH SALMON

2 ounces thinly sliced smoked salmon

Served on a leaf of green lettuce, garnished with red onion slices and a thin slice of twisted lemon, capers and a rosette of whipped cream cheese. Served with toast points and English ale. Serves 1.

Hyatt Del Monte
Monterey, California

GREEN DIP

2 tablespoons capers, chopped   1 ounce anchovy paste
2 tablespoons parsley, chopped   1½ tablespoons Dijon mustard
1½ teaspoons basil leaves, crushed 8 ounces sour cream
1 clove garlic, chopped and   8 ounces mayonnaise
   crushed

Combine all ingredients and blend well. Let sit approximately 12 hours before serving. Serve with assorted fresh relishes. Makes 1 quart.

The Carmel Butcher Shop
Carmel, California

VINAIGRETTE

1 jar Dijon mustard   ½ onion, pureed
1½ cups olive oil   1 tablespoon chopped parsley
1½ cups salad oil   Garlic
1 cup good vinegar   Salt
1 tablespoon tarragon   Pepper
1 tablespoon thyme   Dash white wine, pernod or
1 tablespoon basil   brandy

Place the mustard in a food processor and, with the machine running, gradually add the oil and vinegar alternately (the mixture should be thick and creamy). Add the remaining ingredients and process for 30 seconds. Keep cool. If refrigerated, let stand at room temperature until ready to serve.

A Catered Affair
Tahoe Vista, California

On October 3, 1981 Dame Judith Anderson visited the Santa Catalina campus to view the film *Medea,* the play written especially for her by Robinson Jeffers, and which was shown at our Performing Arts Center during the third annual Tor House Festival.

"Aioli covers a multitude of sins — it transforms cold foods, Valentine's roast beef, Monterey Bay prawns, lobster, artichokes . . ."

PETER'S AIOLI

4 medium to large cloves garlic
2 extra large Carmel valley egg
* yolks*
1½ cups extra-virgin California
* olive oil*

1-2 tablespoons chopped fresh
* basil*
Juice of 1 lemon

Mince the garlic very fine, add to the yolks and whisk thoroughly. Slowly dribble in the oil, whisking constantly. Add the basil and lemon juice to taste.

Peter Fox
A Moveable Feast Caterers
Carmel Valley, California

GREEN GODDESS SALAD DRESSING

1 cup mayonnaise
1 minced clove of garlic
2 teaspoons anchovy paste
¼ cup finely minced chives
¼ cup finely minced parsley

1 tablespoon lemon juice
1 tablespoon tarragon vinegar
½ teaspoon salt
Ground black pepper
½ cup sour cream

Combine all the ingredients. The above is the classic Green Goddess dressing created for George Arliss while staying in San Francisco at the Palace Hotel. Our recipe varies slightly since we use institutionally packaged premixed spices not available to the public. But start with the above and with a little experimentation, you will no doubt produce something as good or better than ours. If the dressing is too thick, substitute a little buttermilk for some of the sour cream. You may also want to increase the garlic, or lemon or add a bit of sugar. Yields about 2 cups.

The Clock Garden Restaurant
Monterey, California

A traditional event at Santa Catalina is the Day Student Party put on entirely by the day students for the boarders. It is a day of games, theme costumes, dinner and entertainment.

COMPANY STORE SALAD SUPREME

½ head red cabbage
½ head white cabbage
1 cucumber
1 carrot

1 tomato
1 small cauliflower
1 avocado

DRESSING:
¼ cup sherry vinegar
½ cup mayonnaise
1 tablespoon honey
½ cup Parmesan cheese
½ teaspoon lemon juice

1 clove garlic, minced
3 teaspoons Super Sauce mustard
½ teaspoon salt
½ teaspoon pepper
2 ounces parsley

Cut all vegetables into bite-sized pieces and combine in a salad bowl. Make the dressing by combining the vinegar, mayonnaise and honey until creamy. Add the remaining ingredients and blend until smooth. Pour over the salad and chill. Serves 6.

The Company Store
Pebble Beach, California

MEAT SALAD

1 pound cooked beef
Salt
Pepper
Thyme
1 green pepper

1 tomato
1 onion
6 spears dill pickles
½ bunch chopped parsley
Pickle juice

Slice the meat and season with salt, pepper, and thyme. Thinly slice the green pepper, tomato, onion and dill pickles. Layer all the ingredients alternately in an attractive bowl. Add enough pickle juice to barely cover the layers and garnish with slices of hard cooked eggs. Refrigerate 3 hours. NOTE: This is an excellent way to utilize leftover roast or prime rib.

Thunderbird Restaurant
Carmel Valley, California

On May 28, 1983, the Grammy Award winning blind pianist and composer George Shearing gave a concert in the Performing Arts Center on behalf of Guide Dogs for the Blind.

BUCHERON-SPINACH TART

1 rich pastry shell
3 tablespoons minced scallion
3 tablespoons sweet butter
1½ cups cooked, chopped spinach
¼ teaspoon nutmeg
¼ teaspoon salt

¼ teaspoon pepper
¼ pound fresh cream cheese
¼ pound Bucheron (French goat cheese)
4 eggs, separated
½ cup heavy cream
1/3 cup fresh bread crumbs

Prebake pastry shell (weighted down) at 425° for 12-15 minutes. Saute the scallion in 2 tablespoons of the butter. Add the drained spinach and spices, and cook, stirring, for 5 minutes. Transfer to a large bowl, and add the cream cheese and Bucheron. Add the egg yolks, one at a time, and the heavy cream; combine well. Beat the egg whites with a pinch of salt until stiff, and fold into the spinach mixture. Pour into the pastry shell, dot with 1 tablespoon butter and sprinkle with crumbs. Bake in a 375° oven for 25 minutes, till puffed and brown.

The Cheese Shop
Carmel, California

CHEESE AND TOMATO TART

1 pastry shell
3 large tomatoes
Salt
Pepper
3 tablespoons olive oil

½ pound Cantal cheese (can substitue fontina d'Aosta, Gouda, or Danish fontina)
1 rounded tablespoon tarragaon mustard (or add ½ teaspoon tarragon to 1 tablespoon Dijon mustard)

Prebake the pastry shell (lined with wax paper and weighed down with beans or rice) for 12-15 minutes in a 425° oven. Reduce the heat to 350°. Cut the tomatoes into thick slices, deseed and remove excess moisture; season well with salt and pepper and baste with olive oil. Marinate 15 minutes, turning 2 or 3 times. Spread mustard over the bottom of the shell and cover with cheese slices. Top with the tomatoes, brush with marinade, and bake for 30 minutes. Turn off the oven and let the tart remain 20 minutes longer. Suggestion: Add garlic, onion, oregano or basil to marinade.

The Cheese Shop
Carmel, California

STUFFED TOMATOES
1 Serving

Medium sized Tomato
STUFFING:

1 ounce mushrooms
1 ounce oyster mushrooms
1 ounce Shitake mushrooms
1 ounce Chanterelles mushrooms
1 whole shallot, peeled and finely chopped
½ clove garlic, mashed

½ teaspoon chopped parsley
3 ounces butter
1 tablespoon sherry wine
Salt
Pepper
Parmesan cheese

Coarsely chop the mushrooms. Saute the mushrooms, shallots and garlic in the butter; add the parsley and flame with the sherry. Season with salt and pepper. (Thicken with a roux if necessary). Core the tomato on the stem side and cut a ¼ inch cavity on the opposite end of the tomato. Place the cooled stuffing in a pastry bag with a star pastry tube; pipe the stuffing into the tomato. Sprinkle with Parmesan cheese and bake in a 350° oven. Serves 1.

Hyatt Del Monte
Monterey, California

CHICKEN CHOWDER SOUP

1 chicken
1 lemon
1 tablespoon basil
5 cups water
3 large potatoes, peeled and diced

3 ribs celery, diced
¼ cup half and half
16 ounces sour cream
Seasoned salt
Pepper

In a large kettle, place the chicken with enough water to cover, and boil with the lemon and basil until tender. Cool, bone, and cut the chicken into bite-sized pieces, reserving the broth. In a separate pot, place the 5 cups water, the peeled and diced potatoes, and the celery and cook until the potatoes are done. Add the chicken and reserved broth; blend in the half and half and the sour cream. Season with salt and pepper. NOTE: If desired, soup may be thickened with cornstarch, flour or potato buds.

A Little Pizza Heaven
Carmel, California

GREEK LEMON SOUP

2 quarts chicken rice soup
¼ pound butter
1 teaspoon powdered chicken
  stock

½ cup sauterne
3 egg yolks
Juice of 2 lemons

To the chicken rice soup, add the butter, powdered chicken stock and sauterne; simmer gently for 20-30 minutes. In a separate bowl, beat until frothy the egg yolks and lemon juice. When ready to serve, whisk 1 cup of the hot soup into the egg-lemon mixture, then pour all back into the soup kettle. Serve immediately garnished with thin slices of lemon or finely chopped parsley. By adding extra rice, as the Greeks do, this makes a fine one-course meal. Serves 8.

The Clock Garden Restaurant
Monterey, California

CREAM OF OYSTER SOUP

1 yellow onion, peeled and
  finely chopped
½ pound butter
½ cup flour
1 quart half and half
1 pint oysters

1 cup dry sherry
1 bay leaf
½ cup chopped parsley
Pinch cayenne pepper
Salt

Cook the onions in the butter until golden; add the flour and cook for a few minutes. In a separate saucepan, heat the half and half to a scald and stir into the roux. Add the bay leaf. In a saucepan, poach the oysters and sherry for 5 minutes and add to cream. Heat to just under a boil. Season with cayenne pepper and salt; top with minced parsley. Serve with oyster crackers. Makes 6-8 servings.

Hyatt Del Monte
Monterey, California

BONGO-BONGO SOUP

1½ quarts half and half
8 large Pacific oysters
½ onion, diced
1 pound chopped frozen spinach,
  thawed
1 clove fresh garlic
1 tablespoon Aromat seasoning

1 tablespoon salt
½ teaspoon ground white pepper
1/8 teaspoon Cayenne pepper
1 ounce Pernod
2 tablespoons cornstarch

Place all ingredients, except cornstarch, in a food blender; blend until very fine. Place in a saucepan and bring slowly to a boil. Add the cornstarch mixed with a little cold water, whisk in with a whip and remove from heat. It should be of medium thickness. Top with whipped cream, or leave plain. Serve with sour dough French bread or lavosh crackers. Serves 6-8.

Mark Thomas Outrigger
Monterey, California

OYSTERS BELVEDERE

24 small to medium-sized oysters
1 cup flour
1 egg, beaten
1 teaspoon finely chopped parsley
1 tablespoon lemon juice
Breadcrumbs, finely ground

1 tablespoon grated Parmesan cheese
½ teaspoon finely chopped sweet basil
Scarpara Sauce
4 thin slices French bread, halved, buttered and toasted

Bread the oysters by dipping first into flour, then into beaten egg mixed with the chopped parsley and lemon juice, then into finely ground breadcrumbs mixed with Parmesan cheese and basil. Grill on a lightly oiled grill or in a saute pan until just golden in color; remove. Place grilled oysters into Scarpara Sauce and simmer from 5 to 7 minutes; remove to serving plate. Serve immediately with toasted halves of French bread.

SCARPARA SAUCE

Prepare this sauce a day ahead to allow time for the flavors to blend properly.

3-4 pounds fresh tomatoes, ground or blended smooth
1 teaspoon finely chopped fresh sweet basil
1 teaspoon lemon juice
1 ounce white wine

1 ounce dry sherry
1 cup cold water, if needed for proper consistency
2 teaspoons finely chopped parsley

Combine all ingredients except water and parsley. Bring to a boil, then lower heat to simmer and continue cooking 12-14 hours, stirring occasionally. Add water ONLY if necessary. Add parsley during the last half hour of cooking as adding the parsley too early will destroy the texture of the seasoning and will darken the sauce.

Bertolucci's
Pacific Grove, California

FRUTTA DI MARE

1 eschallot
2 cloves garlic
½ cup fresh parsley
1 medium onion
2 ounces olive oil
3 ounces butter
4 (16 ounce) cans tomato sauce
  or 36 fresh pear tomatoes,
  peeled and seeded

1½ pounds clams with broth
1½ dozen prawns, peeled and
  deveined
12 washed mussels
1 pound cleaned calamari
8-10 scallops, cut in halves
2-3 pounds cooked pasta

Together, chop the eschallot, garlic, parsley and onion; saute in the olive oil and butter. Add the tomato sauce or fresh tomatoes, if desired, and cook over low heat for 45 minutes. To cook the clams, saute 1 teaspoon garlic in 1 tablespoon butter for 2 minutes. Add 4 cups water and the washed clams; cook for 5 minutes. Remove the clams, reserving the broth. Shuck the clams and add to the tomato sauce with the clam broth; add the prawns, mussels, calamari and scallops and cook for an additional 20 minutes. Serve over cooked pasta. Serves 6-8.

Alioto's
San Francisco, California

LINGUINI PESCADORI

8 scallops (20 to a pound)
8 prawns (15 to a pound)
2 tablespoons olive oil
2 whole tomatoes, seeded,
  peeled, crushed
1 tablespoon fresh basil
1 tablespoon garlic, chopped fine
4 sprigs parsley, chopped

8 fresh clams
¼ cup water
16 ounces thin noodles, cooked
  al dente
2 tablespoons sweet butter,
  unsalted
2 tablespoons heavy cream
1 tablespoon Parmesan cheese
Salt

Saute the scallops and peeled prawns in 1 tablespoon of the olive oil in one pan. In another pan, put the remaining tablespoon of olive oil and add the tomatoes, basil, garlic and parsley. Put in the clams and add ¼ cup water. Let simmer until clams open, then combine all in one pan. After the noodles are cooked and drained, add sweet butter and heavy cream; toss until hot and blended. Put noodles on a platter, and remove mixture with a slotted spoon and place on top of the noodles. Sprinkle with Parmesan cheese. Serves 4.

The Rogue
Monterey, California

PRAWNS ST. JAMES

18 prawns or jumbo shrimp
Beer
1½ pounds crab meat
¾ cup lemon juice
1 cup grated Parmesan cheese
1 cup cracker meal or fine bread
  crumbs

5 egg yolks
1 cup chopped parsley
6 hard-cooked eggs, chopped
1 cup shredded Swiss cheese
1 cup Hollandaise Sauce

Shell prawns and split them open, butterfly style. Marinate at room temperature in enough beer to cover. Combine all other ingredients except the Hollandaise for the stuffing. Preheat oven to 350°. Drain prawns and place them in a shallow casserole. Divide the stuffing among them and top each with 1 teaspoon of Hollandaise. Bake for 20-30 minutes.

HOLLANDAISE

10 egg yolks
Juice of 1 lemon
1 dash Tabasco sauce

1 dash Lea and Perrins
2 pounds butter, melted

Combine the egg yolks and lemon juice in the top of a double boiler. Beat with a wire whisk constantly while cooking over hot water (not boiling) until the mixture thickens. Remove from heat and stir in the butter and remaining ingredients.

The Sardine Factory
Monterey, California

Mrs. Trevenen James of London, guide in England on the great houses and garden tours, presented a slide-show and lecture on the architecture of 13th Century London to our student body, faculty and the Monterey community in our Performing Arts Center, on October 29, 1981.

SEAFOOD CASSEROLE "NEWBURG"

8 ounces scallops
8 ounces lobster meat, cut in 1
inch pieces
8 ounces halibut, cut in 1 inch
pieces
8 ounces shrimp meat
10 prawns, peeled and deveined
10 crab cocktail claws
10 medium mushrooms,
quartered

3 ounces melted butter
3 ounces brandy
1/8 ounce paprika
4 ounces dry sherry
1½ pints Cream Sauce (see note)
8 ounces half and half
Salt
Pepper
10 fleurons for garnish

Lightly saute the fish and the mushrooms in the melted butter; add the brandy and flambe. Sprinkle with paprika, add the sherry and reduce. Stir in the cream sauce and the half and half and season with salt and pepper; let simmer for a short time to finish cooking the fish. Place in 5 individual casseroles, garnish with 2 fleurons each, and sprinkle with fresh parsley. NOTE: To make a cream sauce, melt 3 ounces butter; add 3 ounces flour to make a roux. Stir in 2 pints scalded milk, simmer for 5 minutes and strain.

Crow's Nest
Monterey Holiday Inn
Monterey, California

VITELLO DUCALE

Prepare Fish Stock and Fish Sauce in advance.

8 scallops or slices of veal, 3-4
ounces each
Salt
Pepper
Pinch finely chopped parsley
Pinch finely chopped oregano
4 jumbo prawns, shelled, cleaned
and butterflied, with shells reserved

1 cup flour
1 egg, beaten
Fish Sauce
8 mushroom caps
1 ounce brandy or sherry
Garnish: 4 sprigs parsley

Lightly pound veal scallops and sprinkle each with salt, pepper, parsley and oregano. Dip prepared prawns into flour, then into the beaten eggs and grill quickly on a lightly oiled grill or in a saute pan until just golden. Remove. Place 1 grilled prawn on top of each of 4 slices of veal. Cover with remaining slices of veal and steady each serving with tooth picks on all 4 sides. Dip each serving into flour, coating both sides, then quickly in and out of egg batter. Grill on both sides until golden. Remove and hold. Line bottom of individual casseroles or 1 large baking dish with half of the Fish Sauce. Layer veal servings on top of the sauce. Garnish with mushroom caps and top with remaining sauce. Just before placing in the oven, pour brandy or sherry over the top. Bake in a preheated 375° oven for 15-20 minutes. Garnish with sprigs of parsley and serve.

FISH SAUCE

¾ cup butter	Pepper
¾ cup flour	Fish Stock
Salt	

Melt the butter and mix in the flour to make a roux. Add salt and pepper to taste. Blend over low heat for at least 5 minutes, but do not brown. Slowly pour in hot Fish Stock, stirring to blend and then cooking rapidly for 5 minutes until creamy. Strain through a sieve to assure that the sauce is smooth.

DINO'S FISH STOCK

1 pound filet of sole or other white fish	3 bay leaves
	4 ounces white wine
Prawn shells	4 ounces cooking sherry
1 onion, cut in quarters	1 to 1½ gallons cold water
2 stalks celery	
1 lemon, cut in half	

Bring all ingredients to a boil. Reduce the heat and simmer for at least 4 hours, reducing stock to approximately 7 cups. Strain.

Bertolucci's
Pacific Grove, California

A visit to the King Tut exhibit in San Francisco's De Young Museum was made by alumnae, students, faculty and parents and friends of the School on 20, 1979 for a private showing. Close to 1000 attended the exhibit.

COURT BOUILLON SAUCE AND FILET OF SOLE

COURT BOUILLON:

1 cup water
1 cup dry white wine
2 shallots
Clove
Thyme

Parsley
Salt
Pepper
¼ lemon
4 filets of sole

SAUCE:

2 tablespoons salted butter
2 tablespoons flour
1½ cups Court Bouillon
¾ cup heavy cream
Salt
Pepper

½ cup crab meat
½ cup scallops
½ cup bay shrimp
1 cup mushrooms
2 tablespoons Calvados

Combine all the ingredients for the "Court Bouillon" in a saute pan. Bring to a boil and simmer 15 minutes. Strain the broth and, keeping it at a low boil, put in the rolled filet of sole. Cook for 4 to 6 minutes. Remove the sole and place in a baking dish. To prepare the sauce, melt the butter over low heat in a heavy saucepan. Stir in the flour gradually, stirring constantly with a whisk. Slowly stir in 1½ cups of the "Court Bouillon" and cook 10 minutes. In another skillet, saute in butter the scallops, shrimp and crabs as well as the mushrooms. Flambe, with Calvados, and pour the sauce over it. Add the cream, stirring constantly. Correct the seasoning. Pour the sauce evenly over the filet of sole and glaze under the broiler. Serves 4.

Pedro de la Cruz
Club XIX, The Lodge at Pebble Beach
Pebble Beach, California

ROASTED PACIFIC RED SNAPPER

2 (3 pound) or 4
  (1½ pound) red snappers,
  cleaned and scaled, heads left on
8 small cloves garlic
½ cup olive oil
Salt
Pepper

½ teaspoon dried thyme
1½ cups fresh anise tops or
  fennel or 1 tablespoon aniseed
2 cups fish or chicken broth
4 ounces Pernod
2 ounces cognac
Parsley

Trim fins from fish. Insert garlic into fish backs. Brush inside and outside of fish with the olive oil; sprinkle with salt and pepper. Sprinkle outside of fish with thyme; fill fish cavities with fresh anise or aniseed.

Place the fish on an oiled rack in a roasting pan. Mix the broth, Pernod and cognac; pour into pan under the fish. Cover tightly with aluminum foil. Bake in a 475° oven for 15-25 minutes, depending on fish size. Remove foil and bake 10 minutes longer. Serve fish with pan juices and garnish with parsley. Makes 4-6 servings.

Whaling Station Inn Restaurant
Monterey, California

POACHED DOVER SOLE

2 pounds Dover sole
2 shallots, chopped
¼ teaspoon salt

1/8 teaspoon white pepper
2 cups dry white wine
6 small crayfish (boil 5 minutes)
Light Cheese and Wine Sauce

Wash and lay sole filets skin side up. Sprinkle filets with the chopped shallots, salt and white pepper, and roll firmly. Line in a baking dish. Pour the wine over the filets and cover lightly with foil. Poach in moderate oven (350-375°) for 20-25 minutes. Drain and serve covered with sauce. Garnish with crayfish and parsley or watercress. Makes 4-6 servings.

LIGHT CHEESE AND WINE SAUCE

¼ cup chopped onion
2 shallots
¼ pound butter
½ cup flour
1 cup dry white wine

1 cup heavy cream
1 cup Swiss or Gruyere cheese
¼ cup Parmesan cheese
Salt
White pepper

Cook the onion and shallots in the butter until transparent, being careful not to burn the butter. Add the flour and cook slowly for 2-3 minutes. Using a whisk, add the wine and blend well; Add the cream and cheeses and continue to whisk. Heat until almost boiling. Season with salt and white pepper (use a little of the poaching liqueur if desired consistency is not reached). Ladle over the poached filets. Serves 4-6.

Hyatt del Monte
Monterey, California

"Delicate lobster mousse rolled in a blanket of thinly sliced provimi veal sauteed with white wine, shallots, mushrooms and herbs, capped with cream sauce."

PAUPIETTES DE VEAU LANGOUSTINE

LOBSTER MOUSSE:
12 ounces lobster meat, uncooked ¾ cup heavy cream
3 ounces shrimp meat, cooked   ½ teaspoon salt
3 egg whites   ½ teaspoon cayenne pepper

Grind lobster meat and shrimp meat in a food processor until very fine. Then add the egg whites while the processor is still going, and then the heavy cream is gradually worked into the mixture. Add salt and cayenne pepper. Place the whole mixture in a bowl, and mix thoroughly with a wooden spatula. The mixture must become thick enough to be shaped.

PAUPIETTES DE VEAU:
1½ pounds of provimi veal loin

Slice the veal loin into 12 equal slices and place them (2 at a time) between a plastic film and pound until slices are thin and approximately 3 x 5 inches in size. Taking one piece at a time and placing approximately 2½ ounces of the lobster mousse on one end of the veal, roll into a cylinder shape. You should have a total of 12 paupiettes when all is finished.
when all is finished.

PAUPIETTES DE VEAU LANGOUSTINE COOKING PROCEDURE:
2 cups sliced mushrooms   1 tablespoon shallots
1 cup flour for dusting   1 cup dry white wine
4 tablespoons butter   2 cups heavy cream

Flour the 12 paupiettes, place in a very hot saute pan with the butter already melted in it. Brown the veal, add the shallots, mushrooms and white wine. Reduce by 1/3 and then add the cream. Lower the heat and simmer for 15 minutes with the saute pan covered. Remove from the pan and place the 12 paupiettes in a heated serving tray, then pour the cream sauce on top. Serves 6.

Anton and Michel
Carmel, California

The Annual Retreat is held for 2½ days and is a time for renewal and a drawing together of the entire Santa Catalina community. Father English comes from the East Coast to participate in the retreat.

FILET OF PORK WELLINGTON

4-6 ounces pork tenderloin,
    completely trimmed

FILLING:
2 ounces veal
2 ounces pork (end cut of
    tenderloin)
1 ounce chopped mushrooms
Fresh breadcrumbs (1 slice
    white bread)
1 egg

3 ounces puff pastry dough
1 ounce goose liver

½ cup fresh cream
1 ounce brandy
Thyme
Salt
Pepper
Parsley

Cook the pork until medium; cool. Make the filling: Finely grind the veal, pork, mushrooms and crumbs. Using a food processor or blender, process the meat mixture with the egg, cream, brandy and seasonings. Roll out the pastry dough into a 6 x 6 inch square. On the bottom portion of the rolled out dough, place the goose liver and half of the filling, cover with the remaining filling and fold the dough to encompass the meat. Place on a baking sheet, seam side down, and bake in a 375° oven for 45 minutes. Serves 1.

Hyatt del Monte
Monterey, California

VEAL WITH COARSE GRAIN MUSTARD SAUCE

8 ounces veal loin
Flour
1 tablespoon olive oil
1 medium shallot, minced
2 ounces dry white wine
2 ounces heavy cream

2 tablespoons coarse grain
    mustard
Chopped parsley
1 tablespoon butter
Salt
Pepper

Cut the veal into 4 slices and pound to ¼ inch thickness. Dredge in flour, shaking off the excess. Heat the olive oil in a pan until almost smoking. Place the veal in the pan and saute 30 seconds on each side; remove to a platter and keep warm. Add the shallots to the pan and saute until translucent. Pour in the wine and reduce to half; blend in the heavy cream and reduce. Using a small whip, incorporate the mustard and parsley into the sauce. Add the butter and season with salt and pepper. Spoon the sauce over the veal. Serves 2. NOTE: This sauce may also be used with shrimp or chicken breasts.

Ventana
Big Sur, California

ESCALOPES DE VEAU DU CHEF

4 ounces thinly sliced veal
Flour
2 ounces butter

1 teaspoon minced shallots
1 fresh lemon
Sprinkle of chopped parsley

Saute the lightly floured veal in butter; drain the excess butter; add the shallots. Squeeze the juice of the lemon over the veal to loosen the pan juices. Garnish with butter and chopped parsley. Serves 1.

The Covey Restaurant at Quail Lodge
Carmel Valley, California

"Penelope R. Williams, Class of 1964, sent this recipe from her restaurant. It has appeared in L.A. Magazine, Gourmet and Bon Appetit."

CHICKEN WITH CHIVES

1 bunch fresh watercress
2 ounces butter
6 ounces shallots, peeled and
   chopped
3 bay leaves
½ teaspoon thyme
1 teaspoon marjoram
6 boneless double chicken
   breasts with skin

Freshly ground salt
Freshly ground pepper
1 pint chicken broth
½ pint whipping cream
6 ounces unsalted butter
Chopped chives
Baby carrots for garnish

Remove the leaves from the watercress and plunge into well salted boiling water and cook for 3 minutes. Pour through a strainer and cool under cold running water. Let drain. Puree in a food processor or blender. Melt the butter in a large shallow pan with a tight fitting lid. Add 2 ounces of the shallots and herbs and cook slowly without color for a few minutes. Season the chicken breasts inside and out with salt and pepper. Tie loosely with string in the middle so they form a nice shape. Place the chicken carefully on top of the shallots and herbs and cover with the lid. Cook slowly over the lowest heat until chicken becomes a little firm to the touch, about 1 hour. Remove the chicken from the pan, scrape off any shallots that cling, and keep warm. Add the chicken broth to the shallots and simmer until almost dry. Add the whipping cream and reduce over low heat to a ½ pint total quantity. Pass this thru a fine strainer and reheat. Using a balloon whip, add the 6 ounces of unsalted butter in small pieces, one at a time. The butter must be at room temperature and you must allow each piece to be thoroughly incorporated before adding the next bit. Remove from heat and check seasoning and keep warm. DO NOT AT ANYTIME BOIL

THIS SAUCE!! To serve, add the watercress puree to the above sauce and pour into 6 hot plates. Sprinkle generously with chopped chives. Remove skin from the chicken, slice lengthwise and arrange on top of the sauce. Garnish with baby carrots. Serves 6.

Penelope's
Santa Barbara, California

"Everyone seems to own a Weber barbecue kettle these days. Nothing cooks roasts, steaks, even turkeys so well with such great flavor. Valentine is our 'pit-master', and here is his technique."

VALENTINE'S ROAST BEEF

*1 New York strip
(10-12 pounds), trimmed
Weber or Happy Cooker kettle
barbecue*

*3-4 pounds hardwood charcoal
Fresh rosemary, sage, or
or marjoram*

In the center of the kettle, build a teepee fire with crumpled newspaper and lots of small kindling. An hour and a half before serving, open the bottom vents of the kettle and light the fire. A fast, hot fire is needed to get the charcoal going. In 15-20 minutes, when the charcoal is burning nicely, shake down the pile and gently break up and distribute the larger chunks evenly around the bottom of the kettle. Replace the grill and kettle lid. Open the lid vents all the way and wait a few minutes for the grill to heat and the fire to even out.

Half an hour before serving, place the roast, fat side down, on the grill. Throw on the coals a few branches of fresh rosemary, sage or marjoram. Leave the lid off just until the fat starts to flame. Replace the lid, close the lid vent, and two of the bottom vents. Wait 10 minutes, and, armed with a wine bottle full of water, open the lid. If the fat flames, toss on a little water. Turn the roast, and again do not replace the lid until the coals are burning nicely. Leave the top vent open enough for the fire to breathe.

After 10 minutes, check the fire and the doneness of the roast. (For medium, the tines of a roasting fork left in the roast for 10 seconds or so should be no warmer than a baby bottle.) If not done, shake down the fire gently, and open more vents, close the lid, and wait. With a good fire, a New York strip should take no more than 30 minutes. It doesn't hurt to let the roast rest on the cutting board for 10 minutes before serving.

Valentine Fine
A Moveable Feast Caterers
Carmel Valley, California

BRAN-PECAN MUFFINS

2 cups flour
2 tablespoons sugar
¼ teaspoon salt
1¼ teaspoons baking soda
2 tablespoons coarsely grated
  orange rind
1½ cups bran

2/3 cup chopped pecans
1/3 cup raisins
2 cups buttermilk
1 beaten egg
½ cup dark molasses
3 tablespoons melted butter

In a large bowl, sift together the flour, sugar, salt and baking soda. Add the orange rind, bran, chopped pecans and raisins and mix well. In a separate bowl, beat together the buttermilk, egg, molasses and melted butter; add to the dry ingredients and stir just enough to mix. Fill greased muffin pans about ¾ full and bake in a preheated 350° oven 25-35 minutes or until done. Cool 5 minutes before removing from pan. NOTE: To reheat, wrap loosely in foil and place in a 450° oven for 5 minutes. Yields 16 2-inch muffins.

The Clock Garden Restaurant
Monterey, California

CHEESECAKE

CRUST:
1 cup sifted flour
¼ cup sugar
1 teaspoon grated lemon peel

½ cup butter
1 slightly beaten egg yolk
¼ teaspoon vanilla

CHEESE FILLING:
5 (8 ounce) packages cream
  cheese
¼ teaspoon vanilla
¾ teaspoon grated lemon peel
1¾ cups sugar

3 tablespoons flour
¼ teaspoon salt
4 or 5 eggs (1 cup)
2 egg yolks
¼ cup whipping cream

For the crust, combine the flour, sugar and lemon peel. Cut in the butter until the mixture is crumbly. Add the egg yolk and vanilla and blend well. Pat 1/3 of the dough on the bottom of a 9-inch springform pan (sides removed). Bake in a 400° oven about 8 minutes or until golden; cool. Attach sides of the springform pan to the bottom and butter; pat remaining dough on the sides to a height of 1¾ inches. For the filling, let the cream cheese soften at room temperature, 1-1½ hours; beat until creamy. Add the vanilla and lemon peel. In a separate bowl, combine the sugar, flour and salt; blend into the cream cheese mixture. Add the eggs and yolks, one at a time, beating after each addition just enough to blend. Gently stir in the cream. Pour into the crust-lined pan. Bake in a 450° oven for 12 minutes; reduce heat to 300° and bake 55 minutes longer. Cool. Loosen sides with a spatula after ½ hour; remove sides at end of 1 hour. Cool 2 hours longer.

Hog's Breath Inn
Carmel, California

CHOCOLATE MARBLE CHEESECAKE

CHEESECAKE:
2 pounds cream cheese
1½ pounds ricotta cheese
2 cups sugar
½ teaspoon vanilla

1½ teaspoons gelatin
1 cup heavy cream
8 egg yolks

CHOCOLATE GANACHE:
6 ounces unsweetened chocolate   *2½ ounces heavy cream*
6 ounces semi-sweet chocolate

Beat cheeses and sugar in mixer until smooth and liquified. Add gelatin to heavy cream and heat *gently* until dissolved. In a bowl over a double boiler combine egg yolks and gelatin mixture, and continue to heat and stir until thick. Combine with the cheese mixture. Pour into a lightly oiled mold. Make the chocolate ganache by grinding the chocolates in a food processor. Bring the cream to a boil and slowly add to chocolate until smooth. Stir 1 cup of the chocolate ganache into the cheesecake for the marble effect. Chill until set, 3-5 hours. To unmold the cheesecake, set mold in hot water for 10 seconds and turn onto a rack or grate. Cover the cheesecake with the remaining chocolate ganache and allow to set in the refrigerator ½ hour. Remove to a serving plate and cut with a knife dipped in warm water. Serve with Coffee Sauce. Serves 10-12.

COFFEE SAUCE

3 cups heavy cream
¼ cup Kahlua

¼ cup Tia Maria
1 teaspoon fresh coffee grounds

Combine in a food processor or mixer at high speed until you reach a smooth consistency.

Penelope's
Montecito, California

Contributors

ADAMS, JEANNE
ADAMS, VIRGINIA
AGHAZADEH, MANIJEH
ALLDRIN, MRS. CALEB
ANDERSON, DOROTHY
ANDERSON, JULIE
ANDERSON, KATHLEEN
ANDERSON, MARIAN
ANDERSON, RUSSELL
ANDERSON, SHIRLEY
ANKA, ANNE
ANKA, PAUL
ANSEL, ROSE MARIE
ARANGO, PENELOPE COREY
ARKLEY, CHERIE PETTIT
ARMANASCO, AUGUST
ATHA, MRS. DONALD
AUCKENTHALER, JANE
BAGGIOLINI, ANNE
BARBER, SUSAN & KENT
BARG, NANCY
BARMBY, GAIL FRICK
BARONE, ADA
BARRES, RUTH
BEACHAM, GRACE
BEARDSLEY, LOUISE
BEAUMONT, ROBERT
BECKER, BEVERLEE
BECKER, SHIRLEY
BECKING, PAMELA
BEDFORD, KIT NELSON
BEESLEY, ARLIENE
BELDEN, CRESSEY JOY
BELDEN, MARIE CRESSEY
BERNDT, AMY
BEROLZHEIMER, ANNE
BERRIEN, MRS. PRICE
BERTELSEN, BONNIE MCWHORTER
BERTHOIN, PAOLA
BETTENCOURT, APRIL ANDERSON
BETTENCOURT, JERRY
BISCEGLIA, JULIE
BISGROVE, MARGORIE
BLACKWELL, MARGARET
BLACKWOOD, MRS. WILLIAM
BLAIR, SHERRY

BROOKS, MARGARET
BRUNO, JANET
BRYANT, WALLY
BUFFINGTON, JANE
BUTTERFIELD, MRS. BILL
BYERS, SUZANNE
BYRNE, TERRY
CANTIN, PAULINE
CARRINGTON, KATHERINE HAYES
CARTER, JANE
CHAMLIAN, CHRISTA
CHANEY, MARIANNE WOLFSEN
CHRISTIE, ELLEN
CHRISTIE, IVAN
CLARK, HILARY WICKERSHAM
CLING, MARY JEAN QUINLAN
CLORAN, ALICE
COHEN, JOANNE
CONIGLIO, ALYSON
CONIGLIO, PAT
COOPER, DANIELLE CHAVY
COOPER, MRS. M. B.
CORRELL, SADIE
COURNEEN, JOAN
COVERT, KAY
COVERT, ROBERT
CRAFT, KATE
CRANE, NANCY
CRAWFORD, AMY
CRAWFORD, ELIZABETH
CRISTOFARO, LINDA
CRISTOFARO, NANCY
BLEVENS, BARBARA
BONDESON, PATRICIA
BONILLA, MARGARET DONLIN
BONORA, EMMA
BOSWELL, WINTHROP
BOWDEN, KATHI
BOWDEN, KIM
BOWMAN, LUCILLE
BOYLE, JUNE
BOYLE, VIRGINIA
BRAZINSKY, APRIL
BRAZINSKY, JENNIFER
BRAZINSKY, JOHN
BRAZINSKY, TERRI

DALTON, ELIZABETH
DANIEL, CHARLOTTE
DAVIS, KITTY
DAY, JANE
DE ASTIVIA, PATRICIA
DE BAUBIGNY, GRETCHEN
DE FOREST, DENISE LE BLANC
DE GUAJARDO, LUCIA
DE LA PORTE, JOY
DEGNAN, MARIE
DEL PIERO, TINA TOMLINSON
DELANEY, PAT
DELIANTONI, NANCY
DEMING, MARSHA
DEMING, MRS. JOSEPH
DEVOTO, CLEO
DICKIE, MARY ANN
DICKMAN, JACQUELINE
DIDION, GLORIA
DOIG, CATHERINE
DOUGLAS, PENELOPE
DRYDEN, ARLENE
DUCATO, CANDY HAZARD
DUDLEY, BEV HARMAN
DUDLEY, LON
DUFLOCK, MARGARET
DUGAN, MELANIE
EASTMAN, GIGI VINCENZ
EGBERT, MEREDITH NINO
ENGLISH, JENNIFER
EPPLER, JEANETTE
ERICKSON, CAROLE
ESCHER, PAULA SULLIVAN
ESTRADA, CAROLYN SULLIVAN
ESTRADA, TERESA
EVANS, MARIAN
EVERSOLE, NORMA
FINNEY, SUZANNE TOWNSEND
FISCHER, KATHLEEN MCPHARLIN
FLY, GIULIA GAGLIOTI
FORD, MARY MALCOLM
FOSTER, MRS. JACOB
FOSTER, PATI
FRANCESCONI, MABEL
FRASSE, WENDY MILLER
FRICK, LINDA
FRICK, MARGARET ANN
GALLAWAY, PAMELA DUPRATT
GAMBILL, PHYLLIS BURNETTE
GAMBLE, JANE MCFARLANE

GANTNER, SUSAN VERBLE
GARDNER, ELLIE HUTCHESON
GARRIHY, VELVA
GASCOIN-RUFFIE, LETICIA
GAZLEY, MARY
GILL, BETH
GIRARD, GILL M. III
GLADSTONE, ROBERTA
GOODFELLOW, JANE HOWARD
GOODRICH, TINA
GOULDEN, JULIA BRAZINSKY
GRANT, CARY
GRAY, NINA DAVIS
GREITEN, KATHLEEN HARMAN
GROW, SHIRLEELYNN ARNAUDO
GRUPE, ANNE
GRYPE, JAN
GUY, BRENDA
GUY, HOLLY
HALE, DORIS
HALL, LINDA
HANSON, ANN CRAIG
HARRIS, LOUISE
HARVEY, CHARLENE
HATHORN, PRISCILLA
HAUSERMAN, JOAN WEAVER
HEYMANN, JANINE
HICKEY, LOIS
HOLL, MARY MUNHALL
HOLL, STEPHEN
HOLODILOFF, FAINA
HOLODILOFF, FRANCES
HOWARD, HELEN
HOWARD, LYNNE
HOWELL, MONIKA
HUGHES, ETHELYNE
HULL, SUSAN
HUMISTON, CAROLYN
HUNTER, JOAN
HUPERT, LILLY
IBABAO, LILIA
IMPEY, MARIAN GUIRY
JANKO, ALBERT BELA
JEKEL, PAT (JEKEL VINEYARD)
JENNINGS, MARGIE
JENSEN, LEILA
JOHNSEN, MARTHA
JOHNSON, BARBARA
JOHNSON, DIANNE
JOHNSON, EMIKO

JOHNSON, KRISTI
JOHNSON, LINDA
JOHNSON, MARGERY BOBBS
JOHNSON, PATRICIA
JOHNSON, SUSAN
JONES, CHUCK
JONES, MARIE
JUD, DORITA
KAGEYAMA, MARIAN
KAJIKURI, AMY
KAJIKURI, DIANE
KEHL, LAURIE MCWHORTER
KELLOGG, CHRISTINA
KELLOGG, MARLENE
KENDALL, SUSAN
KENNEDY, HEIDI
KENNEDY, JUDITH
KINCADE, NANCY QUINLAN
KING, DIANA
KING, DIANNE
KIRK, DOROTHY
KLEPPE, JULIANNA
KLOS, ELEANOR HILLS
KNOKEY, ANN QUINLAN
KNOOP, GRACE
KNOOP, LAURA
KOO, MRS. RAYMOND
LAMBERT, JULIE
LAMSON, SHEILA
LANGER, CATHERINE
LANSBURGH, OLIVE
LATHAM, NICOLA
LAUERMAN, STELLA SINNER
LE BLANC, LANI
LEIST, VELMA
LIMOV, DOROTHY
LINDEMANN, JACQUIE
LOTZ, MARGARET
LOVE, MOLLIE
MACKENZIE, CAROLINE LORD
MADDEN, PATTY
MADSEN, LINDA
MAHANEY, BARBARA
MANASSERO, MR. & MRS. JAMES
MANUEL, YOLANDA SCACCIA
MARASCO, JANICE KOHT
MATHEWS, SHEILA
MATTHEWS, MELISSA KING
MAY, JOANNE
MAY, THERESA

MAZZEO, KATIE CLARE
MCCORMACK, JOHN & NANCY
MCFADDEN, MARIANNE
MCFARLANE, ANNE
MCGREGOR, JANINE
MCGUIRE, TOM
MCNEELY, MRS. DONALD
MCNEIL, NANCY
MCNULTY, PIPER
MEDANICH, URSULA
MEGHETTI, CAMERON MILLER
MERRIMAN, EARLENE
MESTRES, JUANA
MICHAELS, JENNIFER
MICKELSON, SUSAN DURNEY
MILLER, JOAN
MILLER, TESIAH
MILOVANOVIC, LJUBINKA
MINK, MYRNA
MISSIG, MARGIE
MOCK, CYNTHIA
MONTEREY VINEYARD
MOORE, BEEZIE LEYDEN
MORGAN, OLIVIA
MUGNAINI, MARLO MUSTO
MUNCKTON, MR. & MRS. JERRY
NAGLE, SALLY
NEAR, PAT
NEBREDA, JULIE
NEISESS, MICHELE
NELSON, LINDA
NENCINI, KAREN
NICHOLS, PENNY
NICHOLS, VERA
NICKLAS, ELLA
NIX, DUDLEY
NOKES, DEADRA
NOMELLINI, KATHERINE
NORDSTROM, JEANETTE
NYMAN, LAURA
O'HARA, HELEN
ORTNER, DIANNE
OSPINA, MARILYN RAMOS
PARODI, SUSAN
PARSONS, MARY ELLEN
PEIRCE, HEATHER
PERRAULT-PERRY, RENEE
PIERCE, MRS. FRANK
PIERCY, JULIETTE
PINCKNEY, SUE

PITTS, MRS. FRANK
POLLACCI, CHRISTY
POST, SALLY
PRICE, GRACE
PROTELL, ELIZABETH HOLT
PULEO, JULIA
QUINLAN, JEAN
RAMOS, MILDRED
RANSOM, DOLORES
RAPPAPORT, MARILYN
REARDON, MAURA
REESE, POLLY
REMBERT, NANCY
RENSHAW, CORINNE
RHODES, PEGGY
RHODES, SALLY SMITH
RICE, MARTHA
RICO, DONNA
ROBBINS, DONNA
ROBINSON, SANDRA
ROGERS, TERESA ANNOTTI
ROMANO, MARY
ROSENAUER, KATHLEEN
ROTHE, TERESA
ROWE, PAMELA
RYAN, KATHLEEN
SAGA FOODS
SAGE, CONNIE
SALIDO, PILAR
SAMMONS, MRS. FRANCIS
SANDERS, MARY KAY
SANTA CATALINA PRE-SCHOOL
SANTA CATALINA SCHOOL, GRADE
SATHER, DEBBY
SAUGIER, DIANNE KLECH
SCACCIA, ELAINE
SCACCIA, SAM
SCHULTZ, LATCHMEE
SEARLE, KRISTIN
SHAPIRO, SONDRA
SHEFIK, PERIHAN
SHIPLEY, KATHY
SIMON, KELLENE KELLOGG
SISTER CARLOTTA
SISTER CLAIRE
SISTER MARY ELLEN
SMITH, RITA
SMITH, SANDRA
SMITH, SUSAN GRUPE
SOLAK-EASTIN, CRI CRI

SOLBERG, TERRI
SOUTHAM, MRS. GORDON
SPARACINO, PATRICIA ALLEN
SPENCER, MRS. ROBERT
STAHL, LAURA
STANTON, VIRGINIA
STAUFFER, DIANE DITZ
STEEN, CAROLE
STEVENS, CAMILLE ANNOTTI
STEVENS, TERESA
STOCK, BARBARA & DAVE
STOCKWELL, JODY
SULLIVAN, CHERI
SULLIVAN, CHRIS
SULLIVAN, EILEEN
SULLIVAN, JAY
SULLIVAN, KATHLEEN
SULLIVAN, MRS. WALTER
SWANSON, ERICA
SWENSON, SANDRA CHIAPPE
SZEMBORSKI, B.J. BURTON
TACK, BASIA BELZA
TALBOT, MARJORIE
TALBOT, SUZANNE
TAYLOR, MARY ANN
TAYLOR, MRS. POWELL HARRISON
TERRELL, ROXANNE
THEIRING, LINDA
TILLOTSON, HELEN
TRAFTON, KATHY
TREDWAY, ANNE
TURGEON & LOHR WINERY
UHRIG, HELEN
UNDERWOOD, SERENA
VAIL, MRS. ROGER
VAN DER PLAS, ELLEN
VESSEY, MARIE
VIOLANTE, ROSEMARY
VOGEL, JILL SHOEMAKE
VON DRACHENFELS, SALLY
WAGNER, GAIL
WAHL, BIA OSMONT
WALTON, JEAN
WARDELL, MOLLY MAHANEY
WARNER, LIBBY
WATERS, LANIE
WEIBEL CHAMPAGNE VINEYARDS
WEIGHT, NANCY
WENTE-BROTHERS WINERY
WESSON, JAMEEN ANN

WESSON, MARY JANE
WEST, VIRGINIA
WEYMANN, MALLORY VAIL
WHITE, MRS. GEOFFREY
WILLIAMS, PENELOPE
WILSON, DONNA
WILSON, PAMELA
WINANS, ELEANOR
WOODWARD, WYNN
WUERFLEIN, CAROLYN
WYKOFF, MARILYN BROWN
YEDLICKA, KAREN
ZAMBO, LESLIE
ZEFF, MRS. WILLIAM
ZENER, UTA
ZUCKERMAN, ELEANOR
ZUCKERMAN, MARGARET

Index

394

404